Challenges and Innovations in Educational Psychology Teaching and Learning

Challenges and Innovations in Educational Psychology Teaching and Learning

edited by

M Cecil Smith
West Virginia University

Nancy DeFrates-Densch
Northern Illinois University

INFORMATION AGE PUBLISHING, INC.
Charlotte, NC • www.infoagepub.com

Library of Congress Cataloging-in-Publication Data

A CIP record for this book is available from the Library of Congress
http://www.loc.gov

ISBN: 978-1-68123-396-3 (Paperback)
       978-1-68123-397-0 (Hardcover)
       978-1-68123-398-7 (ebook)

CONTENTS

SECTION I

TEACHING LEARNING THEORIES FOR EDUCATORS

SECTION II

TEACHING MOTIVATION FOR TEACHERS AND EDUCATIONAL PSYCHOLOGISTS

SECTION III

TEACHING HUMAN DEVELOPMENT FOR TEACHERS

SECTION IV

TEACHING RESEARCH METHODS, STATISTICS AND ASSESSMENT FOR THE NEXT GENERATION OF EDUCATIONAL PSYCHOLOGISTS

CONTRIBUTORS

Eric M. Anderman	*The Ohio State University*
Allison G. Butler	*Bryant University*
Matthew L. Bernacki	*University of Nevada, Las Vegas*
Catherine M. Bohn-Gettler	*College of St. Benedict–Saint John's University*
Kyung Sun Chung	*The Pennsylvania State University*
Christopher Collen	*The Ohio State University*
Jessica Cooper	*Auburn University*
Reagan Curtis	*West Virginia University*
Jennifer G. Cromley	*University of Illinois at Urbana–Champaign*
Ting Dai	*University of Illinois at Urbana–Champaign*
Denise H. Daniels	*California Polytechnic State University, San Luis Obispo*
Nancy DeFrates-Densch	*Northern Illinois University*
Florian C. Feucht	*University of Toledo*
Helenrose Fives	*Montclair State University*
Abraham E. Flanagan	*University of Nebraska-Lincoln*
Terri Flowerday	*University of New Mexico*
James Folkestad	*Colorado State University*
D. Jake Follmer	*The Pennsylvania State University*
Zornitsa Georgieva	*West Virginia University*
Misook Heo	*Duquesne University*
Janet K. Holt	*Southern Illinois University–Edwardsville*
Brett D. Jones	*Virginia Tech*
Kenneth A. Kiewra	*University of Nebraska–Lincoln*
Shaunti Knauth	*National-Louis University*

Daniel K. Lapsley	*University of Notre Dame*
You Joung Lee	*The Ohio State University*
Linlin Luo	*University of Nebraska–Lincoln*
Gwen C. Marchand	*University of Nevada, Las Vegas*
Tammy M. Mills	*Montclair State University*
Connie M. Moss	*Duquesne University*
Louis S. Nadelson	*Utah State University*
Charles Okonkwo	*The Ohio State University*
Jeanne Ellis Ormrod	*University of Northern Colorado*
Tony Perez	*Old Dominion University*
Markeya S. Peteranetz	*University of Nebraska–Lincoln*
Sarah E. Peterson	*University of Texas–El Paso*
Phillip M. Reeves	*The Pennsylvania State University*
Aaron S. Richmond	*Metropolitan State University of Denver*
Daniel H. Robinson	*Colorado State University*
Desiree Rones	*Northern Illinois University*
Diane Salmon	*National-Louis University*
Jennifer A. Schmidt	*Northern Illinois University*
Marlene Schommer-Aikins	*Wichita State University*
Gregory Schraw	*University of Nevada, Las Vegas*
James B. Schreiber	*Duquesne University*
Neal Shambaugh	*West Virginia University*
David M. Shannon	*Auburn University*
Lee Shumow	*Northern Illinois University*
M Cecil Smith	*West Virginia University*
Rayne A. Sperling	*The Pennsylvania State University*
Alexander L. Towle	*The Pennsylvania State University*
Lindsey N. Weber	*Bryant University*
Diana Zaleski	*Illinois State Board of Education*

PREFACE

M Cecil Smith
West Virginia University

Nancy DeFrates-Densch
Northern Illinois University

We see a critical need for a book like this one for at least three reasons. First, there is the important matter of adequately preparing the next generation of educational psychology faculty members to teach the knowledge, methods, and practices of our discipline to students in education and human services. Educational psychology is about understanding the psychological constructs that are embedded in instructional activities and learning processes. Those who teach educational psychology do well to put into practice what a century of research in the field has taught us about effective teaching and learning in and out of classrooms. This book attempts to convey some of this through a variety of examples of instructional practices carried out by well-regarded educational psychologists who excel in the classroom.

Second, many graduate students in the field are well versed in both content and research, but they are often not afforded the opportunity to teach courses in their programs; such as an undergraduate course in educational psychology. And, if they are assigned to teach such a course, they may be placed in the classroom having little preparation and without the benefit of mentoring faculty members. While this book cannot take the place of a mentor teacher, the knowledge about effective instructional methods that

Challenges and Innovations in Educational Psychology Teaching and Learning, pages xi–xxii
Copyright © 2016 by Information Age Publishing
All rights of reproduction in any form reserved.

is contained in the collected chapters can serve to inspire, influence, and direct novice faculty to innovate and experiment as well as to provide proven methods for teaching educational psychology.

In a related manner, we have observed that several of our recent doctoral students have obtained faculty positions at smaller institutions that have heavy teaching responsibilities. Frequently, they are the only educational psychology faculty member at their institution and, thus, they have few colleagues with whom they can discuss ideas about teaching educational psychology. Even when our graduate students land at larger comprehensive and research-intensive institutions, the mentoring that they receive from colleagues often focuses on research productivity rather than teaching proficiency. The implicit message for them is they will learn how to teach educational psychology by teaching educational psychology. We would like to suggest that there has to be a better way to learn to teach educational psychology (or, really, any disciplinary field) than simply by trial and error. After all, educational psychologists have decades of research on learning that demonstrates the importance of induction and mentoring in the development of effective PK–12 teachers and there is little reason to doubt that such practices are important in higher education, too.

Third, there are few professional outlets that have published research and professional development articles specific to instruction that teaches students about educational psychology. The online journal, *Teaching Educational Psychology*, was published for a decade under the guidance of the Teaching Educational Psychology Special Interest Group, an organization of the American Educational Research Association. However, since that journal has been discontinued, there are now no publication outlets that focus attention on instructional matters within our field. This book is an effort to address this gap.

As we conceptualized the contents for this book, as well as the authors who might best contribute to a book focusing on teaching educational psychology, we asked two questions: "What is the content knowledge of the field?" and "What is most important for students—both undergraduate and graduate students—to learn, understand, and know about educational psychology?" We began with our own preparation and experiences in the field, as well reflecting upon the content knowledge that we are teaching to our students. But, we also attempted to look beyond our limited perspectives on the discipline. The three major editions of the *Handbook of Educational Psychology* (Alexander & Winne, 2006; Berliner & Calfee, 1996; Corno & Anderman, 2015), of course, lay out extensive and critical summaries of the major theoretical and empirical advances in the field over the past two decades. The extent to which these reference works inform the content of instruction within educational psychology courses is uncertain, however.

Nolen (2009) surveyed the contents of six leading educational psychology journals published in the early years of the twenty-first century. She found that the following topics were the most common foci of investigations published in these journals: classroom achievement; learning and memory; learner affect, motivation, and beliefs; and cognition and reasoning. Alternatively, Mitchell and McConnell (2012) focused attention on a single leading educational psychology journal, *Contemporary Educational Psychology*, during the period from 1995 to 2010, to examine the themes, trends, and topics of the papers published in the journal at that time. They observed that three theories dominated and guided the investigations that were published in CEP in the examined years: behaviorist, constructivist, and cognitivist theories. The attention of educational psychology researchers to these topics suggests that these topics are likely to be covered in educational psychology classrooms.

ORGANIZATION OF THE BOOK

We have organized the chapters around the "core domains" of the field: learning and cognition; assessment; motivation; and human development. We also have included research methods and statistics because these topics are frequently taught by educational psychologists or by those who closely align with the field.

Learning theories constitute the "heart" of educational psychology and occupy a significant portion of many undergraduate courses and graduate seminars in the field. As is true in any scientific field, particular theories may be replaced by more current, more parsimonious, explanatory theories; yet, many theories of human learning are long-standing "legacy" theories. Teaching these older theories provides, in part, a history of the field and a basis for understanding contemporary perspectives on learning. The range of complex models and theories of learning in educational psychology makes it challenging to adequately compare, contrast, and evaluate these learning theories in the classroom.

Teaching the topic of motivation (i.e., theories of motivation, motivation concepts, and methods for motivating students) is one of the most challenging topics for educational psychologists to address in courses for undergraduate teacher candidates and in graduate seminars. There are a number of prominent theoretical perspectives of human motivation (i.e., goal theory, expectancy-value theory, self-determination theory) that argue for different cognitive, affective, or behavioral antecedents to, and consequences of, motivation. Much of the terminology used within and across these different perspectives is confusing, with different terms referring to the same or similar constructs. Frequently, it is difficult to turn theoretical knowledge of motivation into meaningful classroom practice—in part because students have few opportunities to immediately put this knowledge into practice.

There are myriad topics that fall under the broad domain of human development that are important for educators and human services professionals (i.e., counselors, speech pathologists, social workers) to know and understand. These topics include genetics and biological processes, physical growth and maturation, cognitive and intellectual development, emotional growth, and the influences of diverse environmental and social contexts (i.e., schools) on child and adolescent development. Typically, most undergraduate and introductory-level graduate courses address these topics in a broad, survey-type approach. Student learning thus tends to be broad and superficial rather than deep and sustaining.

Although many of the faculty members who teach research methods and statistics courses are not educational psychologists, a good many faculty who identify themselves as educational psychologists teach courses in assessment (i.e., classroom testing; measurement), research methods (both qualitative and quantitative research designs), and statistics. While many graduate students express great reluctance—even anxiety—at the prospect of enrolling in these courses, they form the methodological core of educational psychology. Therefore, it is essential that students have excellent preparation in these subjects and skill areas.

The Chapters

The eight chapters included in Section I focus on teaching learning theories and related educational psychology content to diverse populations of students, ranging from undergraduate teacher education candidates to graduate students in engineering.

In the first chapter on teaching learning theories, Jeanne Ormrod advocates for a "big ideas" approach to organizing educational psychology courses that moves instruction away from a focus on individual theories in isolation from one another. A "big ideas" approach organizes educational psychology content around several general principles that tend to transcend the specific theories.

Although no longer in vogue in education, Rayne Sperling, Phillip Reeves, Jake Follmer, Alexander Towle, and Kyung Sun Chung discuss the importance of teaching behaviorism as a foundational theory. Significantly, behaviorism supports the development of self-regulation of behavior. Sperling and her coauthors describe a behavior modification activity in which their students identify a problematic behavior of their own to modify and attempt to do so using behavioral principles (e.g., reinforcement, transfer). Students track their behavior and summarize the results of their self-monitoring.

Next, Kenneth Kiewra, Abraham Flanagan, Linlin Luo, and Markeya Peteranetz describe a "SOAR-driven approach" to teaching the important learning theories that teachers-in-training need to know. "SOAR" stands for *selecting* (relevant information from text), *organizing* information (in graphical rather than linear form), *associating* ideas to one another and to prior knowledge, and *regulating* one's learning through self-testing. SOAR has been demonstrated to be a superior approach to learning than are students' preferred study methods.

Generally, teacher education students come into educational psychology courses with established beliefs about learning based on their own educational experiences and observations. Some of these beliefs may be simplistic and resistant to change. Sarah Peterson and Connie Moss describe their approach to transforming students' beliefs about learning that is based on a framework of systematic, intentional inquiry. Through a series of activities, they challenge their students to recognize their assumptions about teaching and learning in light of theory and research and then use these theories and research findings to evaluate, defend, and modify their decisions about teaching practices.

College students often use ineffective learning strategies, partly because they are unaware of the strategies that are most effective. Aaron Richmond discusses the importance of teaching students which learning strategies are likely to benefit them and how to use these strategies effectively. He advocates for active learning instruction to teach students about effective learning strategies. Active learning instruction is that in which students are actively engaged with the course material in a meaningful way. Richmond suggests that we "practice what we preach" when teaching educational psychology, and concludes with a list of studies that have evaluated the effects of instruction for a variety of learning strategies.

Neal Shambaugh profiles three courses in which graduate students learn to connect their beliefs about learning to theory, to help students learn to ground their instructional decisions in learning theories and research. He describes the instructional activities that he uses in these courses to achieve this goal. Students identify their beliefs about learning, identify the formal theoretical principles that align with their beliefs, and then apply those principles in an educational context.

Allison Butler and Lindsey Weber use popular movies to engage students in their educational psychology courses. They select excerpts from movies that illustrate relevant course content and use these to spur student discussion. Along with a list of movies used in their courses, they identify the themes and concepts each movie illustrates, along with their associated instructional objectives. Evidence regarding the efficacy of their practice indicates that students find this film-based approach to learning is engaging and enhances their learning.

Education and social science students are not the only students who enroll in educational psychology courses. Marlene Schommer-Aikins teaches educational psychology to engineering graduate students who aspire to university faculty positions. She describes her first effort at teaching the course to a small group of students and the unique challenges involved when such students lack background knowledge of pedagogical concepts and psychological constructs. In subsequent semesters, the engineering graduate students were integrated with educational psychology students in heterogeneous classes. Schommer-Aikins addresses the challenges presented by this new arrangement, as well as how she confronted and resolved these challenges.

The eight chapters included in Section II address several of the challenges that educational psychology instructors confront when teaching students about human motivation. Terri Flowerday adopts a broad, inclusive approach to teaching education and educational psychology students about motivation as she strives to address all of the major motivation theories in her courses. Because she teaches many Native American and Hispanic students, she emphasizes the relevance of motivation as a foundation for academic success for not only these, but all students. Brett Jones describes his approach to teaching about motivation by using his MUSIC model. The model focuses on instructional strategies that can foster students' motivation in school. According to the MUSIC model, students are motivated during instruction when they perceive that they are *em*powered, believe that what they are learning is *u*seful, feel they can be *s*uccessful at a given task, are *i*nterested in learning, and feel *c*ared for by others in the learning environment. Jones describes several instructional strategies that are associated with these components of his model.

Maslow's Hierarchy of Needs is a foundational humanistic theory of human motivation that has garnered much attention in education over the past 70 years. Helenrose Fives and Tammy Mills suggest that it is important for educators to understand Maslow's theory because doing so enables them to focus on the whole child—their health, happiness, and functioning—rather than simply the student's academic performance. They describe three classroom techniques and assignments that they have employed to teach their students about Maslow's theory: a simulation game that explores students' needs and motivations; a series of brief vignettes in which students' analyze the needs of different individuals; and a case analysis that requires comparison of Maslow's theory to other motivation theories.

Eric Anderman, Charles Okonkwo, You Joung Lee, and Christopher Collen describe several promising practices for teaching pre-service teachers about goal orientations. Goals are obviously important to learning, and goal orientation theory connects the reasons why students participate (or not) in academic tasks—for instance, to master the material or avoid showing low competence—to their academic achievement. Pre-service teachers must possess thorough understanding of goal orientation theory, have principles of motivation repeatedly emphasized throughout their teacher coursework, and be able to practice applying the theory during practical student teaching experiences.

Gwen Marchand and Greg Schraw describe their efforts to find common ground among different motivation theories for the purpose of teaching students about the theories. In doing so, they rely upon constructs from self-efficacy (i.e., social-cognitive) theory—which describes the role of one's beliefs about their abilities to perform an action—and self-determination theory—which describes the role of the innate psychological needs of autonomy, competence, and relatedness in motivating behavior. They advocate for helping students understand the similarities as well as the differences among theories as well as understanding the general process of motivational change. Systematic comparisons of theories are useful in this regard.

Lee Shumow and Desiree Rones more explicitly describe teaching a specific component of self-determination theory—autonomy—to educators. In particular, they emphasize the role that autonomy support has in helping individuals to fulfill their potential. Teachers' ability to demonstrate autonomy support for students has significant impacts on academic performance. Autonomy-supportive practices including providing choice and control to students, promoting the relevance of school subjects and academic tasks, and accepting others' perspectives and alternative ideas. The authors describe classroom examples of these practices.

Engaging in autonomy-supportive practices in the classroom establishes a learning environment in which flow may occur. Flow is a state of optimal experience that is marked by intense concentration, a merging of action and awareness, having the perception of control over one's actions, enjoyment, and a sense that time has passed very quickly, according to Jennifer Schmidt. Flow is important for educators because it has been shown to relate to student motivation, engagement, and achievement. Schmidt describes three approaches to teaching university students about flow and its' relevance to learning. These approaches include guided discussion, observations of flow conditions in classrooms, and collection of data about the flow experience.

Neal Shambaugh employs project-based learning (PBL) to demonstrate to educational psychology students how PBL can be used to engage and motivate student learning. PBL is a teaching method that engages students in learning activities through an extended inquiry process that uses authentic tasks. Shambaugh suggests that PBL can tap into students' curiosity and help them develop self-regulation skills. He describes how he implements

PBL projects in two different educational psychology courses to directly demonstrate the effects and value of PBL.

Section III contains six chapters that are devoted to describing instructors' efforts to teach development concepts, principles, and theories in the context of human development courses. Such courses are often required in the teacher education programs as well as in graduate programs in educational psychology.

Denise Daniels observes that, frequently, students' underlying beliefs and assumptions lead them to disregard the practical value of developmental theories when teaching children. She describes several promising practices that can help foster students' learning about child development that will, in turn, inform appropriate educational practices. Daniels acknowledges the difficulty of altering students' beliefs about children's development in the relatively brief duration of a college course, yet finds evidence that students' beliefs can be positively affected when they have opportunities to compare what they believe to what is known about child development and then reflect on the difference.

Catherine Bohn-Gettler's chapter articulates some of the principal difficulties present when teaching students about information processing theories of cognition and cognitive development. Information processing accounts of changes in cognitive abilities comprise a number of perspectives, theories, and sub-theories that can be difficult for students to integrate into a coherent whole that explains human thinking and reasoning. Bohn-Gettler describes a classroom activity in which students work collaboratively to achieve an integrated perspective that involves describing, elaborating upon, and identifying applications of the various theories.

M Cecil Smith describes a graduate course on adolescent development organized around understanding the critical developmental task of identity formation during the adolescent years. Rather than limiting coverage of identity development to a single lecture, identity is emphasized throughout and saturates all aspects of the course. Students determine, discuss, and evaluate the many dimensions of and influences in adolescents' identity formation through structured small group discussions. They analyze video cases of real adolescents who talk about their lives and experiences in and out of school, and write case analyses that draw upon specific developmental theories. The course helps students appreciate the salience of identity to adolescents' well-being, enables them to apply theory to interpret and explain adolescent identity strivings, and contributes to their own identity strivings—which has benefits to their academic and professional growth.

Florian Feucht uses the story of Anne Frank, as told in her biography, *Anne Frank—Diary of a Young Girl*, to illustrate important developmental concepts in adolescent development. Treating Anne's diary as a data source for a case study, Feucht's students write brief essays in which they describe diary excerpts that illustrate developmental concepts. Students also write essays in which they relate the development concepts in Anne Frank's diary to their own development and roles as future teachers. Feucht concludes with several tips for teachers who want to use the Anne Frank assignments in their human development courses.

Human development, of course, occurs in specific contexts. Such contexts include the family, neighborhoods, and the larger communities in which families and neighborhoods are located. Lee Shumow describes the variety of pedagogical approaches that she has employed to teach students—ranging from teacher certification candidates to school administrators—about the important and diverse roles of families, neighborhoods, and communities in shaping children's and teens' development. One activity requires students to design an applied project to identify a school or community need, gather and analyze appropriate data, and implement a program to address the identified need.

Similar to identity development, moral development is a topic that is often given scant attention in courses on human development. Recognizing the perils of ignoring moral development in teacher training, Daniel Lapsley presents three responses to the challenge of preparing teachers for the "moral work" of teaching. These are: (1) the Best Practice model, rooted in constructivism, which guides the formation of "good learners;" (2) broad character education which build character strengths in learners; and (3) intentional moral-character education which transforms the good learner into a moral self.

The final section of the book contains 10 chapters that address many of the challenges present when educational psychologists and their colleagues teach students about methods of assessment, research design, program evaluation, and data analytic procedures—in particular, statistics. We begin with a subsection that contains four chapters focusing on teaching introductory statistics—a course that may be a boon or a bust for many educational psychology students.

Greg Schraw and Matthew Bernacki argue that, when statistics instructors properly scaffold students' understanding, then statistics need not be stressful to learn. They advocate for a "big ideas" approach to statistics that focuses on core concepts, application with actual datasets, and distributed practice in applying statistical methods. Jennifer Cromley, Tony Perez, and Ting Dai draw upon principles from the research in academic achievement motivation to structure their introductory statistics courses. They emphasize conceptual understanding and practical applications, give students ample opportunities for practice to build mastery, provide rapid feedback, and demonstrate the relevance of statistical methods, among other methods.

Reagan Curtis and Zornitsa Georgieva, like Schraw et al. and Cromley et al., acknowledge the fear and trepidation of many students in statistics courses. Yet, they suggest, students' "statistical anxiety" can be leveraged to support their learning in statistics courses. They assess students' anxiety around statistics at the outset of the course. They then treat these data as an authentic dataset that personalizes statistical data (e.g., individual student anxiety profiles) and makes statistical methods relevant for the students. Daniel Robinson and James Folkestad have adopted a team-based learning (TBL) approach to teaching statistics. Four components of TBL—heterogeneous groups of students work together throughout the course, students take readiness tests that prepare them for instruction, team members work together on a statistics problem and challenge one another, and members provide feedback to promote team development—lead to enthusiastic, accomplished learners.

James Schreiber and Misook Heo confront a more challenging statistics course—teaching large-scale data analyses. Large-scale data refers to data that is collected at the population level, such as U.S. Census Bureau statistics. Focusing on developing students' data visualization skills and statistical modeling procedures, Schreiber and Heo require their students to complete several related assignments and projects. Students must employ path analysis, confirmatory factor analysis, and structural equation modeling to analyze their selected data set, and must write up a narrative that includes the methods, results, and limitations of their project

Multilevel modeling (MM), a regression-based analysis method that is appropriate for hierarchically structured or nested data, is often used in educational analyses because of the natural nesting of these data (e.g., students nested within classrooms, and classrooms nested within schools). Janet Holt and Diana Zaleski teach MM to graduate students in education and the social sciences. They observe that learning MM is facilitated when students have knowledge and experience with regression methods. Their chapter explores the essential content in a MM course, challenges of a MM course from both instructor and learner perspectives, and suggests pedagogical approaches that foster and accelerate understanding of MM.

Student assessment is an increasingly important topic in education, although teachers generally obtain little pre-professional preparation regarding best practices. Diane Salmon and Shaunti Knauth have developed a course that employs a practice-based approach for instructing in-service teachers in the uses of formative assessments in their classrooms. They suggest that formative assessment can be a powerful means of advancing teachers' professional knowledge and skills.

It is increasingly important for graduate students in educational psychology—particularly those who aspire to higher education faculty positions—to have opportunities to publish research. Louis Nadelson describes how he has successfully embedded authentic research experiences into a research methods course where students collaborate on a team-based research project. He has coauthored several published research reports with various groups of students using these embedded research experiences. Qualitative research methods are equally essential to statistics for the educational psychology researcher. Florian Feucht describes how he teaches a particularly critical skill for students who want to gather qualitative data: how to develop coding schemes for analyzing such data. A coding scheme is used to identify, capture, and triangulate evidence to corroborate an emerging or existing theory to address one's research questions. Feucht describes eight cognitive principles that support the development of application of coding schemes in qualitative research.

The evaluation of various educational programs, curricula, and interventions is essential to identifying "what works" in education. Program evaluation requires strong skills in assessment, statistics and qualitative methods (e.g., interviews, observations), and data analysis and interpretation, as well as the ability to communicate findings to stakeholders. David Shannon and Jessica Cooper describe their authentic, real-world approach to teaching program evaluation competencies and prepare educational psychology students to conduct such studies in a variety of educational settings.

We note that several gaps exist in this book's coverage of topics that are often addressed in educational psychology courses. To give adequate attention to these and related topics might require several volumes! Among the topics that are not examined include the psychology of instructional design and applications of educational technology (e.g., online instruction) to learning, as well as the psychology of school subjects (including mathematics and science, and language arts). The critical issue of learner diversity, and how differences in students' backgrounds, experiences, and abilities affect their learning and achievement in school is not directly addressed. Affective dimensions of learning (e.g., attitudes, beliefs, and emotions) are not described insofar as demonstrating effective methods for teaching about the role of affect in learning and development. Finally, the nature, scope, and consequences of student-teacher relationships in the classroom are not addressed, although educational psychology students should be informed about the impact of these relationships on students' learning and achievement.

ACKNOWLEDGMENTS

We are exceedingly grateful to the individuals who contributed chapters to this book. We thank them for writing well-crafted, thoughtful, and informative contributions. We also acknowledge and thank several colleagues for their support and encouragement throughout the development and production of this book. First, we extend our gratitude to our many colleagues in the Teaching Educational Psychology Special Interest Group of the

American Educational Research Association. Cynthia Bolton-Gary, Sandra Deemer, Greg Goodman, Laurie Hanich, Angela O'Donnell, and Martha Strickland were particularly enthusiastic about this project. Greg Schraw, General Editor for the Educational Psychology series at Information Age Publishing, provided invaluable encouragement and editorial support. Lisa Paylo Myers has been a tireless contributor to this book, providing outstanding copy editing, with a keen eye for finding the tiniest of errors. We take responsibility for any errors that remain. We also acknowledge Hannah Greenbaum for her assistance with several last-minute details. Finally, we express our love and appreciation to our respective spouses, Ellin and Greg, for their unselfish support of our work.

REFERENCES

Alexander, P. A., & Winne, P. H. (2006). *Handbook of educational psychology* (2nd ed.). Mahwah, NJ: Erlbaum Associates.

Berliner, D. C., & Calfee, R. C. (1996). *Handbook of educational psychology* (1st ed.). New York, NY: MacMillan.

Corno, L., & Anderman, E. M. (2016). *Handbook of educational psychology* (3rd ed.). New York, NY: Routledge.

Mitchell, A. W., & McConnell III, J. R. (2012). A historical review of Contemporary Educational Psychology from 1995 to 2010. *Contemporary Educational Psychology, 37*, 136–147.

Nolen, A. L. (2009). The content of educational psychology: An analysis of top ranked journals from 2003 through 2007. *Educational Psychology Review, 21*, 279–289.

SECTION I

TEACHING LEARNING THEORIES FOR EDUCATORS

CHAPTER 1

TEACHING *ACROSS* RATHER THAN *WITHIN* THEORIES OF LEARNING

A "Big Ideas" Approach to Organizing Educational Psychology Courses

Jeanne Ellis Ormrod
University of Northern Colorado

As members of an exponentially expanding discipline, we educational psychologists have published thousands of articles and presented countless papers about effective instructional strategies for teaching various topics in our field. Well-crafted lectures, small-group cooperative and collaborative activities, case studies, problem-based discussions, independent readings—all of these strategies and many others can enhance our students' ability to understand and apply principles and theories of learning, development, motivation, instruction, and related topics. In this chapter I try to move the conversation in a different direction to address the question, "How can we best *organize* what we teach in educational psychology courses?" To be consistent with the subtitle of this volume's subsection—*Teaching Learning*

Challenges and Innovations in Educational Psychology Teaching and Learning, pages 3–13
Copyright © 2016 by Information Age Publishing
All rights of reproduction in any form reserved.

Theories—my focus here will be on how we might organize the things we have collectively discovered about human learning.

Traditionally, many of us have organized our instruction about human learning into discrete theory-specific units—units that each focus on a particular "ism." For example, we might create separate units on, say, behaviorism, social cognitive theory, information processing theory, constructivism, and sociocultural theory. Most textbooks, too, take a theory-by-theory approach, reflecting a legacy that goes back to the middle of the twentieth century (e.g., see Hilgard & Bower's classic *Theories of Learning*, 1966). There are probably two overlapping reasons for such an organizational scheme. First, as a professional group, many of us have had trouble thinking outside the, *this-is-how-it's-always-been-done* box. And second, when educational psychologists write textbooks that are organized in a very different manner, so few instructors use them that the authors and publishing companies have little incentive to follow up with a second edition. (I have an old friend who discovered this the hard way; he put a lot of work into an ingenious approach that only briefly saw the light of day.) As a textbook writer myself, I can say with confidence that diverging too far from the traditional organizational path meets considerable resistance from most instructors of educational psychology classes. If they choose to use someone else's book over mine, I don't get many readers, which means I can't have much of an impact on teacher education. If I *want* to have an impact, then, I need to toe the line.

This traditional approach certainly reflects how the field was growing as late as the 1980s, with advocates for any particular theoretical framework talking almost exclusively among themselves rather than communicating with adherents to alternative perspectives. In this twenty-first century, however, most educational psychologists of diverse theoretical persuasions regularly talk with one another, sharing and building on one another's ideas, and many of them view various theories as complementing rather than competing with one another (e.g., see Sawyer & Greeno, 2009). Isn't it time that we instructors focus on the commonalities and complementarity of our theories rather than on their differences?

I think we can all agree that the primary goal in an educational psychology class is to get students to think about how they might effectively *apply* what they are learning to real-world situations and problems—and ideally to actually put that knowledge to use in their future professional practices. I argue here that a theory-by-theory approach isn't the best way to accomplish such a goal.

PROBLEMS WITH A THEORY-BY-THEORY ORGANIZATIONAL STRUCTURE

In my own 40 years of experience in teaching and writing about educational psychology and learning about colleagues' instructional practices, I have observed several problems with a theory-by-theory, isms-based approach. First, when we *begin* instruction by presenting one or another theory, we are starting with an abstraction that can appear irrelevant to students' everyday, concrete realities and future professional needs (Anderson et al., 1995; Patrick, Anderman, Bruening, & Duffin, 2011; also see Nathan, 2012). In such a situation, motivation to truly master the subject matter can suffer, and students may be tempted to simply rote-memorize the information they think they'll need in order to "get by" on assignments and exams.

Such problems can be compounded when instructors ask students to focus on comparing and contrasting theories, in which case the underlying message is that various theories are rigid belief systems that hold no promise of being applied in combination. Apparently some instructors really do see various theories of learning as being incompatible. As an illustration, I recall a reviewer of one of my books who complained about my use of the word *retrieval* in a discussion of constructivism. The term originated with information processing theory, the reviewer said, and thus had no place in any description of constructivist ideas.

In addition, some instructors—and, I might add, many papers and articles—communicate the premise that certain theories are high on some elusive "rightness" scale, whereas others have little credence or value. In some instances such a view is accompanied by a deification of particular theorists. For example, over the past 20 years, several reviewers of my books have requested that I include photographs of, say B. F. Skinner, Albert Bandura, Jean Piaget, or Lev Vygotsky; if I were to do this, I would be focusing my readers' attention on particular theorists and consequently taking their attention away from things that are far more important: the theorists' *ideas.*

Finally, an organizational scheme based on specific theories does not match the kinds of questions that teachers and other practitioners are likely to ask when they are in real classrooms or other professional settings. For example, when faced with challenging situations and problems in their classrooms, I suspect that teachers rarely ask themselves questions such as these:

- "What might a social cognitive theorist do in this situation?"
- "How would a behaviorist solve this problem?"
- "How is constructivism different from information processing, and which one should I apply when I'm developing lesson plans?"
- "In what ways does sociocultural theory enhance my students' understanding of classroom learning and behavior?"

Instead, they're more likely to ask themselves questions along this line:

- "How can I design lessons in such a way that my students will genuinely understand important classroom topics?"

- "What can I do to help my students develop better study habits?"
- "Some of my students are getting misinformation from Internet searches and Facebook postings. How can I help them critically evaluate the things they see online?"
- "How can I help Julie acquire better social skills when she interacts with her peers?"

Novice teachers are more likely to retrieve principles and theories relevant to such questions if their educational psychology courses have been organized around such issues.

"BIG IDEAS" AS AN ALTERNATIVE ORGANIZATIONAL SCHEME

A Big Ideas approach organizes content around general principles and recommendations that in many cases transcend particular theories—hence the title of this chapter, "Teaching *Across* Rather Than *Within* Theories of Learning." Big Ideas approaches to curriculum planning and instruction have been advocated for many other disciplines, especially at the elementary and secondary school levels (e.g., see Brophy, Alleman, & Knighton, 2009), and they underlie both the Common Core standards that many U.S. states have adopted and the content-area standards that a number of discipline-specific professional groups have developed. In educational psychology, we took a preliminary step in this direction with the American Psychological Association's *Learner-Centered Psychological Principles* (1997; also see McCombs, 2005). However, these principles provide only very general guidance, and they focus almost entirely on what happens inside of learners and within learners' immediate instructional environments, with little regard for large-scale contextual factors or ongoing reciprocal *interactions* between learners and their environments.

Here I offer some Big Ideas that might be useful for organizing some of what we educational psychologists have learned about learning. I put these ideas into four categories that reflect more general ideas—*Mega Ideas*, if you will—beginning with (a) intra-individual variables (e.g., cognitive processes, temperamental characteristics); and then moving to (b) immediate environmental factors influencing learning; (c) broader-scale environmental factors influencing learning; and finally (d) reciprocal influences among intra-individual and environment variables. I accompany each Big Idea with concepts or principles from particular theories and occasionally with more specific ideas that don't necessarily "belong" to a particular theoretical perspective.

My list is not meant to be exhaustive, nor are its items meant to be mutually exclusive or prescriptive. Rather, the list is intended to suggest some of the across-theory principles that might be especially useful in teaching future teachers and other future practitioners. As I briefly discuss each of the following 26 Big Ideas, please forgive me if I too easily attribute certain concepts and principles to a particular theoretical perspective. In fact, many researchers and theorists—including *yours truly*—really do not like to be pigeonholed!

INTRA-INDIVIDUAL VARIABLES AFFECTING LEARNING

Some knowledge is explicit. Other knowledge is implicit, in that it lies partially or entirely below the level of conscious awareness. This Big Idea highlights a basic distinction that is often mentioned only in passing, and yet it is fundamentally important for true understanding of the many forms that learning might take. Historically, much of our instruction has been about the acquisition of explicit knowledge, especially when taking an information processing or constructivist perspective. Yet, many motor skills, attitudes, and classically conditioned responses are partly or entirely implicit in nature.

Attention is important for explicit learning. This Big Idea is a key principle in information processing theory, but we also see it in the behaviorist concept of *orienting response* and in social cognitive theorists' list of prerequisite conditions for successful modeling (i.e., attention, retention, motor reproduction, and motivation).

People tend to construct rather than absorb their explicit knowledge. This Big Idea pervades many cognitively oriented theories; for instance, we see it in constructivists' notion of *knowledge construction*, in sociocultural theorists' concept of *mediated learning experience*, and in information processing theorists' concept of *elaboration*. But we also see hints of it in the active *information seeking* that some contemporary behaviorists describe.

Learning and studying are typically more effective when people relate new information and ideas to their prior knowledge. Such learning might take the form of *chaining* two or more previously acquired S-R associations (a behaviorist notion), *assimilating* a new event into existing schemes (a Piagetian perspective), or drawing on an existing *script* to interpret a new situation (an idea from schema theory).

Prior "knowledge" that consists of inaccurate understandings or beliefs can impede effective learning. This Big Idea is most prominent in information processing theory and constructivism, but it can also come into play in traditional behaviorist views of *interference*.

People can consciously attend to and think about only so much at a time. This Big Idea emerged from information processing theory's concept of *short-term memory* and, later, *working memory.* It is also the basic premise underlying contemporary *cognitive load theory.*

Many people are relatively naive about how they can best learn and keep themselves on task when they are working or studying independently. This Big Idea encompasses both the concept of *metacognition* (for which cognitive developmental psychologist John Flavell was an early advocate) and social cognitive theorists' concepts of *self-regulation* and *self-regulated learning.*

People benefit more from learning experiences when they can accurately self-evaluate their performance and progress. Although this Big Idea is probably most prominent in social cognitive theorists' discussion of self-regulation, it also plays a role in behaviorists' early conceptualizations of *programmed instruction* and *computer-assisted instruction,* and it underlies information processing theorists' concepts of *calibration* and *comprehension monitoring.*

Especially in this age of the Internet, effective learning requires critical evaluation of available information and ideas. This Big Idea has probably never been a theory-specific one. Certainly, concerns about the importance of *critical thinking* have been around for many centuries. But they have reached an all-time high as members of literate societies have gained increasing access to Internet postings and other materials that convincingly offer inaccurate and occasionally counterproductive versions of the "truth"—versions that sometimes espouse beliefs that undermine human societies' collective efforts to maintain a healthy planet and to ensure respectful regard for individuals with diverse backgrounds and characteristics.

For better or for worse, certain dispositional characteristics influence thinking and learning. Much of the work on dispositions has come from research related to temperament, personality, and motivation, but we have become increasingly aware of its implications for learning. Key concepts related to this Big Idea include not only critical thinking (in this case as a disposition rather than a cognitive process) but also such temperamental and personality variables as *effortful control, need for cognition, epistemic curiosity, open-mindedness,* and *need for closure.*

IMMEDIATE ENVIRONMENTAL VARIABLES AFFECTING LEARNING

Close contiguity of two or more events increases the probability that people will form associations between those events. The concept of *contiguity* has historically been associated with behaviorist views of both classical and operant conditioning. But it also plays a prominent role in contemporary views of information processing: Two pieces of information are most likely to be associated in long-term memory if they have been in working memory at the same time.

Consequences of people's behaviors influence their future learning and behaviors. In some cases, these consequences are external to the learner; for example, they might take the form of a concrete *reinforcer,* a brief *time-out,* or *verbal feedback.* In other cases, they may be entirely internal ones; for example, social cognitive theorists talk about *self-reaction* as being an important aspect of self-regulation, and developmental theorists have documented the roles of *shame* and *guilt* as essential contributors to moral development. A noteworthy corollary to this Big Idea is that people must have an accurate *awareness* of the contingency, as noted in both social cognitive theory and attribution theory.

Regular feedback about performance levels, including suggestions about how to *improve* performance, can greatly enhance learning over the long run. From a theoretical standpoint, the importance of regular feedback probably first emerged in behaviorists' ideas about reinforcement. Subsequently, many cognitivists, social cognitivists, and attribution theorists have helped us understand that the *nature* of the feedback is an important factor in its impact and effectiveness.

People benefit from hearing or reading the ideas of others. Cognitive developmentalist Lev Vygotsky was probably the first psychologist to stress this Big Idea. It has also been an underlying assumption of behaviorist and information processing theorists, who have either explicitly or implicitly advocated for the value of expository instructional materials in classroom learning. The idea is reflected, too, in sociocultural theorists' proposal—and none of us can really deny it—that any long-standing social or cultural group passes along a good deal of collective knowledge to successive generations (more on this point in Big Idea #21 below).

People often work with peers or more experienced individuals to co-construct new understandings. Some constructivists and sociocultural theorists have proposed that people often acquire more complex and sophisticated understandings when they learn *with* rather than *from* other people. On some occasions co-constructed understandings are created at a single sitting involving only two or a few individuals. On other occasions, they evolve over a lengthy period of time; for instance, the physical, life, and social sciences and many other academic disciplines (e.g., philosophy, literature) have evolved over many decades through a process of studying, testing, modifying, and sometimes rejecting the ideas of those who have gone before.

Many behaviors and thought processes have their origins in social activities, with individual learners gradually internalizing them for independent use. The influence of Vygotsky's concept of *internalization* is obvious in this Big Idea. A corollary is the sociocultural notion of *appropriation:* In the process of internalizing others' behaviors, strategies, and ways of thinking, people often tweak them in one or more ways so that they better serve personal circumstances and needs.

Age-appropriate challenges foster learning and development. We see this Big Idea in concepts from many theories; for example, it underlies Piaget's *disequilibrium,* Vygotsky's *zone of proximal development,* Kohlberg's *moral dilemmas,* and behaviorists' *shaping.* We also see it in information processing theorists' belief that learners develop more complex cognitive strategies only when instructional demands require them to do so, as well as in social cognitivists' belief that *self-efficacy* is better enhanced when learners succeed at challenging, rather than easy, tasks.

People can more effectively tackle challenging tasks if they have appropriate guidance and supports to help them in their efforts. Such guidance and supports might take the form of *scaffolding* (sociocultural theory), *retrieval cues* (information processing theory), or *discriminative stimuli* (behaviorism). More recently, this Big Idea has appeared in contextual theorists' concept of *distributed cognition:* People can more effectively carry out complex tasks if they have physical or cognitive tools (e.g., computers, concepts and principles of chemistry, mathematical symbols and equations) or collaborating social partners that enable them to offload parts of those tasks onto something or someone else.

People are more likely to apply (transfer) school subject matter to new situations when they have previously learned and practiced using that subject matter in real-world contexts. This Big Idea crosses many theoretical perspectives, including behaviorists' notion of *generalization,* information processing theorists' views about *retrieval,* constructivists' endorsement of *authentic activities,* and sociocultural theorists' concepts of *legitimate peripheral participation* and *communities of practice.*

In instructional settings, people are most likely to master important ideas and skills when assessment tasks require mastery of those ideas and skills. Classroom assessment practices are, in part, the focus of this fourth section of this text on the challenges of teaching educational psychology topics, and I would be negligent if I didn't include a Big Idea related to assessment here. Legitimate assessment activities might involve either a traditional *paper-and-pencil* test or assignment (a strategy often attributed to behaviorist or information processing perspectives) or *authentic assessment* (a strategy often attributed to constructivist or contextualist perspectives). In any event, teachers must always keep in mind that assessment activities invariably influence what learners study *before* and *after* the assessment and what they learn *during* an assessment. In a very real sense, then, assessment *is* instruction.

BROAD-SCALE ENVIRONMENTAL VARIABLES AFFECTING LEARNING

Large social and cultural groups typically create and then pass along many physical and cognitive tools that facilitate accomplishment of challenging tasks. As previously noted for Big Idea #18, physical and cognitive tools provide many support mechanisms (e.g., digital technologies; concepts and principles of various academic disciplines) that can significantly enhance people's thought processes and performance. In Big Idea #21 (which has its roots in Vygotsky's work), we shift the focus to the originators of such tools: particular social or cultural group members, who conceive and create them and then instruct future generations in their use.

Virtually any cultural group instills certain worldviews—certain ways of interpreting various physical and social phenomena—that often lie below the level of conscious thought. For example, long before the concept of *ecological systems* gained prominence in elementary and secondary school biology lessons, some Native American cultural groups consistently instilled in their children the belief that plant and animal species regularly interact with and influence one another (see Atran, Medin, & Ross, 2005). I have seen allusions to people's worldviews in a variety of places, although more frequently in general psychology journals than in educational psychology literature. In any event, such implicit belief systems can have profound effects on what people learn—and in some cases *don't* learn—from science-based information related to, say, evolution or climate change.

The multiple layers of any society influence learning in a variety of direct and indirect ways. This Big Idea rests squarely on Bronfenbrenner's ecological systems theory and bioecological model, which describe the many layers of environment—not only one's family, friends, and close neighbors but also local and national agencies, government policies, and national and international events—and *how they interact* to either directly or indirectly influence a single individual's learning, development, and behavior.

In any large social group, people tend to specialize in certain topics and skills and draw on one another's expertise when dealing with problems for which they have little or no relevant knowledge. The gist of this Big Idea is that no single individual can possibly be master of all trades but must instead learn how to work collaboratively with others in communities or other group settings. Sociocultural and contextualist concepts such as *community of practice* and *distributed knowledge* are relevant here.

RECIPROCAL INFLUENCES AMONG INTRA-INDIVIDUAL AND ENVIRONMENTAL VARIABLES

People's behaviors, internal traits and mental processes, and environments mutually influence one another. Social cognitive theorists' concept of *reciprocal causation* obviously provides the basis for this Big Idea: Behavioral, personal, and environmental variables continually interact in their influences on learning and development, both over the short run and for the long haul. I've also seen a hint of this idea in behaviorists' concept of *behavioral cusp*.

People actively seek out or create environments that are a good fit with their existing characteristics and behaviors. Although this idea is implied by the reciprocal causation described in Big Idea #25, it has occasionally surfaced in developmental psychology as well—for instance, in the concept of *niche-picking* (e.g., Scarr & McCartney, 1983) and in research on heredity/environment interactions in intellectual development.

CLOSING THOUGHTS

A focus on Big Ideas has at least three advantages over a focus on *-isms*. First, Big Ideas are far less controversial than *-isms*; most theorists agree with them to some extent. (As an example, when I changed the title of the "Constructivism" chapter to "Knowledge Construction" in one of my textbooks—thus changing it from an *-ism* to a Big Idea—I received more consistently positive comments from reviewers.) Second, Big Ideas typically describe general principles of learning and/or instruction that lend themselves readily to concrete classroom applications; in contrast, experts do not always agree regarding the specific applications of various *-isms*. Finally, a focus on Big Ideas allows us to draw from two or more *-isms* simultaneously when developing classroom applications—perhaps to analyze the effectiveness of authentic activities in promoting transfer or to talk about teacher scaffolding when discussing ways to foster effective study strategies.

In closing, I must repeat two points I made earlier: The 26 Big Ideas I have just described for human learning are hardly an exhaustive list, and I have almost certainly omitted some of the ways in which various theoretical perspectives have contributed to these ideas. Furthermore, I must stress that we should continue to teach various theories of human learning *as theories*, because they provide essential foundations on which most Big Ideas rest. At the same time, one of our most central messages should be that all perspectives have practical value for teachers and other professionals. No single theory can ever be "best."

REFERENCES

Anderson, L. M., Blumenfeld, P., Pintrich, P. R., Clark, C. M., Marx, R. W., & Peterson, P. (1995). Educational psychology for teachers: Reforming our courses, rethinking our roles. *Educational Psychologist, 30,* 143–157.

Atran, S., Medin, D. L., & Ross, N. O. (2005). The cultural mind: Environmental decision making and cultural modeling within and across populations. *Psychological Review, 112,* 744–776.

Brophy, J., Alleman, J., & Knighton, B. (2009). *Inside the social studies classroom*. New York, NY: Routledge.

Hilgard, E. R., & Bower, G. H. (1966). *Theories of learning* (3rd ed.). New York, NY: Appleton-Century-Crofts.

McCombs, B. L. (Ed.). (2005). *Learner-centered principles: A framework for teaching*. Mahwah, NJ: Erlbaum.

Nathan, M. J. (2012). Rethinking formalisms in formal education. *Educational Psychologist, 47*, 125–148.

Patrick, H., Anderman, L. H., Bruening, P. S., & Duffin, L. C. (2011). The role of educational psychology in teacher education: Three challenges for educational psychologists. *Educational Psychologist, 46*, 71–83.

Sawyer, R. K., & Greeno, J. G. (2009). Situativity and learning. In P. Robbins & M. Aydede (Eds.), *The Cambridge handbook of situated cognition* (pp. 347–367). Cambridge, England: Cambridge University Press.

Scarr, S., & McCartney, K. (1983). How people make their own environments: A theory of genotype environment effects. *Child Development, 54*, 424–435.

CHAPTER 2

TEACHING BEHAVIORISM TO SUPPORT SELF-REGULATION, INTEGRATION, AND TRANSFER

**Rayne A. Sperling, Phillip M. Reeves, D. Jake Follmer,
Alexander L. Towle, and Kyung Sun Chung**
The Pennsylvania State University

In this chapter, we address the teaching of behaviorism to undergraduate students and share an instructional strategy that we implemented within this broad topic domain to address the primary goals of our course. The strategy was designed to combat challenges encountered when teaching learning theory for transfer given students' low prior knowledge and few prior or concurrent experiences. These challenges are compounded, as noted by Kiewra and colleagues (this volume), because of the inherent complexity of learning theories and the perceived lack of practical implications and applications of theory within classrooms. Our overarching goal when teaching educational psychology is transfer of student learning at several levels (e.g., Perkins & Salomon, 1988). These include transfer within the course, across the college's curriculum, and ultimately to contexts that

Challenges and Innovations in Educational Psychology Teaching and Learning, pages 15–28
Copyright © 2016 by Information Age Publishing
All rights of reproduction in any form reserved.

students will face in their personal and professional practice. The implementation and subsequent discussion of this activity created the opportunity for transfer and served as a model to provide vital connections between theory and practice (e.g., Anderman et al., this volume).

COURSE CONTENT AND ORGANIZATION

We believe educational psychology is the most important course any student can take as an undergraduate, especially when the essential connections among topics in the course and between course content and application are made salient. An understanding of behaviorism is necessary for future application in professional settings, in part because the application of behavioral techniques can serve as support for effective individual self-regulation. For example, through the use of behavioral techniques, self-knowledge is enhanced and, when monitored and graphed, feedback can reinforce and support individual behavioral change. Such an approach is commensurate with observations of those who cite the importance of self-monitoring for college students (e.g., Zimmerman & Paulsen, 1995) as well as by those who propose graphing as a metacognitive and self-regulatory tool (e.g., Manning, 1991).

One strand or theme of our course is teaching the important role of self-regulation during the learning process. We target students' own self-regulated learning and often discuss how to model, scaffold, and support others' effective regulation. Therefore, the instructional strategy we used to facilitate learning behaviorism also aided our intent to promote our students' self-regulated learning through effective monitoring, evaluation, and feedback.

Application of the principles taught in educational psychology courses provides the foundation for many concepts that can buoy individuals' navigation during everyday life experiences in addition to establishing the principles of effective instructional practice. Among other related topics within the scope of behaviorism content, our course covers principles of both classical and operant conditioning, the mechanisms of reinforcement and punishment, schedules of reinforcement, reinforcer potency, satiation, the benefits of reinforcement over punishment, types of reinforcers, temporal aspects of effective reinforcement, generalization and discrimination, as well as an introduction to shaping and Applied Behavior Analysis.

Key connections between behaviorism and other course content include connecting broad classes of behavioral theories and other learning theories, using graphing as a regulatory and management tool, demonstrating how monitoring enhances effective self-regulation and strategy use, and understanding how behavioral views of learning support effective instructional strategies for learning and management strategies for teaching.

Behaviorism, in our view, is critical and essential content for educational psychology courses taken by emerging professionals.

COURSE POPULATION

The behaviorism content in our course is typically found in learning and instruction classes and often is taught within the context of pre-service or master's level teacher education programs. Most introductions to educational psychology texts include related content (e.g., Eggen & Kauchak, 2012; O'Donnell, Reeve, & Smith, 2011). At our large research university, the course is taught in lecture halls to classes of up to approximately 190 students per section. Students generally enroll in the class early in their academic careers and many have not yet taken a post-secondary development or psychology course.

Further, students from a variety of majors enroll in our course. For example, all pre-service teachers enroll, including those specializing in kinesiology, music, and art education among others as well as special education, early childhood, elementary, and secondary education of all subjects. Rehabilitation services students, speech communication disorder students, some psychology and human development and family studies students, along with those in an integrated undergraduate program with science, and individuals seeking post-baccalaureate certification also enroll. A handful of students elect to take the course as they consider the possibility of future teaching or corporate training. The combination of the diversity of the students, lack of connection to a field experience, timing of the course within the unique curriculum plans of numerous majors, as well as the size of the course (i.e., number of enrolled students) present interesting challenges for instruction and learning. These difficulties are evident when attempting to provide support for transfer to practice given the many different career paths these diverse students want to pursue.

Additionally, our course serves as a prerequisite for special education majors and as a foundational course for students who are communication disorders majors. Subsequent course content in both of these majors relies heavily on behavioral foundations. Many of the remaining students who enroll in our course later register for a special education course for non-majors, and some may later complete an applied behavior analysis certificate program, which is recognized as one of the premier programs in the country (http://www.worldcampus.psu.edu/degrees-and-certificates/applied-behavior-analysis-for-special-education-certificates/overview). In short, many students will need to transfer foundational understanding of behaviorism and the application of behavioral principles to their future coursework as well as to professional practice in their careers.

Finally, we teach this course from a department comprised of school psychology, special education, counselor education, counseling psychology, rehabilitation, as well as educational psychology scholars. Taken together, these contextual elements make it necessary to provide an adequate foundation for students' future coursework and experiences.

BEHAVIORISM: HOW RELEVANT IS IT?

Most instructors of educational psychology would suggest that there is simply too much content to cover within our learning and instruction courses. Behavioral theories of learning have witnessed less attention in undergraduate educational psychology curriculum as evidenced by a limited inclusion of content in several course textbooks that we examined. In addition to the vast amount of content to cover in such courses, this reduction is also due, in part, to increased influence of cognitive, social cognitive, and constructivist views of learning and effective teaching. References to the changing views of behaviorism have been recognized and debated in the literature (e.g., Schlinger 2010; Wyatt, Hawkins, & Davis, 1986). At our institution, we have had to answer direct questions from colleagues outside of our department regarding why we teach behaviorism at all in our courses. Given the questions and, at times, objections from academic communities regarding the relevance of behaviorism, one clear challenge we must address through pedagogy is the relevance of the content for student learning and later practice.

Behaviorism is critical content to include in introductory educational psychology courses for numerous reasons that only minimally relate to historical foundations and for the purpose of situating contrasting views among mechanisms of learning across theories. Behaviorism is relevant to educational psychology in order to facilitate students' understanding when learning content but also because of the relevance of behavioral theories to the management of self and others' behaviors. Regarding within-class transfer, our students must have foundational understanding of behaviorism to best understand pedagogical strategies, such as precision teaching, and instructional strategies designed to support the learning of declarative knowledge and basic skills. Further, understanding behaviorism is critical for later integration of course content that addresses the principles of classroom management and the characteristics of effective feedback and praise.

TEACHING BEHAVIORISM

One of the biggest challenges of teaching learning theories to undergraduate students is the same challenge instructors always face: the students' lack of adequate prior knowledge and skills. Regarding educational psychology, previously learned information, and so-called folk psychologies (e.g., Daniels, this volume) also impede effective knowledge construction. Students in undergraduate educational psychology courses have spent considerable amounts of time learning in and out of classrooms. These experiences have led to perceptions of effective learning and teaching that directly influence their views of behaviorism. Many, for example, embrace punishment as an effective learning tool. Further, students hold misconceptions about the technical aspects and terms of behaviorism, in particular operant conditioning. These misconceptions, such as confusions among types of reinforcement (i.e., the belief that negative reinforcement and punishment are synonymous) have, unfortunately, often been strengthened by inaccurate examples and references in the mass media as well as by ineffective instruction in high school psychology courses.

In addition to limited and erroneous prior knowledge, students struggle to learn behavioral learning theory in our courses because of a large amount of vocabulary, the conceptual depth of the content we cover, and a lack of clear application to their current or future lives. Students often attempt to memorize the terms and mechanisms but fall short when learning outcomes require conceptual application.

In our course, we push beyond the typical examples of dogs and pigeons and seek conceptual understanding and transfer often unsupported by texts designed for the course. For instance, most students learn that if a reinforcer is presented, future behavior will likely increase. However, factors that influence the effectiveness of consequences, such as satiation, are not emphasized in many texts (e.g., Abramson, 2013). As a result, students may not fully realize the nuances of behavioral principles that necessitate analysis of both the person and the environment in order to optimize learning or behavioral change. We believe that a deeper understanding of behavioral views of learning, garnered through personal application and practice, enhances the likelihood of future application.

In teaching behaviorism over several years, we have relied on hundreds of examples of learning, reinforcement and punishment, and the nuances of behavioral theory based in everyday experiences and in classrooms to aid in transfer. However, some students were often still unable to connect behaviorism to other course content and their career goals, a concern echoed by Fives and Mills (this volume) regarding students' learning of Maslow's hierarchy. In short, we found that we were falling short on some of our instructional goals for the course.

Given these challenges and what we deemed as less than stellar success, we piloted a behavior modification and graphing activity to illustrate an application of behavioral theory. The implementation of graphing is not a new strategy for teaching behaviorism but the scope of our application and our intent was broader. We felt that, through the activity, students would see a direct application of behaviorism. They also would connect behaviorism to self-regulation through the mechanisms of monitoring, evaluation, and feedback. Students would also practice graphing and recognize graphing not only as an important skill but also as a teaching and management tool, and would actively connect theory and practice throughout the course.

INSTRUCTIONAL STRATEGY

Our piloted behavior modification activity was electively completed by 149 students in an undergraduate educational psychology course. The purpose of the activity was to facilitate the application of behavioral theories and principles of learning. Students who completed the assignment were given 1% extra credit. The activity centered on the selection of a target behavior and the application of behavioral principles to achieve a desired increase or decrease in the target behavior. An instructional scaffold (the exact materials are available from the authors) supported the activity and provided a series of steps that facilitated students' successful completion of the activity. These steps were: (1) selecting the target behavior; (2) selecting whether an increase or a decrease in the behavior was desired; (3) establishing a reinforcer; (4) determining the unit of analysis (e.g., frequency, time, distance etc.); (5) determining how the behavior was measured; (6) determining how the behavior was tracked or recorded; (7) implementing the reinforcement plan; and, (8) summarizing the results of the activity. Students were provided general recommendations for structuring and planning the graphing activity. The selection of the target behavior was open to the students. Required baseline recording of the target behavior occurred consecutively for three days.

After the tracking and recording of baseline data for the target behavior, students were encouraged to begin the implementation of a behavior modification plan. In the interest of time allocated for the activity, this occurred concurrently with the tracking of behavioral change over seven consecutive days. Some students developed more elaborate plans with the inherent goal of achieving behavioral change over an extended period of time (e.g., a plan to shape behavior gradually over the course of the rest of the semester) while some students' "plans" were simply to attempt change. These variations were acceptable given that the tracking and graphing of behavioral data were important components of the assignment. Student examples of longer-term modification plans were mentioned in class as related to introductory Applied Behavioral Analysis and discussion of more complex shaping content taught in the course.

Students were provided with potential example methods for both tracking (e.g., clickers, notepads) and recording (e.g., bar graphs, line graphs) behavioral change. At the completion of the activity, students were required to submit descriptions of the target behavior, descriptions of the methods utilized to track and record behavior, the graphs or representations produced, and an analysis of the effectiveness of the activity in leading to behavioral change. To facilitate conceptual understanding of the activity and integration of the activity with behavioral theories and principles of learning, and to further promote transfer, students were given a series of questions that encouraged critical thinking and analysis of the effectiveness of the activity. Example questions included: "For what other behaviors do you think this strategy might or might not work? Why?" "After completing this assignment, would you use an activity like this in your professional future? Why or why not? If so, how?" and, "How important do you think behaviorism is as a topic in this class? Explain your response." Written responses to these questions were also collected and coded.

Students were told that they could select any behavior that they may have wanted to increase or decrease. Numerous possible behaviors were mentioned (e.g., nail biting, exercise behaviors, water consumption). Students were encouraged to think about the frequency of behaviors that they might want to target given the need to record daily and also given the relatively short time of the activity. Students' selected behaviors were coded into nine broad categories based upon clustered similarities, including: electronics/ social media use, dietary behaviors, exercise behaviors, personal habits, swearing behaviors, sleep behaviors, academic behaviors, substance use, and miscellaneous behaviors. Table 2.1 outlines proportional engagement by students in each of these categories.

The units of measurement utilized by the students varied depending upon their chosen behaviors. Several common units of measurement

TABLE 2.1   Summary Information of Behavioral Categories and Proportions Within Categories

Category Number	Behavioral Category	Number of Participants	Percentage (%)
1	Electronic/Social Media	14	9.40%
2	Diet/ Health Behavior	50	33.56%
3	Exercise Behavior	22	14.77%
4	Personal Habits	15	10.07%
5	Swearing Behavior	13	8.72%
6	Sleep Behavior	12	8.05%
7	Academic Behavior	12	8.05%
8	Drug/Alcohol Behavior	4	2.68%
9	Miscellaneous	7	4.70%
	Total	**149**	**100.00%**

emerged, however, including: frequency of behaviors, duration of behaviors, as well as specific measurable quantities of behaviors, such as daily dietary intake in calories or money spent in dollars and cents.

Information regarding students' methods of behavioral tracking was also recorded. Students commonly relied on tally marks and time stamps recorded in their notebooks or on their mobile devices. Additionally, some students used tangible frequency counters, such as beads, coins, or paperclips, which they stored on their person and then moved to specific locations, such as a pocket, whenever they engaged in the target behavior.

Data representing students' use of reinforcers or punishers were also collected and are shared in Table 2.2. Typical reinforcers included food, beverages, money, extra time engaging in desired activities, such as television watching or social events, and the purchasing of desired tangible items, such as clothing. Of importance for later use of the strategy, some students reported that the activity and their progress and improvement in altering their behaviors through the activity, was intrinsically rewarding in itself.

Typical punishers included removal of social time, social media outlets, or electronic devices, as well as additional time spent exercising. There was wide variation in the timed application of these reinforcers and punishers. While some students chose to reinforce or punish immediately following their behaviors, others chose to reinforce or punish at the very end of the tracking period, which may have contributed to differing perspectives of the effectiveness and success of their self-selected modification strategies.

Next, information regarding the characteristics of students' behavioral changes was recorded. Approximately two-thirds of the participating students selected behaviors they desired to decrease, while the remaining

TABLE 2.2 Categories for Student-Selected Reinforcers/Punishers

Reinforcer/Punisher Type	Percent
Food or beverages	45.65
Relaxation time (including personal hobbies)	12.08
Health-related activities (including exercise)	9.40
Shopping	7.38
Using behavioral tracking	6.71
Social activities (with friends, family etc.)	5.37
Social media engagement	2.68
Money	2.01
Beauty routines	2.01
Sleep	2.01
Academic activities	1.34
Not specified	3.36

third selected behaviors they desired to increase. A majority (79.19%) of the students recorded findings that were consistent with their modification desires, although some reported evidence of no change. It is likely, however, that at least some of the students fabricated or dramatized their tracking data in order to be consistent with their expectations and desires, both for their own sense of behavioral improvement and for the purpose of gaining extra credit, although extra credit was not contingent on actual behavior change.

As students were tasked with graphing their behavioral changes, data were also recorded on the nature of their graphing techniques. Four major types of graphing were observed: line graphs (64; 42.95%), bar graphs (83; 55.71%), both bar and line graphs (1; .67%), and a pie chart (1; .67%). Figures 2.1 and 2.2 share examples of graphing strategies students used for the assignment.

Last, data regarding the students' beliefs about the utility of the assignment for their personal and professional lives, as well as the importance of teaching behaviorism, were recorded. The majority (86.58%) of students reported that they would use a behavioral modification and tracking strategy again in the future for their own personal use. Additionally, the majority of students (89.94%) reported that they would use a behavioral modification and tracking strategy again in their future professional careers. The overwhelming majority (99.33%) of students reported that they believe the teaching of behaviorism in educational psychology is important. It is

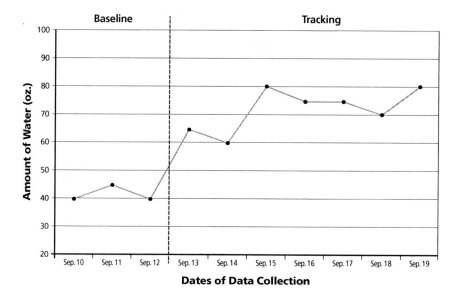

Figure 2.1 Student-submitted example graph: Daily water consumption.

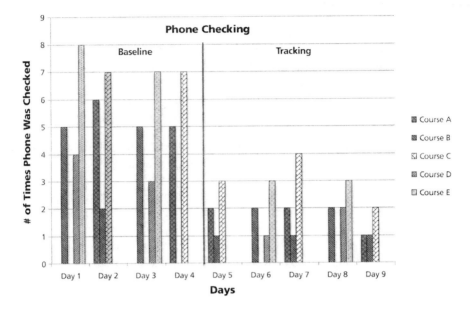

Figure 2.2 Student-submitted example graph: Frequency of phone checking in classes.

relevant to note, however, that these percentages reflecting fairly choral support for the teaching and application of behaviorist principles in educational programs is likely inflated by the students' desire to appease their instructor, whom they would perceive feels that there is value in the content by virtue of having administered the assignment. Still, there is unquestionably some evidence of support among students for the use of the activity and for application in teaching and learning behaviorism.

OBSERVATIONS AND CONCLUSIONS

We concur fully with Ormrod (this volume) when she asserts,

> I think we can all agree that the primary goal in an educational psychology class is to get students to think about how they might effectively apply what they're learning to real-world situations and problems—and ideally to actually put that knowledge to use in their future professional practices.

The purpose of the instructional strategy we employed to teach behaviorism aligns with this intent.

Given the views that supporting students' self-regulation is important, that modeling effective pedagogy is critical, that activities that require application are beneficial to students' conceptual understanding and transfer, and that behaviorism is important content to teach in undergraduate educational psychology courses, we piloted a new instructional strategy. Our intent was that, through additional application as required by the behavioral monitoring activity, students would generate deeper understanding and better integrate course content. The pilot of this activity was sufficiently successful to suggest revision and future use as an instructional tool. We feel the activity could be successfully implemented to teach behavioral learning theory content in undergraduate and graduate courses after modifications to account for students' prior knowledge.

Some of the success of the activity is apparent in that, despite the small payoff (i.e., 1% of course grade in resultant extra credit), 149 students completed the activity. Many students noted enjoyment in the activity and the results of their efforts related to personal behavior change. Others shared that the activity made them think about their target behaviors more often and helped them to attend to behavior change. Some noted it helped them to observe the effects of tangible monitoring of target behaviors.

Given the goal of supporting students' own self-regulation and mechanisms to scaffold others' monitoring, the behavioral modification activity presented students with strategies to monitor their future behavior and track and evaluate their progress toward goals. The graphs provide inherent feedback. We made sure to note in follow-up class discussions that a host of behaviors could be monitored through similar methods. These examples included study behaviors and strategies known to support academic success. For example, we shared that similar methods could be used to track and support distributed study practice and monitoring accuracy in homework problem completion.

The activity also provided ample opportunities to support integration and transfer of course content. As an example, connections among subsequent course content were delineated between this activity such as the role of effective reinforcement and the use of behavioral views of learning applied to classroom management. The activity was recounted and the role of graphing as an effective instructional strategy to indicate progress toward mastery in content learning was also discussed.

To connect other class content to the activity, in addition to the self-regulated learning content, we linked the use of the activity to principles of operant conditioning. We also connected the use of the activity and the selection of reinforcers to the frequency of reinforcement. The activity also provided a referent for future student contributions to class discussion. In diverse class sections that we teach in large lecture halls, increasing students' participation is one of our ongoing goals that this activity has helped us to attain.

As noted, students in this class often enroll in subsequent classes for which behavioral learning theory is important foundational knowledge. This activity provided a richer learning opportunity for students to hold for later transfer to course content on tracking students' learning and behavior and also for use as our students enroll in courses that target behavioral analysis and interventions as well as those that advocate precision teaching strategies.

Despite the success of this activity to meet many of our instructional goals for student learning and transfer, we recognize some limitations and room for modification in the activity as we prepare to teach our course again. First, the activity will become a required assignment and will replace one of the ten standing course assignments. Students' course grades are comprised of three multiple-choice tests and ten application and transfer assignments. These assignments are designed to provide practice for course content and also an opportunity for transfer in the form of application. The instructional strategy we described in this chapter fits within the scope of these assignments as it is designed to facilitate several levels of transfer (e.g., Perkins & Solomon, 1988).

Although a large portion of our students completed the activity for extra credit, others did not. Therefore, not all students took advantage of opportunities to learn and transfer understanding from the activity. This limitation was mediated slightly through instructor examples from the activity and related experiences. Nonetheless, the activity generated effects from which all students could benefit as they learn and apply course content.

A second modification we will make and recommend to those employing the activity is to strengthen a priori instruction for behavior recording and graphing and for selecting effective reinforcers. University students should know how to interpret and create graphs. The understanding of graphs and graphing skills are included in K–12 standards within several academic domains. For example, the National Assessment of Educational Progress, the Next Generation Science Standards, the Common Core State Standards, and the Social Studies Standards all address aspects of understanding or generating graphs. Nonetheless, as educational psychologists, our research indicates that students struggle to comprehend graphs (e.g., Peeples, 2013). Our students struggled with how to generate effective representations of their behavior tracking. Increased direct instruction on graphing will support our future students. Of note, graphing is discussed as a powerful tool in our class, and our students enroll in subsequent special education courses that require a working understanding of graphing behavior.

We used the activity as an instrument to discuss selection of reinforcer and reinforcer potency. Of those students who reflected upon the effectiveness of the activity for behavior change, several suggested they wished they had a 'better' or 'more effective' reinforcer. It may be that the success of the activity for application in class and for transfer would benefit from both a priori and post-activity attention to reinforcer selection.

A final recommendation, beyond the scope of our class but perhaps especially appropriate for those considering application of this activity for a higher level educational psychology course, is to extend the time and complexity of the activity. A longer duration activity that includes more than three days of baseline and perhaps additional, more authentic intervention designs will better facilitate understanding and transfer regarding the intricacies and nature of effective behavioral interventions.

In this chapter, we shared the pilot administration of an instructional strategy to enhance learning, integration, and transfer of behaviorism as a learning theory in undergraduate educational psychology courses. Through this activity, we were able to connect content from our class to K–12 academic standards. We also increased students' comfort with use of technical vocabulary terms, and enhanced class discussion of the effects of reinforcers and of recording behavior. Consistent with our overall class goals, we implemented this activity within the context of supporting the self-regulated learning of our students and provided a tool for their later use to scaffold others' regulation. The use of the activity realized opportunities for us to connect course content to the career goals of a diverse population of students.

REFERENCES

Abramson, C. I. (2013). Problems of teaching the behaviorist perspective in the cognitive revolution. *Behavioral Sciences, 3*(1), 55–71.

Anderman, E. M., Okonkwo, C., Lee, Y. L., & Collen, C. (this volume). Teaching pre-service teachers about goal orientations. In M C. Smith & N. DeFrates-Densch (Eds.), *Challenges and innovations in educational psychology teaching and learning.* Charlotte, NC: Information Age.

Daniels, D. H. (this volume). *Teaching child development to prospective educators.* In M C. Smith & N. DeFrates-Densch (Eds.), *Challenges and innovations in educational psychology teaching and learning.* Charlotte, NC: Information Age.

Eggen, P. D., & Kauchak, D. P. (2012). *Educational psychology: Windows on classrooms* (9th ed.). Upper Saddle River, NJ: Pearson.

Fives, H., & Mills, T. M. (this volume). Making motivation meaningful by mastering Maslow. In M C. Smith & N. DeFrates-Densch (Eds.), *Challenges and innovations in educational psychology teaching and learning.* Charlotte, NC: Information Age.

Kiewra, K. A., Flanigan, A. E., Luo, L., & Peteranetz, M. S. (this volume). *Teaching learning theories: A SOAR-driven approach.* In M C. Smith & N. DeFrates-Densch (Eds.), *Challenges and innovations in educational psychology teaching and learning.* Charlotte, NC: Information Age.

Manning, B. H., (1991). *Cognitive self-instruction for classroom processes.* Albany: State University of New York Press.

O'Donnell, A. M., Reeve, J., & Smith, J. K. (2011). *Educational psychology: Reflection for action.* New York, NY: John Wiley & Sons.

Ormrod, J. E. (this volume). *Teaching across rather than within theories of learning: A "big ideas" approach to organizing educational psychology courses.* In M C. Smith & N. DeFrates-Densch (Eds.), *Challenges and innovations in educational psychology teaching and learning.* Charlotte, NC: Information Age.

Perkins, D. N., & Salomon, G. (1988). Teaching for transfer. *Educational Leadership, 46*(1), 22–32.

Schlinger, Jr., H. D. (2010). The long good-bye: Why BF Skinner's Verbal Behavior is alive and well on the 50th anniversary of its publication. *The Psychological Record, 58*(3), 1.

Wyatt, W. J., Hawkins, R. P., & Davis, P. (1986). Behaviorism: Are reports of its death exaggerated? *The Behavior Analyst, 9*(1), 101.

Zimmerman, B. J., & Paulsen, A. S. (1995). Self-monitoring during collegiate studying: An invaluable tool for academic self-regulation. *New Directions for Teaching and Learning, 63,* 13–27.

CHAPTER 3

TEACHING LEARNING THEORIES

A SOAR-Driven Approach

**Kenneth A. Kiewra, Abraham E. Flanigan, Linlin Luo,
and Markeya S. Peteranetz**
University of Nebraska–Lincoln

Learning theories are an integral part of the teacher education curriculum. Prospective teachers might take a learning theories course or learn about them in an educational psychology course. Either way, learning theory instruction is meant to help teachers understand human learning and to design instruction compatible with learning principles. This chapter: (a) explains the importance of learning theories for teacher training; (b) specifies challenges associated with teaching learning theories; (c) offers a promising practice to meet this challenge; (d) demonstrates this practice; and, (e) concludes with instructional recommendations for teaching learning theories.

Challenges and Innovations in Educational Psychology Teaching and Learning, pages 29–43
Copyright © 2016 by Information Age Publishing
29

THE IMPORTANCE OF LEARNING THEORIES
FOR TEACHER TRAINING

We begin by offering three instructional scenarios followed by some questions.

Scenario A: *Abbey waves her arms feverishly and calls, "oh, oh," each time she volunteers to answer her teacher's question. Her teacher has called on her in the past, but now wants this behavior to stop. Why does Abbey do this? What should the teacher do to stop it?*

Scenario B: *When studying for his astronomy test, Baker makes flash cards with each card showing a planet name on one side (e.g., Mars) and a planet fact (e.g., orbit speed = 15,000 miles/hour) on the other. He reviews by going through the cards in random order again and again. What is wrong with Baker's approach? What alternate study method should the teacher suggest?*

Scenario C: *Cassidy gets a math test back and sees that she got a 65%. When speaking to the teacher about it, Cassidy blames her low performance on "being bad in math." What's wrong with Cassidy's reasoning? How should Cassidy's teacher react?*

How should teachers react to these scenarios? Fortunately, there exists a science of learning that can guide teacher understanding and intervention. That science is called learning theory. Actually, there are many learning theories that explain how learning occurs and provide the basis for teacher understanding and intervention strategies. Let's see how learning theory helps teachers in Scenarios A–C.

In Scenario A, operant theory helps the teacher understand that Abbey's hand waving and moaning persist because they are positively reinforced by the teacher calling on Abbey. Operant theory also provides an intervention, extinction, which involves—from here on out—ignoring Abbey's previously reinforced behaviors. If Abbey is not chosen to answer when she waves or moans, then eventually those behaviors will decrease.

In Scenario B, information-processing theory helps the teacher understand that Baker' piecemeal and rote approach is not conducive to understanding and remembering information. The same theory suggests that the teacher should encourage Baker to seek relationships among planet facts. For example, if Baker examines planets' orbit speeds relative to their distance from the sun, then he will learn this important relationship: As planets move farther from the sun, their orbit speeds decrease.

In Scenario C, attribution theory helps the teacher understand that Cassidy is making a faulty attribution when she blames poor performance on low math ability. Armed with an understanding of attribution theory, the teacher should council Cassidy that people are not inherently good or bad in math and that the cause of low performance is most likely the result of insufficient effort or weak math strategies—both of which can be fixed.

In summary, learning theories are the foundation for understanding the learning process and for making instructional decisions. All prospective teachers should be taught about learning theories and their implications for instruction. With learning theory information in hand, teachers become *meta-teachers* who reflect on and amend their teaching practices in accord with learning theory.

CHALLENGES ASSOCIATED WITH TEACHING LEARNING THEORIES

Three challenges for teaching learning theories are discussed. The first challenge is complexity. Learning theory has a long history, comprised of many theories and sub-theories, and much detail. To give you a flavor for this complexity, consider that learning theories date back to the times of Plato and Aristotle (around 400 B.C.), that current learning theory textbooks cover about 20 unique theories or sub-theories, and most theories contain multiple parts. Hull's Hypothetico-Deductive theory, for example, includes 17 laws and 133 specific theorems. This complexity makes it difficult for students studying learning theories to comprehend relationships within or across theories. For example, a student might be uncertain how different theories interrelate in terms of time (i.e., Which came earlier, classical or operant theory?) or classification (i.e., Is Guthrie's theory one of contiguity or contingency?). Or, how certain theories or their components compare and contrast (i.e., How are Pavlov's and Watson's conditioning theories alike and different? How are operant theory's positive and negative reinforcement components alike and different?).

A second challenge associated with teaching learning theories is that instructional implications are not always specified or tied to theory. Learning theory texts are commonly written for a general audience and do not necessarily include instructional implications for teachers. Educational psychology texts do present instructional implications, but these are not always tied to theory. Kiewra and Gubbels (1997), for example, found that several educational psychology texts presented theoretical information about behaviorism in one chapter and presented applied information about behavior management in a later chapter without linking theory and practice.

A third challenge is that students use ineffective techniques when they try to learn material, whether it pertains to learning theories or other content. They tend to make four errors reflective of shallow, non-meaningful processing that limit learning: (a) incomplete note taking; (b) poor organization; (c) piecemeal learning; and, (d) redundant strategies. In terms of note taking, students record incomplete notes (about 35%), which is problematic because amount of notes and achievement are positively correlated (Titsworth, 2004). In terms of organization, students rarely reorganize notes; when they do, they tend to create lists or outlines. Unfortunately, such linear organization actually restricts relationship learning (Kauffman & Kiewra, 2010). Most students also overlook potential relationships among ideas as they study one idea at a time in a piecemeal fashion. Piecemeal learning is akin to trying to figure out the end product of a puzzle by examining each puzzle piece one at a time rather than by how they fit together. Piecemeal learning is associated with low achievement (King, 1992). Finally, most students use redundant strategies like rereading, recopying, and reciting. These passive study techniques are also associated with low achievement (Callender & McDaniel, 2009).

In summary, learning theory instructors are apt to drown in the sea of learning theory information, not recognize the relationships among or within theories, and miss the potential instructional implications of those theories. Meanwhile, their students are apt to use shallow and ineffective learning techniques that limit learning.

SOAR: A PROMISING PRACTICE FOR TEACHING LEARNING THEORIES

One means to overcome these teaching and learning challenges is SOAR, a system developed by Kiewra (2009) meant to address common teaching-learning problems. SOAR is an acronym for the system's four components: select, organize, associate, and regulate. Students can soar to success by *selecting* all relevant information by taking complete notes (rather than incomplete ones), *organizing* information graphically (instead of linearly), *associating* ideas to one another and to prior knowledge (rather than learning in a piecemeal fashion), and *regulating* learning through self-testing (rather than employing redundant strategies). SOAR methods can be directly applied by students or prompted by teachers who, for example, provide complete notes, present graphic organizers, make relationships explicit, and offer practice test questions. And, SOAR methods have empirical support and are based on learning theory. Research confirms that students using SOAR materials outperform students using their preferred study methods when learning from text (Jairam & Kiewra, 2009) and from computer-assisted instruction (Jairam & Kiewra, 2010) and that SOAR studiers also outperform students who study materials based on a competing study system: SQ3R (Jairam, Kiewra, Rogers-Kasson, Patterson-Hazley, & Marxhausen, 2013). Meanwhile, SOAR fits with information-processing learning theory. As shown in Figure 3.1, SOAR's select component fosters attention,

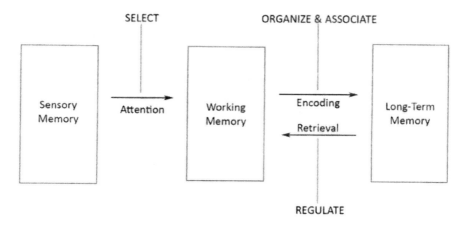

Figure 3.1 How SOAR fits with information processing theory.

the process by which important information enters into working memory. SOAR's organize and associate components foster encoding, the recoding process by which information enters long-term memory. And, SOAR's regulate component fosters retrieval, the process by which stored memories are returned to working memory. Unlike students' preferred study methods, which are linked with shallow, non-meaningful processing, SOAR methods are linked with deep, meaningful processing.

DEMONSTRATING SOAR FOR TEACHING
LEARNING THEORIES

In this section, we describe the empirical support for SOAR and demonstrate how a teacher educator could present information about a particular learning theory (operant theory) using the SOAR method. Operant theory was chosen because it includes concepts already familiar to readers such as reinforcement and punishment. In the end, you see how SOAR meets the three challenges of teaching learning theory: theory complexity is reduced, theory relationships and implications are emphasized, and students' ineffective learning techniques are replaced with effective ones.

Select

As previously mentioned, most students never give themselves a chance to succeed academically because they take incomplete lesson notes—recording just one-third of critical ideas. This is a big problem because the number of notes recorded is positively related to achievement. Moreover, note taking is useful because it serves process and product functions (Williams & Eggert, 2002). The process of taking notes aids in sustained attention during lessons. The product derived from taking notes provides an external record that can be studied later.

There are four proven ways to bolster note completion and aid the selection process. Instructors can provide: (a) complete notes; (b) skeletal notes; (c) cues; and (d) pauses.

Complete Notes

One obvious way to increase the completeness of students' notes is to simply give them a set of complete notes. Studying provided notes that are complete results in higher achievement than studying one's own notes, which are often incomplete. One study (Kiewra, 1985) went as far as to show that students who did not attend a lecture but later reviewed a set of provided notes achieved more than students who attended the lecture, recorded notes, and later studied them. Figure 3.2 shows a set of complete notes that might be provided to students for the operant theory lesson.

Skeletal Notes

Some instructors might be opposed to simply giving students a set of complete notes to study, believing that students should be active participants in information selection. Skeletal notes are a good alternative for those instructors (and their students). Skeletal notes get their name because they are akin to the bones on a skeleton. They contain the lesson's main ideas (bones) with spaces between them where students record lesson details (the flesh on the bones). Recording notes on skeletal frameworks leads to more notes and higher achievement than does recording notes without skeletal frameworks. One study (Kiewra, Benton, Kim, Risch, & Christensen, 1995) showed that students using skeletal notes recorded 22% more lesson ideas than students recording notes without a skeletal framework. Skeletal notes for the operant theory lesson might include just the bolded portions of Figure 3.2 with blank spaces for note taking following each bolded segment.

Lesson Cues

Teachers can also increase note taking by presenting cues throughout a lesson. Two types of cues have bolstered note taking: importance cues and organizational cues. Importance cues signal critical lesson information. Instructors can deliver such cues verbally when they say things like, "this is critical," or "note this;" non-verbally, perhaps by waving their arms or nodding their head; and, by using voice inflections such as speaking louder, softer, or slower. One proven way of importance cuing is jotting key words

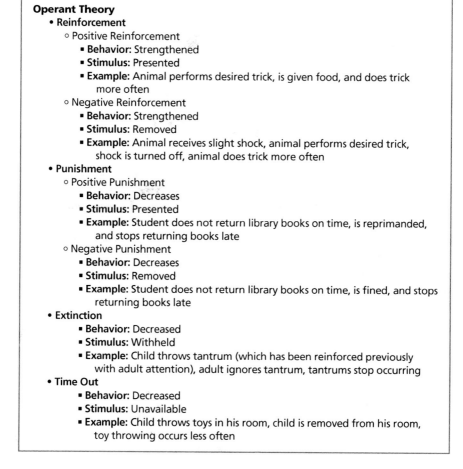

Figure 3.2 A set of complete notes for the Operant Theory lesson.

on the board. Students record nearly 90% of information written on the board. When teaching about operant theory, a teacher might supply importance cues like the following:

- "Note that the stimulus is removed for negative reinforcement."
- "It's crucial that you distinguish withheld stimuli from unavailable stimuli."
- "You surely see that "p-p-p-p-positive techniques involve the p-p-p-p-presentation of stimuli."

Organizational cues alert students to the lesson's organization and where they presently are within that lesson by signaling the topic and the category being addressed. When teaching the operant theory lesson, a teacher might say: "Now, we will discuss positive punishment (the topic) with respect to the behavior produced (the category)." Research confirms that inserting such organizational cues throughout a lesson bolsters notes in terms of both organizational points (in this case, the terms *positive punishment* and *behavior*) and detail points (in this case, noting that behavior is *increased*) and also raises achievement compared with an un-cued lesson (Titsworth & Kiewra, 2004).

Pauses

Students' incomplete note taking might be, in part, the result of physical limitations. Most lectures are presented at a rate of about 150 words per minute. And, although adults can listen at a rate of about 200 words per minute, they can only transcribe about 50 words per minute. That is why pauses interspersed throughout a lecture are useful; they give students more time to record lesson notes they might have missed originally. A recent study (Luo, Samuelson, & Kiewra, 2014) confirmed that interspersing three five-minute pauses during a 14-minute lecture led to greater note taking and higher achievement than providing the same amount of pause time immediately following the lecture. When teaching about operant theory, a teacher can provide occasional pauses for students to supplement their notes.

Organize

Students often have trouble learning from lessons because information is presented in a piecemeal fashion and organized linearly so that relationships among ideas are obscured. When possible, it is better to organize material in a hierarchy, sequence, or matrix. The matrix is the most powerful organizer because it is a cross-classification table, extended from hierarchies and sequences, which highlights comparisons among steps displayed in a sequence or elements displayed in a hierarchy. (See Kiewra, 2009, for descriptions of organizer types). For example, it is difficult to discern operant theory relationships from the linear display in Figure 3.2. The matrix in Figure 3.3, however, reveals quickly that positive and negative reinforcement both increase behavior. The benefit of matrices over text or linear displays is well supported. In one representative study (Kauffman & Kiewra, 2010), college students studied wildcat information displayed in text, outline, or matrix form. The matrix group learned up to 22% more facts and 21% more relationships than the other groups.

Matrices are instrumental for addressing the complexity-of-learning-theories challenge mentioned earlier. The matrices presented in Figures 3.3–3.5 illustrate how complex information is tamed. The Figure 3.3 matrix

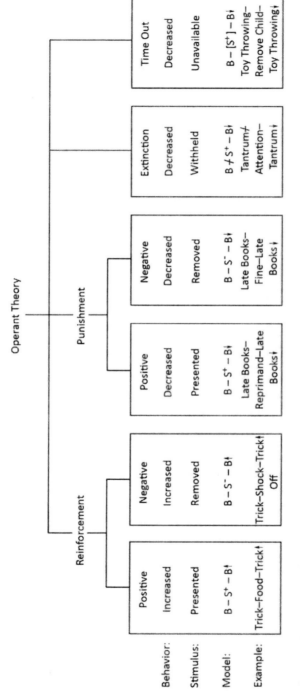

Figure 3.3 Operant Theory matrix organizer.

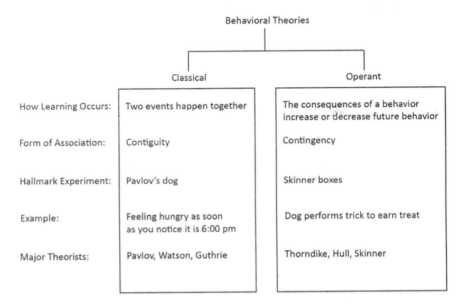

Figure 3.4 Matrix organizer comparing two behavioral theories.

on operant theory reveals the material's overriding classification structure (operant theory includes six techniques: two are types of reinforcement, and two are types of punishment) with just a glance. Similarly, Figure 3.4 displays how operant theory compares with another behavioral theory, and Figure 3.5 displays how behavioral theory compares with other theory classifications.

Associate

Organized information is of little value if studied one idea at a time in a piecemeal fashion. Instead, information should be associated. When associations are made, students learn more facts and, especially, learn more relationships. There are two types of associations: internal and external. Internal associations are those made within the new material being learned. External associations are those made between the new material and ideas outside that new material, usually stemming from the learner's prior knowledge. When teaching operant theory using the matrix in Figure 3.3, the following internal associations, among others, might be made:

- Reinforcement increases behavior, whereas punishment decreases behavior.
- Positive techniques involve stimulus presentation, whereas negative techniques involve stimulus removal.

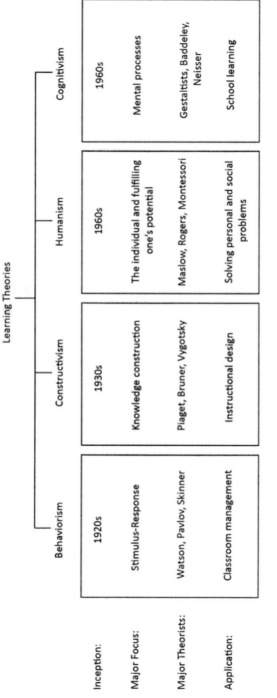

Figure 3.5 Matrix organizer comparing four learning theories.

- Punishment, extinction, and time out all decrease behavior.
- The stimulus is presented or removed in punishment, withheld in extinction, and unavailable in time out.
- An animal trick is an example of a behavior. Giving the animal a treat is an example of a presented stimulus. And, the animal doing the trick more frequently is an example of an increased behavior.

And, here are some external associations that might be made:

- An example of positive reinforcement is when a teacher hands out a gold star for high marks and the student earns even more high marks.
- An example of negative punishment is when a referee penalizes a football team 10 yards for holding and they do not hold thereafter.
- To remember information about extinction, think that the dinosaur population *decreased* and eventually went *extinct* because food was *withheld*.
- A teacher who wants to strengthen polite social behaviors should positively reinforce those behaviors.

Associations are instrumental for handling the lack-of-relationships-and-implications challenge mentioned earlier. Internal associations unveil important relationships within and across theories, and external associations are a means for providing teacher implications.

Regulate

Effective learners regulate learning. This means that they check their understanding before their teachers test them. Teachers can help students regulate learning by questioning them or by providing practice tests in advance of real ones. Students who regulate learning through practice testing outperform those who use other non-regulatory study methods (Karpicke & Roediger, 2007).

When teaching learning theories, teachers can provide students with practice questions that tap various learning outcomes such as facts, relationships, concepts (the recognition of new examples), and skills. Returning to the operant theory material, a teacher might provide these sample practice items: Fact items:

- For which technique does behavior decrease due to the removal of a stimulus?
- In extinction, is the stimulus presented, removed, withheld, or unavailable?

Relationship items:

- Which two techniques involve stimulus removal?
- Which two techniques involve an increase in behavior?

Concept items:

- When the baby cries at night, the parents ignore the crying. After several nights of this, the baby stops crying during the night. What operant technique did they use?
- When Johnny gets his chores done on time, his parents allow him to play computer games for 30 minutes. As a result, Johnny gets his chores done on time most every day. What operant technique are the parents using?

Skill items:

- A student is quiet and only occasionally speaks up in class. Come up with a plan based on operant theory that gets this student to speak up more in class.
- A child pulls books from a bookshelf whenever his father is around. The father believes that the child is doing this to gain attention from him. Describe how the father can use (a) extinction; and (b) time out to resolve this problem.

In summary, using SOAR methods addresses the three challenges of teaching learning theories. The graphic organization of ideas reduces information complexity. The association of ideas showcases relationships within and among theories and can include instructional implications. Overall, SOAR methods ameliorate the ineffective learning techniques students commonly employ.

RECOMMENDATIONS

Prospective teachers need to learn about learning theories so they can teach students in ways compatible with those theories. The problem is that prospective teachers, like most students, might use ineffective learning strategies themselves. They might record incomplete notes, fail to organize those notes, study those notes one idea at a time, and then try to commit noted ideas to memory using redundant strategies like re-reading and rehearsal. This chapter introduced an antidote to ineffective strategies called SOAR. Using SOAR, students: (a) select all the important information, not just one-third of it; (b) organize information in comparative matrices and other graphic forms rather than in linear forms that obscure relationships; (c) associate ideas rather than try to learn them one at a time; and, (d) regulate learning through practice testing rather than mindlessly repeating information over and over.

There are two methods that learning theory instructors can use to help students soar to success. The good-teaching method is accomplished when teachers develop SOAR-compatible materials and simply provide them to students. Teachers, for example, provide students with a complete set of notes (select) organized in matrix form (organize). Teachers also provide internal and external associations (associate) and practice test questions (regulate). The problem with the good-teaching method is that student learning depends entirely on the nature of instruction. Ideally, educators want students to learn under all circumstances, even when teaching is not so good. For that to happen, students must be taught how to learn and taught how to use SOAR strategies independently. This teach-students-how-to-learn method is accomplished by embedding strategy instruction (in this case, SOAR strategies) in content instruction (in this case, learning theory instruction).

Here is how students are taught how to learn. As the learning theory teacher is presenting information about operant theory, for example, she can embed the teaching of SOAR strategies such as organization. Strategy instruction includes four components: introduce, sell, perfect, and generalize. When teaching organization, the instructor can introduce the matrix strategy by presenting a matrix like that in Figure 3.3 and explaining how to create one using columns and rows. She can sell the strategy by describing and demonstrating why a matrix is more effective than a linear display for comparing learning theories or their components. The teacher can perfect the strategy by providing various opportunities to practice the matrix strategy while covering operant theory. The teacher can also generalize the strategy by suggesting other opportunities to use matrices, such as when comparing various behavioral theories or when comparing behavioral theory and cognitive theory. Such strategy instruction over time enables students to use SOAR strategies independently.

In conclusion, a SOAR-based perspective can help learning theory instructors design effective learning theory instruction and teach their students how to employ SOAR strategies on their own. To appreciate these two approaches, recall the old adage that giving a man a fish feeds him for a day while teaching him how to fish feeds him for a lifetime. That adage fits the two approaches presented here. Using the good-teaching method bolsters student learning for today. Using the teach-students-how-to-learn method bolsters student learning for a lifetime.

REFERENCES

Callender, A. A., & McDaniel, M. A. (2009). The limited benefits of rereading educational texts. *Contemporary Educational Psychology, 34*, 30–41.

Jairam, D., & Kiewra, K. A. (2009). An investigation of the SOAR study method. *Journal of Advanced Academics, 20*, 602–609.

Jairam, D., & Kiewra, K. A. (2010). Helping students soar to success on computers: An investigation of the SOAR study method. *Journal of Educational Psychology, 102*, 601–614.

Jairam, D., Kiewra, K. A., Rogers-Kasson, S., Patterson-Hazley, M., & Marxhausen, K. (2013). SOAR versus SQ3R: A test of two study systems. *Instructional Science*, 1–12. doi: 10.1007/s11251-013-9295-0

Karpicke, J. D., & Roediger, H. L. (2007). Repeated retrieval during learning is the key to long-term retention. *Journal of Memory and Language, 57*, 151–162.

Kauffman, D. F., & Kiewra, K. A. (2010). What makes a matrix so effective? An empirical test of the relative benefits of signaling, extraction, and localization. *Instructional Science, 38*, 679–705.

Kiewra, K. A. (1985). Learning from a lecture: An investigation of note taking, review, and attendance at a lecture. *Human Learning, 4*, 73–77.

Kiewra, K. A. (2009). *Teaching how to learn: The teacher's guide to student success.* Thousand Oaks, CA: Corwin Press.

Kiewra, K. A., Benton, S. L., Kim, S., Risch, N., & Christensen, M. (1995). Effects of note taking format and study technique on recall and relational performance. *Contemporary Educational Psychology, 20*, 172–187.

Kiewra, K. A., & Gubbels, P. S. (1997). Are educational psychology courses educationally and psychologically sound? What textbooks and teachers say. *Educational Psychology Review, 9*, 121–149.

King, A. (1992). Comparison of self-questioning, summarizing, and note taking-review as strategies for learning from lectures. *American Educational Research Journal, 29*, 303–323.

Luo, L., Samuelson, L., &, Kiewra, K. A. (2014, April). *Revising lecture notes: The effects of pauses and partners on note taking and achievement.* Paper presented at the annual meeting of American Educational Research Association, Philadelphia, PA.

Titsworth, B. S. (2004). Students' note taking: The effects of teacher immediacy and clarity. *Communication Education, 53*, 305–320.

Titsworth, B. S., & Kiewra, K. A. (2004). Spoken organizational lecture cues and student notetaking as facilitators of student learning. *Contemporary Educational Psychology, 29*, 447–461.

Williams, R. L., & Eggert, A. C. (2002). Note taking in college classes: Student patterns and instructional strategies. *Journal of General Education, 51*, 173–199.

CHAPTER 4

USING BELIEF TRANSFORMATION AS A THEORETICAL FRAMEWORK FOR TEACHING EDUCATIONAL PSYCHOLOGY

Sarah E. Peterson
University of Texas at El Paso

Connie M. Moss
Duquesne University

Everyone thinks of changing humanity; no one thinks of changing himself.
Our world is hungry for genuinely changed people.
—Tolstoy

OVERVIEW

When it comes to quality teachers, there is general consensus that beliefs matter. Research has shown that teachers' beliefs influence their teaching practices, their professional learning experiences, and their responses to reform efforts (Woolfolk Hoy, Davis, & Pape, 2006). Beliefs also play an

Challenges and Innovations in Educational Psychology Teaching and Learning, pages 45–58
Copyright © 2016 by Information Age Publishing
All rights of reproduction in any form reserved.

important role in formal teacher preparation programs. Aspiring teachers enter their teacher education programs with firmly established beliefs based on their years of experience as students. Coined as the "apprenticeship of observation" by Lortie (1975), these beliefs are often limited and simplistic, because they are developed from a student point of view. In addition, beliefs are usually implicit, difficult to articulate, and resistant to change (Wolfolk Hoy et al., 2006). Thus, aspiring teachers tend to graduate with their beliefs intact, which is problematic when they are expected to use teaching methods that differ from how they were taught. In fact, Darling-Hammond (2006) has identified confronting the apprenticeship of observation as one of the three major challenges in teacher education.

In this chapter, we provide an overview on beliefs and present a case for articulating clear, defensible outcomes when addressing the beliefs of aspiring teachers in educational psychology classes. We have developed an alternative approach to belief change that differs from most approaches in teacher education. We address the challenges inherent in transforming beliefs of aspiring teachers and describe our approach to facilitating belief transformation in our educational psychology courses, concluding with reflections on our experiences. Although our discussion is framed within the context of educational psychology courses, we believe that our approach can be used throughout teacher preparation curricula.

BELIEF CHANGE VERSUS BELIEF TRANSFORMATION: CLARIFYING THE TARGET

Teachers' beliefs have been defined as "tacit, often unconsciously held assumptions" (Kagan, 1992, p. 65). In spite of the important influences they have on teaching, the mechanisms by which beliefs influence practice have not been clearly established. Based on an extensive review of the research literature, Fives and Buehl (2012) proposed a model in which beliefs serve three functions to: (a) *filter* how experiences are interpreted, including what is learned about teaching; (b) serve as *frames*, influencing how teachers interpret classroom problems; and, (c) serve as *guides* for implementing teaching practices. The role of beliefs as filters has been of particular interest in teacher education programs because they influence what students learn about teaching and how they interpret what they learn. There has been less discussion in teacher education of beliefs as frames and guides, presumably because these functions focus more directly on teaching decisions and enactments of teaching practice. Nonetheless, we believe that each belief function plays a crucial role in teacher education, and our educational psychology courses have been designed to engage our students with all three.

Numerous accounts have documented teaching interventions designed to address the beliefs of aspiring teachers. The interventions range from one semester to entire programs and usually involve reflective learning activities designed to raise students' awareness of their beliefs. Example strategies include structured group activities, refutational text, augmented activation, and course assignments requiring reflection, professional placements, and direct experiences with learners (Fives & Buehl, 2012; Mansfield & Volet, 2014). Results of interventions have been mixed, but some factors that seem to influence effectiveness include making connections to classroom practice through field experiences and/or student teaching, length of the intervention (e.g., one course versus entire teacher education program), building on previous beliefs, and addressing both cognitive and affective aspects of change (Fives & Buehl, 2012; Wideen, Mayer-Smith & Moon, 1998).

Most interventions focus on changing pre-service teachers' beliefs with the intervention being deemed successful if the desired belief change is documented. We have several concerns about this focus on belief change. First, attempts to change aspiring teachers' beliefs are based on the implicit assumption that aspiring teachers enter their teacher education programs with faulty beliefs in need of change (Mansfield & Volet, 2014; Woolfolk Hoy & Murphy, 2001). On the one hand, we acknowledge that research supports this assumption (Wideen et al., 1998; Woolfolk Hoy & Murphy, 2001). If we as teacher educators, however, argue that our students should question their implicit beliefs, then we must also recognize the role played by our own unquestioned assumptions about our students' beliefs. By viewing all aspiring teachers' beliefs as faulty, we begin our work using a deficit model focused on fixing them. In fact, research has also shown that aspiring teachers sometimes enter their programs with perfectly acceptable, although perhaps not sophisticated, beliefs about the nature of teaching and learning (Woolfolk Hoy & Murphy, 2001).

A second concern with focusing on belief change is that no one has yet developed an appropriate set of beliefs that should be taught and ultimately adopted by aspiring teachers and those who educate them. Much of the current literature on belief change has emphasized the promotion of constructivist beliefs that are currently in vogue and reflected in professional standards (Darling-Hammond, 2006; Raths & McIninich, 2003). Such change often requires that students abandon beliefs of teaching as transmission of information, formerly thought to be "right." As new theory and research have emerged, our beliefs about good teaching have changed. We find ourselves in a conundrum when we try to identify a set of beliefs to be taught to aspiring teachers, for what is considered to be a good belief today might not be supported by research tomorrow (Raths & McIninch, 2003). Furthermore, when we appoint ourselves up as judge and jury on the beliefs that aspiring teachers should hold, we do them a disservice by not shaping them in a way that encourages them to be forever vigilant of their beliefs. In essence, when we promote a finite list of important beliefs for them to adopt during their pre-service years, we communicate that there is no need for them to continue to challenge their beliefs throughout their professional careers.

Due to the inherent limitations in focusing on changing aspiring teachers' beliefs, Raths (2001) proposed a different way of conceptualizing teacher education. Arguing that it is impossible to determine a complete set of beliefs that should be developed, Raths proposed that we focus, instead, on strengthening dispositions. He identified three possible dispositions important for teaching: valuing professional knowledge; colleagueship; and, advocacy. Although intriguing, we believe that attempting to develop a complete set of desirable dispositions leaves us in the same quandary as attempting to identify a complete set of desirable beliefs. When we focus instead on developing teachers who systematically and intentionally reveal and challenge their beliefs against the best theory and research, then we develop teachers who can look at their beliefs as evolving rather than fixed.

A third concern about targeting belief change is based on findings in the research literature: beliefs are resistant to change, beliefs are not always consistent (Woolfolk Hoy et al., 2006), and we still don't completely understand the mechanisms by which beliefs influence learning about teaching (Fives & Buehl, 2012). As a result, some have argued that fostering the development of new beliefs in aspiring teachers may not be a necessary condition for effective practice, but there is no question that making effective teaching decisions is crucial. They suggest instead that the best place to start might be to teach effective practices, which might result in an eventual change in beliefs (Raths & McAninch, 2003). On this debate, we wholeheartedly agree with Fives and Buehl (2012) that beliefs should not be discounted, but considered as important precursors to teaching practices, and efforts should be made to understand why beliefs and practices are not always consistent. In the absence of compelling data addressing this question of how beliefs relate to teaching decisions, it seems plausible that a focus on helping aspiring teachers learn to reveal and challenge their beliefs must be balanced with a focus on helping them learn to make effective teaching decisions. Therefore, our approach to teaching educational psychology has emphasized learning how to weigh the effectiveness of instructional strategies and classroom decisions using relevant theory and research and, in doing so, engendering a continuous process of belief transformation.

A final concern is that the majority of the literature on the role of teacher beliefs has been based predominantly on studies of White, middle class, female teachers (Woolfolk Hoy et al., 2006). Teachers from underrepresented or marginalized populations may hold different beliefs about teaching, and therefore view themselves and their tasks very differently. Alternative, and perhaps transformative, perspectives of minority teachers are not represented in the research base and deserve to be voiced. Simply pursuing the target of having aspiring teachers adopt a set of "changed beliefs" connotes that the beliefs of the majority culture represented in the literature is more useful than the beliefs of educators who experience education from different frames of reference.

To move beyond the goal of belief change, we contend that teacher educators should engage aspiring teachers in processes and experiences that actively foster intentional inquiry into their beliefs about teaching and learning. By redirecting our focus, we move beyond the dilemmas posed above. Based on existing research, we argue that teacher education should help aspiring teachers develop the knowledge and skills to engage in systematic and intentional inquiry focused on using theory and research to continuously reveal, examine, and challenge their beliefs instead of teaching them that they must necessarily change their beliefs (Cunningham, Schreiber, & Moss, 2005; Peterson, Schreiber, & Moss, 2011). Our goal as teacher educators, therefore, should not be to teach aspiring teachers *what* to believe or convince them they *must* change their beliefs; rather our goal should be to help them learn how to recognize, uncover and challenge their beliefs through the lenses of theory and research. In doing so, we intentionally foster both an appreciation for the role that beliefs play in their decisions of practice and the importance of systematic and intentional inquiry. Learning this process sets in motion the potential for lifelong learning as it fosters healthy skepticism about the validity of the beliefs we hold.

CHALLENGES IN TRANSFORMING BELIEFS

Beliefs are often implicit, simplistic, difficult to articulate, and resistant to change—even in the face of strong contradictory evidence. Our collective years of experience teaching educational psychology courses have borne out these observations for several reasons. First, aspiring teachers have developed their beliefs from their own limited perspectives as students. They have not had opportunities to view teaching from the teacher's perspective with all of its complexities, and are novices at thinking like a teacher (Darling-Hammond, 2006). For example, students in an educational psychology class might believe that high school students learn best by copying notes from a Powerpoint slide simply because they themselves were successful in doing so. Lacking knowledge of learning theory or understanding of diverse students' learning needs, they may fail to grasp the complexity of teaching, settling for supporting simple solutions that have worked for them.

A second challenge is that aspiring teachers have rarely, if ever, been asked to think about their underlying beliefs and assumptions. Furthermore, they have yet to develop the professional language to describe complex concepts related to teaching and learning. Aspiring teachers routinely believe that they won't actually learn how to teach until their student teaching experience and, therefore, often do not recognize the value of education courses as connected to the real life work of the classroom. We agree with Daniels (this volume) that they may come into their educational psychology classes expecting to confirm what they already "know." As a result, being asked to uncover their beliefs and assumptions about teaching is difficult, at first. Furthermore, being asked to share their beliefs publicly can be threatening and uncomfortable.

A third challenge is that aspiring teachers lack teaching experience to which they can make connections between beliefs and teaching practices. Going back to our previous example, suppose pre-service teachers are planning a lesson for an educational psychology assignment, in which high school students will take notes from a Powerpoint slide—an experience with which our pre-service students are very familiar. Based on their pre-existing beliefs, initially they think they are proposing excellent teaching. After learning about scaffolding, however, they now have a more sophisticated lens that offers the potential for them to discover the gap between teaching and learning for their high school students. However, simply learning about scaffolding is not sufficient for closing the gap—they need to consider both what is taking place in the lesson, as well as what is missing. Juxtaposing their new conceptual understanding and language for scaffolding, with a new awareness of their previously held belief about good teaching as lecturing with Powerpoint notes, creates a state of disequilibrium in which they begin to experience genuine doubt about their beliefs, setting the stage for belief transformation. Therefore, deep learning requires that they gain conceptual understanding of theoretical concepts, that they enter into a state of ambiguity about their previously held beliefs, and that they can make meaningful connections to authentic teaching (Moss, 2002).

Given these circumstances, it is not surprising that the process of revealing and challenging beliefs is challenging for students, especially in the initial stages. One of the methods by which we have been most successful in overcoming these challenges is to scaffold the process by asking our students to complete the following prompt: "I used to think that _____ but now I know that _____, because _____." While the prompt appears simplistic at first blush, it provides students with an entrée to connecting what they propose to do in their classrooms to the beliefs they hold. It also helps in developing an understanding that their beliefs are what they use to determine the effectiveness of their teaching and what they will count as evidence that student learning has been positively impacted. In this way, belief transformation happens by leading students into a state of disequilibrium. Belief transformation only happens when the person reaches "genuine doubt," a cognitive process where individuals try to reconcile what they experience with the beliefs that they hold (Cunningham et al., 2005). When individuals' beliefs do not make sense, they must either refine their beliefs or discard them for new ones.

Teachers of educational psychology must address all three of these challenges while being mindful of how they are inter-related. Learning experiences must be designed to help students learn to transition from thinking as a student to thinking as a teacher; students must be given plenty of opportunities to identify their tacit, explicit beliefs about teaching and learning. They must also understand how these learning opportunities connect to authentic teaching activities. Next, we describe how we have tackled these challenges by establishing the connection between course assignments and effective teaching within authentic contexts, regardless of whether or not field experiences are involved.

PROMISING PRACTICES FOR BELIEF TRANSFORMATION

Our educational psychology courses have been based on a framework of systematic and intentional inquiry developed by the second author. This framework has been used in undergraduate and graduate courses in educational psychology and child/adolescent development, as well as graduate level courses in learning and motivation, in both face-to-face and online environments. We have used the same theoretical framework of systematic and intentional learning, along with a focus on transforming beliefs (Peterson et al., 2011).

All of our educational psychology courses have several crucial components in common: (a) learning objectives that focus on belief transformation as well as course content; (b) development of authentic teaching projects or case studies through which to consider theory operating in effective practice; (c) critical analysis of projects using theory and research to identify elements that are supported by theory and research, as well as to identify areas in need of improvement; (d) using theory and research to propose specific changes that will make the project more theoretically sound; (e) identification and reflection on assumptions and beliefs in light of new learning about theory and research; (f) reflective summary reports; and (f) analytic rubrics guiding the writing and evaluation of student papers (see Table 4.1). Each of these components is described briefly.

Learning Objectives

Although objectives are tied to the specific content in the courses, our major learning objectives have always been to develop an understanding of

TABLE 4.1 Rubric for Learning Project Analysis Assignment

	Levels of Performance			
	(D) Unsatisfactory	(C) Basic	(B) Proficient	(A) Distinguished
Project Abstract (×5)	Project summary does not highlight learning goals, major learning activities, and products and/or performances from the project. The abstract does not summarize the developmental stages and characteristics of the students in the class. Little mention is made of context for the learning project.	Project summary presents learning goals, major learning activities, and products and/or performances that represent the project. Project is set in context.	Learning goals, professional standards, major learning activities, and products and/or performances presented clearly indicate to reader the significance of the learning project. In addition, the abstract summarizes the developmental stages and characteristics of the students in the class. Project is set in context.	Learning goals, professional standards, major learning activities, and products and/or performances presented clearly indicate to reader the significance of the learning project. In addition, the abstract clearly summarizes the developmental stages and characteristics of the students in the class. Contextual anchors provide the reader key information with which to consider the goals and activities.
Analysis Using Theory and Research (×25)	Aspiring teacher displays minimal understanding of key principles involved in the teaching-learning process. Key principle and underlying theory & research are not set in the context of the learning project.	Aspiring teacher displays basic understanding of key principles. Key principle and underlying theory and research are considered in the context of the learning project.	Aspiring teacher displays solid knowledge of key principle. Theory and/or research from the text are cited within the context of the project. Demonstrates analysis of the project using the key principle, describes connections between the key principle and the learning of students, and provides insight for further developing and refining the project.	Aspiring teacher displays extensive knowledge of key principle. Theory and/or research from the text are cited in support of claims about the project. Demonstrates critical analysis of the project using the key principle, explicitly describes connections between the key principle and the learning of all students, and provides important insight for further developing and refining the project.

(continued)

TABLE 4.1 Rubric for Learning Project Analysis Assignment (continued)

	Levels of Performance			
	(D) Unsatisfactory	(C) Basic	(B) Proficient	(A) Distinguished
Assumptions of Practice (× 20)	Assumptions are not identified, analyzed, or discussed. Validity of assumptions is not considered.	Tentative assumptions are identified in broad, general terms. Validity is considered, but not connected to specific theory or research.	Assumptions are accurately identified. Specific theory and research is connected to decisions regarding the validity of the assumptions. Consideration of assumptions provides insight for refining the project.	In addition to accurate identification and specific analysis of the validity of the assumptions, theory and/or research are cited from the text to support the basis for the validity of decisions. Consideration of assumptions provides significant insight for refining the project.
Changes & Refinements (× 20)	Changes/Refinements do not reflect consideration of theoretical knowledge.	General changes or refinements are listed that connect to general theory and research.	Specific changes or refinements are listed that demonstrate clear connections to specific theory and research.	In addition to being clearly connected to specific theory and research, specific changes or refinements listed, when considered as a group evidence careful consideration of the dynamic nature of the learning project.
Connections to the Themes and Domains of the LTP (× 5)	Connections are vague or inaccurate and demonstrate minimal understanding of the themes and domains of the LTP.	Connections are general and demonstrate basic understanding of the themes and domains of the LTP.	Connections are explicit and demonstrate solid understanding of the themes and domains of the LTP.	Connections to current analysis and key principle are explicit and comprehensive and demonstrate significant insight into the meaning of the themes and domains of the LTP.
Quality of Writing (× 25)	Writing contains many grammar and syntax errors. Repeated patterns of mechanical and usage errors seriously interfere with writer's purpose. Vocabulary is not on a professional, formal level, may be inappropriate, vague, or used incorrectly.	Grammar and syntax are correct. Professional vocabulary is limited but appropriately used. Most thoughts are expressed formally.	Writing is on a formal and professional level. Communication of ideas is clear and accurate. Language reflects correct usage of a professional vocabulary. Ideas borrowed from other sources are professionally cited.	Writing is of publishable quality. The language used reflects a careful choice of words and a vocabulary that documents a growing professional knowledge base that includes increased use of previous key principles. Ideas borrowed from other sources are professionally cited.

relevant theory and research operating in effective practice (Peterson et al., 2011). We want students to: (a) understand theory and research as lenses through which to consider effective practice; (b) recognize, reveal, and challenge their assumptions about teaching and learning in light of theory and research; and (c) use theory and research to evaluate, defend, and/or modify their decisions of teaching practice. Examples of objectives specific to belief transformation include: (1) develop the ability to reveal, examine, and challenge beliefs about motivation; and (2) engage in reflective practice that focuses on revealing and challenging personal and collective beliefs using the theory and research that guide effective educational practice.

Development of Authentic Teaching Projects

Our educational psychology courses are built on the assumption that a crucial element for professional education courses is the need to anchor students' learning in authentic contexts so that they learn inside practice. Ideally, they learn most meaningfully when they can use their knowledge of theories and research in actual classrooms (e.g., observe in classrooms through field experiences). Planning effective lessons, however, also reflects actual classroom practice and even though educational psychology classes are not always tied to field experiences students can still develop knowledge and skills by engaging in this real work of classroom teaching, an important component of which is effective research-based instructional planning. With these fundamental ideas in mind, we ask each student to begin the course by proposing a learning project to serve as the context for investigating relevant educational theory and research that supports effective teaching. Learning projects consist of a unit or program of study that our students intend to teach in their anticipated professional positions. For each unit of educational psychology, students file Learning Project Analyses that include the following components:

Overview of the Learning Project

Students write an overview that includes a description of the targeted learners, intended learning goals, major learning activities, and products and/or performances used to assess achievement of the learning goals. They also identify five initial assumptions they make about teaching and learning.

Analysis of Projects Using Theory and Research

As the course progresses, students use theories and research to analyze and refine their projects, submitting learning project analyses for each unit of study. We ask students to use theoretical concepts and research from the unit to analyze decisions of practice in their learning projects.

They identify elements of their project that are and are not supported by theory and research. In this process, their beliefs serve as attentional filters as they make decisions about which concepts to use/not use in their analyses. As they analyze their units for elements that are supported or not, their beliefs also serve as frames to guide them in conceptualizing and analyzing problems of teaching.

Changes and Refinements

Having analyzed their projects for elements that are supported or not supported, students then propose ideas for refining, replacing, or changing those decisions when warranted to make their project more theoretically sound and research based. In this process, their beliefs serve as guides for making effective teaching decisions.

Reflection on Beliefs

Students are asked to identify at least one belief that has become explicit in light of new learning about theory and research. They discuss if it is a new belief, a modified belief, or a belief that has changed completely. They cite theory and/or research in support of their consideration of the validity of these beliefs.

Reflective Summary Reports

At the end of the course, students prepare a reflective summary report highlighting, first, their areas of significant learning. They are asked to explain why each area is significant and how it relates to effective teaching practice. Second, they generate a list of theoretically supported beliefs they now hold about the teaching-learning process. They indicate if these beliefs are newly developed beliefs, previous beliefs that have been modified as a result of their learning, or previous beliefs that are now supported by theory and research. Students also discuss how their beliefs are related to effective teaching practice, either within the context of their project or other teaching contexts.

Analytic Rubrics

For all writing assignments, students are given detailed rubrics to guide their writing and we use the rubrics for grading students' papers (Table 4.1). Criteria focus on the above learning/thinking processes, as well as depth of content learned and applied to authentic teaching decisions, but never on getting the "right" answer or saying what the teacher wants to hear.

Therefore, we believe these rubrics allow us to gather valid evidence of students' belief transformations because they do not have to report belief change to get a good grade.

REFLECTIONS ON BELIEF TRANSFORMATION

Although students initially treat these assignments as requirements to be completed for a grade, they begin to see that planning lessons and units of study require more than assigning fun classroom activities or providing a lecture with Powerpoint. As students begin to justify their lesson plans against theories of human development, cognition and learning, motivation, instruction, and assessment and grading, they become increasingly aware of what an effective lesson requires and acutely aware of the shortcomings of their original plan.

Because their original unit plan is an undeniable snapshot of their beginning beliefs and knowledge of effective teaching, analyzing it during each learning cycle leads the students deeper into disequilibrium. As they gain experience in challenging their beliefs, they also gain experience as teachers who can plan theoretically sound and research-based lessons for learners at a specific developmental level. In doing so, they transition from thinking like a student to thinking like a teacher; and, as they increasingly frame their task as improving a lesson they will teach to their future students, they are able to make more sophisticated connections to theory and see connections among theoretical frames. For example, they become able to explain how an effective lesson could be justified using theories of schema development, social cognition, and self-efficacy. For us, the power of the process we have put into motion becomes clear as students compare their first lesson analysis to their final analysis. The growth in their knowledge and skill as teachers coupled with their sophisticated approach to revealing and challenging their own beliefs as part of effective classroom practice becomes evident. The process we have used addresses the challenges in belief transformation and promotes learning inside of practice to raise students' consciousness about effective teaching.

Reflecting on the role of beliefs as filters, frames, and guides, we have analyzed hundreds of student papers, identifying instances where students: (a) ignored information that was incompatible with their beliefs, thus filtering out important information; (b) focused on information that was contrary to prior beliefs, thus using filters as attentional mechanisms to embrace cognitive dissonance and gain significant new insight into teaching; and (c) focused on information that confirmed their prior beliefs, again using filters as attentional mechanisms to develop more sophisticated beliefs. Note that in the first instance, no belief transformation took place, whereas in the second and third instances, there was belief transformation. In the second instance, beliefs were changed, and in the third, beliefs were transformed when students were able to support prior beliefs with theory and research. We have found that approximately 20% of students' exiting beliefs are previously held beliefs that are now supported with theory and research; 50% are prior beliefs that have been modified but, again, are more sophisticated because they have more nuanced understandings; 20% are new beliefs; and, 10% are beliefs that have completely changed. Our experiences and analyses confirm that the goal of belief transformation is not only viable, but also important for developing teachers who are aware of their beliefs and also willing to challenge their beliefs in light of theory and research.

RECOMMENDATIONS AND CONCLUSIONS

We have argued that teacher educators should provide aspiring teachers with opportunities to reveal, examine, and challenge their beliefs about teaching and learning to attain two important goals. The first goal is to help students develop the habit of mind to constantly reveal and challenge the beliefs that they hold. The second is to create conditions that hold the potential for leading our students into genuine doubt and belief transformation. These opportunities may or may not result in belief change but they result in something much more important—teachers who understand the need to constantly hold their beliefs and practices up to scrutiny. It is this process of constantly examining one's beliefs that allows a teacher to engage in continuous and intentional professional learning focused on raising instructional effectiveness. Clearly, we believe it is important to scaffold critical self-assessment and self-regulation for our students. Teachers who approach their profession as a continuous process of examining their practice against theory and research create a very different trajectory for their careers. This habit of self-excavation, self-monitoring, and self-regulation is the engine that drives thoughtful professionals who can continue to transform their beliefs throughout the whole of their educational practice.

REFERENCES

Cunningham, D. J., Schreiber, J. B., & Moss, C. M. (2005). Belief, doubt and reason: C.S. Peirce on education. *Educational Philosophy and Theory, 37*(2), 178–189.

Darling-Hammond, L. (2006). *Powerful teacher education: Lessons from exemplary programs.* San Francisco, CA: Jossey-Bass.

Fives, H. & Buehl, M. M. (2012). Spring cleaning for the "messy" construct of teachers' beliefs: What are they? Which have been examined? What can they tell us? In K. R. Harris, S. Graham, & T. Urdan (Eds.) *APA educational psychology handbook: Vol. 2. Individual differences and cultural and contextual factors.* Washington, DC: American Psychological Association.

Kagan, D. M. (1992). Implications of research on teacher belief. *Educational Psychologist, 27*, 65–90.

Lortie, D. (1975). *Schoolteachers: A sociological study.* Chicago, IL: University of Chicago Press.

Mansfield, C. F., & Volet, S. E. (2014). Impact of structured group activities on re-service teachers' beliefs about classroom motivation: An exploratory study. *Journal of Education for Teaching: International Research and Pedagogy, 40*(2), 155–172. doi: 10.1080/02607476.2013.869967.

Moss, C. M. (2002, April). *In the eye of the beholder: The role of educational psychology in teacher inquiry.* Paper presented at the annual meeting of the American Educational Research Association, New Orleans, LA.

Peterson, S. E., Schreiber, J. B., & Moss, C. M. (2011). Changing preservice teachers' beliefs about motivating students. *Teaching Educational Psychology, 7*(1), 27–39.

Raths, J. (2001). Teachers' beliefs and teaching beliefs. *Early Childhood Research & Practice, 3*(1), 1–11.

Raths, J., & McIninch, A. C. (2003). *Teacher beliefs and classroom performance: The impact of teacher education.* Greenwich, CT: Information Age Publishing.

Wideen, M., Mayer-Smith, J., & Moon, B. (1998). A critical analysis of the research on learning to teach: Making the case for an ecological perspective on inquiry. *Review of Educational Research, 68* (2), 130–178.

Woolfolk Hoy, A., Davis, H., & Pape, S. J. (2006). Teacher knowledge and beliefs. In P. A. Alexander & P. H. Winne (Eds.), *Handbook of educational psychology* (2nd ed.). Mahwah, NJ: Lawrence Erlbaum.

Woolfolk Hoy, A., & Murphy, P.K. (2001). Teaching educational psychology to the implicit mind. In B. Torff & R. J. Sternberg (Eds.), *Understanding and teaching the intuitive mind: Student and teacher learning.* Mahwah, NJ: Lawrence Erlbaum.

CHAPTER 5

TEACHING LEARNING STRATEGIES TO PRE-SERVICE EDUCATORS

Practice What We Preach!

Aaron S. Richmond
Metropolitan State University of Denver

"If simple techniques were available that teachers and students could use to improve student learning and achievement, would you be surprised if teachers were not being told about these techniques and if many students were not using them?" (Dunlosky, Rawson, Marsh, Nathan, & Willinghmam, 2013, p. 5) Unfortunately, the answer to this question is *no* because educational psychology textbooks and instructors are failing to emphasize and teach this essential educational topic. As pre-service educators are most often taught learning strategies in educational psychology courses and that they then enter K–12 classrooms and promote learning strategies to their students, it is imperative that we teach our students accurately and effectively. What, then, can we do to correct this problem? To answer this question, the goals of this chapter are to: (1) illuminate the significance of teaching learning strategies;

Challenges and Innovations in Educational Psychology Teaching and Learning, pages 59–70
Copyright © 2016 by Information Age Publishing
All rights of reproduction in any form reserved.

(2) identify obstacles to teaching learning strategies; (3) describe and assess an instructional method (active learning) for teaching learning strategies; (4) provide strategies on how to implement learning strategies into an educational psychology course; and (5) ultimately, practice what we preach.

THE NUTS AND BOLTS OF LEARNING STRATEGIES

Before jumping into the significance of teaching learning strategies, it is important to define these concepts. Generally speaking, a learning strategy is any technique used to enhance learning. Moreover, learning strategies are a set of intentional cognitive operations outside of what is typically required to complete a task used to achieve a learning goal (Pressley & Harris, 2006). Learning strategies can come in several forms. Visual mnemonic strategies, such as the keyword mnemonic or the method of loci, require learners to connect to-be-learned information to visual images. For example, to learn the definition of *amygdala*, a student might remember "Think of either a *MIG* coming right at you and, of course, making you afraid, or picture a scary *wig* with *dollars* in it." (McCabe, 2010, p. 16) They can also be elaborative strategies such as self-explanation or elaborative interrogation (EI). Elaborative strategies require learners to generate or explain to-be-learned information and relate it to prior learning. Other forms of learning strategies include organizational strategies (e.g., concept maps or note taking) and rehearsal strategies (e.g., flashcards, rereading, etc.). Furthermore, Dunlosky and colleagues (2013) suggest that learning strategies can also take the form of practice testing (i.e., self-testing), interleaved practice (i.e., studying on a specific schedule and a multitude of skills at the same time), or distributed practice (i.e., spreading out studying over time). As is evident by the definition and numerous examples of learning strategies, this topic is complicated and it is incumbent upon instructors of educational psychology students to provide guidance on how to navigate these theories.

WHY, OH WHY, IS IT IMPORTANT TO TEACH LEARNING STRATEGIES TO PRE-SERVICE EDUCATORS?

Among the myriad of topics taught in typical undergraduate and graduate educational psychology courses, teaching learning strategies to future educators is paramount for several reasons. Of most concern, educational psychology textbooks are the primary source for students to learn about learning strategies. Yet, this topic is often insufficiently covered with little up-to-date research and without any analysis of efficacy and generalizability (Dunlosky et al., 2013). Second, learning strategies are rarely taught to pre-service educators outside of educational psychology courses. Because educational psychology courses can be a foundation for other teacher education courses, teaching learning strategies effectively may allow educational psychology students to transfer these skills to other teacher education courses and consequently improve learning of teacher education content. Third, many educational psychology students will become K–12 teachers and will be responsible for teaching these strategies to future generations of students. If they cannot effectively assess and use these strategies, the likelihood of their future students accurately using these strategies is marginal at best. Thus, receiving proper instruction on learning strategies falls solely on the shoulders of educational psychology instructors.

Not only is it important to teach learning strategies in educational psychology because this is the best chance to do so, but it is also important because many educational psychology students are poor users of learning strategies (Cao & Nietfeld, 2007). For example, instead of using more effective learning strategies (e.g., EI or interleaved practice), 72% of college students surveyed report using the ineffective learning strategy of highlighting, 66% do not use distributed practice (i.e., cram instead), and 62% regularly use poorly constructed flashcards (Hartwig & Dunlosky, 2012). Additionally, students report rarely using effective elaborative strategies (Gurung, Weidert, & Jeske, 2010).

Whereas educational psychology students commonly use learning strategies ineffectively, when taught correctly, these students can use strategies to improve their academic performance. For instance, Einstein, Mullet, and Harrison (2012) used an active learning instruction method to teach psychology students about the benefits of practice testing. When students experienced the testing effect, they scored significantly higher in their knowledge of this effect and performed significantly higher on a subsequent comprehensive exam. Additionally, they reported using practice testing more often. Students also benefit by correcting their misconceptions about learning strategies. For example, Gurung and colleagues (2010) found that by teaching about the weaknesses of rehearsal strategies, students corrected their misconception that rehearsal strategies are one of the most effective forms of learning strategies. As demonstrated in several other studies (e.g., Carlston, 2011; King, 1992), students can greatly benefit from learning about learning strategies. Considering these findings provides a compelling rationale to teach educational psychology students to evaluate and assess learning strategies.

TEACHING LEARNING STRATEGIES: HURDLING THE PROVERBIAL BRICK WALL

Teaching learning strategies should be an important topic in every educational psychology course. However, it may come with its own set of obstacles and challenges. First, like many other psychology students, educational psychology students come to class with a myriad of pre– and misconceived perceptions of psychology theories. For instance, many of these students believe that the best learning strategy is rehearsal and that cramming is better than distributed practice (e.g., Cao & Nietfeld, 2007; Gurung et al., 2010). These misconceptions can be very difficult to overcome. However, with well-planned and effective instruction methods, students can overcome their biases and misconceptions towards specific learning strategies.

Second, learning strategy research is—like many psychology theories—complex, nuanced and, consequently, requires a specific level of expertise to understand. For instance, students often do not know when and where to use a given strategy (e.g., keyword mnemonic for vocabulary based declarative knowledge vs. conceptual knowledge). This issue is further complicated because learning strategies are barely covered in most educational psychology textbooks (Dunlosky et al. 2013). Therefore, we cannot expect students to independently learn about these strategies with a great deal of success. As a PhD, it is a daunting task; imagine, then, as a freshman or sophomore, having to sift through journal articles to assess the efficacy of various learning strategies. Thus, it is the job of the educational psychology instructor to present these theories in a meaningful, understandable, accurate, and applicable manner so that students can learn and successfully implement these strategies.

Finally, student individual differences/characteristics can impact one's teaching of learning strategies. Dunlosky and colleagues (2013) suggest that students may struggle with learning strategies because of prior domain knowledge, level of fluid intelligence, motivation, their self-efficacy towards learning strategies, and previous experience with given learning strategies. For example, if educational psychology students do not have experience with psychological theories, they may have difficulty using EI or self-explanation strategies. Again, although there may be several obstacles that hinder the teaching learning strategies, sound instructional methods can mitigate these issues.

TEACHING LEARNING STRATEGIES ACTIVELY: PRACTICING AND PREACHING

Research suggests that educational psychology students generally employ ineffective learning strategies (Cao & Nietfeld, 2007). Also, there is only cursory, sometimes inaccurate, information on learning strategies and their potential benefits to learning within and beyond the classroom contained in educational psychology textbooks (Dunlosky et al., 2013; Gurung et al., 2010; Hartwig & Dunlosky, 2012). Thus, there is a clear need for research on how instructors of educational psychology can best teach learning strategies to pre-service educators. Unfortunately, to date, no studies have been conducted to assess the efficacy of teaching about *several* learning strategies to educational psychology students. Yet, there is evidence that suggests students improve academically when taught individual learning strategies such as concept maps (e.g., Buehl & Fives, 2011), keyword mnemonic (McCabe, 2010), or rehearsal strategies (e.g., Golding, Wasarhaley, & Fletcher, 2012).

The question then becomes, what instructional method is best used to teach educational psychology students about different types of learning strategies? Because studies have demonstrated that active learning can be an effective form of instruction for educational psychology students, can significantly increase higher-level learning (Richmond & Kindleberger Hagan, 2011), and has been successfully used to teach learning strategies (e.g., Einstein et al., 2012), I decided to implement this method to teach learning strategies. Active learning focuses on student accountability and active engagement with course material, learning in a meaningful way, and the teacher's is a facilitator of learning (Richmond & Kindelberger Hagan, 2011). In contrast, I used a typical form of higher education instruction (i.e., lecture based direct instruction) to compare the efficacy of teaching learning strategies to educational psychology students.

Therefore, I recently conducted a study to address several questions about the efficacy of teaching learning strategies. First, does active learning instruction significantly improve educational psychology students' (i.e., pre-service educators) knowledge of learning strategies over that of direct instruction? Second, based on past research demonstrating that active learning instruction increases higher-level learning (e.g., Richmond & Kindleberger Hagan, 2011), does active learning instruction significantly increase higher-level learning over that of lower-level learning? Finally, do these effects persist over time (i.e., 4-week retention test)?

Thirty-eight pre-service early childhood education and elementary educators enrolled in two separate sections of an undergraduate educational psychology course at a large urban state university participated in this study (90% female). Students were pulled from a high population of first-generation college students, non-traditional, and ethnically diverse students.

To answer my research questions, I used a mixed-factor experimental design. For the first factor (between-subjects), I taught the students in one section of the educational psychology using active learning instruction. I taught the students in a second section of the educational psychology using direct instruction. The second factor (within-subjects) consisted of level of knowledge (higher vs. lower) of learning strategies. The dependent variable was a 20-item multiple-choice recognition test.

All students were assessed on their immediate and long-term (4-week) retention of knowledge of learning strategies using the recognition test.

Three trained blind coders categorized the 20 recognition questions into either higher- or lower-level questions (95% agreement). Nine items were considered lower-level questions based on whether they attempted to assess general knowledge and comprehension of learning strategies. For example, Elaboration strategy is defined as:

a. Knowledge and beliefs about one's own cognitive processes.
b. The attempt to learn and remember information by repeating it over and over.
c. Beliefs about what knowledge is and how it is acquired.
d. *The process of using prior knowledge to embellish new information and thereby learn in more effectively.*

Eleven items were considered higher-level questions based on whether these questions assessed analysis, synthesis, evaluation, or application of learning strategies. For example,

Charles is trying to learn all the parts of the brain and their corresponding functions. He creates flashcards and studies them each week over an 8-week period. What learning strategy is Charles using?

a. *Rehearsal*
b. Organization
c. Elaboration
d. Visual imagery mnemonics.

All students were administered this recognition test immediately following the lesson on learning strategies and again four weeks later as part of the midterm exam. Scores were converted to percentage correct for both lower- and higher-level learning.

Procedure

Direct instruction. Participants ($n = 19$) over two classes (1.5 instructional hours) were taught learning strategies using direct instruction via a traditional 20-slides PowerPoint lecture. First, students were given the definition and several specific examples of each learning strategy and associated concepts. These included rehearsal strategies (i.e., flashcards), organizational strategies (i.e., concept maps), elaborative strategies (i.e., EI or self-explanation), and visual mnemonic strategies (i.e., the keyword mnemonic). Additionally, students were given the definitions and examples of interleaving, summarization, highlighting/underlining, practice testing, and distributed practice. Finally, students were also provided with information on the efficacy and utility of these learning strategies according to Dunlosky and colleagues (2013). During the lesson, students were encouraged to ask as many questions as they wanted.

Active Learning Instruction

Over two class periods (1.5 instruction hours), 19 students were taught various learning strategies using active learning instruction. First, the instructor presented the same information on learning strategies, and their respective definitions, via 20 PowerPoint slides, as with the direct instruction class. Then, students engaged in a number of different active learning techniques designed to experience, activate, and connect new information to prior knowledge. For example, to experience and understand rehearsal strategies, students were divided into groups of 2–3 persons and instructed to discuss their personal uses of rehearsal strategies (often flashcards) with their group members. Discussions included how effective students thought these strategies were, how they created the flashcards, and how often they practiced with flashcards. In another example, after learning the definition of organizational strategies, students generated concept maps of learning strategies (Beuhl & Fives, 2011) and other elements of cognitive theory (e.g., model of memory).

Results

To determine if type of instruction affected lower vs. higher-level learning and retention of the knowledge of learning strategies, I conducted two 2 (Instruction type: Active vs. Direct) × 2 (Level of Learning: Higher vs. Lower) mixed-factorial analyses of variance (ANOVAs). For the immediate test, there was a main effect of instruction type, $F(1, 36) = 11.31$, $p = .002$, $\eta_p^2 = .24$. This result indicated that the use of active learning instruction significantly increased students' knowledge of learning strategies ($M = .81$, $SD = .18$) compared to when students received direct instruction ($M = .53$, $SD = .31$) for both higher- and lower-level learning. There was, however, not a main effect of level of learning, $F(1, 36) = 0.04$ $p = .849$, $\eta_p^2 = .001$. There was a significant interaction between level of learning and instruction type, $F(1, 36) = 4.45$, $p = .042$, $\eta_p^2 = .11$. This demonstrated that when students received active instruction, they performed significantly better on higher-level questions than when they received direct instruction. See Figure 5.1(a) for an illustration of the effects.

To determine if this result persisted over time, a mixed-factorial ANOVA was conducted on the 4-week delayed recognition test. Consistent with the immediate recognition test, there was also a main effect of instruction type, $F(1, 36) = 13.28$, $p < .001$, $\eta_p^2 = .13$. This result indicated that students

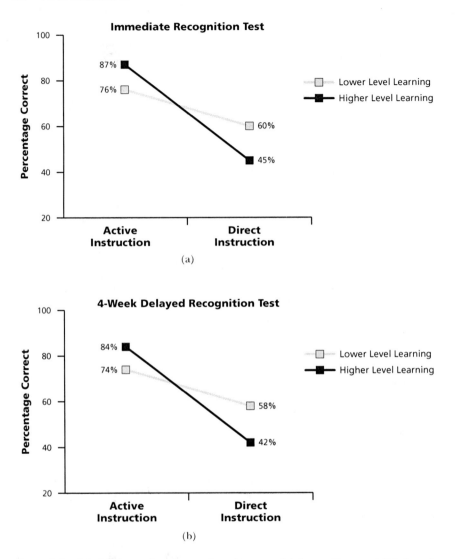

Figure 5.1 Academic performance of students on (a) Immediate and (b) 4-week delayed recognition tests by instruction type and level of learning.

who received active instruction ($M = .78$, $SD = .18$) had significantly higher scores than those who received direct instruction ($M = .51$, $SD = .27$). Also consistent with the immediate recognition test, there was no main effect of level of learning, $F(1, 36) = 0.15$, $p = .70$, $\eta_p^2 = .004$. Inconsistent with the immediate recognition test, there was not a significant interaction between instruction type and level of learning, $F(1, 36) = 73.73$, $p = .061$, $\eta_p^2 = .094$. See Figure 5.1(b) for an illustration of the effects.

Some Observations

As the results suggest, teaching learning strategies through active learning instruction can significantly improve educational psychology students' knowledge of learning strategies compared to a direct instruction approach. Additionally, this positive effect was observed over time. It is likely that active learning instruction allowed my students to process the information at a deeper level, connect their knowledge of the strategies to their personal studying experiences, and practice using the strategies in a meaningful way. Furthermore, there was mixed support that active learning instruction differentially affected higher-level learning. While students taught using active learning instruction did not do significantly better on higher-level compared to lower-level learning, they did perform better overall compared to direct instruction students.

Of course, this small-scale field experiment was limited, having a small sample, and was conducted in only two classes that I taught. Also, there was no direct measure of students' uses of the various learning strategies (i.e., to determine strategy transfer). However, classroom studies, like this one, are helpful in promoting best practices in teaching psychology.

RECOMMENDATIONS FOR INSTRUCTION

Based on the findings of my classroom study and the findings of other investigators, I offer several recommendations for implementing an active learning approach to teaching learning strategies in educational psychology courses. First, if a goal of your course is to increase your students' higher-level learning of various learning strategies, you may want to consider adopting active learning instruction (as described previously in this chapter). There is a growing body of research which suggests that active learning and strategy instruction can increase higher-level learning (e.g., Richmond & Kindleberger Hagan, 2011). Second, to maximize the potential benefits of teaching your students about learning strategies, you should introduce the topic as early in the semester as possible. For example, after the initial chapter that introduces the topic of educational psychology, spend some time teaching your students about specific learning strategies and their benefits. Finally, leverage the students' acquired knowledge of learning strategies to help them study other educational psychology concepts within the course. That is, infuse and scaffold learning strategy use throughout the course. Some examples include:

- Students create keyword mnemonics for structures of the brain
  (e.g., "The cerebellum helps in coordination and balance. Picture

your favorite athlete with *bells* all over his or her body (hanging from the clothes, hands, feet, etc." McCabe, 2010, p. 18).

- Students take weekly practice tests of class material to practice self-testing
- Students create elaborative flashcards, and use distributed practice (i.e., create and practice the flashcards each week), and practice interleaving (i.e., mix and study these flashcards with other educational psychology concepts).
- Students create concept maps of the main theories in educational psychology (e.g., cognitive, developmental, behavioral, etc.) to compare and contrast the main concepts and/or principles of each theory

To assist your effort to create innovate ways for incorporating learning strategies into the classroom, there are peer-reviewed resources available (see Table 5.1).

CONCLUSION

Although teaching pre-service educational psychology students about learning strategies is challenging, research suggests that it is beneficial to

TABLE 5.1 Source and Description of Studies Assessing the Teaching of Learning Strategies

Learning Strategy	Source and Description
Encoding Strategies	Schellenberg et al. (2011) had students create a cue card containing organizations, elaborations, and visual imagery of educational psychology concepts
Visual Mnemonics	For a comprehensive review of how to use all types of mnemonics (e.g., pegword or method of loci) in the classroom, see McCabe (2010).
EI	In a classroom study, King (1992) taught students to effectively apply EI techniques to learn instructional strategies (e.g., discovery learning).
Concepts Maps	Buehl and Fives (2011) used evolving concept maps to conceptualize topics such as adolescent and learning and cognition.
Survey, Question, Read, Recite, and Review (SQ3R)	In a classroom study, Carlston (2011) had students use SQ3R to increase comprehension and retention of various psychology concepts.
Testing Effect	Einstein et al. (2012) described a demonstration used to illustrate the testing effect and the benefits of practice testing.
Rehearsal	Golding et al. (2012) used flashcards to study various introductory psychology concepts.

students. Through our collective efforts as educational psychology instructors, we can correct many of the misconceptions that our students have about learning strategies. As demonstrated by the results of the study I reported in this chapter, an effective way to improve both lower- and higher-level knowledge of learning strategies is to use active learning instruction. I have attempted to practice what I preach and I challenge you to do the same, as we all share the goal of improving our teaching and our educational psychology students' learning.

REFERENCES

Beuhl, M. M., & Fives, H. (2011). Best practices in educational psychology: Using evolving concept maps as instructional and assessment tools. *Teaching Educational Psychology, 7*(1), 62–87.

Cao, L., & Nietfeld, J. L. (2007). Examining the relationship between achievement goals, study strategies, and class performance in educational psychology. *Teaching of Educational Psychology, 2*(1), 1–20.

Carlston, D. L. (2011). Benefits of student-generated note packets: A preliminary investigation of SQ3R implementation. *Teaching of Psychology, 38*(3), 142–146.

Dunlosky, J., Rawson, K. A., Marsh, E. J., Nathan, M. J., & Willingham, D. T. (2013). Improving students' learning with effective learning techniques promising directions from cognitive and educational psychology. *Psychological Science in the Public Interest, 14*(1), 4–58.

Einstein, G. O., Mullet, H. G., & Harrison, T. L. (2012). The testing effect: Illustrating a fundamental concept and changing study strategies. *Teaching of Psychology, 39*(3), 190–193.

Golding, J. M., Wasarhaley, N. E., & Fletcher, B. (2012). The use of flashcards in an Introduction to Psychology class. *Teaching of Psychology, 39*, 199–202.

Gurung, R. A., Weidert, J., & Jeske, A. (2010). Focusing on how students study. *Journal of the Scholarship of Teaching and Learning, 10*(1), 28–35.

Hartwig, M. K., & Dunlosky, J. (2012). Study strategies of college students: Are self-testing and scheduling related to achievement? *Psychonomic Bulletin & Review, 19*(1), 126–134.

King, A. (1992). Facilitating elaborative learning through guided student-generated questioning. *Educational Psychologist, 27*(1), 111–126.

McCabe, J. A. (2010). *Integrating mnemonics into psychology instruction.* A publication of the Society for Teaching of Psychology. Retrieved from http://teachpsych.org/resources/Documents/otrp/resources/mccabe11.pdf

Pressley, M., & Harris, K. R. (2006). Cognitive strategies instruction: From basic research to classroom instruction. In P. A. Alexander & P. H. Winne (Eds.), *Handbook of educational psychology, Volume 2* (pp. 265–286). Mahwah, NJ: Lawrence Erlbaum.

Richmond, A. S., & Kindelberger Hagan, L. (2011). Promoting higher-level thinking in psychology: Is active learning the answer? *Teaching of Psychology, 38*(2), 102–105.

Schellenberg, S., Negishi, M., & Eggen, P. (2011). The effects of metacognition and concrete encoding strategies on depth of understanding in educational psychology. *Teaching Educational Psychology, 7*(2), 17–24.

CHAPTER 6

UNDERSTANDING LEARNING THEORIES BY UNPACKING LEARNING BELIEFS

Neal Shambaugh
West Virginia University

WHY LEARN LEARNING THEORIES?

Students of educational psychology can realize three related benefits from learning about learning theories. First, learning theories provide a foundation from which to teach, meaning that any teaching decision can be explained from what we know about learning and how specific learning principles extracted from theories can be applied to educational settings. Second, embracing learning theories as tools to think with, rather than as vague ideas, helps educators to make informed teaching decisions. To be of value to educators, however, learning theories need to be applied in the form of learning principles. Learning principles are based on what research has confirmed as valid and reliable mechanisms for action—if X is tried, then Y will result. Third, applying learning theories provides educators with multiple teaching options, assuming a stance that there are multiple ways to teach. Thus, teaching learning theories empowers educators in these ways: "I can explain what I am doing as a teacher and why," "I can try

Challenges and Innovations in Educational Psychology Teaching and Learning, pages 71–81

this strategy in order to accomplish this outcome and make changes" and, "I see that a blend of approaches makes sense for my students and what they need to learn."

Teachers do not come to school thinking about learning theories, but rather embracing a set of decisions or "moves" that can be identified from a teacher's personal philosophy and "what works." The teaching decisions of public school teachers tend to revolve around the selection of teaching strategies and learning activities in lessons and units. Meanwhile, many beginning college instructors have a limited foundational basis for teaching, based partly on how they were taught in school and limited exposure to learning theories. College faculty may be more aware of teaching approaches that serve specific teaching goals (e.g., inquiry, critical thinking, social learning, knowledge recall) and that are appropriate for particular learning settings (lecture, large classroom, lab).

This chapter describes three online courses in which students unpack their learning beliefs and connect them to learning theories. These approaches involve: (1) examining one's educational history and culture in an educational psychology course; (2) learning a systematic design process in an instructional design course; and (3) examining the context of trying out new teaching models within a models of teaching course. In all three, one's learning beliefs are "placed on the table" for examination and connected to learning theories through the application of learning principles. Rather than learn the theory and the principles, students' learning beliefs provide the "starting point." The three courses are described in terms of how a typical student experiences the learning tasks. The chapter concludes by summarizing the challenges of having students in educational psychology courses unpack their learning beliefs and connect them to learning theories and principles.

THREE COURSES, THREE APPROACHES, THREE STUDENTS

Three student examples will illustrate how students engage in the learning tasks for these three courses.

Educational Psychology Course: Historical-Cultural View of Learning Theories

An educational psychology course is one of the first graduate courses in education-related academic programs. The students, consisting of teachers, trainers, corporate staff, and those who have never taught before, include a mix of master's and doctoral students, and varying ages and work experience. Richard is now student teaching in a post-bachelor's program and is hoping that the course can help him with classroom management issues and new teaching strategies in his middle school placement. Driscoll (2005) is used as the course textbook, because of its survey of learning theories and the use of visual organizers, which help students see the conceptual organization of each chapter. The course learning outcomes include: (a) recall the important features of learning theories; (b) match learning principles to learning theories; and (c) apply learning principles to educational settings. As the learning tasks have no right or wrong answers, student responses reveal different ways that learning principles can be implemented across grade levels and content areas. For those who have never taught, the tasks prompt their thinking about decisions they might make in educational positions they hope to have in the future.

An overview of learning theories gives students a "big picture" to their major differences. Students then develop a "top ten" list of learning beliefs and match a learning theory with the belief statement. Richard's list includes a view of teaching that "learning should be fun" and that teachers should provide a positive learning environment, change lesson plans, be willing to change, and have clear expectations. In his list, Richard also views learners as "humans who should be treated like their age," and that students and teachers have mutual needs for respect.

The lists of learning beliefs provide the basis for online discussion. Richard cites in a posting the value of seeing "what the other students had to say about their beliefs." During an online chat each student identifies one learning belief and how that belief statement is explained by a learning theory. Like many students in the course, Richard matches positive reinforcement of behavioral learning theory to establishing a positive learning environment. Punishment, when listed, is almost always mistaken with negative reinforcement. Teachers tend to understand punishment, according to Richards, as "detention for being late to class." Rewards tend to be identified as another match of learning principle to learning theory, but the textbook chapter on behaviorism helped Richard to rethink the strategy of "giving stickers for being good will cause more students to want the tokens to exchange for things," as a strategy he thought not useful for middle school." Instead, he favored the use of extra credit to reward students.

Many learning beliefs tend to be a mix of folk theory and ideology (e.g., "learning should be fun"). Students discover that some beliefs can be attributed to multiple theories, although they try to identify just one theory. For example, Richard posted two examples from what he saw as features of a cognitive psychology that "students learn at different rates" and "not everyone learns the same way." Students also discover that their belief items connect to multiple theories, although a few students favor one theory over another (e.g., behavioral, cognitive, social constructivist). Issues of learning differences and learning styles tend to be raised early in the discussion, so the online chat provides a lot of issues to address. If anything, students are left with more questions than answers, all of which provides an excellent starting point for the remainder of the course.

In a capstone activity students design a teaching lesson that specifies learning outcomes, teaching options, and they identify the learning theories and major supporting learning principles that are in use. Richard, for example, developed and taught a lesson to help his seventh grade history students write a research paper, a developmental skill he believed would be of value for middle school students. He cited a social constructivist stance on using age-specific topics to increase students' engagement. The teaching lesson gives students a relevant learning task to keep learning principles in mind as they think through the details of the intervention.

Although students may have had an undergraduate educational psychology course, most have difficulty when writing a learning principle. They want to find a match between their teaching and an available list of effective learning principles, so they tend to look for principles and choose those that resonate with their experiences. Recognizing and writing a learning principle is a high level intellectual task, and confidence in writing and applying learning principles is not easily achieved in a single course.

Instructional Design Course: Systems View of Learning Theories

An instructional design (ID) course gives students an opportunity to incorporate learning principles in the design of instructional interventions. Course learning outcomes include: (1) learning a systematic and structured process to design instruction; (2) applying this process to the design of an educational intervention; and (3) learning about what influences their design decisions. The principal activity and assessment is a project, which demonstrates students' understanding of ID phases, including how learning principles have been applied in their design decisions. The course uses the classic ADDIE model of instructional design (i.e., Analysis, Design, Development, Implementation, Evaluation phases), but is supplemented by two preliminary phases: Learning Beliefs and ID Models.

Mallory is an experienced elementary teacher whose priority remains "helping students to become life-long readers." She is interested in the latest comprehension strategies to meet new learning standards. During the initial ID phase, Learning Beliefs, students read the first chapter of the textbook (Shambaugh & Magliaro, 1997), which summarizes three major perspectives on learning: behavioral, cognitive, and social constructivism. Students develop a top ten list of learning beliefs and identify which of the three theories apply to each belief statement. Students prioritize the list to include the top three items, which simplifies the matching task. Mallory's first item saw learning as an engaging and life-long process, which she matched up to all three theories, and cited "humans continue to learn throughout their lives" as a learning principle. Mallory's second item stated that learning is most effective when the task is authentic. Applying this belief, Mallory cited a social constructivist principle as "the task must be relevant to students," a principle which might be applied to all three theories. Her third item was that teaching should be student-centered, a feature of social constructivism, although she was reminded that a behavioral perspective also stresses individualized learning. She cited a learning principle for this belief-theory match as the "teacher acts as a facilitator and the learner solves problems."

Next, students are introduced to six ideologies or views of curriculum, based on a chapter in *The Educational Imagination* (Eisner, 1994). The intent is to raise students' awareness that everyone has a view of curriculum and "rationalizations of what schools teach" (p. 87), and that these ideologies, as "orientations that have guided thinking about what shall be taught in school" (p. 107), might help students to better understand learning theories.

From their list, students then develop a mission statement. Some students copy and paste the statements together, while others work through multiple versions to develop and synthesize a more enduring guiding statement. Mallory wrote that "Learning is an engaging, reflective, and life-long process that is student-centered. The teacher acts as a facilitator and guide imparting knowledge by providing authentic tasks in a safe, compassionate, and motivating environment." Mallory, an experienced elementary teacher, commented that she revised the statement many times and said that "this assignment was a work in progress and I can see myself going back over the beliefs and refining what I wrote." As students make decisions about learning outcomes, instructional sequence, assessment, teaching, and technology, they are reminded to reference learning principles as a means to ground their design decisions in research-based approaches.

To reinforce the value of the learning beliefs phase of the ID process, students are informed that their mission statements will be used to assess their final ID project; specifically, to what extent their beliefs are written in a mission statement incorporated into their design decisions? Mallory's project developed a teacher workshop on standards-based comprehension strategies for 3rd–5th grade level teachers and supporting staff. The four sessions provided teacher time to design and discuss the use of the cognitively based comprehension strategies (Duke & Pearson, 2002), including making connections, questioning, visualizing, and inferring in teachers' classrooms. In the sessions, she used discussion, graphic organizers, collaboration, and practice. Her project was partially assessed based on her adherence to what she espoused in her mission statement—that is, engagement, reflectivity, and authentic tasks.

The mission statement keeps learning beliefs and learning theories "on the table" and visible for the students as they design instruction. As one student said, "I have theoretical and process experience background to support my claims when making decisions for course development in the future." The mission statement helps to keep their teaching philosophy in front of them within the ID project.

Principles of Instruction Course: Contextual View of Learning Theories

In a course called Principles of Instruction students explore the realities of trying out new teaching models. Course learning outcomes include: (a) identifying views on teaching and students; (b) summarizing one's experience as a student and other teachers; (c) applying teaching models to face-to-face and online settings; (d) demonstrating the teaching model in a video; and (e) writing a teaching plan using one or more teaching models. Students use *Models of Teaching* (Joyce, Weil, & Calhoun, 2014) as a way to structure learning theories by categorizing teaching models into learning theory-based families (i.e., behavioral, cognitive, social, and personal). Throughout the course, the family framework introduces students to different teaching options that embrace both psychological and philosophical perspectives. Five learning products are used to implement learning principles, which are the basis for the teaching models.

Andrea, a high school social studies teacher who has returned to school to earn her doctoral degree, has enrolled in this course to learn new strategies to engage adolescents in history and social studies. The first learning product, Teaching Lens, prompted students to record three words that characterize their views on teaching, students, their role in an educational setting, and how they believe others see them. To label her teaching, Andrea recorded the words, "hands-on, interactive, and multifaceted." How she views students was noted by "curious, diverse, and technologically-driven." The words "guide, resource, and facilitator" summarized her role in the educational enterprise. Finally, in terms of how she believes others see her, Andrea noted "motivating, creative, and driven." The purpose of this activity was to raise students' awareness of how one "sees" teaching will influence how one sees students and how one plans, teaches, and assesses.

A Teaching Profile assignment had Andrea first write about how influential educators influenced her learning. Andrea wrote about a sixth grade teacher who varied daily classroom activities and differentiated activities based on her concern and knowledge of individual students. Andrea then recorded her own teaching approaches and views of learning, teaching, and students. She realized that she was not only teaching social studies, but also life skills for young adults, such as study skills and reading strategies. She wrote that she now uses classroom time to discuss helpful learning strategies, so that others might benefit from having more options. She takes advantage of her students' innate curiosity, taps into technology in project-based learning, and understands that her role is as a guide who helps her students to discover the world.

Next, an outside person was required to react to the Teaching Profile document. Andrea's student teacher commented on the impact of her personality in the classroom and how she was able to make visible different student's understandings. Andrea's approach improved the classroom atmosphere around formative assessment.

Students then wrote two-page Model Application Summaries to describe how examples from teaching model families (behavioral, cognitive, social, and personal) could be taught in both face-to-face (F2F) and online learning settings. The summaries were organized using the Joyce et al. (2014) categories for summarizing a teaching model, including purpose, procedures, conditions for optimal use, student reactions, and instructor adjustments. Andrea wrote about direct instruction in both F2F and online settings to help students write essays. She learned from the text that direct instruction is more than simply lecturing to students, but involves the important steps of reviewing, and guided and independent practice. In an online application of direct instruction, Andrea wrote about using a learning management system to house resources and student work and shifting instruction to video—an awareness that occurred before the "flipped classroom" approach became a popular method among educators. She wrote that her students "are extremely independent and would like to grow intellectually at their own pace." For her other models, Andrea choose advanced organizers from the cognitive family to teach governmental structures, and role playing from the social family to help her students "experience" current events. Carl Rogers' non-directive, student-centered model from the personal family was used to help her students feel more comfortable in brainstorming and problem solving activities.

Students next produced a Teaching Video, which documented their actual teaching of a model. Most students recorded a F2F teaching activity, although a small number of students used a screencasting product to record what happened online when they used a teaching model. The video was assessed by model demonstration, model explanation, and production quality. Andrea's teaching video recorded the use of cooperative learning for group inquiry.

The final learning product had students write a Teaching Plan identifying an overall teaching approach using one or more teaching models in addition to recording general purpose strategies that all learning environments have. Students documented either a plan for F2F or online settings. The teaching plan was organized by the Joyce et al. (2014) models of teaching framework, including intent, prior teaching, learning setting, model purpose, procedures, conditions for optimal use, student reactions, and instructor adjustments. Finally, in a move to reinforce the study of one's teaching, students were prompted to identify two research questions and data sources to answer those questions. Andrea's Teaching Plan implemented direct instruction to help high school students analyze primary source documents. She documented instructional procedures for orientation, presentation, and guided and independent practice. Andrea's research question asked, "How does using direct instruction to teach the analysis of primary sources change students' outlook on learning history?" The Teaching Plan demonstrated that multiple strategies and models could take place in a classroom, and that different models served different instructional purposes and goals.

In the doctoral level principles of instruction course, students learn that there is more than one effective way to teach and that multiple models can be used within a lesson, unit, or semester-length course. While the teaching model framework organized different philosophical and theoretical perspectives, the students' priorities in this course always focused on teaching approach first, as opposed to a learning theory perspective. One student commented that applying models to both F2F and online "made me think about how to apply them both F2F and online. It made me think and explore new possibilities. It also clarified misconceptions I had about models such as Advance Organizer, where my perceived definition of it had evolved through more tacit discussions."

The course forced everyone to "try out" one or more new models, rather than document what they currently do. Those who did not have online teaching experience recognized how little they knew about translating teaching models within an online environment. Choosing the same teaching model for both F2F and online helped them to see how a teaching model might differ, depending on other course decisions and how learning outcomes and activity complexity and procedures might differ.

Unpacking Learning Beliefs: Implications for Educational Psychology Instructors

The three educational psychology courses profiled here provide three opportunities to help students connect their beliefs about learning to formal learning theories. The three approaches, historical/cultural, systems, and context of teaching, prompt students to connect statements of learning beliefs to formal learning principles, so that their teaching decisions are more understood as partially grounded in theory and to some extent, research. The educational psychology course taps into what students know historically—from what and how they were taught—and how learning principles can be applied to their teaching. The instructional design course uses a systems approach to incorporate learning beliefs across their design decisions. Finally, in the principles of instruction course, students learn how teaching models are based on specific learning theories as well as philosophical views of education. They see how these multiple models, with a theoretical foundation, can be applied in actual classroom settings.

Summarized in another way, the three courses begin by having students *view their personal history* for learning beliefs, then *step outside of their experience* to examine an instructional problem using a structured system called instructional design and, finally, *face the contextual realities* of educational settings as they consider research-supported and learning-theory based teaching models. In all three courses, students make connections between learning beliefs and learning principles, and apply learning principles as educators in the settings that are of interest to them. A visual summary of the three courses is provided in Table 6.1, including the differences in focus, the basis for understanding learning principles, and the learning tasks.

Recommendations

The following recommendations are suggested when unpacking students' learning beliefs.

- Course learning outcomes. If the application of learning principles is a learning outcome, one approach is to reverse the typical approach of beginning with the learning theories. This chapter suggests that you begin where the students are, in terms of the beliefs they have about students and teaching, and connect the theories to their beliefs in ways that shape the beliefs toward appropriate instructional practices.
- Assessment. An assessment plan across multiple instructional activities helps to determine the extent to which students connect learning principles to how they actually teach.
- Understanding learning principles. Asking students to identify learning principles has been problematic, even following instruction that explains what learning principles are and why they are important to instruction. Students need practice at connecting learning principles to their teaching. A thorough examination of one's learning beliefs usually requires an entire course, rather than being limited to a single reflection activity or assignment.

TABLE 6.1 Comparison of Three Courses That Extract Learning Principles From Learning Beliefs

	Masters Educational Psychology Course	Masters Instructional Design Course	Doctoral Principles of Instruction Course
Course focus	Applying educational psychology theories	Learning a systematic design process	Trying out new teaching approaches
Basis for understanding learning principles	HISTORICAL–CULTURAL: applying learning principles to educational settings	SYSTEMS: incorporating learning beliefs into design decisions	CONTEXT: realities of implementing new teaching models based on learning outcomes
Learning tasks	1. Top 10 list 2. Apply items 3. What's a learning principle? 4. Items—theories 5. Teaching plan	1. Top 10 list of beliefs matched with theories 2. Curriculum ideologies 3. Mission statement 4. Incorporating learning beliefs in ID project	1. Teaching lens 2. Teaching profile 3. Model applications in F2F, online settings 4. Teaching video 5. Teaching plan

- Value of teaching experience. The value of any course increases for students if they can apply the knowledge and skills that they acquire or develop in the course. Having a practicum connected to a course, such as is the case in a teacher education program, is invaluable to giving students opportunities to implement learning principles and sharing the results with one another. Another way is to tap into students' current employment in a school or training setting. Learning beliefs can also be unpacked by those students that have no teaching experience, but their thinking has to be connected to their prior learning experiences, as well as their future goals as educators.
- Examining learning beliefs over multiple courses. Some students in these courses are new to teaching and are "still trying to figure out our teaching capabilities." Many of the students have enrolled in all three of the courses described in this chapter, enabling them to re-examine their learning beliefs across courses. Not all faculty members will buy into this approach, but if they do, then encourage them to work together across courses or sections to determine how the learning principles can be extracted from students' learning beliefs.

Learning theories and learning principles can be considered problematic for teaching practitioners. Theories, according to Dewey, can "guide the formation of new experience and new knowledge through a rigorous exploration of the past" (Elkjaer, 2009, pp. 87–88). Attempting to unpack educators' learning beliefs contributes to purposeful inquiry and reflectivity, which ultimately enhances the value of learning theories in educational settings.

REFERENCES

Driscoll, M. P. (2005). *Psychology of learning for instruction* (3rd ed). Boston, MA: Pearson.

Duke, N. K., & Pearson, P. D. (2002). Effective practices for developing reading comprehension. In A. E. Farstrup & S. J. Samuels (Eds.), *What research has to say about reading comprehension* (3rd ed., pp. 205–242). Newark, DE: International Reading Association.

Eisner, E. (1994). *The educational imagination: On the design and evaluation of school programs* (3rd ed.). Boston, MA: Pearson.

Elkjaer, B. (2009). Pragmatism: A learning theory for the future. In K. Illeris (Ed.), *Contemporary theories of learning: Learning theorists in their own words* (pp. 74–89). New York, NY: Routledge.

Joyce, B. R., Weil, M., & Calhoun, E. (2014). *Models of teaching* (9th ed.). Boston, MA: Allyn and Bacon.

Shambaugh, N., & Magliaro, S. G. (1997). *Mastering the possibilities: A process approach to instructional design*. Boston, MA: Allyn and Bacon.

CHAPTER 7

LESSONS FROM
THE KARATE KID

Using Popular Movies
in Educational Psychology

Allison G. Butler and Lindsey N. Weber
Bryant University

OVERVIEW

Popular movies have been used successfully to promote learning and engagement in a variety of courses and disciplines in higher education. However, the educational psychology literature currently lacks a framework for how professors can best utilize popular movies. In this chapter, we discuss a model for integrating popular movies that illustrate educational and psychological concepts in a traditional educational psychology course. In addition, we report our findings on students' perceptions of the specific reasons why watching popular movies is useful for their engagement and learning of course material. Educational psychology is particularly well-suited for a movie-based instructional approach because of the large numbers of popular movies with teaching and learning related themes.

Challenges and Innovations in Educational Psychology Teaching and Learning, pages 83–95
Copyright © 2016 by Information Age Publishing
All rights of reproduction in any form reserved.

RATIONALE FOR TEACHING WITH POPULAR MOVIES

Professors have reported great success with using popular movies in many academic disciplines within higher education, yet very little has been written about the integration of popular movies in educational psychology courses. This is fairly surprising, given that popular movies have also been used to teach concepts in developmental psychology (Boyatzis, 1994), psychopathology (Ramchandani, 2012), and positive psychology (Niemiec & Wedding, 2008). Zoccolillo (2009) is a strong advocate of using popular movies to teach general psychology because films provide "a multi-sensory presentation and [opportunity for] guided critical discussion to aid students in comprehending difficult or abstract subject matter" (p. 4). Overall, the existing literature on the effectiveness of incorporating movies in college classes points to several benefits for students.

Student engagement highlights students' active role in educational processes (Kuh et al., 2005). In noting that most higher education studies of engagement focus on institutional level engagement, Handelsman, Briggs, Sullivan, and Towler (2005) called attention to the need to better understand engagement at the course level. Engaged students are effective learners, and good teaching stimulates and sustains student engagement (Handelsman et al., 2005). Teaching with popular movies has the power to enhance student engagement at the course level, and movies appeal to the technology-driven millennial generation of students who fill college classrooms (Considine, Horton, & Moorman, 2009). Further, as Lammers and Smith (2008) point out, popular culture is a mechanism for instructors to convey enthusiasm and build rapport with students. The best movies capture the attention and interest of an audience and often create an emotional connection. Appealing to students' interests and emotions is an effective way to foster intrinsic motivation and, in turn, promote learning (Pintrich, 2003).

Studies suggest that using movies as a pedagogical tool enhances student learning in a variety of ways (Zoccolillo, 2009). From an information processing perspective, viewing movies that illustrate course concepts allows students to engage in deeper, more meaningful thinking about the material. As complements to course readings and lectures, movies can provide powerful elaborative experiences that increase the likelihood that students will remember and use the course material later. Roberts, Cohen, and MacDonald's (1996) work suggests that films evoke an emotional response that allows more information to be processed with less effort. Additionally, popular movies take abstract concepts and make them tangible and useful (Zoccolillo, 2009). This application of course material to everyday life increases relevancy for students, which increases recall. Further, using popular movies in conjunction with class discussion provides an important opportunity for students to engage in critical thinking about the material (Boyatzis, 1994).

Notably, little to no research exists on the effectiveness of using popular movies in educational psychology courses. Educational psychology is particularly well suited for a movie-based instructional approach because of the large numbers of popular movies that address themes of teaching, learning, and motivation.

Instructional Context

In this chapter, we will document our experience revising a traditional educational psychology course so that scenes from popular movies are integrated with course content throughout the semester. We developed a systematic method that should be easily replicable by other instructors of educational psychology. Additionally, even though previous research suggests clear learning and engagement benefits of using popular movies in higher education settings, less is known about the specific ways in which students perceive the use of popular movies as beneficial. Thus, we will share narrative student feedback that we gathered in order to elucidate the reasons why students find popular movies to be useful for learning.

The Course

Educational Psychology is one of the course offerings in the Department of Applied Psychology at our university. The course is roughly divided into two parts. In the first part, the focus is on the theoretical foundations of educational psychology, including theories of cognitive, social, and emotional development, as well as major learning theories. In the second part of the course, those theories provide a foundation for considering the more applied aspects of educational psychology, such as teacher behavior, instructional strategies, and assessment techniques.

The typical instructional format for the course includes interactive lectures, class discussions, small group work, and other learning activities, in addition to the showing of popular movies. Currently, the textbook used is Woolfolk's (2013) *Educational Psychology* (12th ed.). Occasionally, supplemental readings are assigned. The class meets for three 50-minute sessions per week, and the typical class size is 35 students.

The Students

The students in our Educational Psychology course are not enrolled in an education program, as there is not currently an undergraduate teacher education program at the university. In one typical semester, 53% of the students majored in applied psychology, 39% majored in a business-related domain, and 8% majored in a liberal arts discipline other than psychology. Fourteen percent of the sample planned to pursue a teaching career within the next three years, while 86% reported that they did not plan to pursue a teaching career within the next three years. Seventy-eight percent of the students were female and 22% were male, and they ranged in age from 19 to 22 years ($M = 21.08$ years). As indicated by self-report, 89% of the participants were White, 8% were Black, and 3% were Hispanic. The course included sophomores (14%), juniors (22%), and seniors (64%) with a variety of college majors.

Using Popular Movies in Educational Psychology Preparation

There are five steps to preparing popular movies to use in an educational psychology course: (1) generating a list of movies that contain scenes that can be connected to course content; (2) viewing each movie and taking detailed notes; (3) reviewing the notes to select key excerpts of no more than 30 minutes in length; (4) creating a cue sheet to facilitate discussion when the excerpts are shown in class; and (5) planning a discussion activity to accompany each film excerpt. Next, we describe in more detail how the first author carried out these steps to use the excerpts in an educational psychology class.

First, we generated a list of popular movies related to educational psychology themes (Table 7.1). Typical themes in an educational psychology

TABLE 7.1   Popular Movies, Applicable Educational Psychology Themes and Concepts, and Learning Outcomes

Movie Title (Year)	Applicable Course Theme(s)	Specific Course Concept(s)	Sample Learning Outcome(s)
			Students will be able to . . .
The Karate Kid (1984)	Learning	Situated cognition; Cognitive apprenticeship	Identify the stages of cognitive apprenticeship demonstrated by Mr. Miyagi and Daniel
Boyhood (2014)	Developmental characteristics of learners Sociocultural influences on development Learning	Gender differences; Parenting styles; Blended family structure; Erikson's psychosocial stages; Piaget's theory	Trace the development of Mason's gender-role identity and compare to his sister Samantha; Identify parenting styles of mother, father, and stepfather and explain their influence; Analyze Mason's development (age 6–18) in terms of Erikson's stages and Piaget's stages

(continued)

TABLE 7.1   Popular Movies, Applicable Educational Psychology Themes and Concepts, and Learning Outcomes (continued)

Movie Title (Year)	Applicable Course Theme(s)	Specific Course Concept(s)	Sample Learning Outcome(s)
Precious (2009)	Sociocultural influences on development	Bronfenbrenner's bioecological model	Identify and analyze the ecological systems that affect Precious
The Blind Side (2009)	Developmental characteristics of learners Sociocultural influences on development	Kohlberg's theory of moral development; Erikson's psychosocial stages; Marcia's identity statuses; Baumrind's parenting styles	Use evidence in the movie to determine LeAnne's stage of moral reasoning; analyze Michael's development of identity and self-concept; discuss parenting styles of Leanne and Michael's birth mother and their impact on Michael's development
Little Man Tate (1991) & *Good Will Hunting* (1997)	Developmental characteristics of learners Individual differences	Definitions of giftedness; Characteristics of gifted students	Recognize shared and distinctive gifted traits demonstrated by Fred Tate, Damon the Math Magician, and Will Hunting; discuss common myths and stereotypes associated with giftedness; explain asynchronous development shown by the characters
Dead Poets' Society (1989)	Teacher behavior	Teacher-directed vs. Student-centered learning	Identify examples of teacher-directed and student-centered learning approaches demonstrated by Mr. Keating and the students at Welton Academy
Mr. Holland's Opus (1995)	Teacher behavior Learning theories	Characteristics of effective teachers; Gardner's Multiple Intelligences; Social learning theory	Recognize qualities of an effective teacher as shown by Mr. Holland; apply Gardner's multiple intelligences to Mr. Holland and students; identify instances of vicarious and enactive learning
Dangerous Minds (1995) & *Freedom Writers* (2007)	Motivation Individual differences Teacher behavior	Sources and types of motivation	Identify examples of goal orientations, learned helplessness, effectance motivation, intrinsic/extrinsic motivation, and determinants of motivation demonstrated by Ms. Johnson/Ms. Gruwell and her students

course include: learning, motivation, developmental characteristics of learners, individual differences, teacher behavior, and sociocultural influences on learning and schooling. When searching for appropriate titles, movies with plot lines centered on teachers and schools came to mind quickly. These movies include such classics as *Dead Poets' Society, Mr. Holland's Opus, Dangerous Minds, and Freedom Writers.* For example *Dead Poets' Society* ties in to the theme of teacher behavior. There are scenes that show the stark contrast between the strict, direct-instruction tradition of Welton Academy and the freer "carpe diem" attitude and student-centered instructional approach endorsed by Mr. Keating. In *Dangerous Minds*, motivation is a central theme, and viewers can witness the techniques that Ms. Johnson employs to foster intrinsic motivation and a mastery goal orientation within her class of at-risk students. In addition to the obvious teacher movies, we also identified a number of films that tapped into course themes and concepts in more unexpected ways, as they did not necessarily depict learning or development in a school context. These movies include *The Karate Kid, Precious, The Blind Side, Little Man Tate, Good Will Hunting,* and *Boyhood.* For example, in *The Karate Kid*, a situated cognition approach to learning is clearly represented in the context of mastering karate. In *Good Will Hunting*, we see a Harvard janitor show characteristics of giftedness, and his giftedness looks quite different than the depictions of giftedness shown in *Little Man Tate. Boyhood,* a coming-of-age drama that was filmed intermittently over a 12-year period, allows students to witness the personal and cognitive development of Mason and his older sister Samantha. Course themes and specific concepts were identified in each of the selected movies, and then desired student learning outcomes were specified.

Once we selected a movie that connected to a course theme, we viewed it in its entirety and took detailed film notes. The notes consisted of a running record of events and dialogue and an accompanying time mark to indicate the exact place in the DVD that a specific scene occurred. See Figure 7.1 for an excerpt from *The Karate Kid* film notes.

A specific procedure was used to identify 15–30 minutes of film that could be extracted from each full-length movie. Because each class meeting is only 50 minutes, film excerpts shown in class are 15–30 minutes to allow ample time for class discussion or an activity. Once film notes for the full-length movie were generated, the key scenes that provide important background information or illustrate a psychological principle were identified. The final scene selections were then determined, reviewed for length and content, and included on a cue sheet to be used by the instructor during class. The cue sheet assisted the instructor in locating specific scenes (e.g., time marks) when searching the DVD in class. It also included a brief summary that was read to the class before the excerpts were shown

Time mark	Episode content:
1:05:30	*Daniel rides bike in to Mr. Miyagi's back yard*
1:06:00	"Hey Mr. Miyagi, this is great, man!"
1:06:29	"What are these?" (sanding disks)
1:06:38	"Right circle, left circle"
1:06:46	"You go. Circle right, a circle left."
1:06:57	"Breathe in, breathe out."
1:07:13	"All the floor, right circle, left circle"
1:07:37	*Darkness, night time; Daniel has sanded the deck all day*
1:07:51	"I'm finished. Mr. Miyagi, I'm beat."
1:08:23	*Daniel leaves*
1:08:50	*Next day. Mr. Miyagi tries to catch fly with chopsticks.*
1:09:03	"Man who catch fly with chopsticks accomplish anything"
1:09:41	"Hey Mr. Miyagi! Look! Look!" (D. catches fly)
1:09:49	"You beginner's luck"
1:09:54	*Paint fence scene begins*

Figure 7.1 Film notes excerpt for use with *The Karate Kid.*

or, often, between scenes, to fill gaps in the storyline. See Figure 7.2 for the cue sheet used with *The Karate Kid.*

The final step in preparing a movie excerpt was to generate discussion questions or learning activities that would provide opportunities for students to apply the course material to movie content and to engage in critical thinking about the material (e.g., a construct or principle). For each movie, discussion activities were linked to the specific learning outcomes identified in Table 7.1.

The Karate Kid

In *The Karate Kid*, Daniel and his mother have recently moved from New Jersey to California. Daniel is teased by a group of boys who know karate. During one fight, Mr. Miyagi, a handyman and caretaker at Daniel's apartment, intervenes to help Daniel. Mr. Miyagi is actually a karate grand master, and he agrees to teach Daniel karate in exchange for doing manual labor tasks at Mr. Miyagi's house.

The relationship between Mr. Miyagi and Daniel grows to exemplify a cognitive apprenticeship, which is a key construct in "situated cognition" perspectives on learning (Driscoll, 2005). According to the situated cognition view, declarative knowledge ("knowing that") and procedural

Synopsis: *Daniel and his mother have recently moved from New Jersey to California. Daniel is getting picked on by a group of boys who know karate. During one fight, Mr. Miyagi, a handyman and caretaker at Daniel's apartment, intervenes to help Daniel. Mr. Miyagi, is actually a karate grand master, and he agrees to teach Daniel karate in exchange for doing some manual labor tasks at Mr. Miyagi's house.*

Time Mark   **Episode Content:**

Chapter 15: Sanding the Deck (begins at 1:05:30)

1:06:29   "What are these" (sanding disks)

1:07:13   "All the floor, right circle, left circle"

1:07:37   *Darkness, night time; Daniel has worked all day*

1:08:50   *Next day, chopsticks*

1:09:41   "You beginner's luck"

Chapter 16: Painting the Fence (begins at 1:09:54)

1:10:32   "No look at me, look at fence"

1:11:08   "Up, down"

1:11:40   "All the fence"

1:12:46   "Very good job. Come morning, start early"

Chapter 17: Paint House (begins at 1:13:09)

1:13:30   *Daniel reads sign about how to paint the house*

1:13:50   *Night again, still painting house*

1:13:57   *Mr. Miyagi returns from fishing, and Daniel confronts him*

1:14:19   "I've been here for four days and I haven't learned a thing"

1:16:33   *Mr. Miyagi puts all the moves together: paint house, wax on—wax off, paint fence, sand floor; Daniel realizes that these jobs have taught him karate skills*

Chapter 18: Learn Balance (begins at 1:18:01)

1:19:23   *At beach, in the waves*

1:19:28   *Daniel sees Mr. Miyagi doing crane technique on post at beach*

1:20:33   *They are confronted by men with beer bottles*

1:20:55   *Mr. Miyagi karate chops the beer bottles and they break*

TOTAL RUNNING TIME: 15 minutes, 25 seconds (1:05:30–1:20:55)

Figure 7.2   Instructor cue sheet: Cognitive apprenticeship in *The Karate Kid.*

knowledge ("knowing how") are seen as integrated. In other words, "what people perceive, think, and do develops [together] in a fundamentally social context" (Driscoll, 2005, p. 157), such as a situation where a novice is learning a skill from a master craftsman. Situated learning theory and the cognitive apprenticeship model suggest that skills should be acquired through authentic contexts and by communicating with experts about those contexts.

A memorable scene illustrates some of the stages of learning that take place within a cognitive apprenticeship: (1) the teacher considers expert-like strategies involved in a task; (2) the teacher designs scaffolds that encourage students to apply the strategies; (3) the activities are situated toward a relevant outcome; and (4) the teacher models strategies and coaches students to apply them (Oliver, 1999). The particular scene that is viewed in class to illustrate these four stages of cognitive apprenticeship shows Daniel working in Mr. Miyagi's back yard:

Daniel has agreed to do some manual labor tasks for Mr. Miyagi in exchange for learning karate. During the scene, Mr. Miyagi assigns Daniel to a series of jobs, including sanding and painting his deck and house. Daniel grows increasingly frustrated, as he has worked from early morning until late into the night for four days, but he has not been taught any karate. It is revealed that Mr. Miyagi asked Daniel to perform these tasks because they require the same focus, perseverance, strength, and physical positioning as karate blocking techniques. Then, with Daniel at the beach, Mr. Miyagi directs Daniel to stand in the rough surf to practice maintaining his balance, as Daniel also observes Mr. Miyagi demonstrating the crane technique.

In this 15-minute excerpt, students observe the four stages of cognitive apprenticeship in action. Mr. Miyagi has identified eye contact, balance, focus, and strength as the important characteristics for mastery of karate (stage 1). He has designed tasks, such as sanding and painting, and standing in rough surf, that enable Daniel to practice karate strategies (stage 2). Mr. Miyagi is training Daniel so that he will be able to defend himself against bullies who have attacked him in the past (stage 3). Finally, he models for Daniel a variety of karate techniques and strategies (e.g., breaking a glass bottle with a karate chop, doing the crane formation) (stage 4).

Integrating Movies into Instruction

A standard procedure is used each time a movie excerpt is shown in the educational psychology course. First, the instructor leads a lecture with discussion that targets the key psychological concepts that are depicted in the movie (e.g., situated cognition, cognitive apprenticeship; ecological systems theory; giftedness). Second, a handout with the learning activity and discussion questions is distributed to students. For example, *The Karate Kid* handout includes a list of cognitive apprenticeship stages and space for students to describe interactions between Daniel and Mr. Miyagi that illustrate each stage. When students watch *Precious*, they fill in a diagram of Bronfenbrenner's bioecological model showing the contextual influences in Precious' life that shape her development. And, when students watch scenes from *Good Will Hunting* and *Little Man Tate*, they are given a handout with a comprehensive, bulleted list of research-supported traits (e.g., related to creativity, social-emotional qualities, intellectual ability, leadership) that are characteristic of gifted students. While they view these latter two movies, students are asked to indicate which characteristics in the handout are exhibited by the three gifted characters—Fred Tate and Damon the "Math Magician" (both from *Little Man Tate*), and Will Hunting. Students write the characters' initials next to each relevant trait on their bulleted list.

For all movies, a plot synopsis is included on the handout, and the handout promotes active listening, close observation, and note taking. The instructor also gives a brief introduction and uses the cue sheet to play the DVD, presenting each excerpt in a predetermined sequence (See Figure 7.2). Finally, the instructor leads a whole class debriefing session or small group session in which students discuss their observations, drawing on the notes they wrote (learning activity).

Students' Perceptions of the Benefits of Movies for Learning

Recently, we assessed our students' perceptions of the benefits of using movies in the educational psychology course. Students were assured that their responses would remain anonymous and have no bearing on their academic standing or course grade. Data on students' perceptions were gathered for each movie. After completing the movie discussion/learning activity, a brief two-item survey was administered that asked students to rate their agreement with each statement using a 5-point Likert scale, 5 (strongly agree) to 1 (strongly disagree). Space was provided for participants to explain their rating.

The engagement item read: "Watching this movie in class helped me to feel engaged in the course material." Students' ratings showed that they perceived the use of movies in class to be beneficial: 100% respondents indicated that they either "agree" or "strongly agree" that "watching this movie in class helped me to feel engaged in the course material."

The learning item read: "*The illustrations of educational psychology topics in this movie helped me to learn the material covered in this unit on* _____" (e.g., situated cognition, motivation). A specific theory or concept was inserted as appropriate for each movie. For all but two movies, 100% of respondents indicated that they either "agree or "strongly agree" with this statement.

A summative measure consisted of three items on a professor-generated course evaluation survey. Two items that closely paralleled the learning and engagement items on the movie-specific measures were included using a 5-point Likert scale. The learning item read: "*The illustrations of educational psychology concepts in the popular movies shown in class helped me to learn course material.*" The engagement item read: "*Watching popular movies in class helped me to feel engaged in the course material.*" Confirming the responses from the in-class film survey, all students (100%) responded "agree" or "strongly agree" on both items. The third item asked if the instructor should integrate popular movies in future Educational Psychology course sections, and 97% of students responded "yes."

Students' Explanations of the Benefits of Movies for Learning

When we examined students' explanations for their ratings on the movie-specific engagement and learning measures, several themes emerged. Separate coding schemes were used for students' narrative data pertaining to the engagement and learning items.

Engagement

Twenty-six percent of students' responses indicated that the movies captured their *attention or interest.* One student commented: "I found myself deeply interested in the movie. Knowing the class material was going to be involved made me even more engaged because there was a challenge to draw connections." Eighteen percent of responses noted the effectiveness of the *class discussion* following the movie. One student wrote: "The class discussion of the movie allowed us to all get engaged and work together to see how the different levels of Bronfenbrenner's model are at play in Precious's experience." Eleven percent of students' explanations highlighted their *emotional engagement* in the film. In response to one movie, a student noted: "The emotional tie—the reactions that the movie's characters enabled—are much more engaging than a textbook." Ultimately, our student feedback suggests that movies capture students' attention and interest, which are critical aspects of engagement, and ultimately, enhance student motivation and information processing (Pintrich, 2003; Roberts et al., 1996).

Learning

Forty-three percent of student responses indicated that the movie excerpts were engaging because they helped them *learn* the course material. For example, one student explained: "Watching this movie definitely helped me to understand the big picture of what we're referring to when we talk about moral reasoning." The strong majority (73%) of all responses to the movie-specific learning items mentioned that the excerpts facilitated learning by providing salient examples of course concepts. As one student explained, "Given the examples, I could easily identify the characteristics of giftedness. [The movies] presented three different examples and helped me to think outside the box of what I would assume giftedness to look like." Fourteen percent of responses emphasized that the excerpts positively impacted learning in a general way. So, for example, one student wrote: "[The movie] helped me to understand in the moment and remember the material covered." Eight percent of responses highlighted the important role that the follow-up *discussion* or learning activity had in improving their learning of course material. One student noted: "The discussion activity really helped with learning the concept. Prior to the movie it was very abstract; discussing the theory in relation to the movie made it much more concrete."

CONCLUSIONS AND CAVEATS

In this chapter, we have described a five-step method for integrating popular movies into an educational psychology course to promote student learning and engagement. These steps are: (1) generate a list of movies that contain scenes having connections to educational psychology course concepts such as motivation or instruction; (2) preview each movie and takes detailed notes; (3) review the notes to select key excerpts of no more than 30 minutes in length; (4) create a cue sheet to facilitate showing the excerpts in a specific, planned sequence; and (5) plan an application or discussion activity for each film excerpt. We recommend that instructors give a brief lecture, followed by class discussion that focuses on relevant course concepts. Distribute a handout having discussion questions or application activities. Debriefing discussions can occur with the whole class or in small groups.

Admittedly, this pedagogical approach is labor intensive, requiring the instructor to select movies, identify appropriate scenes to excerpt, and design activities and discussion prompts for students. Notably, Ramchandani (2012) cautions that popular movies sometimes depict stereotypes rather than authentic people and situations. So, instructors should be mindful to ensure that psychological concepts are conveyed authentically. Finally, instructors may be concerned about taking up valuable time with showing movies. However, a 15–30 minute excerpt can effectively capture students' interest and illustrate important course concepts. While using valuable class time to show popular movies may be seen as a pedagogical risk, it is certainly a risk worth taking because students are likely to be more engaged and find learning of educational psychology concepts to be interesting, relevant, and enjoyable.

REFERENCES

Boyatzis, C. J. (1994). Using feature films to teach social development. *Teaching of Psychology, 21*(2), 99–101.

Considine, D., Horton, J., & Moorman, G. (2009, March). Teaching and reaching the millennial generation through media literacy. *Journal of Adolescent & Adult Literacy, 52*(6), 471–481.

Driscoll, M. (2005). *Psychology of learning for instruction* (3rd ed). Boston, MA: Allyn and Bacon.

Handelsman, M. M., Briggs, W. L., Sullivan, N., & Towler, A. (2005). A measure of college student course engagement. *The Journal of Educational Research, 98*(3), 184–191.

Kuh, G. D., Kinzie, J., Schuh, J. H., Whitt, E. J., & Associates (2005). *Student success in college: Creating conditions that matter.* San Francisco, CA: Jossey-Bass.

Lammers, W. J., & Smith, S. M. (2008). Learning factors in the university classroom: Faculty and student perspectives. *Teaching of Psychology, 35*(2), 61–70.

Niemiec, R. M., & Wedding, D. (2008). *Positive psychology at the movies: Using movies to build virtues and character strengths.* Cambridge, MA: Hogrefe and Huber.

Oliver, K. (1999). *Situated cognition and cognitive apprenticeships.* Retrieved from http://www.edtech.vt.edu/edtech/id/models/powerpoint/cog.pdf

Pintrich, P. R. (2003). A motivational science perspective on the role of student motivation in learning and teaching. *Journal of Educational Psychology, 95,* 667–686.

Ramchandani, D. (2012). The downside of teaching psychopathology with film. *Academic Psychiatry, 36,* 154–155.

Roberts, D. S. L., Cowen, P. S., & MacDonald, B. E. (1996). Effects of narrative structure and emotional content on cognitive and evaluative responses to movie and text. *Empirical Studies of the Arts, 14*(1), 33–47.

Woolfolk, A. (2013). *Educational psychology* (12th ed.). Boston, MA: Pearson.

Zoccolillo, A. M. (2009). Using popular movies to teach general psychology. *Academic Exchange Quarterly, 13*(1), 1–7.

CHAPTER 8

TEACHING EDUCATIONAL PSYCHOLOGY IN CROSS-DISCIPLINARY COURSES

A Case Study of Teaching Engineering Graduate Students

Marlene Schommer-Aikins
Wichita State University

Basic principles derived from educational psychology have wide applicability. I would claim that the field of educational psychology is underutilized due to its almost obscure presence among the general public. In other words, the field of educational psychology would benefit from introducing ideas to individuals outside of the social sciences. One such place is engineering. This chapter will present a self-reflective case study of an educational psychology course that was taught to graduate level engineering students. Names and dates will not be revealed in order to maintain confidentiality. However, I can give you some detail about the instructor. I have taught at the university level for 25 years. I am a professor of educational

Challenges and Innovations in Educational Psychology Teaching and Learning, pages 97–106
Copyright © 2016 by Information Age Publishing
All rights of reproduction in any form reserved.

psychology, and I conduct research on epistemological beliefs, comprehension, metacomprehension, and openness to diversity. I was department chair at the beginning of the study. At the time, STEM issues were (and remain) at the forefront of our national concerns. This case study came into fruition when the deans of the College of Education and the College of Engineering attempted to brainstorm new ideas to improve engineering student retention.

EDUCATIONAL PSYCHOLOGY TO HELP FILL A NEED

The field of engineering seeks to prepare engineers for the twenty-first century. In that quest, researchers of engineering education have reached out to other disciplines to inform their instructional practice (Vanasupa, Stolk, & Herter, 2009). Recruitment of diverse students and retention in the field of engineering are dismal. Adams et al. (2011) report that "... there is strong evidence that academic *disengagement* increases steadily over the undergraduate engineering experience... In the United States only a third of students who graduate with an engineering degree actively seek engineering jobs" (p. 100). In the case study being presented, the dilemma of retention was at the forefront of challenges. The college of engineering dean at a Midwestern U.S. university set a goal for the college to increase student retention.

The engineering dean met with the College of Education dean in an effort to generate a plan to enhance retention. Through their discussions they came upon the idea that the faculty teaching engineering courses needed to improve their instructional and testing techniques. However, the engineering dean also knew that the existing faculty would not be receptive to insinuations that they lacked teaching skills. She needed a way to convince the faculty that teaching and learning principles comes from systematic research inquiry; and, that teaching is both an art and a science. Hence, the two deans strategized that the starting point should be with graduate students instead of existing faculty.

The deans then approached me and proposed that I teach a graduate level educational psychology class to engineering graduate students who planned to obtain a university faculty position. I thought it was a great idea and did not consider the workload that would arise. And so it goes: Some of the best plans are merely knee jerk responses.

First Course: A Learning Curve or a Learning Mountain?

The first attempt at conducting an educational psychology class strictly for engineering students was full of adventure. Apparently our tacit philosophy was, "create a course and they will come." The College of Engineering had an education facilitator. He tried to get the word out to prospective engineering graduate students during the fall semester that a psychology of learning class would be available for engineering students in the following spring semester. One week before the course was to begin, only one student had signed up for the course. I called the sole student and said that the course would be closed due to lack of enrollment. The student (pseudo name, Lila) asked what she could do to keep the course afloat. I simply told her to persuade some of her fellow students to sign up for the course. Apparently, this engineering student was enterprising. The course was able to stay on the books with five engineering students.

The course was titled "Learning and Instruction for Engineer Education." It was predominately cognitive psychology applied to learning. I revised the course normally taught to graduate students in the social sciences, such as educational psychology, school psychology, and communication sciences and disorders. My attempts to revise the course before I met the students turned out to be shots in the dark.

On the first day of class, the students slowly entered the classroom. They were all international students. The classroom was in a building some distance away for the engineering building. Ten minutes after the start time, all the students had found the building and the classroom.

The first thing I did was to have them form a semi-circle. The students were not accustomed to looking at each other. Already they were experiencing something novel. The goal was to maximize exchange of ideas. As the students introduced themselves, I found myself straining to understand a couple of students' thick accents. I asked them to tell us a little about themselves and why they were taking the course. Lila was teaching as a graduate assistant and she had taught in an earlier career. She had no formal training in teaching or learning theory. She had simply tried her best based on her own personal experiences with being taught and her natural inclination to interact with people. Three other students were teaching assistants. They were struggling to teach and to construct tests. They also struggled with getting respect and cooperation from the students that they were teaching. The fifth student was new in the graduate program and anticipated a faculty position. The one thing in common among these students was that Lila was persuasive in getting them to at least come to the class the first night. If they would come back a second time was yet to be seen. I took note that this course needed to seem relevant, interesting, and within the students' grasp.

I then asked the students how many have had any psychology courses either at the undergraduate or graduate level. Only Lila had taken a course. A couple of students enjoyed psychology as presented in the popular press. I discovered that many students with international degrees in STEM do not have any requirements for social sciences, or at least not psychology. I took note that background knowledge would need to be infused in the instruction to facilitate students' understanding of the textbook that they would be reading. Adjustments on instructional objectives would need to be made because these students would be starting with the basics.

I was also aware that the graduate level textbook I assigned would be difficult for several reasons. First, this was out of their field of engineering. Second, with little to no psychology whatsoever, some terms would be misunderstood from a colloquial sense. Third, they were doctoral students having a heavy workload of engineering classes and assistantships. Fourth, reading in English was no doubt difficult, especially when the terms were not engineering. With these challenges in mind, I asked students to read as best as they could. They were encouraged to understand the key ideas. I provided a list of the key concepts for each chapter. In addition, each week they were to journal about the assigned reading materials. They were to select four key concepts and generate a personal or professional example of the concept. They were also to write three questions that came to their mind as they read the chapter. The journaling was to be turned in at the beginning of the following class.

In subsequent classes, I provided background material to facilitate the students' comprehension of the textbook chapter. Students automatically set up the semi-circle of tables and chairs. By the end of the second class, students were feeling more comfortable talking with one another about the course content. The one rule that I made was that all students should feel free to express their ideas and questions. Any personal examples that were discussed in the class were never to be repeated outside of the class. Confidentiality was considered important in the event students wanted to talk about their own experiences as university students of engineering.

The third class was abuzz with dialogue. Students were eagerly asking for clarification of concepts. On the way out of the class that night, one student walked with me down the hallway to my office. He told me that the first night, when he was walking across campus to get to the education building, one of his fellow engineering students stopped him and asked why he was on the other side of campus. When he told his fellow student that he was taking a psychology of learning class, his colleague told him that he was wasting his time. He urged him to drop the class. Now at the third week of class, he was already seeing the value in learning educational psychology. He was beginning to see that his own attempts as a teaching assistant were random hit and misses of ideas. And now he was beginning to develop strategies that will help his students understand him better. That night I walked home with a skip in my step.

Key changes were made to make the course more relevant to teaching in higher education and teaching in the sciences. Three unique (to my engineering students) projects were added to the course. The first unique project was for students to conduct classroom observations. After four weeks of instruction that introduced many basic principles of educational psychology, the students were to attend a class in engineering and make observations of the teaching in the class. They then completed a matrix of what instructional techniques they saw, what learning principle the techniques represented, and whether the techniques helped or hindered the learners. This was to be the focus of discussion in the following class period.

The following class discussion evolved from what they had observed in the classroom to what they, themselves, had experienced in past college level classes. Observations they had seen the week before varied from poor to good examples of educational psychology principles. More important, having the engineering students engage in observation and then process the psychological concepts more deeply triggered memories of their past. Some memories were positive. For example, they reported that some of their professors would come to class prepared to teach. They always felt free to ask questions. Class projects felt relevant to the course. Students were allowed to ask challenging questions of the professor.

However, some memories were exceptionally negative. For example, several of the students described how one particular engineering class was conducted. Students are all seated and ready for class. The professor walked in and looked straight ahead at the chalkboard that is in the front of the classroom. He continued to face the chalkboard and started lecturing and writing on the board at the same time. He wrote on the full width of the chalkboard. When the board was full, he erased everything and continued writing and talking. When the class session ended, for the first time he turned to the class and stated, "Class dismissed." Hence, for that class, there was no eye contact, and it could be assumed that no questions should be asked. The burden of keeping up with note taking and comprehension was solely upon the students. These are very challenging conditions for students whose first language is not the same as the professor's. Another example of a negative memory is recalling when professors embarrass or humiliate students when they ask questions that seem to challenge the professor.

As the students continued to open up, they moved from the behavior of their professors to those of fellow students who felt they needed to do *anything* to survive their courses. I will share one example but will use an alias to avoid too much disclosure. One of my students said, "You know we have a saying among us engineering students. It's 'Follow the Dejas.'" Upon hearing this, the rest of the class laughed. They all knew what it meant. I innocently asked, what does it mean? The student who was sharing said that the Dejas had a system. They filled the room the first day of class and determined if they could handle the class or not. They studied the syllabus and then contacted other Dejas who had taken the course before. If the course looked very difficult, they had connections to get old tests and/or old test keys. If they could not get these survival aids, they did not return to the course. Hence, "follow the Dejas" meant that there was a system among the students that could help them survive. If the Dejas did not return to the class, there was not a system in place.

I was astounded to hear this story. These students had opened up to me. They said they never followed the Dejas and were upset that such an underground student system existed. However, they also understood that some classes seemed impossible to survive if you had to rely on the professor for the content or for questions. My engineering students survived their courses by being good readers of English and contacting any tutors who were available. They also pondered why some of their professors did not have any knowledge about learners or about teaching.

I suggested that they could start to change the world of college instruction in engineering. They could be the leaders of today—even if they were only teaching assistants at this early stage of their careers. And, they could be the leaders of tomorrow as future university professors. Indeed, they commented that what they were learning in my educational psychology course was helping them become better learners as well.

The second project unique to this class was what I called, "teach a buddy." My students were to find a friend or relative and teach them an educational psychology concept. They were to document how they planned to incorporate educational psychology concepts in their teaching, how they assessed what their buddy had learned, and what they would do differently the next time they taught a buddy. I created this project because some of my students were not teaching assistants at the time of taking my course. Those who were teaching assistants could modify this task and use the self-reflection documentation to describe teaching their own class.

The class session following this assigned task was used to discuss the teach-a-buddy activity. For the most part, the students demonstrated systematic approaches to teaching using psychology principles, such as activating prior knowledge, presenting material in a logical fashion, providing visual aids, and asking their buddy to engage in an activity to deepen their cognitive processing. Success in teaching their buddy varied and ideas for improvement were in abundance. The candidness of my students was most apparent as I went from student to student, asking them to share their ideas of what actions to change. One student smiled and said, "The next time I will get a new buddy. This one did not take it seriously." We all had a good laugh. However, my student wanted a genuine experience. The next teaching buddy experience, was indeed, with a new buddy.

The third unique project was to write a teaching philosophy statement. This was due at the end of the semester. It gave me an opportunity to see how well they had incorporated the educational psychology principles in their minds. And, I saw how they could understand the application of these principles to their future teaching.

At the end of the semester, I received e-mails from my students that indicated that they now saw the world of teaching in a whole new light. They felt like better learners themselves as a result of the many concepts that they had learned. And, they had a new found respect for the social sciences. Some students experienced insight into themselves as learners:

> Learning psychological principles for the first time was just cool. Having never taken any type of psychology class before, it was very educational and provided a lot of insight into how and why I do things a certain way, how I study, how I reason, how I learn.

Some students saw the value for teaching and for looking beyond the world of engineering:

> Most graduate students, whether they are interested in teaching or not, would benefit from the educational psychology class. It just broadens your perspective on how the human mind works. In the very least, it gives us one-dimensionally minded engineers something more interesting to talk about! But for someone who is interested in teaching, this class should be required. And they should take the class early in their career before they get set in their ways.

Some students saw the need for educational psychology for all faculty members:

> If we could get professors to start thinking differently about their teaching, to critique their own styles, consider the curriculum from a different perspective, it may be possible to improve engineering education and perhaps bring in even more creative thought to the field. I sometimes wonder whether many of the students who drop out of engineering, drop out because they learn differently. And the regular chalkboard lectures simply just make it impossible for them to learn. I guess this could lead into a philosophical discussion, so in short, I believe it would benefit the college of engineering if professors were educated in educational psychology.

Economic Demands Result in Heterogeneous Classes

The economy was depressed at the time and that put pressure on curriculum demands and limited the course offerings within the College of Education. The dean had made it clear to me that having five students in the class was not acceptable on a regular basis. I was then required to add engineering students to my regular Learning and Instruction Class. With this in mind, I decided to use a flexible semblance of a class-within-a-class format. It started with the syllabus. The main body of the syllabus was the same for all students. Some projects were common to all students. Some projects were unique to either social science students or to engineering students. That meant that sections for grading were unique for each constituent group. And the weekly assignment section in the syllabus was composed of columns with the following headings: (a) All Students; (b) Educational Psychology Students Only; and, (c) Engineering Students Only.

All students wrote journal entries for their weekly reading. They read the same chapters. They all had a culminating experience of teaching our class for 30 minutes. Educational psychology students conducted a small research project and wrote a theory paper. Engineering students did classroom observations, the teach-a-buddy project, and each wrote a teaching philosophy statement.

For the first test of the semester, I met with students individually and had brief interviews with them in a quiet sequestered place. My two important interview questions were, "How is the class going for you?" and "How can I improve this class?" I learned a great deal from these informal interviews. Students did not hesitate to tell me when I was difficult to understand. The educational psychology students were excited to engage in discussion with the engineering students. It gave the educational psychology students new insights into learners very different from themselves.

The most important lesson that I learned in one of these interviews was about communication. One of my engineers said that the discussions were difficult to follow. He explained that every person in the class (meaning everybody, including White Americans) had a unique accent. And because English was his second language, he needed to acclimate to each and every person. Furthermore, he was taught English with a New York accent. And the farther away the person's accent was from New York, the harder it was for him to understand us. Whew! That was a lesson for me, indeed. The next week in class I shared this issue with the entire class. "Hey everybody, we all have accents. We all need to slow down in our speech." The entire class was amazed and found a new sense of respect and courtesy for their fellow students.

Classroom discussions in this heterogeneous class provided a rich environment for all to learn. When the class engaged in discussions meant to elaborate on psychological principles, the engineering students provided examples from various fields within engineering or from different cultures. The educational psychology majors typically gave U.S. classroom examples or examples from their own families. Each constituent group amazed and informed each other. The culminating experience of teaching our class was very enriching as well. Both the group of educational psychology students and I learned concepts from an academic field far from our own. I also realized how different my life might have been if I had been exposed to the exciting world of engineering as a child. The engineering students found a new respect of educational psychology. They found applicability to their future as university faculty members and as parents.

Challenges Teaching Students Outside of the Social Sciences

The field of educational psychology has wide applicability. Today's innovative universities are encouraging cross-disciplinary instruction, degrees, and research. Cross-disciplinary instruction comes with many challenges. Table 8.1 summarizes the many challenges that both my students and I faced, but also the benefits that derived from the class. Mixed classes at the

TABLE 8.1   Challenges and Benefits of Teaching Educational Psychology to Engineering Graduate Students

Issue	Challenge	Benefit
Lack of prior knowledge	No coursework in psychology; Knowledge limited to popular psychology; Students must deal with ill-structured concepts.	Dispel pre-conceived, possibly incorrect, ideas about psychology. Bring insight into human learning for their future teaching and for their own self-improvement.
Students speak, read and write English as a second language	Students contribute infrequently to class discussions; Textbook difficult to understand; Lecture difficult to understand; Spoken accents difficult to understand; Students do not ask questions.	Develop new assignments and activities that do not rely upon texts. Develop techniques that implicitly provide wait time for students to think and feel better prepared to share ideas.
Cultural differences among students	Students not comfortable interacting with one another; Teaching one another is difficult; Students do not ask questions; Students unfamiliar with pedagogical methods, such as sitting together in a circle.	Raise awareness of cultural and language diversity among learners. Expose students to new, and different, pedagogical methods.
Cross-discipline mix of students	Educational psychology students must be patient with engineering students; Assignments must be unique to students from different disciplines; Academic jargon familiar to some, not others.	All students gain insights into their own teaching abilities. Students have greater appreciation for diversity in academic disciplines and in ethnicity. Stereotypes of either psychologists or engineers are challenged.

graduate level means that educational psychology students must be patient when other majors do not know the basic concepts of our discipline. Each discipline has its own jargon. Hence, each student needs to be able to follow the conversation or feel free to ask for clarification. University faculty members (from other disciplines) need to see the value of educational psychology for their discipline. These faculty members can either encourage their students to take an educational psychology course (or dissuade them from doing so). Educational psychology faculty should reach out to faculty members in engineering and other disciplines outside of education to inform them about how their students can benefit from learning about the psychology of learning and instruction.

The Future of Educational Psychology Infused With Other Academic Disciplines

Some engineering educators are already collaborating with educational psychology to create new approaches to instruction (Adams et al., 2011; Johri & Olds, 2011). The field of educational psychology has great growth potential. A most logical improvement to higher education is to provide one or more foundational courses in educational psychology for all teaching faculty of higher education. If innovative cross-discipline case studies, such as the engineering/educational psychology case just described, result in success for students in other disciplines, then both faculty and students in these disciplines may see the added value of preparing faculty to teach college students effectively. If educational psychologists can begin these conversations with other disciplines, then applied educational psychology will become valued by others who have never heard of our field. In the best of all worlds, educational psychology will change from being an obscure discipline to a core course for future instructors of higher education.

REFERENCES

Adams, R., Evangelou, E., English, L., De Figueiredo, A. D., Mousoulides, N., Pawley, A. L., & Wilson, D. M. (2011). Multiple perspectives on engaging future engineers. *Journal of Engineering Education, 100,* 48–88.

Johri, A., & Olds, B. M. (2011). Situated engineering learning: Bridging engineering research and the learning sciences. *Journal of Engineering Education, 100,* 151–185.

Vanasupa, L., Stolk, J., & Herter, R. J. (2009). The four-domain development diagram: A guide for holistic design of effective learning experiences for the twenty-first century engineer. *Journal of Engineering Education, 98,* 67–81.

SECTION II

TEACHING MOTIVATION FOR TEACHERS
AND EDUCATIONAL PSYCHOLOGISTS

CHAPTER 9

USING MOTIVATION
TO TEACH MOTIVATION

Terri Flowerday
University of New Mexico

Teaching courses in educational psychology to college students is what we do. It is the most important thing that we do as professors of educational psychology. The research that we conduct contributes to the literature, furthers our understanding of psychological principles and their application, and informs our teaching. And, our teaching reaches educators at every level. Pre-service teachers in undergraduate education programs, graduate students who will become the faculty in higher education, and other students from across the university will learn these principles and take them into their own classrooms, counseling offices, businesses, and homes. Our students will use the theories to improve their own learning strategies, and will pass this knowledge on to their students, colleagues, and family members. We have important opportunities to encourage lifelong learning in many sectors of society, and to improve learning experience for countless individuals. These are the reasons why I get excited about teaching, and why I devote energy and time to teaching, and engage in extensive reflection about my efforts when it comes to teaching educational psychology.

Challenges and Innovations in Educational Psychology Teaching and Learning, pages 109–121
Copyright © 2016 by Information Age Publishing
All rights of reproduction in any form reserved.

One area about which I am most passionate is motivation theory, in particular, theories of self-efficacy (Bandura, 1977) and self-determination (Deci & Ryan, 1985), both of which are core theories in our field. I have been interested in this topic since my first days in college when I entered the field of education in the 1980s. My personal journey is all about motivation. I am a first-generation college student. My grandmother grew up on the Rosebud Sioux Indian reservation in South Dakota, later moving the family to Nebraska. I did not finish high school, dropping out in tenth grade. Not because I didn't enjoy learning; I very much enjoyed my coursework and was hungry for knowledge. However, life can take unexpected turns; my parents divorced and we moved several times. I landed in a school with little student support and much gang activity. I was afraid to go to school and so I quit. I did, however, earn a GED. I then applied to college and, because someone had faith in me, I was admitted. To shorten the story, I earned a degree in education, taught high school history, returned to earn an MA in educational psychology, and taught community college courses in psychology for several years. My personal education goals were accomplished while raising two children as a single mother. I was motivated!

These personal experiences gave me rich insight into the goals, challenges, and motivation of students in diverse educational settings. Upon returning to the university for doctoral work, I sought the best mentors that I could find. These professors taught with passion and purpose, and guided me by using every possible motivation principle. They modeled motivation theory and practice at every turn, and learning was a joy. Many thanks to my mentors; you know who you are.

For 25 years, I have been teaching educational psychology courses. I have also taught at three higher education institutions, working with undergraduate pre-service teachers in their junior or senior year of college as they prepare for K–12 classrooms. I have also taught graduate students at two universities who were actively teaching in K–12 classrooms while earning their degrees. In my own family, two of my children have become high school teachers, and my third child is majoring in psychology. These experiences keep me close to the real world, the front line of teaching and learning—and are what motivates me to continuing learning and teaching others how to learn effectively.

Most recently, I have been teaching and mentoring graduate students in educational psychology. Most of these students are from rural areas in New Mexico, and come from middle to lower SES backgrounds. Many of my students live in American Indian communities, often on Native Nation reservations. I have established a research lab (Indigenous Research Lab, IRL) to mentor a new generation of Native scholars. In addition, a number of my students are Hispanic and from rural communities. I therefore teach, and I write this chapter from an indigenous perspective. Considerations of culture, language, and community are woven into each of my lesson plans. We discuss the diversity of motivation: Different things motivate different people at different times and in different ways. And, language and ways of thinking, cultural knowledge and background, and community values influence each person's motivation profile. My students have responded positively to my approach. I have, over the past 15 years, mentored many Native and Hispanic students who have graduated with MAs and PhDs, and I have a wonderful group in the preparation pipeline. I wake up each morning, excited about their futures and hopeful that they will love teaching and mentoring as much as I do. I am therefore humbled to share some of my ideas about teaching motivation to college students within a multicultural context.

SETTING THE STAGE

As I consider the format and scope of my motivation course, I strive to meet the students where they are, in terms of their knowledge and experiences. I know that they will come to class with unique personal experiences, and varying degrees and sources of motivation. Each student will remember times when engagement and learning was easy and their motivation was high. They will also remember times when their motivation for school work was low, and competing assigned activities or personal circumstances made their lives difficult. They may have been introduced to the basic concepts of important learning theories in previous courses, but their understanding of these concepts needed to be affirmed. In each case, students' perspectives, interests, and goals are considered. It is critical that the students see themselves within the content addressed in my class, including the motivation research that we read and discuss.

In the first weeks of class, I work to ensure that my students have the basic, foundational knowledge upon which to further build their understanding of motivation theory. For this reason, I begin the course by checking their prior knowledge through question-and-answer discussions, rather than with tests and quizzes. I introduce and review social cognitive theories, especially Bandura's work, and the learning processes and strategies that are associated with these theories. After the introduction, I explain the relevance of motivation theory and practice. Basic information processing models, encoding and retrieval strategies, vicarious learning and modeling, and the components of self-regulation: These principles are the foundation upon which the study of motivation is built. While some students have this background knowledge, many others do not. My review serves to make prior knowledge connections to new information, establishing a knowledge foundation upon which to build, and prepares students to be successful in the class.

My hope is that every student develops individual interest in motivation, or better still, that each comes into the course with this interest in place. However, it helps to be explicit about motivation. I therefore explain the content's relevance, and the utility of understanding motivation theories as well as their application to teaching and learning. This reinforces any interest-based motivation that students bring to the class.

One of the greatest fears of new teachers is their feeling of being ill-prepared for classroom management. Novice teachers have little self-efficacy for managing disruptive behavior or responding to students' acts of defiance or their lack of motivation. As well prepared as teachers might be in pedagogical style, content knowledge, and lesson planning, they have little experience with adolescents who refuse to engage or seem determined to undermine their own or others' learning.

The appropriate application of motivation theories can, however, provide much needed strategies to address students' learning and behavior challenges. Teachers' knowledge of motivation, when effectively employed, can minimize problem behaviors in the classroom. My message to new teachers is that motivation is the frontline in the battle for student engagement. My pre-service teachers snap to attention when they hear this, and their interest in learning the theories of motivation increases because they see the relevance of these theories to classroom practice and behavior management.

What Is Motivation?

Motivation is a psychological state that directs and sustains behavior. Having motivation does not insure that one will act, however. For example, I might be motivated to use my treadmill, but will not do so if I have an opportunity to visit friends instead. Herein lies the challenge for teachers who wish to encourage their students' motivation for academics. It is necessary to find an effective combination of motivators, or incentives, for learning such that their cumulative power outweighs one's motivation for other activities. In the classroom, the best way to accomplish this is by understanding students' interests and incorporating their interests into assigned learning tasks. Emphasizing the relevance of learning tasks also serves to complement students' interests.

Students are confronted with numerous, often confusing, definitions of motivation in textbooks and research articles. I provide ample opportunities for my students to read about and discuss what motivation means to them. I ask them for their ideas about the characteristics of, strategies for, and challenges associated with motivation. Students quickly discover that they know a lot because of their personal experience with motivation. And, they feel efficacious about their ability to learn more, which helps establish a sense of personal relevance.

Next, we look more closely at motivation in educational settings, work, and careers, and in homes and families. "Some of my students just aren't motivated." I hear this all the time. I tell my students that every person is motivated; they are motivated to do something, as well as motivated to not do something else. This conception of motivation is important for my students to understand because it suggests that teachers should never give up on their students. Within every student is a spark of interest or a desire to learn something, and teachers can build upon this bit of motivation to help students achieve both their personal and academic goals.

Using Motivation Theories to Inform Practice

Typically, two class sessions are devoted to each motivation theory that I cover in my educational psychology course. Among the topics addressed are self-determination, self-efficacy, and goal orientation theories, and community building/caring, relevance, and task value. As we move through these basic theories and concepts, I explain their relevance and application by using multiple examples across many and varied contexts (e.g., school, family, community) and problems. It is essential to describe contexts that students understand and to which they can relate. My examples tend to focus on rural school settings, community and family based issues, and cultural aspects of education as these are relevant to my Native and Hispanic students. By framing my examples in settings familiar to my students, they can connect the new information to existing schema, and can elaborate with additional examples using personal experiences to anchor their understanding.

For example, many of my students live in communities where family and kinship is a central focus. Thus, including aspects of family life into examples is useful. In addition, Native and Hispanic students have unique histories related to education policy—often not pleasant or positive. Students may come from circumstances in which formal education is viewed with suspicion and disdain. For example, forced removal from homes and families to attend distant boarding schools where language and culture was punished is the legacy of formal education in many Native communities. Hispanic students too, have histories of language oppression, and cultural genocide. It is important, therefore, to understand this history and acknowledge it.

I give my students positive examples of teachers using motivation principles in everyday practice. Then, these motivational practices are given their theoretical names. Students read research articles, including several older, seminal works (Deci & Ryan, 1985) that explain foundational motivation theories, as well as recent work (Flowerday & Shell, 2015) that describes contemporary revisions and innovations. As students read these research studies (about 4 each week), they write journal entries about each article. The journaling requires them to reflect and make connections to their personal motivation experiences. Among the questions that I ask my students to consider are these:

- When have you used this theoretical principle to motivate yourself or others? Was it successful? Why did it work, or not work?
- When applying these motivation principles, with what assumptions do you begin? How do you decide which theory to look at and apply first? Second? Third?
- How do you know when your strategy is working?

I encourage students to write additional questions for discussion in the following week's class.

Key Theories for a Multicultural Context

Next, I discuss four theoretical perspectives that are most relevant for my students. I begin with interest and intrinsic motivation; next, I address the role of goals as motivators of behavior; then, I describe the concepts of self-efficacy and competence and their relations to motivation; finally, I address the most salient constructs in motivation—relatedness and sense of community. I focus on these four theoretical concepts because they resonate most strongly with my students and each is essential to understanding and modeling motivation.

Interest and Intrinsic Motivation

Interest is a powerful motivator (Hidi & Harackiewicz, 2000; Hidi & Renninger, 2006). Nurturing students' interest is key to promoting student engagement and persistence for academic work (Hidi & Renninger, 2006). Existing interests (i.e., personal interest) can be reinforced, and new interests can be cultivated (i.e., situational interest) through the use of interest-targeted lesson plans and activities. But, to do so, teachers must first determine their students' interests and passions. Intrinsic motivators such as enjoyment and intrigue are based on individuals' inherent interest in something. When intrinsically motivated, students will engage freely and pursue task-related goals enthusiastically, according to self-determination theory (Deci & Ryan, 1985). Although extrinsic motivators, such as praise and task value, may often initiate students' engagement, intrinsic motivation is more likely to sustain students' long-term interests.

Teachers can use their knowledge of students' interests to create lessons and implement curriculum. For example, I recently worked with a community elementary school in a remote area of a Native American Nation to implement a curriculum that focused on horses. My research had revealed that the children were interested in learning more about horses. I suggested to the principal, teachers, and school director that we brainstorm ways to use horses in our lessons. The school had a barn on the property, and school administrators had decided to keep horses for the students to work with and to learn basic principles of horsemanship, as well as responsibility and discipline. Teachers then devised ways to use students' knowledge of horses (e.g., characteristics, uses for agriculture, sport, travel, culture etc.) in their lesson plans for math, science, and language arts. In addition, we held fund-raising events to buy new books for the library on various aspects of horse care, riding, history, and storybooks for the younger children. The teachers reported that students demonstrated renewed interest in reading, and were checking out books (not only the books about horses) from the library. Obviously, not all schools can provide horses for students; but, the larger point is that teachers need to identify students' interests, incorporate these interests into the math, science, and language arts curricula, and their lessons, assignments, and related activities.

Goals

Interest is also fundamental to goal orientation theories (Ames, 1992). Goal theories describe two types of student goal orientations that can be developed as a consequence of classroom instruction. These are a mastery goal orientation and a performance goal orientation. A mastery goal orientation refers to a student's level of motivation that is based on his or her inherent pleasure, desire for learning, and interest. Of course, we all hope that these are the primary motivators for all of our students. Goal orientation theory suggests that, in order to develop a mastery goal orientation, students must shift from a performance orientation (what other people are thinking about them) to an internal locus of control (Eccles & Wigfield, 2002). Qualities of the classroom environment, as well as the teacher's instructional approach, can facilitate an internal locus of control. Such qualities include a safe space for exploration of ideas, respectful dialogue between teacher and students, and among peers, and positive social interactions. I encourage my students' development of mastery goals by creating interesting and intellectually stimulating lessons and enjoyable classroom activities. Participation is encouraged, risk-taking and mistakes are welcomed, and a sense of community is nurtured.

In the most positive sense, performance goals focus on the future value of a learning task. A student may be motivated to do well so that she can earn good grades and get into college or secure a good job. These performance goals can be powerful and instrumental in getting students to engage. Performance goals are important for my students to learn about and understand. They can see how these goals help to sustain their effort at challenging tasks. Understanding the "value" of a concept, a task, or a class is crucial for my students' engagement. They want to know why they need to learn an assigned theory, complete a particular assignment, or enroll in a specific course, and how these activities relate to their individual circumstances and opportunities. Relevance is a primary motivator for my students. After relevance and reasons for engaging have been explained, students will embrace learning to its fullest.

Less useful, and not as relevant to motivation is the performance avoidance construct. My students are not particularly competitive and are not so much influenced by the need to "look good" or perform better than their peers. Students tend to support one another and encourage achievement for all, especially my Native and Hispanic students. Clearly, this will not be so for all students.

Self-Efficacy and Competence

Self-efficacy is an assessment of one's competence in a specific area, or the likelihood that one can successfully perform a task or achieve a goal. It is closely associated with achievement outcomes. We care about self-efficacy because, without an optimal level of self-efficacy, a person will not attempt a task, engage in an activity, or persist in the face of difficulty. Stated plainly, if I don't think I have a chance of success, I won't even try. Self-efficacy develops largely from one's past experiences. If a student has not been successful in his science classes, then it is unlikely that he will attempt more science classes. In addition, students who have no role models that can demonstrate achievement in a particular endeavor will not likely choose to engage in that activity. In many cases, my students have not been privileged with excellent educational experiences and opportunities for success. Coming from rural, under-resourced schools, they have been unable to take advanced high school courses or achieve educational goals that other students take for granted. They often have no role models who have successfully completed high school or attend college and earned degrees. Thus, their self- efficacy for academics is often quite low.

It is important, therefore, for me to encourage the development of positive self-beliefs among my students. They need to have multiple experiences of success before they believe they can do the coursework, learn the material, and achieve their academic goals. Opportunities for success and for developing a sense of competence are, therefore, built into every class session. Students work in groups and are assigned key roles to play. Each person contributes and each person leads. Assignments are developed with the zone of proximal development (Vygotsky, 1978) in mind. Students will be challenged, but they can and do succeed in my class.

Another aspect of self-efficacy to be considered in my class is self-efficacy for teaching. Many of my students are currently teaching, or will become teachers. Teacher self-efficacy—the belief in one's competence as a teacher—is strongly related to the teacher's classroom performance (Ashton & Webb, 1986). Self-efficacy for teaching may be low among pre-service teachers because they have little or no experience in classroom management, and they are concerned about their abilities to keep students on task. They may, however, feel more competent in their pedagogical skills and knowledge of the content. Nonetheless, they wonder how they will be able to motivate and keep their students engaged. The theories and applications learned in my motivation course can help them create classroom environments that encourage learning and minimize behavioral problems. We discuss these aspects of self-efficacy, and read about the implications for teacher self-efficacy in terms of the current political climate—in which teachers often have little autonomy and are subjected to critical assessment by parents, administrators, and school reformers.

Relatedness: Creating Community Through Personal Connections
By now, interest, relevance, and self-efficacy and competence have been demonstrated and discussed, and the most important motivation principle—relatedness—is introduced. Relatedness is a key concept in self-determination theory, but one that is often overlooked or deemphasized. Self-determination theory posits that there are three essential human psychological needs: autonomy, competence, and relatedness (Deci & Ryan, 1985). Although much attention in the literature has been given to autonomy and competence, it is my view that relatedness is the most salient to learner motivation among under-represented and marginalized student populations.

Therefore, I begin early in the semester to help my students develop as a community of learners. Through a variety of classroom exercises and discussions, they get to know one another, work together, and assume responsibility for their peers' success, as well as their own. For example, I assign small group discussions around students' experiences with teaching and learning and ask them to explain how these experiences can be viewed through the lens of different theories of motivation (e.g., describe a great teacher that you have had. What did your teacher do to make you feel connected to, and cared for, by him or her? How did the teacher demonstrate concern for your success? Walls, Nardi, von Minden, & Hoffman, 2002).

A sense of community is beneficial for most students (Summers & Svinicki, 2007), but especially for those from under-represented groups (Cabrera et al., 2002) because they often feel isolated and ill-suited to the mainstream college experience. A connection to family, friends, and others within one's community is essential for learning in both Hispanic and American Indian cultures (Aseron, Greymorning, Miller, & Wilde, 2013). Understanding community takes time and effort, however. I therefore tell my students:

> Know your students! Do your research ahead of time. Learn where your students come from, and what their community means to them. Learn about what has influenced their identities as learners by talking not only to your students, but also to their parents and family members, and visit their home communities. Give your students opportunities to talk about aspects of their identities in a safe, respectful way.

One activity that I use is called Unique Self/Common Self. In small groups of 4–6 students, I ask them to find, through discussion and inquiry, three characteristics that are unique about each person within their group, and three characteristics that no other group member can claim. Next, they determine three characteristics that they all have in common. This activity requires students to talk to and learn about one another. Then, one spokesperson from each group describes the shared characteristics of their group. Finally, each person introduces him- or herself, and describes their three unique characteristics.

Thus, everyone in class learns about each classmate, and this knowledge helps establish a greater sense of community: Three students discover that they have all traveled to Mexico City. Two students learn they have both been raised in Gallup, New Mexico. Four students are avid basketball players, and two more participate in rodeo. Students use this information to make connections with peers, develop a sense of cohesion and community, and communicate more effectively. Their group rapport and social connections positively influence their attendance, peer support, and achievement.

Drawing upon students' needs for relatedness to establish a classroom community is time well spent because it leads to cooperation and mutual concern (Osterman, 2000). Such qualities are particularly important for some cultural groups, including American Indian and Hispanic students, particularly in terms of persistence and academic achievement and persistence (Sánchez, Colon, & Esparza, 2005).

DISCUSSION AND REFLECTION

Familiarity with the core tenets, constructs and principles of theories of motivation increases students' understanding of the utility of these theories for the benefit of their learning and achievement, and informs their instructional practices when they become teachers themselves. My students become more confident in and optimistic about themselves and their abilities to learn and to teach as their understanding of motivation increases. Vygotsky (1978) points out that most learning takes place through human interaction. This is the reason why I encourage my students to relate motivation to their lived experiences so they can make connections to the theoretical constructs. They reflect on personal situations that a specific theory can explain in terms of their behaviors or those of another student or family member.

Understanding motivation theories and the teaching practices that are rooted in these theories helps students develop a toolkit of strategies for improving their own learning, as well as helping their students to learn once they are teaching. Thus, as you consider the motivation theories that you want to teach your students, it is essential that you make each theory come alive and relevant to your students' personal interests and professional goals. Present the theories through the research literature. Model the applications of each theory in class. Demonstrate the theories throughout your lessons, assignments, and classroom activities. Help your students to experience, reflect upon, and internalize the theories, as each offers unique perspectives on the development of academic motivation and learning.

Teaching motivation to students from under-represented-populations requires that you understand the cultural and educational backgrounds of your students—no small task! You should strive to base your teaching strategies and establish the classroom environment on a model that is optimal for Native and Hispanic students. In my years of working with Native and Hispanic students, I have observed that relatedness (i.e., community building), self-efficacy, and an emphasis on relevance to goal attainment are very powerful factors for many of these students.

My recommendation for working with under-represented populations—specifically Native American and Hispanic students—is to teach motivation theories and practices early on in the educational psychology program, and to reach out to students of similar backgrounds that are non-majors to encourage their enrollment in these courses as well to build a community of learners that share similar experiences. Motivation theories should be appropriately applied and evaluated in every aspect of practice. Because many Native American and Hispanic may not have had prior academic achievements, and may lack role models for academic success, it is critical to provide them with multiple and varied opportunities to demonstrate (to themselves and others) that they are capable. As a consequence of engaging in these and related practices, my students often tell me

- "Learning about educational psychology and research is really fun."
- "I am feeling so confident and competent; I know I can do this."

- "I can't wait to join the field and bring Native/Hispanic perspectives to educational psychology, and work in my home community for the good of the people."

These students are—without a doubt—motivated!

At the University of New Mexico, we now have a steady stream of Native and Hispanic students who are registering for educational psychology courses, and an increasing number of these students are entering our program to become educational psychologists. My colleagues and I apply many of the motivation principles that I have described in this chapter to our coursework and student mentoring activities. The success of our motivation-focused efforts is evident by the number of Native and Hispanic graduate students in our educational psychology program: 10 PhD and 14 master's degree Native and Hispanic students have graduated over the past six years. These data indicate that our motivation-based recruitment and retention strategies are working. Our graduates have become community leaders and several have taken positions in the academy. They are conducting research in their communities, providing valuable knowledge that will benefit society, and bringing new perspectives to the field.

REFERENCES

Ames, C. (1992). Classrooms: Goals, structures, and student motivation. *Journal of Educational Psychology, 84*, 261–271.

Aseron, J., Greymorning, S. N., Miller, A., & Wilde, S. (2013). Cultural safety circles and Indigenous Peoples' perspectives: Inclusive practices for participation in Higher Education. *Contemporary Issues in Education Research, 6*(4), 409–416.

Ashton, P. T., & Webb, R. B. (1986). *Making a difference: Teachers' sense of efficacy and student achievement.* New York, NY: Longman.

Bandura, A. (1977). Self-efficacy: Toward a unifying theory of behavioral change. *Psychological Review, 84*(2), 191–215.

Cabrera, A. F., Crissman, J. L., Bernal, E. M., Nora, A., Terenzini, P. T., & Pascarella, E. T. (2002). Collaborative learning: Its impact on college students' development and diversity. *Journal of College Student Development, 43*(1), 20–34.

Deci, E. L., & Ryan, R. M. (1985). *Intrinsic motivation and self-determination in human behavior.* New York, NY: Plenum Press.

Eccles, J. S., & Wigfield, A. (2002). Motivational beliefs, values, and goals. *Annual Review of Psychology, 53*(1), 109–132.

Flowerday, T., & Shell, D. (2015). Disentangling the effects of interest and choice on learning, engagement, and attitude. *Learning and Individual Differences, 40*, 134–140.

Hidi, S., & Harackiewicz, J. (2000). Motivating the academically unmotivated: A critical issue for the 21st century. *Review of Educational Research, 70*, 151–179.

Hidi, S., & Renninger, K. A. (2006). The four-phase model of interest development. *Educational Psychologist, 41,* 111–127.

Osterman, K. F. (2000). Students' need for belonging in the school community. *Review of Educational Research, 70*(3), 323–367.

Sánchez, B., Colón, Y., & Esparza, P. (2005). The role of sense of school belonging and Gender in the academic adjustment of Latino adolescents. *Journal of Youth and Adolescence, 34*(6), 619–628.

Summers, J. J., & Svinicki, M. D. (2007). Investigating classroom community in higher education. *Learning and Individual Differences, 17*(1), 55–67.

Vygotsky, L. S. (1978). Mind in society. In M. Cole, V. John-Steiner, S. Scribner, & E. Souberman (Eds.), *Mind in society: The development of higher processes.* Cambridge, MA: Harvard University Press.

Walls, R. T., Nardi, A. H., von Minden, A. M., & Hoffman, N. (2002). The characteristics of effective and ineffective teachers. *Teacher Education Quarterly, 29,* 39–48.

CHAPTER 10

TEACHING MOTIVATION STRATEGIES USING THE MUSIC MODEL OF MOTIVATION AS A CONCEPTUAL FRAMEWORK

Brett D. Jones
Virginia Tech

OVERVIEW AND PURPOSE

The study of motivation is important to teachers, instructional designers, and others because students who are motivated tend to learn more and perform at higher levels than students who are not as motivated (Schunk, Meece, & Pintrich, 2014). The importance of motivation in the field of educational psychology is evidenced by its prominent role in educational psychology journals, handbooks, and textbooks. Because most textbooks that broadly cover educational psychology devote at least one chapter to motivation, educational psychology-related courses often include learning objectives related to motivation. These types of courses are common at colleges and universities with teacher education programs because educational

Challenges and Innovations in Educational Psychology Teaching and Learning, pages 123–136
Copyright © 2016 by Information Age Publishing
All rights of reproduction in any form reserved.

psychology topics are generally viewed as foundational courses and are often required for students to obtain a state K–12 teaching license in the United States. Motivation courses are also offered for graduate students interested in a variety of fields, such as educational psychology, learning sciences, psychology, and the K–12 content areas (e.g., mathematics, science, literacy, and social studies). Students enrolled in these courses may become instructors at community colleges, professors at universities, research scientists conducting basic or applied research in a university or research organization setting, instructional designers, or professionals within non-profit organizations.

Authors of educational psychology textbooks for undergraduate and master's-level courses usually provide a combination of theory and practical teaching strategies because many students want and need to learn practical strategies for their teaching careers. Teaching implications of motivation theories are also usually part of the learning objectives in graduate courses that focus on conceptual understanding of motivation constructs, the measurement of constructs, and/or research methodologies. However, because the field of motivation is comprised of numerous constructs and "mini-theories" (Reeve, 2005), it can be difficult for instructors to teach these concepts in ways that help students to learn and remember them. The purpose of this chapter is to address this difficulty by explaining how I developed and have used the MUSIC Model of Motivation to teach students practical instructional strategies based on current motivation theories and constructs.

CURRENT MOTIVATION THEORIES AND CHALLENGES IN TEACHING STUDENTS ABOUT MOTIVATION

To understand how I developed the MUSIC Model of Motivation, it is helpful to understand the variety of current motivation theories and constructs. In Table 10.1, I present some of the motivation theories and constructs included in three different types of books that were edited or authored by well-known authors in the field: a recent handbook (*Handbook of Motivation at School*, Wentzel & Wigfield, 2009); a textbook focused on motivation in education (*Motivation in Education: Theory, Research, and Applications*; Schunk et al., 2014); and a motivation chapter from an educational psychology textbook (*Educational Psychology: Developing Learners*; Ormrod, 2014). To show the similarities of the theories and constructs across books, I aligned the theories and constructs in each row to the extent that it was possible to do so. This table shows that these three books are fairly consistent with respect to the motivational theories and constructs presented and, thus, provides evidence that these are currently some of the most important theories and constructs in educational psychology.

TABLE 10.1 Motivation Theories and Constructs Presented in a Recent Handbook and Textbooks

Handbook of Motivation at School (Wentzel & Wigfield, 2009)a	Motivation in Education (Schunk, Meece, & Pintrich, 2014)b	Educational Psychology, Chapter 11: Motivation & Affect (Ormrod, 2014)c
Attributional approach (Ch. 2)	Attribution theory (Ch. 3)	Attributions
Self-theories of intelligence (Ch. 7)		
Self-determination theory (Ch. 9)		Self-determination
	Intrinsic motivation (Ch. 7)	Intrinsic and extrinsic motivation
		Relatedness
Achievement goal theory (Ch. 5) and Goal-directed behavior (Ch. 6)	Goals and goal orientations (Ch. 5)	Goals
Self-efficacy theory (Ch. 3)	Social cognitive theory (Ch. 4)	
Self-regulation (Ch. 12)		
Self-worth theory (Ch. 8)		Competence and self-worth
Expectancy-value theory (Ch. 4)	Expectancy-value theory (Ch. 2)	Expectancies and values
Interest (Ch. 10)	Interest and affect (Ch. 6)	Interests
Engagement and disaffection (Ch. 11)		Affect; Anxiety; Arousal
		Maslow's theory

Note: The theories included in this table are not intended to be comprehensive or to represent all of the theories presented in these sources. Rather, because they are chapter titles or headers, they represent broad conceptions of motivation in education. Often, a theory shown in one book, but not in one or both of the others, does appear somewhere in the other books.

a This list only includes the chapters in the "Section 1: Theories" section of the handbook because they present "overviews of the major theoretical perspectives that address children's motivation at school, its antecedents, and development" (p. 4).

b This list includes only theories that are named in the chapter titles.

c This list includes only theories listed in a major heading within "Chapter 11: Motivation and Affect."

Because of the large quantity and variety of motivation theories and constructs, it can be difficult for students to remember them and the teaching implications associated with them. In my educational psychology courses, I became frustrated with students' inability to integrate the teaching strategies for student motivation into a meaningful and practical model that they could or would use as teachers. And who could blame them? Generally, I only allotted one or two weeks for students to think about these motivational concepts because my courses included many other educational psychology concepts, such as learning, cognition, development, and assessment. Thus, I faced a problem: I was unable to prepare students with the motivation strategies they needed when they needed them most, such as when they were planning and implementing instruction. There is need for more integrated models that retain the complexity of current motivational constructs, yet are simple enough for practitioners to use. This need was also recognized by Wentzel and Wigfield (2009).

THE MUSIC MODEL OF MOTIVATION

The Process of Developing the MUSIC Model

To address the need for an integrated model of teaching strategies for student motivation, I created the MUSIC Model of Motivation using an inductive and iterative approach that spanned over a decade. I reviewed the practical motivation implications and strategies in many textbooks, handbooks, journal articles, and other sources. I noted that many authors provided implications for each motivation theory or construct along with the theory or construct, but did not provide a means of presenting the strategies in a manner that was easy to remember. To develop a more integrated conceptual model, I grouped motivational strategies by similarity, often because they emerged from similar constructs (e.g., self-efficacy and expectancy for success). For example, the strategy, "teachers should establish quality relationships with students" is similar to the strategy "teachers should get to know their students," regardless of the fact that these strategies originated from different theoretical perspectives or constructs. I am not suggesting that theories are unimportant. However, when motivation strategies are presented in a text along with each theory or construct, and there are many theories and constructs, this results in a long list of strategies that are redundant. My solution was to organize similar strategies together to reduce this redundancy to help students remember the strategies and be more likely to use them in practice.

I tested different conceptual groupings of motivational strategies by using them in undergraduate and graduate educational psychology-related courses at a variety of universities (e.g., Duke University, University of South Florida St. Petersburg, and Virginia Tech) with different students for many years. I implemented many different variations of groupings until I found those that were inclusive of most motivation theories represented in educational psychology books and current research. When I was satisfied that the conceptual groupings were easily understandable to students and would help them in their careers as they designed and implemented instruction, I presented the five groupings formally in an article (Jones, 2009) and a conference presentation (Jones, 2010).

The Five Components of the MUSIC Model

Each of the five conceptual groupings of motivational strategies can be summarized by a general principle. Students are more motivated during instruction when they: (1) perceive that they are *empowered*; (2) believe that the content is *useful*; (3) believe that they can be *successful*; (4) are *interested*; and (5) feel *cared* for by others in the learning environment. I named these groups with one key word that would be descriptive to instructors and avoid academic jargon (e.g., self-efficacy, self-concept, utility value) that can be confusing to practitioners. By chance, the key words—eMpowerment, Usefulness, Success, Interest, and Caring—provide a memorable acronym, MUSIC. I named these five conceptual groups the *MUSIC Model of Academic Motivation* (which can be shortened to the *MUSIC Model of Motivation*) to emphasize that these five principles work together to create a learning environment that is motivating to students.

Factor analyses of items related to each of these MUSIC components demonstrated that, as predicted, the five components were correlated yet distinct from one another in samples of middle school students (Jones & Wilkins, 2013b) and university students (Jones & Skaggs, 2012; Jones & Wilkins, 2013a), thus providing empirical, quantitative evidence for the MUSIC model. Since then, I have examined the use of these five strategy groupings in a variety of contexts (see www.MUSICmodelofmotivation.com for citations).

Teaching Strategies Associated with the MUSIC Model

Examples of motivational teaching strategies that relate to each component of the MUSIC model are presented in Table 10.2, along with some theories and constructs that align well with each component. Note that some theories and constructs can lead to teaching strategies that span more than one MUSIC model component. The *empowerment* component of the MUSIC model refers to strategies related to providing students with control

TABLE 10.2 Motivation Strategies Associated with Components of the MUSIC Model

MUSIC model components	Motivational strategiesa	Related theories and constructs
eMpowerment	• Give students control over their learning (p. 215) • Support students' autonomy (p. 175) • Provide choices when possible (p. 183) • Give students opportunities to talk (p. 184)	• Need for autonomy
Usefulness	• Highlight the implications of the content to students' everyday lives (p. 216) • Use an approach that focuses on solving significant problems (p. 156)	• Utility value • Future time perspective
Success	• Provide children with mastery experiences (p. 61) • Provide positive competence feedback and encouragement (p. 214) • Attribute successes and failures to internal, controllable causes to help students believe that they can succeed with effort. (pp. 20, 134). • Clearly communicate expectations for behavior and performance (p. 306)	• Self-efficacy • Expectancy for success • Self-concept • Self-worth • Need for competence • Achievement goals • Attributions • Incremental views of intelligence • Anxiety
Interest	• Express interest in the subject matter (p. 216) • Select text that is surprising, vivid, and easy to comprehend (p. 199) • Create pleasurable experiences (p. 64) • Relate new subject content to students' existing interests (p. 216)	• Situational interest • Need for arousal • Affect • Flow • Intrinsic motivation
Caring	• Increase students' feelings of relatedness with their teacher and peers (p. 215) • Be willing to provide help (p. 307) • Provide emotional support (p. 307) • Create a community of scholarship (p. 158)	• Caring • Need for relatedness • Belonging • Attachment

a All of these strategies and the associated page numbers refer to the *Handbook of Motivation at School*, edited by Wentzel and Wigfield (2009). These are only samples of the types of strategies provided in this handbook and are not a comprehensive list.

over their learning; that is, these strategies promote students' autonomy. The *usefulness* component involves strategies that demonstrate the usefulness of the coursework (e.g., assignments, activities, readings) to students' short- or long-term goals. The *success* component focuses on strategies that can help students believe that they can succeed if they put forth the appropriate effort. The *interest* component generally refers to *situational* interest, which involves strategies that capture students' attention and lead to the short-term enjoyment of instructional activities. The interest component can also refer to longer-term *individual* interest that involves students valuing the content. The *caring* component includes strategies that instructors can use to demonstrate that they (or others in the learning environment) care about their students' well-being and their success in their coursework.

Students can be motivated in a course even when all of the MUSIC model components are not perceived to be present at high levels. For example, students who are not *interested* in course topics and are not *empowered* to make choices may still be motivated in a course because of the *usefulness* of the course to their future goals. To increase the chances that all students will be motivated, however, it is logical that instructors should try to use strategies that address all of the MUSIC components. Because the components are related to one another (Jones & Skaggs, 2012; Jones & Wilkins, 2013a, 2013b), it is possible that when teachers increase students' perceptions of one component, they might also increase students' perceptions in one or more of the other components.

THE MUSIC MODEL AS AN ORGANIZATIONAL SCAFFOLD TO TEACH MOTIVATION STRATEGIES

Elements of Instruction

My approaches to teaching motivation strategies in courses that focus on educational psychology and motivation have usually involved one or more of the four elements explained in this section, although other approaches are certainly possible. I honed these approaches through my knowledge of effective teaching practices and the use of student feedback in undergraduate and graduate courses that I taught either face-to-face or online.

Element 1: Present the MUSIC Model

At the beginning of a motivation course or a motivation unit in an educational psychology course, I present the MUSIC Model of Motivation by having students complete one or more of the following: (a) read the Jones (2009) article; (b) read the main content sections of the MUSIC model website (www.MUSICmodelofmotivation.com); and/or (c) watch a 10- to 15-minute video presentation (available on YouTube.com) in which I explain the five key MUSIC principles and provide example strategies. Students complete these activities on their own outside of class time, although I encourage them to ask me clarifying questions. I used to present the MUSIC model at the *end* of a motivation course or unit, but students prefer to see the MUSIC model at the beginning because they like to use it as a type of advance organizer and conceptual framework for the teaching strategies presented throughout the course or unit.

Element 2: Connect Theoretical and Research Implications to the MUSIC Model

Throughout a motivation course or at the end of a motivation unit in an educational psychology course, I ensure that students are able to connect the instructional implications for each motivation mini-theory and construct to the MUSIC model conceptual framework (see Table 10.2 for examples). For face-to-face classes, the students and I can discuss these connections explicitly through class activities. For online courses, I rely on the information presented in Element 1 above, the course readings, and/or the videos I created to help students understand these connections.

Element 3: Analyze Instruction Using the MUSIC Model

As an in-class activity, an out-of-class assignment, or both, I ask students to use the MUSIC model to analyze a video of instruction or a written case study of a teacher, and to then identify ways in which the instructor is consistent or inconsistent with the motivational strategies in the MUSIC model. This analysis requires students to consider what effective motivational strategies "look like" in an instructional setting. One way I do this is by providing students with the following directions to a "Motivation Investigation" assignment:

> (1) read the Jones (2009) article (or the MUSIC model website); (2) watch [insert link to an online video] which shows an instructor in a "real" classroom and note how the teacher is consistent and inconsistent with the MUSIC model strategies; (3) for each of the five MUSIC components (i.e., empowerment, usefulness, success, interest, and caring) summarize your notes into a paragraph of consistencies and a paragraph of inconsistencies; (4) rate the instructor on each of the five MUSIC components on a scale from 1 to 4 (1 = *unsuccessful,* 2 = *somewhat successful,* 3 = *successful,* and 4 = *very successful*); and (5) provide a one-paragraph explanation of why you chose each of the ratings.

I provide students with a template to insert their answers because when their answers are formatted similarly I can grade them faster, which allows me to use the assignment in courses having more than 50 students.

This analysis assignment can teach students several important points about motivation. It demonstrates that instruction should not be viewed as either motivating or not motivating for students; rather, instructors may be stronger in some aspects of the MUSIC model and weaker in other aspects. It also identifies specific weaknesses that instructors can work on to improve and strengths that they can build upon. Furthermore, it provides an example of how students can evaluate their own or others' instruction in the future. I intentionally select videos and case studies in which the instructor has both strengths and weaknesses to ensure that students have opportunities to consider both.

Element 4: Discuss the Analysis

In my face-to-face courses, I provide time for students to discuss their analyses in small groups of three or four students and then I moderate a whole-class discussion. These discussions may also work well online (although I have not yet tried them online). When there is not time for small group discussion, I allot time for whole-class discussion. These discussions are important because students often disagree with one another about the effectiveness of the instructor with respect to some of the MUSIC components. Hearing other students' perspectives can lead to a deeper understanding of these motivational principles. For example, some students may believe that a teacher's explanation is clear and fosters success beliefs, whereas others may find the explanation too informal, vague, and confusing, leading to anxiety and lower perceptions of the possibility of success. The whole-class discussion provides students with a broader range of perspectives and I can ensure that this variety of perspectives is considered (i.e., I play devil's advocate for positions that few or no students want to support openly). These discussions can show that there is often a consensus among students' perceptions of the MUSIC model components; yet, at other times, reasonable students can have different perceptions. These disagreements demonstrate to students why the same instruction may be motivating to some students and not to others.

Outcomes of the Four Elements

Using these four elements allows me to model instruction that is consistent with the MUSIC model strategies. The instruction analysis and discussion allow students to share their ideas, which can empower them. Students may find these elements *useful* because they help them remember the motivation teaching strategies and allow for application to "real-world" instruction similar to what they might experience as future instructors. The structure of the elements (e.g., clear explanations) can help students believe that they can *succeed* in implementing the motivation strategies, especially when we practice an analysis during the class session before they begin a graded analysis assignment that they complete on their own. The real-world aspects of the analysis and the novelty of the video or case study can also *interest* students. The other students and I can demonstrate *caring* by listening to their ideas and respecting differing opinions during Element 4.

In the following section, I provide specific examples of how I have used these four elements in three different types of courses. In two of the courses described below, students responded to the following item on an end-of-course evaluation: "The MUSIC Model of Academic Motivation is useful in helping me to remember instructional strategies that motivate students" (rated on a 6-point Likert-type scale with the following descriptors: 1 = *strongly disagree*, 2 = *disagree*, 3 = *somewhat disagree*, 4 = *somewhat agree*, 5 = *agree*, and 6 = *strongly agree*). On average, students rated this item between *agree* and *strongly agree*, which provides evidence that the MUSIC model helped students remember motivational strategies ($M = 5.42$, $SD = 0.62$, $n = 31$ for the online undergraduate course, *Motivation in Education*; $M = 5.28$, $SD = 0.96$, $n = 29$ for the online graduate course, *Psychological Foundations of Education for Pre-service Teachers*). In the next section, I provide results from other measures specific to each course.

Examples of the Elements Used in Courses

Motivation in Education

I used the MUSIC model in my online undergraduate *Motivation in Education* course that upper-level undergraduates (typically majoring or minoring in psychology) select as an elective course. Students are expected to learn motivation theories and constructs (and related instructional strategies), such as self-efficacy, expectancy-value theory, self-theories of intelligence, attribution theory, interest, self-determination theory, self-worth theory, self-regulation, attachment theory, control-value theory, and emotion.

After beginning the course by reading the introductory chapter of the *Handbook of Motivation at School* (Wentzel & Wigfield, 2009), students read the Jones (2009) article and watched a 13-minute video about the MUSIC model that reinforced the concepts in the article (Element 1). I assessed students' knowledge of these concepts using an open-book, multiple-choice quiz. Students proceeded through the assigned handbook chapters (not all chapters were assigned) and watched 10- to 20-minute videos I created for each chapter. The videos followed a similar organization whereby I began by explaining the major concepts in the theory. Near the end of the video, I presented the instructional implications provided by the chapter authors, followed by an explanation of how these implications fit into the conceptual framework of the MUSIC model (Element 2; see Table 10.2 for examples). Students also completed "Motivation Investigations" that required them to apply motivation theories to "real" cases or students (Element 3).

In an open-ended item at the end of the course, I asked students whether this teaching approach motivated them and helped them to learn the concepts related to the teaching implications of motivation theories. Most of the students reported that the instruction motivated them and helped them learn the teaching implications, as demonstrated in comments from the following three students: (a) "Reading the article on the MUSIC Model at the beginning of the course was extremely beneficial as it served as a good introduction to the course, while laying a strong foundation in the teaching implications of motivation theories"; (b) "It was helpful that the MUSIC Model of Academic Motivation reoccurred often throughout the course"; and (c) "I think the MUSIC model helped to motivate me because it broke everything down into simpler terms."

For one of the assigned "Motivation Investigations" I asked students to watch a 35-minute online video (available at www.videolectures.net) of a university professor teaching a lesson titled "Lecture 2: Discovery of Nucleus." I provided students with the instructions listed in the Element 3 section above. At the end of the course, students rated the following question using a 6-point scale (1 = *strongly disagree*, 2 = *disagree*, 3 = *somewhat disagree*, 4 = *somewhat agree*, 5 = *agree*, 6 = *strongly agree*): "This assignment helped me to apply motivation theories to practical examples." All of the students, except one who disagreed, reported values from 4 to 6, indicating that they agreed with this statement ($M = 4.9$, $SD = 1.0$, $n = 31$).

Psychological Foundations of Education for Pre-Service Teachers

I used the MUSIC model in an online educational psychology course designed for pre-service teachers, titled *Psychological Foundations of Education for Pre-service Teachers*. Most students were first-year master's students or undergraduate seniors who were, or planned to be, enrolled in a master's program to obtain a state K–12 teaching license. The textbook was Ormrod's (2009) *Essentials of Educational Psychology*, in which one of the 10 chapters was specifically devoted to motivation and affect, although issues related to motivation were included throughout the textbook. Students were expected to learn motivation constructs and theories in the Ormrod (2009) textbook.

Near the middle of the course, after reading Ormrod's (2009) "Motivation and Affect" chapter, students completed an online, multiple-choice quiz to assess their knowledge of the chapter's contents. Next, students read the main content pages of the MUSIC model website to understand the five components of the MUSIC model (Element 1). Then, students completed an assignment in which they read a case study of a teacher (Element 3). What follows is a summary of the directions that accompanied this assignment.

As you are reading [the case study], make a list of 10 behaviors (or activities) in which the teacher motivates students by meeting one or more of the MUSIC model components. Your assignment is to list: (1) the page number in the [case study] where you found the behavior and a short description of the behavior to which you are referring; (2) which of the MUSIC components the behavior met; and (3) your rationale for why you claim that it meets each of the components that you listed.

At the end of the course, students rated the following question using a 6-point scale (1 = *strongly disagree,* 2 = *disagree,* 3 = *somewhat disagree,* 4 = *somewhat agree,* 5 = *agree,* 6 = *strongly agree*): "The [case study] assignment helped me to apply motivation theories to practical examples." All of the students reported values of 4 to 6, indicating that they agreed with this statement ($M = 5.6$, $SD = 0.6$, $n = 29$). In an open-ended item that asked what was useful and/or not useful about the ways that the MUSIC model and motivation theories were taught, most students reported that the assignment helped them to apply theory to practice. Many students reported that the MUSIC model was easy to understand and use, and thought it would be helpful to them in the future.

Motivation and Cognition

This is another graduate course I have taught, but face-to-face rather than online. Enrolled students were a combination of doctoral and master's students seeking degrees in a variety of disciplines, including educational psychology, engineering education, and mathematics education. The readings for the course consisted primarily of journal articles and handbook chapters written by prominent authors in the field (e.g., an article on *self-efficacy* by Schunk and Pajares [2002]). Students were responsible for learning most of the motivation theories and constructs shown in Table 10.1.

Students read the Jones (2009) article and two other articles related to the MUSIC model for the second week of class (Element 1) after having completed an introductory reading for the first week. During the second week, I showed students a video and led a discussion about how the instruction in the videos was consistent or inconsistent with the MUSIC model strategies (Elements 3 and 4). I also modeled how to use the 4-point rating scale described previously in this chapter. On their own, students completed the Motivation Investigation assignment described above and I provided feedback and assigned a grade to each student's work. During the class session after the assignment was due, I led a short whole-group discussion of students' perceptions of the video (Element 4).

I implemented Element 2 by connecting the teaching implications of each theory to the MUSIC model teaching strategies throughout the course. When I asked students about the extent to which I referred back to the MUSIC model throughout the course, 19 of 20 students reported that they appreciated the references back to the MUSIC model as a conceptual framework.

SUMMARY AND CONCLUSION

My approach to teaching motivation strategies involves four primary elements: (a) presenting the MUSIC Model of Motivation to students as a conceptual framework; (b) connecting implications of theories and research to the MUSIC model framework; (c) requiring students to analyze instruction using the MUSIC model; and (d) facilitating a discussion of the instructional analysis. Using the MUSIC model to organize motivation strategies can be an effective approach for instructors for a few reasons. First, the framework of the MUSIC model can decrease the cognitive load students can experience when learning motivation strategies by assigning the strategies to one of five broad categories. Limiting the strategies to five categories is a practical way to scaffold students' learning so that they actually remember the main concepts. It is unreasonable to expect all students to want or need to understand all of the subtleties among motivation constructs, especially in courses where motivation may only be included as the primary focus for one or two weeks. As students become more familiar with motivation theories and research, they can understand more of the nuances within each of the five MUSIC components. This more complex understanding may happen while students are enrolled in a course, or it may happen later, as they begin to teach and apply the strategies. To summarize, I contend that the MUSIC model provides a usable model that includes the major motivation strategies in a manner that students can easily remember and apply when they are teaching.

REFERENCES

Jones, B. D. (2009). Motivating students to engage in learning: The MUSIC Model of Academic Motivation. *International Journal of Teaching and Learning in Higher Education, 21*(2), 272–285.

Jones, B. D. (2010, October). *Strategies to implement a motivation model and increase student engagement.* Paper presented at the annual meeting of the International Society for Exploring Teaching and Learning, Nashville, TN. Retrieved from http://www.MUSICmodelofmotivation.com).

Jones, B. D., & Skaggs, G. (2012, August). *Validation of the MUSIC Model of Academic Motivation Inventory: A measure of students' motivation in college courses.* Research presented at the International Conference on Motivation 2012, Frankfurt, Germany.

Jones, B. D., & Wilkins, J. L. M. (2013a). Testing the MUSIC Model of Academic Motivation through confirmatory factor analysis. *Educational Psychology: An International Journal of Experimental Educational Psychology, 33*(4), 482–503.

Jones, B. D., & Wilkins, J. L. M. (2013b, May). *Validity evidence for the use of a motivation inventory with middle school students.* Poster presented at the annual meeting of the Society for the Study of Motivation, Washington, DC.

Ormrod, J. E. (2009). *Essentials of educational psychology* (2nd ed.). Columbus, OH: Pearson.

Ormrod, J. E. (2014). *Educational psychology: Developing learners* (8th ed.). Columbus, OH: Pearson.

Reeve, J. (2005). *Understanding motivation and emotion.* Hoboken, NJ: Wiley.

Schunk, D. H., Meece, J. L., & Pintrich, P. R. (2014). *Motivation in education: Theory, research, and applications.* Columbus, OH: Pearson.

Schunk, D. H., & Pajares, F. (2002). The development of academic self-efficacy. In A. Wigfield & J. Eccles (Eds.), *Development of achievement motivation* (pp. 239–266) San Diego, CA: Academic Press.

Wentzel, K. R., & Wigfield, A. (Eds.). (2009). *Handbook of motivation at school.* New York, NY: Taylor & Francis.

CHAPTER 11

MAKING MOTIVATION MEANINGFUL BY MASTERING MASLOW

Helenrose Fives and Tammy M. Mills
Montclair State University

Maslow's Hierarchy of Needs is a foundational humanistic theory of motivation that spans multiple fields within the discipline of psychology. This topic is found in introductory educational psychology, general psychology, and human development texts and courses. Within educational psychology, Maslow's Hierarchy of Needs (MHN) is often presented with achievement motivation theories, although the distinction of this theory as focusing on overall well-being rather than academic achievement is often underscored. Further, the lack of empirical evidence to support the hierarchical nature of the identified needs has often caused Maslow's work to be relegated to the sidelines rather than seen as a foundational conceptualization of human motivation (Tay & Diener, 2011). In this chapter, we argue that the theory is essential to understanding human motivation and humanist ontology. Therefore, we describe Maslow's theory, the challenges in teaching it, our three-pronged approach to teaching the theory. We conclude with recommendations for other instructors.

Challenges and Innovations in Educational Psychology Teaching and Learning, pages 137–149
Copyright © 2016 by Information Age Publishing
All rights of reproduction in any form reserved.

MASLOW'S HIERARCHY OF NEEDS

Maslow's (1943) Hierarchy of Needs is foundational to humanist theories of motivation. This theory provided the backdrop for Alderfer's (1969) ERG theory, Mathes' three-levels of motivational needs (1981), Glasser's (1993) five basic needs of human belonging, and Ryan and Deci's (2000) self-determination theory. Understanding MHN and the humanistic approach to psychology provides a meaningful context for knowledge construction within human needs, motivations, and behavior. Maslow's theory provides a particularly salient socio-historical juxtaposition to behaviorism—which was prevalent in the 1940s and 1950s, and is still featured in many educational psychology texts.

Maslow based his theory on the assumption of the importance of overall well-being of the individual beyond academic achievement. Maslow's premise is decidedly affirmative, based on the belief that behavior is a consequence of choice and that people are: (a) inherently good; (b) free to act; and (c) able to learn, grow, develop, and reach their potential with impunity (Wilson & Madson, 2008).

Maslow (1954) posited that humans have a hierarchy of needs ranging from the lowest level physiological needs to the highest level of self-actualization. His categorization of these needs into six levels is based on the assertion that each lower need must be met before the next higher need can be met. The first four needs are described as *deficiency needs* and include: physiological, safety, love and belonging, and esteem. These needs are marked by the ability to be satisfied. That is, one's deficiency needs (e.g., physiological needs of food, water, sleep) can be fully met in a given moment of existence. Further, these needs can be "over satisfied" to the point where potential problems can arise. For instance, one can be overfed, or feel overly safe or good about him- or herself. In contrast to deficiency need, the three needs at the top of this hierarchy are referred to as *growth* or *being* needs. These needs are for knowledge, aesthetic appreciation, and self-actualization. They are generative such that the more one experiences each need, the more the person wants of each. For instance, the more one learns, the more one wants to learn. Or, a person who hears a beautiful piece of music, rarely says "That was good, I don't need to hear that again." In fact, the opposite is generally true!

Due in part to issues related to measurement and vagueness of language and concept, Wahba and Bridwell (1976) suggested a paucity of evidentiary support for Maslow's theory. The hierarchal structure was questioned with regard to its use as an organizational scheme (Alderfer, 1969) and with regard to Maslow's claim that lower levels must be met for higher levels to be pursued or satisfied (O'Connor & Yballe, 2007). However, O'Connor and Yballe (2007) redirected readers to the position that Maslow (1954) himself acknowledged about his theory: MHN is an over simplification of daily life and, in temporal moments, multiple basic (deficiency) needs can be simultaneously satisfied. In this way, one particular action on the part of a person, like going to work, can be motivated by a desire to satisfy all of the person's deficiency needs and possibly some growth needs. A person goes to work in order to purchase food and health care (physiological needs), pay for rent and car repair (safety needs), be part of a collegial community or engage in social interaction (love and belonging), and feel a sense of contribution to society that leads to subjective self-worth (esteem needs). Thus, while the notion of the hierarchy when strictly interpreted and tested has been questioned, Maslow did not necessarily intend for such a strict interpretation.

MASLOW'S HIERARCHY OF NEEDS FOR EDUCATORS

Who Do We Teach?

The educational psychology students (EP students) whom we typically teach are pre-service teachers. In our institution, educational psychology is a prerequisite to the teacher education program, so most EP students in the class are in their first or second year of university coursework and are deciding whether or not they want to pursue teacher certification. A second group of EP students are enrolled in the subject-area Masters of Arts in Teaching or our Post Baccalaureate Teacher Certification Programs. These groups differ in their majors (e.g., science education, math education, English education), as well as their career history.

Why Teach MHN?

Viewing learners through Maslow's lens allows pre-service teachers in educational psychology classes to consider their future students' overall subjective well-being beyond a narrow focus on academic achievement. Our goal is to prepare pre-service teachers to reach the *whole child*. Evidence suggests that a positive correlation exists between need fulfillment and subjective well-being (Tay & Diener, 2011). To help learners experience well-being, teachers and other school personnel need to understand the relationship between human need fulfillment and subjective well-being. This suggests a more human-centered goal than achieving high scores on state-mandated tests.

Maslow (1954) suggested that fulfillment of needs is likely to enhance a person's sense of well-being. Building upon Maslow's theory, researchers and scholars across a number of disciplines (e.g., psychology, sociology, anthropology) have posited that societies enjoying a higher quality of life contain people having a stronger sense of well-being (Tay & Diener, 2011). MHN highlights the multi-disciplinary nature of teaching; it can provide pre-service teachers WITH a frame for capturing a broader view of education within a larger societal context.

What Should Be Learned?

Maslow took a humanistic view of psychology. He argued that people were able to access happiness, health, and functionality when they took responsibility for fulfilling their needs (Ventegodt-Merrick & Anderson, 2003). With respect to EP students and future teachers, it is important that they understand the nature of a humanist ontology. Maslow's theory provides an example of this perspective that is intuitive, complex, and accessible. Pre-service teachers should be able to recognize the distinction and possible consequences of deficiency and growth needs and how each may lead to different responses from their future students. As a foundational perspective on human motivation, MHN can be used as an advance organizer for understanding other, more current, motivation theories.

Maslow did not intend for people to conceptualize the needs hierarchy as one of rigid completion of a stage before progressing to the next, or that completion of a stage ensures completion of a subsequent stage (O'Connor & Yballe, 2007). EP students may need help in seeing the dynamic and fluid nature of MHN. By overlaying other motivational theories onto Maslow's, instructors can help EP students use MHN as a lens to examine other motivation theories (e.g., Ryan & Deci, 2000). Additionally, it is essential that instructors ensure EP students have a grasp of the situational and recurring nature of needs (Walker & Greene, 2009). A need that has been met may reoccur in any given situation. EP students, as future teachers, will be working with individual students in schools situated within communities. Knowing Maslow's conception of how his needs theory influenced societal constructs may help teachers consider their work and relationships from a larger perspective (Tay & Diener, 2011).

What Challenges Emerge When Teaching Maslow?

The challenge in teaching about MHN to pre-service teachers rests in (1) the seeming simplicity of the theory; and (2) students' tendency to forget it as new topics are examined in class. First, MHN seems to make intuitive sense for most EP students, and consequentially, they sometimes fail to consider the multiple components of the needs hierarchy simultaneously when applying it to practice. Further, as discussed previously, the humanist ontology in which Maslow's theory is rooted needs explication for EP students—particularly in preparation for exposure to other perspectives (e.g., mechanistic or organismic ontologies). These overarching perspectives are frequently challenging for students new to psychology to grasp and, yet, they can offer learners a helpful organizer for understanding the field at large. Thus, when a theory seems overly simple for EP students, they may accept it too readily and not engage in a cognitive interrogation of the concept that would lead to deeper learning.

Pre-service teachers' attempts to apply this theory to classroom based cases, in our context, frequently leads to the same kinds of errors that were found as critiques of the theory. For instance, EP students sometimes fail to question how love and belonging needs may be part of the way that esteem needs are met or created. To illustrate, there will be classroom situations in which future students will possess both sets of needs. Our pre-service teachers sometimes make faulty assumptions about the importance of maintaining the hierarchy and make a direct application of the theory without critical reflection and consideration of the dynamic nature of these needs in lived contexts.

A second challenge is that EP students rarely transfer their understanding of MHN theory into other problems we discuss in educational psychology or, later, to their teaching practice. For instance, when we discuss metacognition, EP students rarely raise the issue that student metacognition, an effortful cognitive act, requires a motivator and that learners may choose to not engage this process when their needs are neither met nor activated. Similarly, EP students do not connect to Maslow when we discuss cooperative learning and social constructivism, both of which rely on interpersonal relations. There is room here for instructors to help pre-service teachers see these connections by asking them to explicitly use Maslow's theory as a lens for critiquing learning theories and instructional methods. For example, cooperative learning and social constructivism can be compared using MHN as a lens of analysis.

Cooperative learning is largely supported by Vygotsky's (1978) theory of social constructivism and, specifically, the zone of proximal development. Successful cooperative learning, according to Johnson and Johnson (2009), requires positive interdependence, individual accountability, promotive interaction, social skills, and group processing. Thus, we move from a conceptualization that learning occurs in the zone of proximal development through interaction and internalization (Vygotsky, 1978) to a classroom practice of cooperative learning (Johnson & Johnson, 2009) that coordinates several theories and underlying perspectives about learning, classrooms, and people. The underlying influence of a humanistic perspective on development and learning can help future teachers see the connections between Vygotsky's theory and the application of that theory to teaching via the practice of cooperative learning.

Related to this challenge of transfer within educational psychology, EP students are also challenged by a limited ability to apply their understanding of MHN to future teaching practices. In our university context, EP students are pre-admission to teacher education and have no field experience (beyond their own lives) from which to consider the course material. Thus, when we discuss ways to apply Maslow to real life contexts, our EP students frequently fall back on obvious and overly simple suggestions. For instance, when faced with a child whose physiological needs are not met, our pre-service teachers frequently respond that they would feed the child or let him or her sleep in class. But when pushed by the extension that, for this fictitious child, the pattern continues, our EP students frequently fail to consider any other possible avenues of support. At the other extreme, they might also have difficulty understanding how a middle or high school student can get caught up in a need to know or to express themselves. In these cases, the response is usually to give the student extra work. These limited applications are not surprising given the ages and limited experiences of our EP students. However, the challenge remains that, by the time our pre-service teachers have developed their craft knowledge rooted in practical experience, their consideration of theories like Maslow's are often forgotten. Thus, the challenge for us is how to provide instruction on this (or any other) theory for students early in their program in ways that they will continue to draw upon as they develop as teachers.

THREE STEPS TO LEARNING MASLOW'S HIERARCHY OF NEEDS

To address the content needs and challenges associated with understanding, applying, and transferring Maslow's humanistic perspective on human motivation, we do so through a three-step progression of activities. These activities include a simulation, vignette series application, and case analysis and theory comparisons. The activities can be completed in one 2.5 hour class session; however, we typically spread them out over 2–3 sessions. By implementing several different pedagogical techniques, we seek to expose students to MHN in multiple ways and to model different approaches to instruction.

Simulation: Survivor-Educational Psychology

We use a simulation game, "Survivor-Educational Psychology" to introduce EP students to MHN. There is no prior preparation for this activity and EP students can come to the lesson "cold." The learning objective for this simulation is for EP students to conceptualize Maslow's seven types of need.

Using a projector, we present the simulation (Table 11.1). EP students, organized into six groups, are told that each group represents a surviving

TABLE 11.1   Lifeboat Simulation Scenarios

Context: *Your cruise ship containing all of your most cherished family and friends has sailed into a cata-strophic hurricane (Hurricane Helenrose) that has forced you to load onto the lifeboats and strike out for safety in the Bermuda Triangle as the Cruise Ship slowly sinks to the bottom of the sea. Given the peculiarities of the Bermuda Triangle and the Rages of Hurricane Helenrose the lifeboats separate and experience very different outcomes... Following each scenario students are told: A Genie appears and offers you one wish (no compounds) for anything but a way off the boat (or island)... What do you wish for?*

Outcome	Level	Actual Responses
Boat 1: Your lifeboat has been floating aimlessly for a week. Emergency supplies ran out 36 hours ago. You are short on water and have no food. There is no land in sight and another storm seems to be starting—given the increasing waves and darkening skies. Shark fins have circled your boat several times and one has even attempted to bite into the bottom of your boat.	Physiological needs (food, water, shelter)	• Speargun • Land in sight • For the boat to be put in Times Square • That our families are safe

Your lifeboat landed on the warm and sunny sands of a deserted island. There is plenty of fresh water and food available. The storms seem to have avoided your island completely.

Boat 2: However, one of your fellow life-boat mates turns out to be a psychopathic serial killer and cannibal trained by the U.S. Navy Seals. In the week that has passed on the island 3 of your fellow lifeboat mates have been murdered.	Safety needs	• For the psychopathic serial killer to *not* be a psychopathic serial killer • For Rambo (for real) to come to the island
Boat 3: However, you do not know anyone on your lifeboat and they all speak a language you do not understand and refuse to even eat with you.	Love and belonging	• A common language • A working radio

And... Your lifeboat was filled with the friends and family you were on the cruise with.

Boat 4: To make life more enjoyable your crew has decided to build a shelter, start fires, etc. However, every time you attempt to assist it lands you in near disaster and inevitably ruins the attempts made. People are getting fed up with your "help." You are quickly becoming known as "Gilligan" (aka, the island screw-up) and being told you are a failure and embarrassment.	Esteem needs	• To not be a screw-up • To be good at something

And... You all have worked hard and have contributed to the building of a nice shelter and community on the island as you wait for rescue.

Boat 5: After 3 weeks on the ½ sq. mile island you have seen everything there is to see, and have heard everyone's stories several times. On a recent walk you discovered a cave with strange carvings and pictographs.	Knowledge	• To understand hieroglyphics • For the people on the island who drew the pictures to be gone or just not be cannibals
Boat 6: All of your fellow islanders have many stories to tell and knowledge to share. However, the island is small and after 3 weeks on the ½ sq. mile island you have seen everything there is to see.	Aesthetic appreciation	• A working hot tub with built in margarita machine • A bigger island • For the island to be Manhattan

lifeboat from a sinking cruise ship on which they were vacationing with family and friends. Due to an unexpected storm (Hurricane Helenrose), the lifeboats separated and each fell to a different fate within the Bermuda Triangle. Each group is then given their "fate" and told that a genie appears (this is the Bermuda Triangle) offering one wish—for anything but a way off the boat or island. EP students are given a limited amount of time to discuss and decide on their wishes. The instructor must move about the room and act as the "genie" to approve wishes or to clarify the rules (e.g., you can't wish for more wishes, or use compounds to wish for many things). Once each group has settled on a wish, they are asked to write their wish on the board next to their lifeboat number. Then groups are invited to compare the posted wishes within their group and to hypothesize about the fate experienced by other boats.

As a whole class, we then go through the wishes. Starting with lifeboat 1 the instructor reads the wish, asks for thoughts from the other lifeboats, and then asks someone in lifeboat 1 to read their fate. This process continues until the fate and wish from each lifeboat is reviewed. At this point the class is asked to explain why they "wished" as they did? What motivated them? What need was satisfied? Through whole class discourse each level of MHN is revealed to the class.

Vignette Application: Sam, Bobby, and Chris

EP students in small groups are presented with a gendered version of one of three student cases and are asked to analyze the case based on their understanding of Maslow. Specifically, they are asked:

- What needs seem to be present? Have any been met?
- What additional information would you like to have? And,
- As the teacher, what are your next steps?

The three vignettes are very brief and provide a limited amount of information about each student. This allows us to help our future teachers become aware of assumptions and it cautions them against making rash conclusions. The vignettes are:

Sam (Samuel or Samantha) had been receiving A's in all classes until about a month ago when everything just started going downhill for Sam. Homework is non-existent, absenteeism is up, and test grades are low. Sam rarely participates in class now and when asked, "What's going on in life?" Sam replied: "Nothing." When you call home to talk to Sam's mother a man answers the phone and claims that he's Sam's dad and you can talk to him about Sam's behavior in school. This is confusing to you since when you met Sam's mom at back to school night she told you that she was a single mother and dad was "Way out of the picture. . . . Thank GOD!"

Bobby (Robert or Roberta) had been receiving Cs and Ds in all classes until about a month ago when everything just started improving. Homework has been completed regularly, attendance is up, and test grades are getting higher. Bobby is frequently attentive in class now and even asks questions. When you comment on the improvement you see, Bobby smiles and says, "Yeah, I'm catching on now." You know that Bobby has recently been cast in the school play and you wonder if there is some connection to that and the improvement in class.

Chris (Christopher or Christine) had been receiving A's in all classes until about a month ago when everything just started dropping. Homework is now regularly missed, absenteeism is up, and test grades are very low. Chris frequently falls asleep in class now. When asked if things are ok—Chris replies—"Sure." When you call home to talk to Chris's parents you are surprised that Mr. Smith answers the phone in the middle of the day. From previous experience with the Smiths you know that Mr. Smith typically works 9–5, in fact, you scheduled special conferences at 7 a.m. just to accommodate Mr. Smith's schedule. Mr. Smith assures you that Chris will be back on track ASAP—but you wonder, was Mr. Smith slurring?

During this activity, EP student groups share with the class their responses to the opening questions and provide a rationale for each. As each student case is presented, we also discuss if any difference occurred across the same case if the student was perceived to be male or female. This frequently leads to questions about other potential assumptions, including those about the age of the student, ethnicity, and socioeconomic background.

Using these small vignettes, EP students are able to identify the needs that are present—both those that seem to be met and those that seem to be motivating (or demotivating) the students' behaviors. The class discussion, when opened up to both a comparison of the three cases and the teachers' reactions to each, allow for a broadening of perspectives about the assumptions that can be made from scant information (EP students are always shocked when I suggest that Mr. Smith might have been home in the middle of the day for a dentist appointment) and how using the Maslow lens can highlight things that they might otherwise miss. In addition, this discussion and analysis can also help these future teachers to see how one event may serve to fulfill several needs.

Case Analysis (Theresa) and Theory Comparison

To further address the challenge of transfer and expand on the contribution of Maslow's Humanistic Psychology, we use EP students' prior knowledge (from the previous two activities) of Maslow as an advance organizer to evaluate and consider additional theories of motivation. This typically takes one full class session (2.5 hours), but it can be adapted to a homework activity or an online collaborative task for students. We begin by presenting our pre-service teachers with a student case (Teresa), developed by Fives (2003) for her dissertation study, to identify knowledge of motivation strategies. The case is designed to present multiple challenges for a teacher with respect to student motivation and to limit "obvious" answers. EP students are presented with the case below:

> **Teresa**, having been retained, is in your class for the second year. Her retention was due to failing grades in three major subject areas as well as high absenteeism. (She missed 60 days of school, approximately one-third of the school year). Teresa rarely does assigned work. However, when she applies herself she is able to earn passing marks. In class, rather than taking notes or following along, she prefers to flip through an entertainment magazine, planning her future career as an entertainer.
>
> Teresa has made it clear that school is of little interest to her and that the subjects have little value for her future. Her interest is occasionally sparked when music, dance, or drama is somehow incorporated into class content or an assignment. However, this often fails to make a real difference in her performance for two reasons. First, she often misses large parts of the work due to lateness or absenteeism. Second, she tends to withdraw from the projects early on claiming that the music is "out of date" or the dance style is "funky" (meaning a bad thing) and that memorizing lines is unessential because in "real-life they have teleprompters anyway."
>
> 1. What do you see as the key problem(s) or concern(s) in this situation?
> 2. What would be the desired resolution of this classroom situation? (Do not explain how that end is accomplished. Simply describe the desired outcome.)
> 3. Please list *as many* strategies, techniques, plans, or actions that you can think of for resolving the aforementioned situation and achieving the desired outcome.

Pre-service teachers share their responses to the questions in small groups or as a whole class (depending on class size). As the discussion unfolds, pre-service teachers are reminded of Maslow's theory and are asked to consider how using the theory can help them address the issues in Teresa's case. Typically, the pre-service teachers note that Maslow does not provide them with strategies for intervening, but the theory helps them to better problematize the situation. We then move to a discussion of multiple motivation theories.

We use a jigsaw technique to examine the motivation theories in relation to Maslow. The class is divided into expert groups and each is assigned one of six foundational motivation theories to summarize, compare with

MHN, and use when analyzing Teresa's case. EP students are encouraged to "map" or align the components of motivation theories onto MHN. Following the development of expertise around a theory, EP students form groups of mixed expertise and revisit Teresa's case, with each expert explaining to his/her group how their assigned theory aligns with Maslow and addresses the case study. Together, the groups then respond to the same three questions without theory and compare their responses.

RECOMMENDATIONS

MHN provides EP students with an introduction to human motivation and humanist ontology. This foundational theory is often neglected in favor of more current conceptions of achievement motivation. Instead, we argue that MHN should be leveraged as a comparative advance organizer for EP students to frame their conceptions of motivation. In this chapter, we have described our three-part approach to teaching Maslow's theory and how we use it to foster understanding of modern theories of motivation.

The simulation game has been used by the first author for over 10 years, with minor adaptations (situations in lifeboats 5 and 6) that yield a less diverse sampling of ideas. This enables discussion of how growth and being needs are unique to individuals. The simulation works well at the beginning of the semester and we have used it as early as the first day of class to introduce the course content and as an icebreaker for EP students' groups. Be aware that some students focus on either "getting home" or "winning the game" by getting home, rather than embracing the actual purpose of the simulation. In these instances, the genie role becomes more salient in helping to foster particular goals. Sometimes the "wishes" do not align with Maslow (e.g., lifeboat 1 wishing for the safety of their family rather than their own). When this occurs we use these to problematize both the theory and how the task was interpreted. Over the years, we have learned that almost any response from students can be used to facilitate further class discussion—which leads to better understanding of the theory.

We strongly recommend that instructors include a discussion activity that allows EP students to consider Maslow's theory in relation to more authentic tasks. We use vignette analysis to help EP students experience using Maslow's theory as a lens for understanding classroom situations and student cases. However, EP students can also reflect on their own lives and identify times that their academic behaviors were (or were not) motivated by a desire to satisfy these needs. Regardless, we have found that when EP students (particularly the early undergraduate students with whom we work) are not guided to make connections to school or life experiences, they tend to only remember the simulation game and not the theory.

It is important to remind students that, while textbook chapters and course units are organized around specific theories or issues, in practice all theories and aspects of learning (e.g., motivation, individual differences, context etc.) need to be considered when engaging with any learning case or experience. The brevity of the vignettes allows the EP students to think about the information they will need when they evaluate students. One of the most important takeaways from the resulting class discussions is how much information teachers need to gather to understand their students. We also talk about the ways that teachers can gather this information without trampling on students' needs for safety, love, esteem, and competence, all of which can be threatened by an overly inquisitive new teacher.

The case and theory comparison provides an opportunity for EP students to engage in a critical evaluation of theories while using prior knowledge as a framework for that evaluation. MHN serves as an accessible comparative advance organizer for EP students who have participated in the simulation and vignette analysis. Because we typically introduce Maslow on the first day of class, and then motivation theory later in the semester; this provides an opportunity for students to see how ideas in educational psychology are connected. The value of this activity is the EP students' attempts to connect Maslow to current perspectives on achievement motivation and to justify the connections (or lack of connections) that they observe.

The case of Teresa is particularly helpful for exploring and comparing a variety of motivational theories. It enables EP students to think about how each theory addresses the issues presented. As described with the vignettes above, students need multiple opportunities to consider how theory can relate to authentic decision making contexts. These connections are further clarified when we share data from Fives (2003) on practicing teachers' responses to Theresa. When EP students compare their own strategies to those of practicing teachers they begin to see how the application of theory helps them to explore more dimensions of the problem than they do when left to their own devices.

The use of simulations, case/vignette analysis and theory comparisons are not new pedagogical innovations for educational psychology courses. These methods are well grounded in practice. The innovation we offer is the explicit integration of these varied methods to introduce, explore, and extend one foundational theory. We have used these activities with pre-service teachers at the undergraduate and masters' levels. While the discussions vary based on the life experiences of EP students in the classes, the activities themselves evoke meaningful learning. Moreover, the approach of using one theory as leverage for understanding other theories can be used extensively and effectively in educational psychology—if course instructors are open to the possibilities for student learning that such a method affords.

REFERENCES

Alderfer, C. P. (1969). An empirical test of a new theory of human needs. *Organizational Behavior and Human Performance, 4*(2), 142–175. doi: 10.1016/0030-5073(69)90004-X

Fives, H. (2003). *Exploring the relationships of teachers' efficacy, knowledge, and pedagogical beliefs: A multimethod study.* Unpublished doctoral dissertation. College Park: University of Maryland.

Glasser, W. (1993). *The quality school teacher.* New York, NY: Harper Collins.

Johnson, D. W., & Johnson, R. T. (2009). An educational psychology success story: Social interdependence theory and cooperative learning. *Educational Researcher, 38*, 365–379. doi: 10.3102/0013189X09339057

Maslow, A. H. (1943). A theory of motivation. *Psychological Review, 50*, 370–396. doi: 10.1037/h0054346

Maslow, A. H. (1954). *Motivation and personality.* New York, NY: Harper.

Mathes, E. (1981). Maslow's hierarchy of needs as a guide for living. *Journal of Humanistic Psychology, 21*, 69–72. doi: 10.1177/002216788102100406

O'Connor, D., & Yball, L. (2007). Maslow revisited: Constructing a road map of human nature. *Journal of Management Education, 31*(6), 738–756. doi: 10.1177/1052562907307639

Ryan, R. M., & Deci, E. L. (2000). Self-determination theory and the facilitation of intrinsic motivation, social development, and well-being. *American Psychologist, 55*, 68–78. doi: 10.1037110003-066X.55.1.68

Tay, L., & Diener, E. (2011). Needs and subjective well-being around the world. *Journal of Personality and Social Psychology, 101*(2), 354–365. doi: 10.1037/a0023779.

Ventegodt, S., Merrick, J., & Anderson, J. N. (2003). Quality of life theory III. Maslow revisited. *The Scientific World Journal, 3*, 1050–1057. doi: 10.1100/tsw.2003.84

Vygotsky, L. S. (1978). *Mind in society: The development of higher psychological processes.* Cambridge, MA: Harvard University Press.

Wahba, M. A., & Bridwell, L. G. (1976). Maslow reconsidered: A review of research on the need hierarchy theory. *Organizational Behavior and Human Performance, 15*, 212–240. doi: 10.1016/0030-5073(76)90038-6

Walker, C. O., & Greene, B. A. (2009). The relations between student motivational beliefs and cognitive engagement in high school. *Journal of Educational Research, 102*(6), 463–471. doi: 10.3200/JOER.102.6.463-472

Wilson, I., & Madson, S. R. (2008). The influence of Maslow's humanistic views on an employee's motivation to learn. *Journal of Applied Management and Entrepreneurship, 13*(2), 46–62.

CHAPTER 12

TEACHING PRE-SERVICE TEACHERS ABOUT GOAL ORIENTATIONS

Eric M. Anderman, Charles Okonkwo, You Joung Lee, and Christopher Collen
The Ohio State University

OVERVIEW OF THE TOPIC

In education, one of the most basic problems is moving research into practice. This has been particularly true in the field of educational psychology (Anderman, 2011). Once students become professional teachers there is little support available to reinforce the importance of many principles.

Perhaps one of the areas that is most often de-emphasized is academic motivation. Education students are exposed to numerous motivation-related concepts during teacher education programs; however, once they get out into the "real world" of teaching, many of these concepts may be undermined by existing policies. Indeed, research clearly indicates that, although many well-intentioned instructional practices related to academic motivation are built upon solid empirical research, they are often undermined by larger school-level policies (Maehr & Midgley, 1996).

Challenges and Innovations in Educational Psychology Teaching and Learning, pages 151–163
Copyright © 2016 by Information Age Publishing

In the present chapter, we focus on achievement goal orientation theory (Ames, 1992; Dweck & Leggett, 1988). As we will describe below, goal orientation theory has a strong empirical base, has been applied to interventions aimed at improving learning, and translates into readily understood instructional principles. In particular, we argue that additional examples of the use of goal orientation theory can be incorporated into coursework *throughout* teacher education programs. If research based theoretical frameworks are repeatedly demonstrated to prospective teachers, and if these future educators also have opportunities to practice the techniques, it is more likely that they will continue to use such practices in their own classrooms.

Explaining the Basics of Goal Orientation Theory

Effectively incorporating goal orientation theory into teacher education programs means that it is imperative for educators to understand the theory. Achievement goals refer to the reasons why students choose to participate in academic tasks. Achievement goals have been explained as two distinct types according to how competence is defined. Various researchers have labeled the two goal types using differing terms, such as task-involvement and ego-involvement goals (Nicholls, 1984), learning and performance goals (Dweck & Leggett, 1988), and mastery and performance goals (Ames & Archer, 1988). The goals labeled as task-involvement, learning, and mastery are associated with a focus on the improvement of competence and mastery of a task (referred to as "mastery goals" in this chapter); goals labeled as ego-involvement and performance are associated with a focus on proving self-competence to others (referred to as "performance goals" in this chapter) (Ames, 1992; Dweck & Leggett, 1988; Elliot, 1999).

Research indicates that mastery goals are associated with adaptive outcomes, such as persistence, self-efficacy, self-regulation and achievement (Ames, 1992; Dweck & Leggett, 1988). The research regarding performance goals indicates less consistent findings. Results of some studies indicate that performance goals are related to adaptive outcomes, such as self-regulation and high performance (Barron & Harackiewicz, 2000), and other studies indicate an association with maladaptive outcomes, such as low self-perceptions of ability (Wolters, Yu, & Pintrich, 1996).

Researchers have divided performance goals into two types, performance-approach and performance-avoidance (Elliot, 1999). An approach orientation involves striving for a potentially positive outcome whereas an avoidance orientation involves avoiding a negative possible outcome. Thus, the conceptual framework of achievement goals was extended to a trichotomous framework of mastery, performance-approach, and performance-avoidance (Elliot, 1999). Performance-approach goals are associated with engaging in a task to demonstrate personal ability in comparison to others; performance-avoidance goals are associated with engaging in a task to avoid showing low competence.

After the trichotomous framework of achievement goals was introduced, it was suggested that mastery goals may also be distinguished by approach and avoidance orientations (Elliot, 1999). Mastery approach goals refer to "striving to develop one's skills and abilities, advance one's learning, understand material, or complete or master a task" (Elliot, 1999, p.181). On the other hand, mastery avoidance goals refer to "striving to avoid losing one's skills and abilities (or having their development stagnate), forgetting what one has learned, misunderstanding material, or leaving a task incomplete or unmastered" (Elliot, 1999, p.181). Researchers today agree that students typically hold multiple goals simultaneously, and that these goals vary across classes and contexts (Pintrich, 2000).

SIGNIFICANCE OF GOAL ORIENTATION THEORY FOR PRE-SERVICE TEACHERS

Goal orientation theory has been a prominent theoretical framework used in guiding research and practice in recent years. The body of research has focused on students and practicing teachers, but there is a potential for the theory to be incorporated into pre-service teacher education. With this in mind, it is important to note that goal orientations can be conceptualized in a variety of ways. Goal orientations can be personal goals (i.e., an individual's goals), or they can be perceived as contextual goals (i.e., the type of goal that is emphasized in a particular classroom or school).

Personal Achievement Goal Orientation

Teachers set the tone in classrooms, which can encourage students to adopt various goals. Personal goal orientations have been studied by a variety of scholars (Ames, 1992; Dweck & Leggett, 1988; Pintrich, 2000). Mastery goal oriented students are self-referenced in their academic progress, instead of comparing themselves to other students. Mastery oriented students want to improve their performance on a task. In contrast, students who exhibit performance goal orientations strive to perform better than other students, showing off their ability and competence (Anderman & Maehr, 1994).

Research indicates that students oriented towards mastery utilize more effective learning strategies (Ames & Acher, 1988), are persistent, put more effort into learning tasks that are challenging, and generally have positive perceptions of their academic abilities and self-efficacy (Wolters, 2004). Consequently, there is ample evidence to suggest that if teachers can help their students adopt mastery goals then beneficial outcomes are likely to accrue.

Classroom Goal Structures

School or classroom goal structures refer to the social and psychological messages that students perceive and receive in learning environments (Kaplan, Middleton, Urdan, & Midgley, 2002). Two basic classroom goal structures have been proposed: *mastery* and *performance goal structures.*

In classrooms in which students perceive a mastery goal structure, teachers encourage students to take ownership of whatever they are leaning, master content, put forth their best effort, enjoy the learning process, and compare their individual progress with their own prior level of understanding. In classrooms in which students perceive a performance goal structure, teachers often communicate to their students that getting the right answer is important; students are encouraged to demonstrate their knowledge relative to others; and, teachers often promote competitive comparison of the students' progress with their peers (Anderman, Anderman, Yough, & Gimbert, 2010; Kaplan et al., 2002).

In classrooms where teachers communicate a mastery goal structure, students tend to recognize the mastery structure and act accordingly by mastering the academic tasks (Maehr & Anderman, 1993). On the other hand, in classrooms where teachers communicate performance goal structures, students tend to recognize and act competitively with their abilities (Rolland, 2012). Similar to classroom goal structures, school-level goal structures are categorized into mastery and performance goal structures. Students tend to perceive school-level goal structures in a similar way to classroom goal structures and to experience similar outcomes.

It is important for pre-service teachers to understand goal orientation theory because the perceived goal structure in a classroom or school is predictive of the types of personal goal orientations that students adopt. As such, classroom and school goal structures are important and predictive of several adaptive outcomes. For example, mastery goal structure of a classroom (school) encourages student engagement and performance (Ames & Acher, 1988). When students perceive their classrooms as emphasizing mastery, they use effective learning strategies (Midgley & Urdan, 2001), exhibit more adaptive coping mechanisms (Kaplan & Maehr, 1999), and report higher academic self-efficacy (Anderman & Young, 1994). In contrast, perceptions of a classroom as being performance-oriented are associated with non-adaptive behaviors such as self-handicapping, avoidance of help-seeking, academic cheating, and disruptive behavior.

It is critical for pre-service teachers to understand that the developmental shifts that occur in personal goal orientations and goal structures. Educators who want to incorporate the principles of goal orientation theory need to understand when and how these shifts occur because they have implications for the timing and types of practices that teachers might select. Several studies have documented a decline in student motivation, collectively, across the transition from elementary to middle school (Anderman & Anderman, 1999; Eccles & Midgley, 1989). For decades, researchers have found early adolescence to be a turbulent, sometimes problematic phase with respect to student academic engagement and performance. Eccles and Midgley (1989) attribute this in part to an ineffective "stage-environment fit," explained as the incompatibility between the developmental needs of adolescents and the opportunities afforded to them, particularly within the realm of academics.

Students' personal goal orientations, and their perceptions of classroom and school goal structures change over time, particularly across the middle school transition. Generally, as students move through the educational system, they place increased emphasis on grades and performance. Research shows that as students enter into their middle school years, performance goals rise significantly whereas mastery goal orientations drop considerably (e.g., Anderman & Anderman, 1999). This means that students' sense of scholastic purpose shifts from the comprehension of content to a greater focus on the demonstration of one's ability relative to others.

Many of these disconcerting trends have been attributed to classroom and school goal-structures. Anderman and Midgley (1997), in a longitudinal study, found that students perceived their fifth-grade classes (while still in elementary school) as more mastery- and less performance-oriented than sixth grade classrooms (after the transition into middle school). To corroborate student perceptions, the self-reported and observed practices of elementary and middle school teachers indicated similar deviations from an emphasis on mastery to an emphasis on performance (Eccles & Midgley, 1989).

Thus, as students move through school, they begin to view the purpose of academic undertakings as a means to prove their competence rather than truly achieving that competence. These perceived changes in classroom goal-structures, in particular declines in perceptions of mastery goal structures, have been correlated with negative changes in cognition, affect, and performance (Urdan & Midgley, 2003). However, some studies have demonstrated that performance-approach goals may serve a more adaptive, motivating function for older adolescents than younger adolescents (Middleton & Midgley, 1997). Nevertheless, during early adolescence specifically, performance goals appear to be associated with self-handicapping and cheating, whereas mastery goals tend to be associated with adaptive outcomes such as persistence, and use of effective cognitive and metacognitive strategies (Wolters, 2004).

In summary, goal orientations are related to important outcomes for students, especially during periods of transition. Teachers can utilize this information to positively affect students' motivation and achievement. An awareness of the developmental shifts in goal orientations and the relations between goal orientations and other valued educational outcomes can greatly enhance instructional practices.

CHALLENGES TO TEACHING GOAL ORIENTATION THEORY TO PRE-SERVICE TEACHERS

It is challenging to teach prospective educators about goal orientation theory for several reasons. As we will discuss, although the theory is intuitively appealing, the principles outlined by the theory often run counter to the policies and practices that are prevailing in schools.

A basic principle of the theory is that mastery goals are beneficial to students. Nevertheless, a focus on "mastery" may be undermined by school-level policies and practices. Consider the following example:

> Mrs. Frank is a fourth grade reading teacher. She believes in encouraging her students to pursue mastery goals in reading. She allows them to work on reading assignments until they reach mastery; she does not penalize them for taking academic risks (e.g., reading a difficult book and needing more time to complete it); she praises her students for exerting effort and for asking questions when they need help.

Now, imagine that the school is simultaneously participating in a project with a local restaurant where students are awarded gift certificates based on the *number* of books that the students read during a grading period. This potentially could create a conflict for Mrs. Frank—she wants to encourage her students to read challenging books and master content, but students will only receive the gift certificates if they read many books, regardless of their understanding of the material. Thus the "mastery goals" that Mrs. Frank is trying to promote in her students may be undermined by the school's participation in the gift certificate program. This is an example of one of the challenges in teaching the principles of goal orientation theory to pre-service teachers. Whereas mastery goals "sound" good, many of the performance-focused practices of schools and communities may undermine teachers' positive intentions.

Another typical example relates to the assessment of learning. When teaching about goal orientation theory, many pre-service teachers might feel that the promotion of mastery goals is virtually impossible when schools are faced with extensive requirements to participate in (and perform well on) standardized examinations. Particularly since many of these examinations are high-stakes in nature, the pressure to have students perform well on those exams seems counterintuitive to the promotion of mastery goals. Many pre-service teachers may feel that it is impossible to promote mastery goals while also trying to get their students to perform well on exams. Nevertheless, as we will review later in this chapter, there are manageable ways to participate in assessments and simultaneously promote mastery goals.

Promising Practices

One of the best ways to integrate motivation principles into practice is to introduce and reinforce these practices while pre-service teachers are learning the trade. It is particularly important to communicate these practices to teachers in training during introductory courses, and then to remind them of the efficacy and utility of those practices in later courses, practicum experiences, and student teaching. When pre-service teachers are repeatedly exposed to evidence about best practices and given repeated opportunities to implement such practices, they will be more likely to adopt and utilize those practices when they eventually have their own classrooms.

As already discussed, achievement goals are related to important outcomes, including achievement, persistence, effort, and the use of effective cognitive strategies. Thus, it is imperative for teacher educators to inculcate strategies into pre-service teachers that will allow them to effectively communicate appropriate achievement goals to their students.

How Do Teachers Communicate Goal Orientations to Students?

Previously we discussed the different levels at which achievement goals operate—personal goal orientations, classroom, and school-wide goal structures. Classroom goal structures are particularly relevant to our discussion. Although goal structures are communicated by teachers to students, goals wield their power through the ways in which students perceive such structures.

Goal structures are communicated to students by teachers in a variety of ways. In general, when teachers emphasize through their daily practices the importance of learning from one's mistakes, the value of effort, and the importance of truly mastering academic tasks, students are likely to perceive a mastery goal structure. In contrast, when teachers emphasize grades, test scores, and how students compare to each other in terms of ability and performance, their students are likely to perceive a performance goal structure (Anderman & Maehr, 1994).

Teachers also communicate goal structures to their students through instructional practices. Teachers who reward students for having chosen to read a difficult novel, for example, may be perceived as emphasizing mastery goals (particularly if the students do not have a formal "test" on the novel after having completed it); in comparison, teachers who reward students for having gotten a 95% or higher on a test may be perceived as emphasizing performance goals. In the former classroom, success is defined by the teacher—success is communicated to students as being related to attempting to engage in a challenging task (i.e., reading a difficult novel), exerting effort during the task, and ultimately completing that task (i.e., finishing the book). In the latter classroom, success is defined by the teacher as having earned a particular grade.

Communicating Goal Orientations to Pre-Service Teachers

How does one effectively communicate and demonstrate these concepts to pre-service teachers? If we want pre-service teachers to incorporate strategies that emphasize either mastery or performance goals into their instructional practices, what can we do to facilitate this? In the following sections, we provide suggestions for ways in which the principles of goal orientation theory can be incorporated into teacher education programs, with the goal of producing teachers who foster the development of adaptive motivational beliefs in their students.

Lesson Planning

During teacher education programs, most pre-service teachers learn how to develop lesson plans, which provide opportunities for them to begin to think about the types of instructional strategies that they will use during lessons to foster the adoption of specific types of goal orientations. Numerous researchers have used the TARGET acronym as a strategy for teachers to use to incorporate instructional practices that promote specific types of goal orientations (e.g., Ames, 1992; Maehr & Anderman, 1993).

The TARGET acronym identifies six instructional domains that can easily be applied during lesson planning. These include the nature of tasks (T), the provision of opportunities for choice or autonomy to students (A), how students are recognized for their achievements and progress (R), how students are grouped for instruction (G), how students are evaluated (E), and how time is used (T). In all six of these domains, the daily plans that teachers make can communicate either mastery or performance goal structures to students. Therefore, when considering academic *tasks* for a lesson, a teacher who selects tasks that allow students to engage in interesting activities, to exert effort (without being seriously penalized for making mistakes along the way), and to achieve mastery with a task, will likely foster the adoption of mastery goals in students (and convey a mastery goal structure in the classroom); in contrast, a teacher who selects *tasks* that force students to compete with each other and that make students' ability differences salient, are likely to foster the adoption of performance goals (and convey a performance goal structure). One simple strategy is for school administrators to include the "TARGET" acronym on each page of teachers' planning materials, so that teachers are encouraged to consider the six dimensions of TARGET during daily planning.

Demonstration of Techniques

During teacher education programs, we also should use our own instructional methods as exemplars. Indeed, there is much research from a social cognitive perspective indicating that students learn from observations of others engaged in tasks in which the students will be involved in the future. Instructors in teacher education courses can demonstrate how they incorporate mastery-focused instructional practices (with the goal of facilitating the adoption of mastery goals in their students) to their students. One way that this can be accomplished is through the use of course syllabi. Instructors also can look at college course syllabi, engage their students in critical analyses of the types of assignments and tasks that are assigned, and whether those tasks are likely to foster the adoption of mastery goals, performance goals, or both. In addition, careful examinations of how assessments are presented on syllabi also may exemplify how educators communicate goal orientations. Such examination of syllabi can provide exemplars for prospective teachers regarding ways to incorporate mastery-focused instructional practices into teaching.

For example, if a final exam is given in a college course, it is useful to engage students in discussions about the types of goal orientations that the exam is producing within the class. There are ways to structure exams so that mastery goals are encouraged, and there are ways to structure exams so that performance goals are encouraged. An exam that fosters mastery goals might be designed so that the students could re-take the exam multiple times until they learn the content well. In contrast, an exam that is given only once and graded on a curve (where only a small number of students can receive an "A") would probably lead to the adoption of performance goals. Here, students are rewarded with higher grades by outperforming other students. Discussions of how students' own goals form in our classes can lead to important insights that students may be able to apply to their own subsequent teaching practices.

Analyses of Classroom Observations

In most pre-service teacher education programs, students are required to spend time in classroom settings observing practicing teachers. Most pre-service teachers are required to take field notes or write in journals during their observations of teachers; in those assignments, they should be asked to describe as much as they can regarding what the teacher asks the students to do and how the students engage with their work. For example, a pre-service teacher might observe that a practicing teacher asks her students to write a paragraph summarizing a text that the class just completed reading, and then the teacher might randomly call on students to share their paragraphs; the teacher and the other students then critique the paragraphs. That practice may have nuanced meanings for students—depending on the language that the teacher uses and other cues that are provided by the teacher, the students may interpret this interaction as focusing on either mastery, or performance, or both (or neither!). If the teacher points out good qualities in each paragraph and then privately provides feedback to students about how they can improve their writing, students are likely to adopt mastery goals; however, if the teacher publicly critiques the paragraphs and compares them in front of the class, students are likely to adopt performance goals.

Assessments of Student Learning

It is important to communicate to pre-service teachers that the assessment of learning does not preclude an emphasis on mastery goals. It is important to engage novice teachers in discussions about this topic throughout their pre-service teacher education programs so they can critically think about this complex issue.

First, when educators focus on "mastery," they are encouraging students to learn material as well as possible. This is not counterintuitive to achieving high test scores; rather, thorough knowledge of a content area is what yields high test scores. Second, when results of assessments are presented to students, those results can be presented in ways that promote performance goals ("You received 82% on the test, most students did better than you") or mastery goals ("You received 82% on the test; you didn't get everything right, but let's review the key concepts that you missed and then you can re-take the test"). With the growth in recent years of standardized assessments that focus on student growth in knowledge over time (referred to as "value-added" assessments), it is more possible than ever to focus on mastery, since teachers can point out to students how their knowledge has changed over time, and thus focus on mastery of content (Anderman et al., 2010).

RECOMMENDATIONS AND CONCLUSIONS

Teacher educators have the potential to shape the careers of the next generation of educators. Student motivation is highly valued by most educators, but exposure to this topic during teacher education is limited. Most pre-service teachers receive only a cursory introduction to the topic in lower-level educational psychology courses. Nevertheless, the motivation literature is replete with replicable ways that teacher educators can expose future teachers to this information and encourage them to incorporate the principles of motivation research into instruction (Stipek, 1996). If pre-service teachers are given the opportunities to observe and practice ways to incorporate the principles of frameworks like goal orientation theory, they will be more likely to use that information when they have their own classrooms.

If educators want to emphasize the importance of the principles of goal orientation theory to their students, substantial collaboration across all of the professionals involved in the preparation of teachers is essential. As previously noted, most students receive a brief introduction to topics such as "motivation" during an introductory educational psychology course. If educators are exposed to the principles of mastery goals early in their training, and if that topic is not reinforced in subsequent courses, then the early learning of those principles is likely to be forgotten.

We propose that if motivation is a valued topic, then all of those who are involved in the preparation of pre-service teachers need to: (a) have a thorough understanding of academic motivation (e.g., goal orientation theory); (b) collaboratively write syllabi so that principles of motivation are repeatedly emphasized *throughout* a variety of courses; and (c) be able to practice applying the theory in classrooms during practicum and student teaching experiences. This is a challenging proposition, but one that has the potential to influence classroom practice if all participants are in agreement about the importance of motivation in learners.

In addition, as we have noted, the recommendations for practice that emanate from goal orientation theory may not align well with schools' policies. Indeed, a focus on mastery goals may contrast with the goals of having students perform well on mandated standardized examinations. Nevertheless, a thorough knowledge of the theory and its correlates might allow teachers to "think out of the box" and incorporate mastery-focused practices into instruction—even when there are very real external pressures to have students perform well on examinations. Educators need to remember that although test scores are important, they are not the only academic outcome worthy of attention. It is lamentable when a student is able to do well on an exam, but never develops an appreciation for the content. If we want to nurture students to become chemists, journalists, or lawyers, then using instructional practices that support the adoption of mastery goals in students may help students to continue to want to pursue chemistry, journalism, or law in the future (Anderman & Weber, 2009).

REFERENCES

Ames, C. (1992). Classrooms: Goals, structures, and student motivation. *Journal of Educational Psychology, 84*(3), 261–271.

Ames, C., & Archer, J., (1988). Achievement goals in the classroom: Students' learning strategies and motivation process. *Journal of Educational Psychology, 80*(3), 260–267.

Anderman, E. M. (2011). Educational psychology in the twenty-first century: Challenges for our community. *Educational Psychologist, 46,* 185–196.

Anderman, L. H., & Anderman, E. M. (1999). Social predictors of changes in students' achievement goal orientations. *Contemporary Educational Psychology, 24*(1), 21–37.

Anderman, E. M., Anderman, L. H., Yough, M. S., & Gimbert, B. G. (2010). Value added models of assessment: Implications for motivation and accountability. *Educational Psychologist, 45*(2), 123–137.

Anderman, E. M., & Maehr, M. L. (1994). Motivation and schooling in the middle grades. *Review of Educational Research, 64*(2), 287–309.

Anderman, E. M., & Midgley, C. (1997). Changes in achievement goal orientations, perceived academic competence, and grades across the transition to middle-level schools. *Contemporary Educational Psychology, 22*(3), 269–298.

Anderman, E. M., & Weber, J. (2009). Continuing motivation revisited. In A. Kaplan, S. Karabenick. & L. DeGroot (Eds.), *Culture, self, and motivation: Essays in honor of Martin L. Maehr* (pp. 3–19). Charlotte, NC: Information Age Publishing.

Anderman, E. M., & Young, A. J. (1994). Motivation and strategy use in science: Individual differences and classroom effects. *Journal of Research on Science Teacher, 31*(8), 811–831.

Barron, K. E., & Harackiewicz, J. M. (2000). Achievement goals and optimal motivation: A multiple goals approach. In C. Sansone & J. M. Harackiewicz (Eds.), *Intrinsic and extrinsic motivation: The search for optimal motivation and performance* (pp. 229–254). San Diego, CA: Academic Press.

Dweck, C. S., & Leggett, E. L. (1988). A social-cognitive approach to motivation and personality. *Psychological Review, 95*(2), 256–273.

Eccles, J., & Midgley, C. (1989). Stage-environment fit: Developmentally appropriate classrooms for young adolescents. In C. Ames & R. Ames (Eds.), *Research on motivation in education* (pp. 139–186). San Diego, CA: Academic Press.

Elliot, A. J. (1999). Approach and avoidance motivation and achievement goals. *Educational Psychologist, 34,* 169–189.

Kaplan, A., & Maehr, M. L. (1999). Achievement goals and student well-being. *Contemporary Educational Psychology, 24,* 330–358.

Kaplan, A., Middleton, M. J., Urdan, T., & Midgley, C. (2002). Achievement goals and goal structures. In C. Midgley (Ed.), *Goals, goal structures, and patterns of adaptive learning* (pp. 21–53). Mahwah, NJ: Lawrence Erlbaum Associates.

Maehr, M. L., & Anderman, E. M. (1993). Reinventing schools for early adolescents: Emphasizing task goals. *Elementary School Journal, 93*(5), 593–610.

Maehr, M. L., & Midgley, C. (1996). *Transforming school cultures.* Boulder, CO: Westview Press.

Middleton, M. J., & Midgley, C. (1997). Avoiding the demonstration of lack of ability: An underexplored aspect of goal theory. *Journal of Educational Psychology, 89,* 710–718.

Midgley, C., & Urdan, T. (2001). Academic self-handicapping and achievement goals: A further examination. *Contemporary Educational Psychology, 26,* 61–75.

Nicholls, J. G. (1984). Achievement motivation: Conceptions of ability, subjective experience, task choice, and performance. *Psychological Review, 92*(3), 328–346.

Pintrich, P. R. (2000). Multiple goals, multiple pathways: The role of goal orientation in learning and achievement. *Journal of Educational Psychology, 92*(3), 544–555. doi:10.1037/0022-0663.92.3.544

Rolland, R. (2012). Synthesizing the evidence on classroom goal structures in middle and secondary schools: A meta-analysis and narrative review. *Review of Educational Research, 82*(4), 396–435. doi:10.3102/0034654312464909

Stipek, D. J. (1996). Motivation and instruction. In D. C. Berliner & R. C. Calfee (Eds.), *Handbook of educational psychology* (pp. 85–113). New York, NY: Macmillan.

Urdan, T., & Midgley, C. (2003). Changes in the perceived classroom goal structure and patterns of adaptive learning during early adolescence. *Contemporary Educational Psychology, 28,* 524–551.

Wolters, C. A. (2004). Advancing achievement goal theory: Using goal structures and goal orientations to predict students' motivation, cognition, and achievement. *Journal of Educational Psychology, 96*(2), 236–250.

Wolters, C. A., Yu, S. L., & Pintrich, P. R. (1996). The relation between goal orientation and students' motivational beliefs and self-regulated learning. *Learning and Individual Differences, 8*(3), 211–238.

CHAPTER 13

FINDING COMMON GROUND WHEN TEACHING MOTIVATION

Examples from Teaching Self-Efficacy and Self-Determination Theory

Gwen C. Marchand and Gregory Schraw
University of Nevada, Las Vegas

OVERVIEW

Teaching motivation to students new to the topic is a deceptively difficult undertaking. On the surface, the definitions appear to be comprised of simple concepts and typically generate substantial student interest. After all, most graduate students in the social sciences, practicing educators, and educators in training are fascinated by questions as to why people behave as they do in learning situations and the "processes that give behavior its energy and direction" (Reeve, 2005, p. 6). The conundrum of teaching motivation, however, is that as students delve beyond the basic definitions of motivational concepts to the specific theories, models, and constructs

Challenges and Innovations in Educational Psychology Teaching and Learning, pages 165–176
Copyright © 2016 by Information Age Publishing
All rights of reproduction in any form reserved.

associated with the broader realm of motivation, things get messy. This messiness occurs for several reasons, which we discuss below, but especially because there is no explicit metatheory of motivation. In our years of teaching motivation, we have come to understand that students crave order and a well-organized theoretical umbrella when learning new concepts. Without some understanding of how all the pieces of the motivational puzzle fit together, it is difficult for many students to make the leap from "this is interesting" to "this all fits together" to "this is useful in everyday life."

The purpose of this chapter is to discuss challenges to teaching motivation and how to find common ground among motivational theories for teaching purposes, using constructs from self-efficacy and self-determination theory (SDT) to illustrate our points. We believe that teaching motivation is enhanced by introducing students to ideas associated with viewing motivation as a general process that is affected by a variety of specific psychological constructs. These include self-efficacy and intrinsic motivation, as embedded within motivation theories such as social-cognitive theory and SDT. When motivation is understood as a process (Wentzel & Wigfield, 2009), teachers grasp how their actions in the classroom influence student motivation and action in school which, in turn, are associated with learning. Very simply, teaching motivation makes explicit the notion that students' beliefs, values, and goals matter to how they participate in school, regardless of the specific type of motivation discussed. Teachers who understand the role of motivation in learning can use this knowledge to determine if performance problems in school are associated with low skill and knowledge or associated with problems due mainly to motivation.

A BRIEF OVERVIEW OF THE THEORIES

Self-Efficacy

The construct of self-efficacy is rooted in Bandura's social-cognitive theory and refers to one's beliefs about their capabilities to perform an action, which in academic settings would refer to learning and performance activities (Bandura, 1977). When individuals have high outcome expectations or beliefs that an action will produce a desired outcome, coupled with strong efficacy beliefs, they are motivated to engage and persist in learning activities. Social-cognitive theory states that human action is explained by a process of reciprocal determinism through which personal factors (e.g., beliefs, emotion), behaviors, and environmental factors (such as social partners) interact in a dynamic manner. In this way, transactions with the environment affect behavior as they are filtered through an individual's cognitions; at the same time, the behaviors of an individual prompt changes in our environment (Bandura, 1978; Schunk & Pajares, 2009). Individuals are active contributors to their own development, but that development shapes, and is shaped by, a developing context.

Speaking specifically to the development of self-efficacy beliefs, Bandura and theorists after him identified four main sources: actual performance, vicarious experience, social persuasion, and emotional and physiological states. These sources influence students' beliefs when students receive feedback about their mastery on academic tasks, when students compare their own performance to that of others, when students receive praise or encouragement from important social partners, and when students experience affective or physiological responses during execution of an academic task. Research supports the notion that mastery responses may be the most powerful source of perceived self-efficacy and that the impact of the sources and efficacy beliefs themselves, vary across different academic domains (Usher & Pajares, 2009).

Why is self-efficacy particularly relevant for the education of educators? Perceived self-efficacy has been demonstrated to influence motivated behavior in many ways. This includes effort and persistence when working on learning tasks. Students with higher perceived self-efficacy beliefs tend to put forth greater effort and persist in the face of failure as they focus on the strength of their capabilities. These students also tend to seek out activities that will provide them with challenges and opportunities to demonstrate competence and improve their skills rather than avoid challenging situations as a self-protective act. Students with a stronger sense of self-efficacy also tend to be more resilient to anxiety and pessimism, facing academic tasks with effort and enthusiasm (for an overview, see Schunk & Mullen, 2009).

Self-Determination Theory

The terms intrinsic and extrinsic motivation may be the most common association with self-determination theory (SDT; Deci & Ryan, 1985) for many individuals. At its core, SDT is concerned with the reasons why individuals (in our case, students) participate in activities. It is considered a "self" theory due to the basic premise that individuals possess the innate psychological needs of autonomy, competence, and relatedness, which act as essential nutriments for healthy psychological development. SDT discusses how the fulfillment of these needs influence action. The social context (e.g., teachers or parents), acts in ways to satisfy or thwart these needs. For example, when teachers act in ways to support a student's need for autonomy, the student should feel that her classroom actions are reflective of her genuine preferences (Ryan, 1993).

By making the fulfillment of autonomy needs a central component of the theory, SDT expanded on traditional views of intrinsic motivation (participating in a task due to the pleasure or enjoyment the task affords) and extrinsic motivation (participating for all other externally driven reasons, including praise and rewards). SDT differentiates different forms of extrinsic motivation depending on the locus of causality; a concept introduced by deCharms (1968), which refers to whether individuals feel like the "origin" or "pawn" of their actions. An internal locus of causality means that individuals experience their behaviors as emanating from the self, thus they are the "origins" of their behavior, whereas an external locus of causality refers to when individuals experience their behaviors as originating from some force outside of the self, thus they are "pawns." SDT argues that intrinsic motivation is always experienced as self-determined but that extrinsic motivation can also be self-determined. Also, there are qualitatively different forms of extrinsic motivation that can be distinguished on the basis of individuals' reasons for why they are performing the task and their experiences of the locus of causality for that task. In this way, not all extrinsic motivation is the same.

Why is SDT relevant for educators? Although teachers do not "cause" intrinsic motivation, teacher actions can support or undermine intrinsic motivation. For instance, when teachers allow students to choose tasks that are in line with their own interests, teachers provide support for intrinsic motivation. Teachers also play an important role in helping behaviors that are more externally controlled to become more self-determined. Students are more likely to internalize the values and goals of school, bringing those values in line with their own preferences and understanding the value of academic tasks, when relationships with teachers are warm and positive. Positive relationships are more likely to develop when teachers support students' social needs for relatedness by demonstrating care to students through provision of attention and resources. Even when they are not intrinsically interested in a school task, if students experience a greater sense of self-determination during academic tasks, they are more likely to be engaged in the classroom—in more enthusiastic and prolonged ways. Thus, teacher motivational support is an important factor for maintaining and increasing school persistence and learning. And, the good news from the self-determination theory viewpoint of intrinsic and extrinsic motivation is that more self-determined forms of extrinsic motivation can be supported in ways that do not put intrinsic motivation at risk (Ryan & Deci, 2000).

FOUR INSTRUCTIONAL CHALLENGES

There are at least four challenges students and instructors face in a class on motivation. We refer to these as naïve beliefs, theoretical diversity, methodological differences, and long-term effects of motivation on learning.

Challenge 1: Naïve Beliefs

We often encounter naïve beliefs about motivation. Students may discuss motivation using language that suggests a trait-like quality, such as "The kids in my class are just not motivated," or "Sally is a motivated student"— suggesting that motivation is a characteristic that students either have or do not have. Further, when asked to define what is meant by "motivation" in these type of examples, students use a range of terms, commonly beginning with ideas associated with students not wanting to work hard or not caring about school, suggesting that the sources of motivation reside solely in the individual. Conversely, when asked if and how motivation for school may be changed, students may turn first to reward-type programs, such as class-room-token economies. We have found it helpful to discuss these beliefs in detail before moving on to a discussion of individual motivational theories and how separate theories relate to one another, and time permitting, re-visiting naïve beliefs at the end of the course in light of research findings.

Challenge 2: Theoretical Diversity

The 2009 *Handbook of Motivation at School* (Wentzel & Wigfield) contains 12 chapters on major theories in achievement motivation, eight chapters on the role of contextual and social influences on motivation, and eight chapters on the relationships among teaching, learning, and motivation. These chapters and the history of the literature in academic motivation demonstrate that the field has generated many vibrant and complex theories; each tending to focus on one or two primary constructs that rarely are explicitly integrated with constructs from other models. The empirical literature also largely stays within these theoretical silos.

We believe students struggle because there is confusion about motivation terminology and a lack of clarity of definitions, a problem acknowledged by the field (Murphy & Alexander, 2000). These are compounded by a diversity of isolated theories in the field, a lack of an overarching metatheory to help students organize the many theories in a meaningful way, and challenges associated with conducting research on motivation, leading many students to question the findings drawn from the literature. Moreover, there is not always a clear translation of the abstract theoretical ideas to actual practice or meaningful action in the classroom (e.g., But what do I actually *do* to support SE in the classroom?).

Challenge 3: Methodological Differences

A third challenge to teaching motivation is the range of methods used to study academic motivation. Many teacher education programs do not train teachers beyond basic courses in research methods. If teachers-in-training are exposed to research methods courses, the "gold standard" of experimental methods is often emphasized. Importantly, many studies of academic motivation do not or cannot use experimental designs characterized by random assignment due to issues of treatment fidelity and nested groups but also because constructs of interest such as self-efficacy and intrinsic motivation are characteristics of individuals beyond experimental control. Instead, researchers often conduct field-based research using correlational designs that model how variables such as gender, abilities, or situational constraints are related to motivational variables such as self-efficacy or intrinsic motivation both concurrently and over time. Often this research requires an advanced knowledge of statistical analytic techniques such as structural equation models. Thus, teachers are faced with a body of research that does not easily conform to their expectations of "good" research but that also exceeds their skill set to be able to critically evaluate the quality of the research. Moreover, the model testing approach does not establish "cause" or "prove" that motivation creates change in academic outcomes, despite the strong evidence that motivation matters to educational outcomes. Some students simply are put off by what they see as too little theoretical integration and too much statistics.

Challenge 4: Long-term Effects of Motivation on Learning

A fourth challenge is to help students understand motivation as a process with long-term developmental implications for learning. After wading through the discrete, specific theories—which are tested by complex methods and statistics that rarely use longitudinal designs—finding the application to practice can be a challenge. One reason is that motivational beliefs change over time due to social scaffolding processes by peers, parents, and teachers. Said differently, the impact of interpersonal support on motivation change is dramatically different than on native ability or innate talents. As a consequence, motivation develops very differently than other "cognitive" phenomena. A second reason is that motivation often affects learning through a complex, indirect pathway rather than directly. For example, self-efficacy may increase engagement and persistence in a task, which in turn, increases task performance and learning. In general, it is a truism that a change in motivation does not have a significant direct effect on learning but, rather, changes other variables known as mediators that exert a direct effect on learning.

FINDING COMMON GROUND WHEN
TEACHING MOTIVATION

Both authors periodically teach a graduate course in motivation that includes teachers, special educators, school administrators, school psychologists, and counselors. Most of these students will only be exposed to motivation theories only in this course. Most are interested in real-life educational applications rather than theory or research. We try to accomplish three main goals in our courses to provide a comprehensive survey of major theories and educational applications. One is to address the four challenges above. A second is to clarify the main assumptions and consequences of each theory. A third is to discuss generic topics that cut across all theories of motivation that bear directly on the teacher-student relationship, including the malleability and domain specificity of beliefs, the role of the teacher and peers in student support, and the link between motivation and positive outcomes. An expanded version of these topics that also includes measurement and development issues is discussed by Wentzel and Wigfield (2009). In the following paragraphs, we touch on each of the points outlined in our third goal and provide references for more in-depth discussions.

Malleability and Domain Specificity of Motivation

Theories of motivation make assumptions about the malleability of constructs, where malleability is viewed as a single continuum that ranges from not at all changeable to completely changeable. This question is extremely important to individuals interested in providing personal and situational support to influence motivational beliefs in a lasting, positive fashion. Self-efficacy is a belief that is driven by individual experiences with the learning environment that is very changeable (i.e., state-like), whereas intrinsic motivation is thought to be an innate property of the individual that is far less changeable (i.e., trait-like) (Ryan & Deci, 2000). However, social partners are important for both theories. Self-efficacy beliefs emerge from a variety of sources including experiences of success and feedback on academic tasks, which are often engineered by teachers, and from specific praise from teachers. Although intrinsic motivation does not "come from" these classroom experiences, teachers can help to maintain or enhance intrinsic motivation by providing opportunities for students to choose and direct their own learning tasks and through positive feedback for activities that hold inherent interest for students.

Further, self-efficacy beliefs are typically treated as more domain-specific, rather than a generalized property that cuts across academic tasks and settings. Reasons for participating in tasks (intrinsic and extrinsic motivation) may also vary to some degree across domains, but are also typically measured as more domain-general orientations toward academic work. In our classes, we encourage students to explore the extent to which sources of motivational change resides in the individual versus the teacher or learning environment. Embedded within this discussion are strategies for how teachers may promote positive motivational change in the student. Often, these focus on providing instructional scaffolding, positive feedback and modeling from teachers and advanced peers, meeting competency needs, and supporting student autonomy to the fullest extent possible.

The Role of the Teacher and Peer Support

All theories of motivation emphasize the role of social support through explicit modeling of skills and behaviors, coaching, and psychological support of needs. Both teachers and more advanced students may provide this support. In the case of self-efficacy, teachers offer specific praise for efforts on a task (social partner support), or provide opportunities for students to demonstrate success on a task (mastery on a performance task). In the case of SDT, teachers provide students with opportunities to choose assignments or tasks, when they explicitly attempt to relate the material to concrete experiences in children's lives (support for autonomy); when they demonstrate warmth and caring to students by stopping what they are doing to listen to children and answer questions or speak to students in a positive manner (support for relatedness); and when they write expectations on the board for behavior and learning, so that students know what they need to do to succeed in the classroom (support for competence).

We have found that students in our classes find it very informative to discuss the underlying mechanism by which social context enhances motivation. For example, self-efficacy theory contends that task-specific efficacy develops through interactive processes between the individual's internal personal factors, environment, and outward behaviors. Improving any of these should increase self-efficacy. SDT contends that students become more self-determined over time via a process of internalization that is driven by feedback loops between teacher supports, student need satisfaction, and student. One outcome of these discussions is for students in our classes to consider what kind of supporting environments they wish to create in their classroom and the role of teacher and peers in creating and sustaining it. For example, we ask teachers to consider that many lesson plans have learning goals or objectives, but what would a motivational goal or objective be for the lesson that day? If the motivational goal was to support intrinsic motivation for reading, what specific steps would be part of that motivational lesson plan? The teacher might make sure that students are offered a choice of literature sources or ask students to relate the story to their own lives. If the motivational goal was to support the development of self-efficacy beliefs, teachers might set time aside for individual feedback sessions with students to improve the calibration of their existing sense of efficacy with their performance and then create individual tasks to allow students to experience success at a task at the upper reaches of their existing skill set.

The Link between Motivation and Positive Academic and Behavioral Outcomes

All motivation theories assume that positive beliefs affect engagement and persistence, which affect academic and behavioral outcomes. We believe it is important to help students understand the mediated process of motivation in which beliefs impact desired outcomes via task engagement and persistence. We try to emphasize the "chain reaction" aspect of this multi-step, mediated process so it is clear that a change in beliefs does not necessarily lead to a change in academic outcomes but, rather, changing beliefs increases engagement activities that help students acquire the knowledge and self-regulatory skills needed to succeed academically. We emphasize as well that this process requires time to change malleable beliefs, foster engagement that enables students to master the skill sets needed to succeed, and apply those skills to desired outcomes. The focus of our classroom discussions is on belief malleability, what type of teacher actions change beliefs, how this process might be accelerated, and how students can be helped to identify achievable academic outcomes.

METATHEORY AND THEORY COMPARISON

Teaching a graduate motivation class is a bit like teaching a survey of world history in which each week brings a new historical epoch with new innovations and societal challenges. We believe it is not enough to teach each theory. Rather, the focus should be on understanding similarities and differences among theories and understanding the general process of motivational change. To do so, we use the final weeks of our courses to consider at least three reasons why a metatheory is difficult to create. One is that unique constructs (e.g., self-efficacy, intrinsic motivation, mastery goals, achievement expectations) are embedded within each theory. A second is that different underlying mechanisms (e.g., personal experience, internal drives, and need for competence) are assumed to play a significant role in some but not all theories. A third is due to different assumptions among theories in terms of the malleability of central constructs. Of course, there may be additional factors that impede the generation of a metatheory that students in our classes identify or choose to explore in more detail.

We strongly believe a systematic comparison of theories facilitates understanding of each theory, as well as its similarities and differences from other theories. Table 13.1 shows a simplified comparison between self-efficacy and SDT—which could be expanded to include other theories as well. Creating a summary matrix (or use of some other graphic vehicle such as tree diagrams or concept maps) helps students to understand each theory at a deeper level and gravitate toward a theory (or specific construct within the theory) that seems consistent with their beliefs and helpful in the classroom. We have found that graphic comparisons greatly facilitate broader, deeper conceptual understanding of motivation theories. Doing so in small focus groups that culminate in group-led discussions has proven to be effective. These activities usually make excellent group projects that contribute to students' grades. In addition, we often ask students to construct analogous summary tables that focus on teacher and peer strategies for changing beliefs.

Finally, we encourage the class to identify general motivation processes that cut across all of the theories that enables them to better help their own students. Most of our classes try to capture the developmental sequence of motivational beliefs. Students discuss whether these beliefs occur concomitantly or in some specific development sequence (e.g., a sense of autonomy precedes self-efficacy), the changeability of beliefs, and whether academic or behavioral outcomes are capable of significant change without a corresponding change in student self-efficacy and autonomy. Other beliefs not addressed herein such as values, mastery, and performance goals, are discussed, as well as the role of internally and externally oriented attributions for success and failure. One critical question that is always worth debating is, how do social and contextual factors affect motivational beliefs? Although a few students may adopt a trait perspective in which beliefs and motivational constructs are viewed as fixed, most students take an incremental perspective in which beliefs change—sometimes dramatically. Our question to these students is, how does the school environment, teachers, parents, and peers contribute to this change?

CONCLUSION

We have found that our greatest successes in teaching motivation to educational practitioners involve: (a) discussion and activities focused on understanding the nature of motivational change; (b) the role of teachers and peers in influencing motivational change; and (c) unpacking motivational theories to discover how motivation impacts student learning, but also to discover commonalities among theories in terms of motivational processes.

TABLE 13.1 Simplified Theory Comparison Table

	Central constructs	Mechanism of Change	Role of Social Context (classroom environmt)	Role of Teacher	Role of Peers
Self-efficacy	Efficacy beliefs and outcome expectancies	Reciprocal determinism	• Subject-specific beliefs • Collective classroom efficacy	Source of development • Feedback • Opportunities for mastery experiences • Domain or task-specific praise	Act as a source of social comparison for learning through vicarious experience, modeling, and providing encouragement
Self-determination theory	Intrinsic and extrinsic motivation (external, introjected, identified, and integrated regulation)	Internalization Need satisfaction	• Climate allowing for expression of individual interest	Need-supportive teaching • Support for autonomy • Support for relatedness • Support for competence	Act to support motivational needs by fostering a sense of peer belonging; group work to foster competence

We encourage those who are teaching motivation to borrow from the various theories being taught to create motivationally supportive climates for learning motivation and ultimately translating academic learning into classroom practice. Within this instructional environment, invite students to summarize, compare, and debate one another about their role in the development of their own students' beliefs.

REFERENCES

Bandura, A. (1977). Self-efficacy: Toward a unifying theory of behavioral change. *Psychological Review, 84*(2), 191–215

Bandura, A. (1978). The self-system in reciprocal determinism. *American Psychologist, 33*(4), 344–358.

deCharms, R. (1968). *Personal causation: The internal affective determinants of behavior.* New York, NY: Academic Press.

Deci, E. L., & Ryan, R. M. (1985). *Intrinsic motivation and self-determination in human behavior.* New York, NY: Plenum.

Murphy, P. K., & Alexander, P. A. (2000). A motivated exploration of motivation terminology. *Contemporary Educational Psychology, 25*(1), 3–53.

Reeve, J. (2005). *Understanding motivation and emotion* (4th ed.) Hoboken, NJ: John Wiley & Sons, Inc.

Ryan, R. M. (1993). Agency and organization: Intrinsic motivation, autonomy, and the self in psychological development. In J. Jacobs (Ed.), *Nebraska symposium on motivation: Developmental perspectives on motivation* (pp. 1–56). Lincoln: University of Nebraska Press.

Ryan, R. M., & Deci, E. L. (2000). Self-determination theory and the facilitation of intrinsic motivation, social development, and well-being. *American Psychologist, 55*(1), 68–78.

Schunk, D., & Mullen, C. (2009). Self-efficacy as an engaged learner. In K. R. Wenzel & A. Wigfield (Eds.), *Handbook of motivation at school* (pp. 291–237). New York, NY: Routledge.

Schunk, D. H., & Pajares, F. (2009). Self-efficacy theory. In K. R. Wenzel & A. Wigfield (Eds.), *Handbook of motivation at school* (pp. 35–53). New York, NY: Routledge.

Usher, E. L., & Pajares, F. (2009). Sources of self-efficacy in mathematics: A validation study. *Contemporary Educational Psychology, 34*(1), 89–101.

Wentzel, K. R., & Wigfield, A. (2009). *Handbook of motivation at school.* New York, NY: Routledge.

CHAPTER 14

TEACHING AUTONOMY SUPPORT TO TEACHERS

Lee Shumow and Desiree Rones
Northern Illinois University

In this chapter, we define autonomy and describe how to foster it. We then explain why it is an important motivational construct for teachers and discuss approaches and challenges for teaching educators about autonomy and autonomy support. Examples of how to implement autonomy supportive practices during teacher education are used to illustrate how the concept of autonomy support can be taught to teachers.

DEFINING AUTONOMY

Deci and Ryan (1991) describe autonomy as the sense of agency people have when they believe that they can affect a particular outcome or situation. Autonomy also can be thought of as a state in which individuals perceive that they can independently determine their own goals and behavior. Outside of the field of psychology, autonomy is defined as having freedom. However, ceding total freedom to students is not a prerequisite for promoting students' self-determination or sense of agency.

Challenges and Innovations in Educational Psychology Teaching and Learning, pages 177–190
Copyright © 2016 by Information Age Publishing
All rights of reproduction in any form reserved.

Theoretical Framework

Self Determination Theory (SDT), an empirically well-supported theory of human motivation, assumes that curiosity is a universal human disposition that drives learning and that autonomy, competence, and relatedness are basic and interconnected human needs (Ryan & Deci, 2000a). To the extent that those needs are satisfied, SDT posits that people will be intrinsically motivated to satisfy their curiosity by learning and will strive to fulfill their goals.

SDT is a comprehensive theory of motivation with a fundamental assumption that intrinsic motivation is far more beneficial than extrinsic motivation and should, therefore, be supported and fostered. Many educators recognize that schooling and the content of schooling are often required by institutions external to, and outside the control of, individuals. Consequently, educators wonder whether and how autonomy fits within that reality. Ryan and Deci (2000b) explain that extrinsic factors operate on a continuum in relation to autonomy. At the most extrinsically oriented end of the continuum, students are enticed to earn rewards or avoid punishment in exchange for engaging in a learning activity. That common and widespread approach in education is seductive for instructional leaders and teachers who perceive that such extrinsic motivators "work" because people often comply in the moment. The unfortunate and undesirable result of this controlling approach, however, is often a counterproductive cycle in which deep learning and engagement are arrested, leading to an escalation in the rewards and punishments offered to counteract that disengagement (Niemiec & Ryan, 2009). The next step in the continuum is offering praise or recognition for task completion. This approach is unlikely to promote internalization, mastery goals, engagement, or learning. The third step of the continuum involves providing an explanation of why tasks, activities, or content are important. Appealing to reason communicates the idea that the individual has some volition. The fourth, and most autonomy supporting and intrinsically motivating, step on the continuum is linking the requirement to a goal, value, interest, or identification of the individual student.

Autonomy Support

SDT views humans as naturally inclined to be active agents in fulfilling their potential. However, achieving optimal development requires support for self-direction and growth. Autonomy is not something that can be transmitted directly to another person, yet it has been well established that educational environments can be structured to facilitate or undermine the autonomy of both students and teachers (Assor, Kaplan & Roth, 2002; Reeve, 2006). Autonomy supportive practices include providing choice and control to individuals, promoting the relevance of subject matter and tasks, and accepting others' perspectives. We focus here on the role of teachers in supporting their students' autonomy.

Choice

Individuals who perceive that they have some choices in what they do and how they do it are more likely to develop a sense of autonomy than those whose work is proscribed and directed. In a classroom, choices can range from relatively small ones—like selecting a topic to write about, choosing a partner, determining which study strategy to use, or the sequence in which work will be completed—to relatively large choices like co-designing long term projects or units and deciding how to go about meeting standards or demonstrating accountability such as with a portfolio of work. Choices work best in promoting autonomy when some structure is provided, either as a scaffold or as a means of clearly communicating expectations or endpoints (Sierens, Vansteenkiste, Goossens, Soenens, & Dochy, 2009).

Control and Responsibility

Ceding control to students or supervisees is not synonymous with permissiveness. Rather, it entails inviting collaboration and cooperation in fulfilling the responsibilities inherent in being a student or a worker. Students are expected to fulfill the obligations of being a student and to learn the subject matter.

Promoting Relevance

An important strategy for promoting autonomy development is to explain how subject matter or requirements are relevant to an individual or why particular behaviors are more productive than others (Assor et al., 2002). When individuals understand the reasons for learning or doing something, they can draw upon that understanding to direct their own behavior. Encouraging students to generate and express their own ideas about how material is relevant may have a more powerful impact on students' feelings of control than simply providing it to them.

Acceptance of Individual Perspectives

Some teachers and leaders support autonomy by being accepting of, and open to, alternate ideas. This means that they listen attentively, treat viewpoints other than their own respectfully, and consider the ideas offered seriously. It is also important to accept negative emotions. Teachers and leaders who attempt to quash negative emotions deny others the freedom to express their true feelings and, thus, undermine a sense of autonomy.

SIGNIFICANCE OF TEACHING AUTONOMY TO TEACHERS

Developmental Importance of Autonomy

According to SDT, autonomy is important throughout the lifespan. However, developmental psychologists who study adolescence describe autonomy as particularly important during adolescence. Independence is a hallmark of adulthood and autonomy is a central factor in that development. Adolescents' cognitive development is focused on attaining mature decision-making skills and rational thinking, which add important elements to their autonomy development. Parents of teens generally do more distal and less proximal monitoring, which supports greater autonomy.

Impact of Autonomy Support

Students

One important reason for teaching about autonomy in education classes is that autonomy supportive teaching is associated with numerous positive outcomes for students. Many education students are practicing or pre-service teachers, so learning about autonomy supportive approaches and putting them into practice is likely to benefit their current or future students. Those benefits include deeper learning, academic engagement, motivation, and emotional wellbeing.

Autonomy supportive teaching has been associated with increased academic performance probably because it impacts students' use of information processing strategies that promote long-term retention of material and better conceptual understanding of the subject matter content (Reeve, 2006). Further, autonomy supportive teaching contributes to students' intrinsic motivation to learn, adoption of a mastery goal orientation, and persistence when challenged (Reeve, 2006). An observational study found that teachers' autonomy support during ongoing instruction was a more powerful predictor of students' behavioral engagement in class than was students' level of behavioral engagement in a prior lesson (Reeve, Jang, Carrell, Jean, & Barch, 2004). Another study using the Experience Sampling Method in high school science classrooms found that during moments when students reported control over their learning, they also perceived themselves as more successful and less anxious (Schmidt, Kackar, & Strati, 2010).

Students of psychologically controlling teachers are at a distinct disadvantage compared to students of teachers who are not. A recent study found that students of psychologically controlling teachers are less likely to use self-regulation strategies and, consequently, do not achieve as well (Soenens, Sierens, Vansteenkiste, Goossens, & Dochy, 2012).

College Students

College students are similar to younger learners in their need for autonomy while learning. In a semester-long study of college students in a chemistry course, students who perceived greater autonomy support from leaders in their small groups made significant increases in self-regulation, including those who, at the beginning of the semester, were identified as low in relative autonomy (Black & Deci, 2000). Another study of college students indicated that by providing a social context that was autonomy supportive, along with an intrinsic rationale for learning the material, students were more autonomous in their motivation to learn, the material was processed more deeply, and students scored higher when assessed over the material. These students were more genuinely engaged, more fully dedicated to learning activities, and reported less superficial processing (Vansteenkiste, Simons, Lens, Sheldon, & Deci, 2004).

Student perception of autonomy is important in course selection, as well as in the actual class itself. Learners have reported more positive experiences in elective than required courses. When students have not chosen a course on their own volition, they can still experience success by receiving interpersonal support, such as through study groups facilitated by leaders who have been trained in autonomy support.

CHALLENGES IN TEACHING AUTONOMY

There are a number of challenges inherent in attempting to foster autonomy development in prospective or practicing teachers and in teaching them how to support autonomy development in their students. These include: (1) the limited prior experience and knowledge about autonomy that students bring with them to educational psychology classes; (2) the prevalent and overarching behaviorist model of motivating students that focuses on external rewards and punishment; and (3) the fear many teachers have of losing control. Finally, the policy climate focusing school and teacher evaluation on students' standardized test scores has resulted in highly controlling and restrictive practices.

Limited Prior Experience and Knowledge

Teachers come to the profession having years of experience as students in schools. Thus, they may be unaware of or inexperienced with autonomy supportive teaching styles. That limited modeling and experience with autonomy supportive teaching constitutes a challenge in teaching about autonomy and autonomy support. Evidence that autonomy support is limited is surprisingly difficult to find. One notable exception was found, however. In that study, 100 sets of field notes from classroom observations were coded for evident autonomy supportive practices (Bozack, Vega, McCaslin, & Good, 2008). Although the researchers identified some use of these practices, students had few opportunities to make choices, understand the relevance of material, share expertise or contribute their perspective.

Most psychology classes do little more than provide information about autonomy and do not demonstrate autonomy supportive practices that could encourage teachers to endorse such practices. For instance, one study showed that pre-service teachers who were exposed to autonomy supportive instructional strategies reported adopting an autonomy supportive style, as contrasted to pre-service teachers who were exposed to control-oriented instruction who did not (Reeve, 1998). Importantly, a mere 80 minutes of training had an enduring impact on pre-service teachers.

However, it is probably insufficient to merely expose teachers to the concept of autonomy. Teachers are unlikely to be able to utilize autonomy supportive practices in the classroom unless they are equipped with guidance and practice in *how* to promote autonomy in everyday instruction. One study of physical education teachers demonstrated the effectiveness of a program in which teachers planned for autonomy and were willing to reflect and change (Tessier, Sarrazin, & Ntoumanis, 2008). After teachers attended an informative session on autonomy supportive teacher behaviors, they participated in group activities that provided time and support for teachers to identify specific ways to incorporate autonomy in their classrooms. Later, they were videotaped and asked to reflect on their instruction. The result was that these teachers demonstrated more autonomy supportive behaviors than their counterparts. That teacher education program was a successful in fostering autonomy support in the classroom. Unfortunately, there are few other examples of such programs.

Behaviorist Tradition of Motivation and Management

Another constraint for educators in practicing autonomy support is that the predominant means of motivating and managing students are drawn from behaviorism, an approach at odds with efforts to develop students' autonomy. The use of controlling approaches to classroom management (Pianta, Hamre, & Allen, 2012) and adherence to behaviorist principles, including punishment, is widespread in K–12 schools (Hulac, Terrell, Vining & Bernstein, 2011). Educational psychology textbooks used in teacher education, practice related articles (Woolfolk Hoy, Davis, & Anderman, 2013) and teacher education classes (Lohse-Bossenz, Kunina-Habenicht, & Kunter, 2013), include and often highlight behaviorist theory as an approach to teaching (see Sperling et al., this volume). As a result of exposure, the behaviorist model is taken for granted as foundational to practice. In a recent study in which the researcher had his university students identify their own topics for a text about educational psychology, behaviorism was selected as the first entry by the students (Seifert, 2010). Also, the U.S. federal government and many states have mandated the use of positive behavioral interventions and supports (PBIS) as a component of response to intervention (Hulac et al., 2011). Although not punitive, the prevalent use of incentives and rewards in PBIS is controlling.

Fear of Losing Control

Yet another constraint—teachers' fear of losing control of their classroom—often arises when attempting to promote teachers' uses of autonomy supportive practices. Not surprisingly, given the traditional definition of teaching that conceptualizes teachers as being in charge—and the current intensive focus on accountability that places tremendous responsibility on teachers alone for student achievement—teachers often fear that they will lose control of their classroom (McCombs, 2012). The first author has often heard both pre-service and in-service teachers express fear about turning over responsibility to their students. Recently, one teacher enrolled in a professional development workshop recoiled after seeing two video clips of exemplary teachers promoting autonomy on a grand scheme. One of the teachers taught using problem based learning (PBL) and the other provided students with an extensive menu of independent project choices including one in which high school students took elementary students and their teachers on field trips that they planned. The teacher attending the workshop insisted that he could never "let go" to such an extent. After discussion, he chose to take a "baby step" by letting his students decide whether to submit their homework on Friday or Monday and see what happened. Interestingly, the other teachers in the workshop predicted disaster. Nevertheless, he gave his students the option and recorded his observations. He found that more homework was returned than ever before and his students' average score on the homework assignment was considerably higher than their average homework score.

Policy Climate

The education policy climate currently undermines teachers' sense of autonomy and their perception that they can support student autonomy development by focusing heavily on high-stakes tests to reward and sanction schools and teachers (Ryan & Weinstein, 2009). Teachers are held responsible for preparing students to perform well on high-stakes standardized tests. The stress to score well is often intense. Research has shown that increased pressure from "above" (administration, government agencies) to affect students "below" causes a great deal of tension for teachers who are caught in the middle and consequently often feel that they are being controlled and need to control their students. Teachers in such positions are less likely to promote self-determined behaviors (Roth, Assor, Kanat-Maymon, & Kaplan, 2007). When teachers feel unable to provide autonomous learning experiences, student motivation and achievement both decrease, and the problem perpetuates.

Educational reforms such as Race to the Top mandate that teachers be evaluated based, in part, on their students' standardized test scores. The premise underlying this mandate is that policy decisions should be data-driven, that the tests are solid measures of student growth and learning, and that teachers alone are responsible for student growth. Such a teacher evaluation system links student performance on a high stakes test with tenure decisions, professional development requirements, compensation, layoffs, and termination (National Council on Teacher Quality, 2013). When careers and livelihoods are in jeopardy, educators are more reticent to relinquish control. According to multiple studies, high-stakes testing causes teachers to feel greater pressure to ensure that students perform well on tests which, in turn, leads to more controlling behaviors (Jones, Jones, & Hargrove, 2003).

INNOVATIONS AND PROMISING PRACTICES

As can be seen by findings that demonstrate the importance of autonomy development, teachers can benefit from understanding and experiencing autonomy support. We could find no analysis of the extent to which autonomy or SDT is included in teacher education curricula. Promising practices and innovations are suggested by a handful of quasi-experimental studies and by the first author's anecdotal experience as a teacher educator.

Quasi-Experimental Studies in the Literature

A set of studies has been published demonstrating that teachers can develop an autonomy supportive style (Reeve, 1998; Reeve et al., 2004). In the seminal study (Reeve, 1998), pre-service teachers were assigned to read booklets about autonomy supportive instructional practices, controlling instructional practices, or neutral practices in regard to autonomy. Compared to the control condition, those pre-service teachers who read about autonomy supportive practices reported a greater inclination to be autonomy supportive teachers immediately after reading about such practices and sustained that inclination at follow-up one month later.

A subsequent study conducted by Reeve et al. (2004) provided more extensive evidence that an autonomy supportive teaching style can be fostered through education. In this experimental study, experienced high school teachers participated in an 80-minute workshop focused on four specific instructional strategies, while a delayed treatment group served as controls. A supplementary website was provided for teachers to use independently in furthering their knowledge about autonomy. Observers, blind to the treatment condition, documented more instances of autonomy supportive practice among teachers who had participated in the workshop. Furthermore, those teachers used all four autonomy support strategies, suggesting that they had developed a holistic style.

Another intervention study with a small group of middle and high school physical education teachers included an informational session, group planning to embed autonomy supportive teaching strategies in classroom activities, and joint experimenter-teacher analysis and discussion of videotaped lessons taught by the teacher. Compared to a comparison group of teachers, this intervention was successful at increasing the teachers' autonomy supportive interactions with their students but did not reduce their use of directive controlling statement (Tessier et al., 2008).

A Personal Example: Fostering Autonomy in Teacher Education Classes

The first author (LS) teaches adolescent development and classroom management classes to pre-service teachers who are pursuing teacher certification and to practicing teachers who are extending their educational credentials or certification. In my classes, I work hard to practice what I preach. That is, I just do not talk about autonomy and autonomy support; I design my classes to support my students' autonomy because I believe that is how they will best learn in the class and how they are most likely to become autonomy supportive teachers themselves.

Required classes pose the challenge, recognized by Ryan and Deci (2000b), of having students that are extrinsically—rather than intrinsically—motivated taking the classes. However, because the students have already chosen to be teachers, they typically perceive the class as somewhat valuable, at least as compared to general education classes. Nevertheless, because the classes are required and need to meet prescribed standards, careful planning is necessary to design an environment that promotes autonomy. The goals are to promote their intrinsic motivation, facilitate their learning, and support their autonomy development as teachers to the extent possible. To accomplish these goals, the class has been structured to maximize student choice, control, responsibility, and intrinsic value. On the first day of class, students receive a syllabus that describes a number of opportunities for students to determine their goals and behavior in class. Numerous choices and ways for students to take responsibility for their learning are presented.

Choices

Students have a number of choices. Most basically, they can choose which grade they wish to earn in the class. Criterion-referenced evaluation is used. Students are provided with the description of what they must accomplish in terms of the amount of work and quality standards that must be met for each grade from A to C; they are told that they will receive a lower grade if they do not meet the C level standards. There are three types of assignments (journal responses pertaining to the reading each week, a presentation to the class that extends a topic introduced in the reading, and a case study), and each one presents students with choices as described subsequently.

Each journal corresponds to assigned readings on a broad topic, such as a chapter title. There are general questions that students are required to respond to in each journal, but they choose the specific topic, which allows students to select and write about content that is meaningful to them. One set of questions asks them to identify one concept or research finding that (a) helped them understand or interpret their own prior experience and beliefs, and another that (b) contradicted their prior belief, and one other that (c) interested them. They are asked to elaborate on their answers. Two other questions pertain to application of the content. One asks them to choose a concept or finding that they think will be useful to them as teachers and another that will be useful for their students to know and to explain why in each case. Another question asks them if they have any authentic questions about the reading. The final question is particular to the chapter. It is usually an application question that prepares them for an in-class activity or discussion and often allows them to take and develop a reasoned stance.

Students choose a presentation topic from a suggested list or can propose a topic if they have an interest or expertise related to the broad topics identified in the class. There are approximately twice as many suggestions as students so that the last student to choose always has many options available. Suggestions include several activities that might appeal to student interests such as: (1) interviewing or observing a phenomenon of interest and presenting the findings in light of the text; (2) using popular culture depictions of students to exemplify concepts or findings presented in the text; or (3) reviewing a program that addresses a particular need of students discussed in the text. The instructions point students to the relevant section of the text and to resources necessary to complete their project (e.g., the name of a popular film, a chapter or web link describing a program), but they do not tell them how to organize or present their findings and conclusions. Students are told that they are responsible for elaborating on the course material in a way that will help their classmates understand the topic or concept. During the second class period of the first week, students work together as a whole class group to construct guidelines for the presentation based on preparatory small group discussion of characteristics of teachers they have had who are engaging and those who are not.

The case study is a semester-long project with multiple facets. Students can find a student (for a development class) or a teacher (in the case of classroom management) to follow throughout the semester, or they can select a subject from a pool of choices that is made available. They need to use class texts to gather and interpret information about the subject and the context for a C grade. The more extended aspects of the case study are selected by students from a list of options and resources to help them collect and analyze either the development, or the classroom management of, their subjects.

Control and Responsibility

Students share responsibility for teaching and learning with the professor. Their activities and presentations significantly shape the class experience. Each student is tasked with providing feedback on every other student's presentation. They are told that this is a serious responsibility that contributes to the learning and development of their classmates and promotes their own learning and development as teachers. Students also have considerable control over the grade they earn because they can revise (one time only) any assignment on which they did not attain the standard using the constructive feedback that has been provided by the professor and/or their peers.

Value

As noted previously, some scholars (Assor et al., 2002) argue that making topics relevant to students promotes autonomy. Researchers have also found that asking students to identify how material is relevant to them increases students' valuing of, and interest in, the subject (Hulleman, Godes, Hendricks, & Harackiewicz, 2010). Accordingly, students are asked to identify content that is especially valuable to them as teachers and content that is most valuable to their students as well as to explain why in their weekly journals. Class generally meets twice each week. Journals are due on the first day of the week. The journals are read and responded to individually in writing. They are also used to plan the second class by incorporating or addressing what students wrote about in the class discussion or activities. Recognizing students' contributions either with individual comments on their journals or by incorporating them into class can be seen as a kind of listening and acceptance of individual perspectives, which supports autonomy.

RECOMMENDATIONS AND CONCLUSIONS

Autonomy, as defined and recognized within SDT, is an important concept for educational psychologists to develop within pre-service and practicing teachers. Teachers need to both receive and provide autonomy support because they and their students work and learn better when they do. Researchers have provided evidence that particular practices enhance autonomy and that those practices and the disposition to use them can be taught and learned. Currently, however, numerous circumstances in education stymie autonomy development in both teachers and students. It is, therefore, more important than ever to provide educators with information about why autonomy support is important and how to implement autonomy supportive practices during their education.

Several broad recommendations can be made for educational psychologists who teach teachers. First, it is necessary to recognize autonomy as a fundamental lifelong need. Second, it is necessary to plan to teach about autonomy, to purposefully model autonomy supportive practices, to provide teachers with the opportunity to both experience and to implement autonomy supportive practices. Third, educational psychologists need to communicate and work with committees within our institutions of higher education and with policymaking bodies as decisions are made about how to educate teachers and with policymaking bodies. It is incumbent upon us to help prepare educators to support autonomy development of our future citizens.

REFERENCES

Assor, A., Kaplan, H., & Roth, G. (2002). Choice is good, but relevance is excellent: Autonomy-enhancing and suppressing teacher behaviours predicting students' engagement in schoolwork. *British Journal of Educational Psychology, 72*(2), 261–278.

Black, A. E., & Deci, E.L. (2000). The effects of instructors' autonomy support and students' autonomous motivation on learning organic chemistry: A self-determination theory perspective. *Science Education, 84,* 740–756.

Bozack, A., Vega, R., McCaslin, M., & Good, T. (2008). Teacher support of student autonomy in Comprehensive School Reform classrooms. *The Teachers College Record, 110*(11), 2389–2407.

Deci, E. L., & Ryan, R. (1991). A motivational approach to self: Integration in personality. In R. A. Diensbier (Ed.), *Nebraska symposium on motivation 1990* (vol. 38, pp. 237–288). Lincoln: University of Nebraska Press.

Hulac, D., Terrell, J., Vining, O., & Bernstein, J. (2011). *Behavioral interventions in schools: A Response-to-intervention guidebook.* New York, NY: Routledge.

Hulleman, C. S., Godes, O., Hendricks, B. L., & Harackiewicz, J. M. (2010). Enhancing interest and performance with a utility value intervention. *Journal of Educational Psychology, 102*(4), 880.

Jones, M., Jones, B., & Hargrove, T. (2003). *The unintended consequences of high-stakes testing.* New York, NY: Rowman & Littlefield Publishers, Inc.

Lohse-Bossenz, H., Kunina-Habenicht, O., & Kunter, M. (2013). The role of educational psychology in teacher education: Expert opinions on what teachers should know about learning, development, and assessment. *European Journal of Psychology of Education, 28*(4), 1543–1565.

McCombs, B. (2012). *Developing responsible and autonomous learners: A key to motivating students.* American Psychological Association: http://www.apa.org/education/k12/learners.aspx.

National Council on Teacher Quality (2013). *Teacher prep review 2013 report.* Washington, DC: Author.

Niemiec, C. P., & Ryan, R. M. (2009). Autonomy, competence, and relatedness in the classroom: Applying self-determination theory to educational practice. *Theory and Research in Education, 7,* 133–144.

Pianta, R. C., Hamre, B. K., & Allen, J. P. (2012). Teacher-student relationships and engagement: Conceptualizing, measuring, and improving the capacity of classroom interactions. In S. L. Christenson, A. L. Reschly, & C. Wyie (Eds.), *Handbook of research on student engagement* (pp. 365–386). New York, NY: Springer.

Reeve, J. (1998). Autonomy support as an interpersonal motivating style: Is it teachable? *Contemporary Educational Psychology, 23,* 312–330.

Reeve, J. (2006). Teachers as facilitators: What autonomy supportive teachers do and why their students benefit. *Elementary School Journal, 106,* 225–236.

Reeve, J., Jang, H., Carrell, D., Jean, S., & Barch, J. (2004). Enhancing students' engagement by increasing teachers' autonomy support. *Motivation and Emotion, 28,* 147–169.

Roth, G., Assor, A., Kanat-Maymon, Y., & Kaplan, H. (2007). Autonomous motivation forteaching: How self-determined teaching may lead to self-determined learning. *Journal of Educational Psychology, 99,* 761–774.

Ryan, R., & Deci, E. L. (2000a). Self-determination theory and the facilitation of intrinsic motivation, social development, and well-being. *American Psychologist, 55*(1), 68–78.

Ryan, R., & Deci, E. L. (2000b). Intrinsic and extrinsic motivations: Classic definitions and new directions. *Contemporary Educational Psychology, 25,* 54–67.

Ryan, R. M., &, Weinstein, N. (2009). Undermining quality teaching and learning: A self-determination theory perspective on high-stakes testing. *Theory and Research in Education, 7,* 224–233.

Schmidt, J. A., Kackar, H. Z., & Strati, A. (2010, May). *Do motivational processes "work" differently for male and female students in science? Examining the role of situational factors and gender in motivational processes among high school science students.* Paper presented at the annual meeting of the American Educational Research Association, Denver CO.

Seifert, K. (2010). Students' priorities as authors of their own text about educational psychology. *Teaching Educational Psychology, 6*(1), 1–19.

Sierens, E., Vansteenkiste, M., Goossens, L., Soenens, B., & Dochy, F. (2009). The synergistic relationship of perceived autonomy support and structure in the prediction of self-regulated learning. *British Journal of Educational Psychology, 79*(1), 57–68.

Soenens, B., Sierens, E., Vansteenkiste, M., Goossens, L., & Dochy, F. (2012). Psychologically controlling teaching: Examining outcomes, antecedents, and mediators. *Journal of Educational Psychology, 104*, 108–120.

Tessier, D., Sarrazin, S., & Ntoumanis, N. (2008). The effects of an experimental programme to support students' autonomy on the overt behaviors of physical education teachers. *European Journal of Psychology of Education, 23*, 239–253.

Vansteenkiste, M., Simons, J., Lens, W., Sheldon, K. M., & Deci, E. L. (2004). Motivating learning, performance, and persistence: The synergistic role of intrinsic goals and autonomy-support. *Journal of Personality and Social Psychology, 87*, 246–260.

Woolfolk Hoy, A., Davis, H. A., & Anderman, E. M. (2013). Theories of learning and teaching in TIP. *Theory Into Practice, 52*(1), 9–21.

CHAPTER 15

TEACHING ABOUT OPTIMAL EXPERIENCE OR FLOW

Jennifer A. Schmidt
Northern Illinois University

As Mihaly Csikzentmihalyi (1990) tells the story, while observing art students in the 1970s, he was struck by their deep engagement. Their focus on the artistic process was so intense that they would often lose track of time, spending hours in the studio working on a painting, neglecting breaks even for food, drink, or to attend to other responsibilities. Interestingly, once the painting or sculpture was complete, the artists seemed to lose interest, putting the work to the side to focus on the next project. Csikszentmihalyi referred to these experiences as "autotelic," signifying that the goal (*telos*) was participation itself (*auto*), as opposed to the production of some final product. This experience of losing one's self in deep engagement was described by research participants as "flowing:" Hence, this experience of deep engagement has come to be known as flow. Because the experience is affectively positive and facilitates growth, it is also referred to as optimal experience.

In the years that followed Csikszentmihalyi's initial observation, the flow state has been studied among adults in a variety of professions ranging from rural farmers and factory workers, to professional athletes, white-collar professionals, and surgeons. Flow has been studied among youth as well, with

Challenges and Innovations in Educational Psychology Teaching and Learning, pages 191–204
Copyright © 2016 by Information Age Publishing
All rights of reproduction in any form reserved.

examinations of the conditions for and experience of deep engagement in academic and extracurricular activities. While the specific activities in which individuals experience flow can vary widely, there is remarkable similarity in the way people describe the flow experience, and in the conditions that tend to underlie this experience.

The Experience of Flow

The descriptions of this optimal experience share a number of features including: (1) intense concentration; (2) a merging of action and awareness; (3) the perception of control over one's actions; (4) enjoyment or interest; and (5) a distorted sense of time (typically that time has passed very quickly).

The Conditions for Flow

Research has identified a number of phenomenological conditions that, when present, make flow more likely to occur. These conditions include: (1) perceiving some sense of choice or control in the activity; (2) perceiving the challenges of the activity as high and in balance with one's skill in that activity; (3) having short-term activity-related goals that are clear and have some value for one's self or others; (4) receiving immediate feedback indicating how effectively one is meeting these goals; and (5) having highly focused, rather than scattered or divided attention.

Certain activities like making music and competitive athletics, by their very nature, are structured such that the above conditions are readily present and, as a result, people experience flow slightly more often when doing them (Csikszentmihalyi, 1990). However, the flow conditions are subjective, suggesting that it is more important for an individual to perceive these conditions as salient than for these conditions to be inherent in an activity.

Certain individuals may be particularly skilled at creating the psychological conditions for flow and producing this optimal experience for themselves across a variety of activities, even when these conditions aren't inherent to the activities themselves. Csikzentmihalyi (1990) referred to this as the "autotelic personality." More recent research has also explored individual variation in the experience of flow in academic contexts (see Shernoff & Csikszentmihalyi, 2009 for a review).

Educational applications of flow principals are typically introduced in the motivation unit in undergraduate educational psychology courses that are part of teacher education programs, or in graduate courses for practicing teachers that are focused on classroom motivation. Research on flow across a variety of domains is often included in graduate level courses focused on motivation research.

SIGNIFICANCE OF FLOW TO EDUCATORS

Student engagement is a primary concern of most educators, and research on engagement has exploded in the past 10 years. A quick search of the keywords "academic engagement" on Google Scholar returns over 1 million articles, books, and published reports in the past decade alone. The flow model has shaped our understanding of the experience of deep engagement and the contextual factors that promote it (Shernoff & Csikszentmihalyi, 2009). The model is a helpful framework for a wide variety of educators because the general principles for fostering flow are not tied to a specific content area, context, readiness level, or to particular educational materials or practices. Instead, the model specifies qualities of the environment that can become salient as a result of activity structures created by the teacher and/or by cognitive parameters that students can learn to create for themselves.

Each of the five conditions for flow described above can be—but often aren't—present and/or manipulated in classrooms. There are myriad ways that learning activities can be structured so that students can feel that they are exercising choice or control. The challenge of a learning activity can be brought into balance with a students' skill level through effective differentiation by readiness and through student awareness of what "good fit" learning activities feel like. Both students and teachers can create short-term learning goals that are valued by students. Immediate feedback can be achieved through ongoing formative assessment by the teacher and (better yet) student self-assessment. Finally, teachers can work to minimize distractions, and students can learn to control their attention to effectively tune out many distractions. As suggested by these examples, each of these conditions can be built into the classroom environment (which is largely created by the teacher), or can be constructed by the student. It is equally beneficial for teachers to work to create these conditions in their classrooms as it is to help students learn how to create these conditions for themselves.

One of the flow conditions—the balance of challenge and skill—has received the greatest attention in both the theoretical and empirical writing on flow, and is highly salient to learning contexts. The relative relationship of challenge and skill within a given task is highly predictive of the quality of one's experience in that task (Csikszetnmihalyi, & Csikszentmihalyi, 1988; Csikszentmihalyi, 1990, Shernoff & Schmidt, 2008). When challenges and skills are relatively high and in balance, one is more likely to experience flow. When challenges are high but skills are low, one feels anxiety, whereas situations characterized by low challenge and high skills tend to produce relaxation (or in the extreme case, boredom). Finally, activities in which challenges and skills are both low tend to produce apathy. These four states—flow, anxiety, boredom, and apathy—are referred to as "channels of experience" in the flow model, and are represented in Figure 15.1. Some scholars have further parsed these four channels into eight or even 16 different states (see Massimini & Carli, 1988), but this level of detail may be of limited utility for educational practice, so the basic model is presented here.

This model is a useful heuristic in that, in very simple terms, it highlights the experiential and motivational benefits of the optimal balance of challenge and skills, and explicitly describes the detriment that can occur when these two factors are not in balance. The model is dynamic, such that, in order for a person to remain in a state of flow, the challenges of the environment and one's personal skills must continually be adjusted. As a person's skill develops, she must take on greater challenges or risk boredom. Conversely, if these new challenges greatly exceed her skill, she will have to work to increase her skills (she will have to learn) in order to avoid feeling excessive anxiety. Thus, the process of maintaining a flow state complements constructivist models of learning, operating in tandem with the zone of proximal development (Vygotsky, 1962).

To the individual, a discussion of "outcomes" associated with flow is irrelevant: The salient "end" in the flow experience is the experience itself (Nakamura & Csikszentmihalyi, 2002). Nevertheless, there is evidence that the deep engagement of the flow state is related to developmental, motivational, and achievement related outcomes. Because flow is experienced as positive and gratifying, individuals select and replicate flow-producing

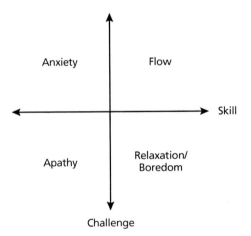

Figure 15.1 Channels of subjective experience.

activities over time—a process that is referred to as "psychological selection" (DelleFave & Massimini, 2003). Ironically, over time, by remaining focused on participation in the activity itself and avoiding focus on the long-term outcomes, one tends to achieve truly exceptional long-term outcomes. For example, the experience of flow during high school is positively related to talent development (Csikszentmihalyi, Rathunde & Whalen, 1993), academic grades (Shernoff & Schmidt, 2008), and longer-term outcomes like choice of college major and college grades (Shernoff & Hoogstra, 2001). This is the take-away message for educators: If you de-emphasize the long-term achievement related outcomes that are the primary focus in contemporary high stakes educational environments and, instead, focus on the more proximal goal of deep and meaningful engagement in learning, you will ultimately realize those same achievement outcomes that are so elusive when focusing on the outcome rather than the process. In the flow model the outcomes are, in a sense, a by-product of achieving this primary goal of repeated engagement over time.

CHALLENGES TO TEACHING ABOUT FLOW

As I prepare to teach about flow, I often joke to my spouse that if the class session(s) in which we discuss this topic are not among the most engaging ones of the semester, I will have truly failed. How could I live with the shame of having a boring class about flow? Fortunately for me (and for my students), the flow experience resonates with most students and seems relevant to their lives. The model is fairly easy to understand, and lends itself well to discussion and application. Many of the seminal pieces describing the model are very well written, and are truly enjoyable to read (e.g., Csikszentmihalyi, 1990; Nakamura & Csikszentmihalyi, 2002). Finally, the methodologies for studying flow are unique and intriguing to students interested in research. A high school physics teacher who was taking my doctoral seminar on motivation once told me that Csikszentmihalyi's (1990) book *Flow* was one of a small number of educational resources that he believed all educators ought to have on their bookshelves. This comment speaks to the relevance to education that many educators find in the flow model. Since interest and relevance do not generally pose barriers, most of the challenges to teaching about flow stem from students' prior experiences with flow and education, with unique features of the flow model as it pertains to education, and with methodological complexities. Each of these challenges is described briefly below.

Addressing the Skeptics: Can Flow Really Happen in Classrooms?

Most people readily recognize the flow experience as it relates to extracurricular interests and hobbies. After all, who could forget that basketball game where there seemed to be nothing that could break the connection between you, the ball, and the net? Or that great novel or video game that you got sucked into last week, at the expense of dinner and a few good nights' sleep? When I ask students to reflect about if/when they have experienced this type of engagement, academic activities rarely enter the conversation. More often, students recognize flow experiences in the sports they have played, in their artistic pursuits, and in video gaming. Indeed, research indicates that students rarely experience flow in school, in spite of the fact that some of the conditions for flow are often present (Schmidt, Shernoff, & Csikszentmihalyi, 2007). So, convincing a roomful of college students that flow is possible in classrooms is often the first hurdle in teaching about flow.

Practicing teachers are frequently the most resistant to the idea that flow can occur in classrooms because they recognize better than most the real and perceived barriers to facilitating flow in this context. The emphasis on high stakes testing promotes practices such as "teaching to the test" that leave teachers feeling like they cannot afford to give students any choice or control, and that they have to remain laser-focused on long term outcomes rather than short term goals. In this framework, teacher feedback is focused on these larger goals, rather than process. In addition, the emphasis on these performance goals over mastery goals creates a situation in which, even when teachers can provide it, appropriately challenging work feels threatening to students rather than motivating. Any given classroom can house a wide range of ability levels; thus, managing the balance of challenge and skill for each student seems an impossible task. Finally, frequent classroom interruptions are often a reality of classrooms that is beyond the teacher's control. To a teacher who deals with these realities on a daily basis, the idea of fostering flow in classrooms may sound like a pipe dream. While flow is certainly not the norm in today's schools, there are numerous examples (described shortly) of how teachers, students, and indeed entire schools have created structures to facilitate this positive experience.

Flow in Classrooms: Standard Rules Don't Apply

The above-mentioned logistical difficulties involved in planning to create flow conditions in the classroom are further compounded because research suggests that these conditions don't operate exactly the same way in classrooms as they tend to do in most other contexts. While challenge and skill tend to be higher in school than in other settings (Csikszentmihlayi, 1990), flow rarely occurs there (Schmidt et al., 2007). This is likely due in part to the fact that school is compulsory, and students are less free to exercise control over their activities (Shernoff & Csikszentmihalyi, 2009). Whereas the challenge-skill balance alone is often sufficient to predict flow experiences in other contexts like leisure or work (see Csikszentmihalyi, 1990 for a review), these conditions are necessary, but not sufficient predictors of flow in classrooms.

Is Flow in The Task, in The Context, or in The Person?

Students occasionally become confused about where flow comes from. Are there certain tasks that make people experience flow? Are there certain features of contexts that make flow, that are not task specific? Are there certain people that are more able than others to find or make flow? The available research and theory on flow suggests that the answer to all of these questions is yes. Certain tasks, like sports, tend to elicit a state of flow more frequently than others. There are features of contexts (the conditions for flow) that tend to promote the flow experience more than others, and these features can exist across a broad range of tasks. Finally, there are individuals who are particularly able to harness their attention, create challenges, rules, and goals when there are none, and to experience more flow. The multiple pathways to flow can create some ambiguity for students learning about the model. The optimist can view this fact as indicating that there are a number of different opportunities for students to experience flow. The pessimist may become frustrated because there is not a single recipe for producing flow that will always be effective. A teacher can do everything in his power to create the conditions for flow in his classroom and, try as he might, his students may still not experience flow. As a subjective phenomenon, flow cannot occur without input from the student.

Recognizing that the experience of flow depends, to a great extent, on the individual, some schools have taken steps to help their students achieve a state of flow on their own, with minimal teacher intervention. For example, the Key Learning Community—a charter public school in Indianapolis (IN) has a "flow center," in which students are expected to perform tasks (largely of their choosing) in which they can engage deeply. Time in the flow center is scheduled into their day, and the rationale is that as students experience the flow state, they will recognize how gratifying it is, learn about what they personally need to achieve flow, and will transfer this knowledge to other academic activities.

Measuring Flow

While issues of measurement do not always come up in introductory educational psychology courses, which are largely directed toward teacher candidates, measuring flow can pose significant challenges for graduate students interested in studying flow. A full description of the complexities of studying flow is beyond the scope of this chapter, but researchers must make decisions about whether to study flow conditions or the flow experience, and whether to seek a qualitative description of flow or to attempt to quantify the magnitude, duration, or frequency of flow. Flow has been studied using interviews, surveys, and the experience sampling method (ESM) —a signal contingent method of data collection in which individuals respond to randomly generated signals to report the quality of their experience (see Csikszentmihalyi & Csikszentmihalyi, 1988; Hektner et al., 2007 for a review of methods).

APPROACHES TO TEACHING ABOUT FLOW

I have found three different approaches to be effective in helping students learn about flow. Students become highly engaged in each of these activities, and have conveyed to me through personal communication that these activities were highly enjoyable and informative for them. In the learning activities that involve the collection of data through observation, survey, or interview (described below), students share with me that they invest an enormous amount of time in these projects, but that it feels like time well spent.

Approach 1: Guided Discussion

I typically introduce the topic of flow to students by initiating a whole class discussion based on prompts from the flow interview protocol, employed by Csikszentmihalyi and colleagues (1993). The prompts read as follows:

> Do you ever do something where your concentration is so intense, your attention so undivided and wrapped up in what you are doing that you sometimes become unaware of things you normally notice? Do you ever do something where your skills have become so "second nature" that sometimes everything seems to come to you "naturally" or "effortlessly"? (pp. 275–276)

As a class, students make a list of all of the activities in which they have had this experience. Through guided questions, students provide details about what this experience feels like. I then ask further questions about the conditions for flow, and we discuss if and how they were present in these recalled experiences. While the vast majority of examples typically involve out-of-school activities, I ask students to think about what would be possible if these experiences did occur in school. Students typically reflect on this question by speculating that if they had experienced flow in their schoolwork, they would have felt better about school, they would have spent more time studying, and they probably would have done better. Students are able to see the relationship between their deep engagement in their flow-producing activities and their skill and interest development in these activities. It is very powerful for them to imagine how this same process can potentially take place with regard to schooling. This is a revelation for some, and immediately sparks a discussion about individual and contextual barriers to the flow experience, and how both teachers and students can overcome these barriers. During or following this discussion, I often show a video of Csikszentmihalyi talking about flow (e.g., http://www.ted.com/talks/mihaly_csikszentmihalyi_on_flow).

Approach 2: Observation of Flow Conditions in Classrooms

I have had students observe in a classroom for some period of time (either a single session or multiple visits) to record evidence of the presence of the conditions for flow, and to make a very basic observation of students' engagement during this time. I have used this type of activity with master's students who are teachers, and with undergraduates in teacher-education programs, particularly when students have access to classrooms, as is the case in courses that include a clinical component. A sample form to use for making this observation is presented in Figure 15.2. While this exercise does not allow students to access the subjective experience of the learners they are observing (a critical component to the experience of flow), it does allow them to assess, in a very basic way, the degree to which teachers can structure activities to maximize the chances that flow might occur. It is important to reiterate in the introduction of this exercise and in the discussion of students' findings that teachers alone cannot just make flow happen for their students, and that they are not always going to be able to simultaneously create all of the conditions for flow for all of their students.

The product of this activity is often a paper and/or a presentation in which students share their observations. Following this activity, students often come to several very important conclusions. First, there is a lot that teachers can (and often don't) do to promote their students' engagement. Second, there are many very real barriers to promoting deep engagement in classrooms. Third, there is an internal, subjective component to

Condition	Examples of Flow-supportive structures and behaviors	Examples of Flow-obstructive structures and behaviors
Choice and Control: • Did teacher offer choice regarding activities, partners, materials, timing, etc.? • Were students given responsibility for managing their work? • Other observations about choice, control, autonomy		
Challenge-Skill Balance: • Did students have to exert effort to complete activity? • Did they complete activity quickly without effort? • Did they seem frustrated? • Other observations about challenge • (Will differ by student)		
Activity-related goals that have value: • Does teacher break down large activities into smaller parts? • Does teacher discuss strategies for completion? • Does teacher emphasize the value of activities for students? • Other observations on goals or value		
Immediate feedback: • Does teacher provide formative or process feedback? • Evidence that students are self-evaluataing? • Other observations on feedback		
Focused attention: • What does teacher do to allow students to focus? • Distractions • Other observations on attention		

On a separate sheet, record your observations of students' level of engagement (this exercise can be modified to focus on a single student, or to make a more global assessment of the class as a whole). Do students appear to be on task? Are they using the time they are given for activities? Do they interact with the teacher and students in ways that suggests they are interested in the activity? Are they constantly looking at the clock?

Figure 15.2 Sample field note guide for observation of flow conditions.

the experience of flow that teachers cannot always manipulate or assess through classroom observation. Learning about the subjective side of flow happens best through another kind of data collection exercise, explained below. The important take-away message is that even if students do not achieve a full state of flow, teachers cannot go wrong by focusing their efforts on engaging students in learning.

To supplement and support this exercise, there are a number of research studies examining alternative school structures (Rathunde & Csikszentmihalyi, 2005), teacher practices (Patrick, Turner, Meyer, & Midgely, 2003), and technological advancements (Coller & Shernoff, 2009) that are particularly good at fostering flow in education.

Approach 3: Methods for Learning About the Flow Experience

In graduate classes, I often have students collect data about the flow experience from some population of their choosing using methods that have been used in prior studies. This exercise provides students with the opportunity to learn about some of the challenges to studying flow empirically. The flow interview (Csikszentmihalyi et al., 1993) can provide a narrative account of how individuals experience flow and in what activities. The Core Flow Questionnaire (Jackson, Martin, & Eklund, 2008) provides information about the frequency and intensity of flow, as well as the type of activities in which research participants experience flow. Products from this exercise are typically a paper and/or presentation in which students present the results of their data collection. When I do this exercise, an important component of the paper or presentation is a reflection about the process of collecting data on flow: What are the challenges, opportunities, and lessons learned from this first attempt? In this exercise, the reflection on the process is more important that the results.

The most common method of collecting data on flow and engagement—the ESM—is highly complex and often not possible to employ in the span of a typical graduate course. However, when we cover flow in my graduate courses, I always include a discussion of the method, the benefits of this method, and the considerations involved in this method of data collection (for a review, see Hektner et al., 2007). I often give interested graduate students the opportunity to analyze ESM data sets for which I have access. For those interested in trying their hand at analysis of ESM data using a flow framework, the Inter-university Consortium of Policy and Social Research (ICPSR) at the University of Michigan houses two ESM databases that can be used for such exploratory purposes. These data sets will be available to institutions that are members of ICPSR, and can be accessed at no cost by visiting https://www.icpsr.umich.edu and searching for the Sloan Study of Youth and Social Development or the 500 Family Study.

CONCLUDING REMARKS

Examining the classroom applications of flow is relevant to teachers who may be taking courses for professional development, and students in certification programs who will soon be faced with the challenge of engaging their own students in learning. The topic is also of use to students who may be interested in issues of data collection, measurement, and analysis pertaining to the empirical study of the flow conditions or experience. In previous sections of this chapter I have outlined what I believe to be very effective methods for teaching each of these student populations. I will conclude here with a few words of caution and advice for teaching these two distinct populations of students.

Recommendations for Teaching Current and Future Educators

The biggest challenge to teaching about the educational applications of the flow model is to convince your learners that flow in education is possible, while maintaining a sense of realism about the aspects of students' classroom experiences that teachers can (and cannot) change. It is important to recognize that offering choices, differentiating instruction so that challenges and skills are appropriately matched, helping students create short-term goals that they value, providing rapid feedback, and removing classroom distractions are all difficult and complex tasks, and cannot be achieved for all students all of the time. Moreover, it would be misleading to give students the impression that, if they could only create all of these learning conditions, then their students would magically enter into a state of flow every day. When the conditions for flow exist, this means only that the flow experience is *more likely* to occur: It is no guarantee that it will occur. It is important to convey that flow is not a state that can be achieved all the time in any context, whether it be sports or leisure activities, or work, or school. However, we know that, regardless of where it occurs, flow is motivating: When we experience this positive kind of deep engagement in activities we tend to seek it out again and again and, in the process of doing so, we develop skills in the domain of the activity and in the process of achieving flow again. Finally, even if students do not achieve the flow state all the time, having teachers focus on the learning conditions that they create and their potential impact on student engagement will always improve instruction and learning.

Recommendations for Teaching Current and Future Researchers

The various methodologies that have been used to study flow have made valuable contributions to our understanding of student engagement. An elusive state to achieve, flow is even more difficult to study. It is my firm belief that the best way to teach students about the complexities of researching a topic is by having them try their hand at it. Once students attempt to collect and analyze data through existing interview and survey protocols, or through experience sampling, they will find—as others have—that while many people can easily recognize the experience of flow, and can describe specific occasions in which they had this experience, even the most reflective people may have a difficult time articulating how and why they experienced flow on some occasions but not on others. Likewise, the ESM can be complex to administer, and requires substantial investment of time by researchers and participants in order to access participants' subjective experiences. The available methods for accessing this information are imperfect and, as is the case with all types of social science research, the realization that there are drawbacks and imperfections to any method (even those that are used widely in published studies and books), can be disheartening to idealistic graduate students.

I believe that learning about any topic requires consideration of the benefits as well as a realistic and critical approach to the limitations of any framework or methodology. I contend without reservation that the limitations and drawbacks to the flow model, both in its educational application and in research, pale in comparison to the value of this model for education and human growth in general. I conclude with a thought from the introduction of our book on the ESM, in which Csikszentmihalyi reflects on the value and limitations of the method. This idea applies to both the research and educational applications of the flow model.

> My inclination . . . is to invoke a variation on the old saying, *If something is worth doing, it's worth doing well.* Abraham Maslow once pointed out that it was equally true that *If something is not worth doing, it's not worth doing well.* Both of these sayings make sense, and we would add a third one that is also true: *If something is worth doing, it's worth doing not well.* In other words, if there is no better way of doing something that needs to be done, it's preferable to do it as well as possible—even if it isn't perfect. (Hektner et al., p. 12)

While current methods for promoting and studying flow in classrooms are imperfect, the value of deep engagement in education merits the use of this framework in educational practice and research.

REFERENCES

Coller, B. D., & Shernoff, D. J. (2009). Video game-based education in mechanical engineering: A look at student engagement. *International Journal of Engineering Education, 25*(2), 308.

Csikszentmihalyi, M. (1990). *Flow: The psychology of optimal experience.* New York, NY: HarperCollins.

Csikszentmihalyi, M., & Csikszentmihalyi, I.S. (Eds.). (1988). *Optimal experience: Psychological studies of flow in consciousness.* New York, NY: Cambridge University Press.

Csikszentmihalyi, M., Rathunde, K., & Whalen, S. (1993). *Talented teenagers: The roots of success and failure.* New York, NY: Cambridge University Press.

Delle Fave, A., & Massimini, F. (2003). Optimal experience in work and leisure among teachers and physicians: Individual and bio-cultural implications. *Leisure Studies, 22*(4), 323–342.

Hektner, J. M., Schmidt, J. A., & Csikszentmihalyi, M. (2007). *Experience sampling method: Measuring the quality of everyday life.* Thousand Oaks, CA: Sage.

Jackson, S. A., Martin, A. J., & Eklund, R. C. (2008). Long and short measures of flow: The construct validity of the FSS-2, DFS-2, and new brief counterparts. *Journal of Sport & Exercise Psychology, 30*(5), 561.

Massimini, F., & Carli, M. (1988). The systematic assessment of flow in daily experience. In M. Csikszentmihalyi & I. S. Csikszentmihalyi (Eds.). *Optimal experience: Psychological studies of flow in consciousness* (pp. 266–287). New York, NY: Cambridge University Press.

Nakamura, J., & Csikszentmihalyi, M. (2002). The concept of flow. In Snyder, C. R. & Lopez, S. J. (Eds.), *Handbook of positive psychology* (pp. 89–105). Oxford, England: Oxford University Press.

Patrick, H., Turner, J., Meyer, D., & Midgley, C. (2003). How teachers establish psychological environments during the first days of school: Associations with avoidance in mathematics. *The Teachers College Record, 105*(8), 1521–1558.

Rathunde, K., & Csikszentmihalyi, M. (2005). Middle school students' motivation and quality of experience: A comparison of Montessori and traditional school environments. *American Journal of Education, 111*(3), 341–371.

Schmidt, J. A., Shernoff, D. J., & Csikszentmihalyi, M. (2007). Individual and situational factors related to the experience of flow in adolescence: A multilevel approach. In A. D. Ong & M. van Dulmen (Eds.), *Oxford handbook of methods in positive psychology* (pp. 542–558). New York, NY: Oxford Press.

Shernoff, D. J., & Csikszentmihalyi, M. (2009). Cultivating engaged learners and optimal learning environments. In R. Gilman, E. S. Huebner, & M. J. Furlong (Eds.), *Handbook of positive psychology in schools* (pp. 131–145). New York, NY: Routledge.

Shernoff, D. J., & Hoogstra, L. (2001). Continuing motivation beyond the high school classroom. *New Directions for Child and Adolescent Development, 2001*(93), 73–88.

Shernoff, D., & Schmidt, J.A. (2008). Further evidence of an engagement-achievement paradox among U.S. high school students. *Journal of Youth and Adolescence, 37,* 564–580.

Vygotsky, L. S. (1962). *Thought and language.* Cambridge, MA: MIT Press.

CHAPTER 16

UNDERSTANDING MOTIVATION THEORIES USING PROJECT-BASED LEARNING

Neal Shambaugh
West Virginia University

TEACHERS VALUE STUDENT MOTIVATION

Motivation deals with the influence of needs and preferences on our behavior. From the viewpoint of any teacher the question is always more specific, such as "Why do students not read the material?" The problem with motivation theories for teachers is the inability of one theory to capture enough of the richness of cases encountered in the classroom. Teachers look to a useful theory to have enough explanatory power that can be applied across many behavioral examples. A theory to researchers, however, may provide explanations of human behavior but without a clear set of principles for action. Even lacking a metatheory (see Marchand & Schraw, this volume) and given the complexity of human behavior, multiple theories provide different ways of looking at and understanding students. Teachers are likely to be more motivated to value motivational theories by first seeing their results.

Challenges and Innovations in Educational Psychology Teaching and Learning, pages 205–215
Copyright © 2016 by Information Age Publishing
All rights of reproduction in any form reserved.

This chapter describes how project-based learning (PBL) influences student engagement, a behavior highly valued by teachers. From my teaching of PBL as a teaching model, both pre-service teachers and experienced teachers become motivated to learn how PBL works *after* seeing engaged and motivated students participating in PBL activities. I begin this chapter by describing the planning, managing, and evaluating of PBL units. Then, I describe how PBL taps into human curiosity and develops academic self-regulation skills, and how motivation can be sequenced within PBL units using Keller's ARCS model (1987). Finally, I describe two instructional approaches to experiencing PBL and motivational theories.

EXPERIENCING STUDENT MOTIVATION IN PBL UNITS

The Buck Institute for Education (BIE), which has provided professional development in PBL for several states, defines PBL as "a systematic teaching method that engages students in learning important knowledge and 21st century skills through an extended, student-influenced inquiry process structured around complex, authentic questions and carefully designed products and learning tasks" (BIE, 2010, p. 5). PBL is not an enrichment activity or reward, but rather a means to apply foundational knowledge and skills (Larmer, 2009). PBL is not based on themes, but rather on a driving question developed out of student curiosity, questioning, and activity. While "hands-on" is definitely a feature in PBL activities, the inquiry may tackle other intellectual activities, such as designing, problem solving, collaborating, and reading and writing.

Planning a PBL Unit

PBL units typically last 2–5 weeks, but briefer week-long units can also introduce students to the process. All grade levels, even kindergarten, can benefit from PBL units. Foundational content and skills are usually needed before PBL can be undertaken. However, by tapping their interests PBL activity gives students a reason for learning foundational knowledge and skills. Thus, PBL taps two important conditions for motivation: attention and relevance.

PBL requires significant preparation time in order to implement key features. Teachers working together around grade levels or content areas can discuss initial ideas for units. The focus for a unit might be the development of specific content area knowledge or skills but, because teachers are sharing control in the classroom and cooperative behavior is needed, social learning outcomes should be specified in the unit plan. If social behaviors are needed in PBL, then they should "count" in the outcomes and corresponding assessment. The scope of the unit frequently gets decided around a cluster of activities and a culminating project. The realities of the school day and calendar will figure prominently into decisions about time.

After thinking through the purpose of a PBL unit and sketching out major activities, the teacher group develops the entry event, an initial activity, which provides the basis for student curiosity and questioning. As students are introduced to the focus of the PBL unit within the entry event, the teacher prompts students to propose a driving question. It is useful for the planning group to think through a possible list of questions from students. To force a driving question is to undercut the potential of PBL and student buy-in for the problem-based inquiry. The teacher's role first involves guiding students to talk about a topic and respond to prompting questions. Out of this discussion students generate a driving question that motivates them to answer or solve or design.

After drafting the schedule and scope of activities, a materials list can be developed. Each group member can be assigned to develop a specific set. Materials must include clear instructions to both teachers and students, and clear explanations about how students will be assessed. PBL requires that teachers think through in advance checklists and rubrics for assessing a range of student performance across multiple categories.

Managing a PBL Unit

PBL planning must also address how the unit will be managed during teaching. One set of decisions involves group work and giving students written and clear instructions and expectations. One suggestion for older students is to develop a PBL work agreement, which helps students to see how cooperative work is negotiated. A valuable PBL activity is to discuss early on what cooperative work entails for both individuals and the overall group. Prior practice with cooperative learning helps the classroom to get up to speed with PBL. A list of tasks specifying rationales (i.e., "why do this?"), explanations, expectations, and deadlines will help students track their progress, develop time-management skills, and see the big picture of their inquiry and results.

Another project management/teaching decision addresses formative evaluation of student work. Informal assessment, which occurs from observing, coaching and prompting, is determined up front. Teaching shifts from teacher-led presentation and solo student activity to listening and providing feedback as students engage in near-authentic activity, related as close as possible to the nature of the content. Benchmark reviews and critiques might be part of the overall assessment plan, and these give students opportunities to share what they have learned and voice their concerns. These formative reviews should be clear as to when they occur and what is being assessed, including knowledge, concepts, skills, and social learning.

Time management is another project management decision. Initially, teachers tend to over schedule activities and underestimate the time necessary for student inquiry and presentation of findings. Teachers should discuss how time is spent in PBL activities across the unit. Planning in some "slack time" enables teachers to adjust activities across the school day and week, as needed.

Evaluating Students and Teachers in PBL Units

PBL units, based on their complexity but also the richness of the student engagement, require both student and teacher to take reflective action, engage in periodic talk out-louds or "temperature checks," and to then revise the activity as necessary to accomplish the project's learning goals. Student projects can be evaluated using checklists or rubrics to assess student performance across performance categories. One challenge for PBL teaching is the need to provide assessment options that match the nature of the activity. Sources of student performance data can include teacher observations, student product and performance rubrics, tests and quizzes, as well as feedback from peers and other adults.

Scheduling time to de-brief gives all participants an opportunity to voice reactions and concerns, feedback that contributes to improvements for future teaching. Project debriefs can range from a simple talk-aloud and written comments to more elaborate celebrations of student projects in the classroom and school building. These memorable events contribute significantly to future learning and motivation, as well as to overall school climate.

Teachers who have invested time in designing and co-teaching PBL units also need to conduct self-evaluations of their work. A question sheet can facilitate reporting out to other teachers and administrators. Archived work allows teachers to demonstrate examples of student products. As classroom space is always an issue, archived work may take the form of digital media. The documentation of student activities by selected students who are motivated to learn media skills is another way that students can learn and also produce records of PBL activity.

MOTIVATING STUDENTS AND DEVELOPING SELF-REGULATION SKILLS WITH PBL

Driscoll (2005) suggests helping teachers by answering two questions: how do we motivate students, and how do we help them develop skills to manage their own learning? Without addressing the second question, developing self-regulation skills, a teacher continually faces the first question. This section answers these questions by discussing how PBL taps human curiosity, and develops self-regulation skills, and I draw upon Keller's (1987) four conditions for motivation within an instructional sequence.

Nurturing Human Motivation

Humans are naturally motivated to satisfy basic needs, such as physiological and safety needs, and are curious and drawn to tasks and situations of interest, including complex problem-solving situations (Keller, 1987). Children love to set their own goals and are motivated to self-assess their behavior and re-adjust (Bandura, 1997). PBL gives students a means to engage their natural curiosity and to engage in problem solving. In classroom settings, however, students need assistance in setting learning goals (competency improvements), as opposed to just performance goals (acceptance or avoidance), and managing their time to achieve those goals (Driscoll, 2005). PBL activities provide structure to help students learn these skills.

In addition to physical needs, curiosity, and attraction to problem solving, students' motivations to learn are influenced by two other factors, which can be nurtured over time: self-efficacy, or beliefs in their abilities to learn, and their expectations (Bandura, 1997; see Marchand & Schraw, this volume). Thus, students' beliefs lead to decisions about the level of effort needed and what actions they will take to achieve an outcome. These actions will depend on students' beliefs in physical effects, social effects, and internal judgments of behavior. A teacher can observe these beliefs indirectly through students' behaviors. Bandura (1997) suggested four sources from which students influence their self-efficacy beliefs, including: (1) past experience on a task; (2) expert or peer modeling of a task; (3) encouragement; and (4) personal instincts. As students are not always capable of integrating these sources, teachers have opportunities to provide assistance. These four sources can be discussed during PBL unit planning, implementation, and evaluation. PBL helps teachers to learn more about individual students and how they perform based on these four sources of students' self-efficacy beliefs.

How then to build on the natural motivations of students in PBL? Driscoll (2005) suggests two factors, the first of which is being aware of student expectations. Students have expectations about what will happen in the classroom in terms of their abilities and rewards for performance. Customary expectations as to what constitutes "school" will be challenged in PBL units, as the roles of teacher and student change, and the expectations of students to perform individually and in groups will need to be re-negotiated. Students' self-efficacy beliefs will also be influenced by the degree of success or failure in applying new skills. Teachers remain involved in whether or not rewards contribute to student success, but they know that it is not necessary to reward students for activity that they already find interesting. Rewards have to be integral to how the task itself is performed, not just in completing an assignment (Bates, 1979). Another value of PBL is the potential that the process of inquiry and the products of inquiry become sources for motivation. In addition, public praise, if warranted, provides a benefit to overall motivation (Keller, 1987). The power of social influence remains useful to help teachers motivate students within and across groups (Bandura, 1997).

In addition to expectancies, a second factor to develop student motivation is being aware of how students credit or blame their performance, an idea informed by attribution theory. Weiner (1992) organized these causes of success or failures along three dimensions: internal versus external; stable versus unstable; and controllable versus uncontrollable. Any student statement about an assignment can be evaluated along these three dimensions. The classic comment that "I don't like math," for example, can be characterized as internal, stable, and uncontrollable.

Internal factors include ability, effort, health, and mood, while external factors include attitudes and actions of peer or the teacher, current events, and task complexity, which will come into play within any PBL activity. Stability addresses how a factor changes over time. One aspect of stability is familiarity with how the school day is spent during PBL, a stability that develops over time. Students view ability as uncontrollable but ability is viewed in attribution theory as a stable factor, while mood or luck are regarded as unstable. Controllability is a factor that characterizes how a student controls an outcome through effort or study skills, for example. Many features of school appear as uncontrollable to students, such as task complexity, teacher expectations, school events, or health. Carefully structured PBL activities can help to address the complexity of inquiry, working together, and taking responsibility for findings and presentation of those findings. A useful teacher exercise is to develop a success/failure grid listing these three dimensions (internal/external, stable/unstable, controllable/uncontrollable) and record their beliefs on student differences across the dimensions.

Developing Academic Self-Regulation Skills

In educational psychology, self-regulation identifies the degree to which students control, monitor, and evaluate their learning. Zimmerman (1994) proposed a conceptual approach that explained academic self-regulation as students needing goals, self-efficacy beliefs, attributions for success, and strategies. Strategies can include self-monitoring, self-judging, decision-making, and designing the learning environment.

Zimmerman's three-phase cycle of self-regulation first involves student planning. Teachers can help students organize PBL inquiry as well as study skill strategies, although older students can sometimes self-organize with teacher feedback. During the second phase—the actual performance—self-monitoring skills require an ongoing cycle of observing one's performance, comparing the performance to an internal or external goal, and adjusting actions to meet or even exceed the goal or standard (Bandura, 1997). Teacher observations and benchmark assessment can help students during this phase. The final phase for self-regulation is reflection where students assign credit or blame, and make decisions on areas they can control. Overall, teachers can support this three-stage cycle in PBL units by sharing control with students, providing them with opportunities to set their own goals and ways to reach those goals, and reflecting alongside students (Driscoll, 2005).

Keller's (1987) ARCS motivational model also provides a sequence for instruction. Four conditions for motivation, as conceptualized by Keller, are attention, relevance, confidence, and satisfaction. These conditions can be sequenced by the teacher. Teachers first attempt to gain students' *attention*, which requires knowing one's learners, an ongoing process by most teachers. *Relevance* connects academic work with the students' world and interests of most immediate curiosity and concern. Keller suggests three strategies for *building confidence*, the third condition and phase for building motivation. First, provide students with clear expectations and task structure. Second, provide students with opportunities for success in sufficiently challenging tasks. Third, give students some choice in tasks when feasible and guide them in helping them become more aware of how they learn, and provide strategies for students to monitor, control, and evaluate. All three confidence-building strategies are essential features of PBL—clear expectations/task structure, challenging tasks, and student choice where possible. In the fourth condition and step for developing motivation, *generating satisfaction* has students applying what they know so that learning has a purpose. PBL inquiry emanates from students' desire to solve a problem or design a solution. Foundational skills are applied to student-relevant and purposeful activity. Even component skills can be motivating if a larger, external goal is present as well as benchmark opportunities to self-assess and share socially. Keller suggests that teachers develop an audience profile using the ARCS conditions to answer the question "Who are the students?" Such an exercise can help teachers rate the degree to which PBL activities address each motivational condition.

EXPERIENCING MOTIVATIONAL THEORIES THROUGH PBL

PBL College Course for Pre-Service Teachers

The best way to learn PBL, of course, is to design, teach, and evaluate actual units. A semester-long PBL course will be outlined, although the sequence can be adapted to a professional development series. My online deliveries of a college PBL course have included as many as 50 pre-service teachers. A total of 28 PBL units were designed, taught, and evaluated involving 35 public school teachers in 19 schools. The pre-service teachers were in their last semester of a five-year, dual-degree teacher education program using a Professional Development School (PDS) model. The teacher candidates observed, tutored, and taught for over 1,000 hours in public schools over three years. Knowing their students and having tried out numerous classroom strategies enabled these pre-service teachers to implement PBL—a relatively complicated form of teaching—with their host teachers. The course, organized over a 4-month PBL cycle, included the following features:

- *Month 1:* Pre-service teachers and host teachers designed a minimum of a week-long unit (3–5 lessons) using a unit structure, which followed state PBL guidelines. The host teacher, a PBL-trained teacher, and the course instructor assessed the unit using a rubric provided by the state department of education. Unit design earned 40% of the course grade.
- *Month 2:* One or more pre-service teachers and host teachers co-taught the unit, along with any specialized educator (e.g., math specialist, special education teacher). The host teacher and PBL-experienced teachers assessed the teaching using a modified rubric developed by the state's department of education. Unit teaching earned 40% of the grade.
- *Month 3:* Each group of pre-service teachers developed a professional development event to report out the PBL experience. Thus, pre-service teachers learned how to create and deliver a professional development activity. A form was used to record feedback. The event earned 10% of the course grade.
- *Month 4:* Based on the above feedback, unit materials were revised and delivered to the public school educators for their use. The revised unit earned 10% of the course grade.

In summary, pre-service teachers were given the same PBL requirements as expected for teachers who might be submitting the units to the state department of education for online publication. The percentages assigned for the four activities were determined from meetings with classroom teachers.

Analysis of designed and taught units identified several key areas of improvement, and findings, which are supported by a state-wide study of PBL use (White & Smith, 2010). PBL units required clearer project guidelines and rubrics. Peer and self-assessment opportunities were new for some teachers, so that practice in the use of these instruments is needed. The challenge for the PBL teacher is to pay attention to students' learning in new ways, and learn how to adjust and provide appropriate feedback during the unit.

Pre-service teachers underestimated the time needed for student inquiry and presentations. Many projects required more time for activities. Pre-service teachers learned that a PBL lesson might need more than one day to complete. Teachers learned how to coordinate and assign planning activities, as well as develop materials and organize classrooms. Unit plans required more attention to the effective use of time by both teacher and students. After having taught or having observed PBL units, experienced teachers responded favorably to this form of teaching. Some teachers expressed reservations about unit development time, although several reported that splitting the responsibilities makes it possible to develop units. A long-term benefit cited by teachers was developing an inventory of tested units for future use.

Experiencing PBL in an Educational Psychology Course

Another option for experiencing PBL is to have pre-service teachers who are enrolled in an educational psychology course develop a PBL activity during the course, and then try it out in a practicum setting. The learning task needs to incorporate key PBL features. A school-based lesson should include learning outcomes (content, skills, social learning) and provide an activity sequence that includes entry event, driving question, and student inquiry. If motivational theories are the focus in the course, then principles from the theories can be identified in the lesson. An observation form with items on engagement, student learning outcomes, and suggestions for improvements will provide pre-service teachers with practice at gathering data. The completed forms can be used to report out in the educational psychology course the results of the teaching, and also describe how motivational theories can be understood and/or applied.

Motivation within Motivating Tasks

PBL taps children's natural curiosity and desire to direct their own learning, particularly if activity is initially focused around their interests. Effective PBL requires sharing of control, providing clear expectations to behavior and task performance, and giving students some say in the direction of inquiry, as opposed to teacher-directed approaches. Most teachers know that one motivational strategy by itself is almost always insufficient to accomplish "X" in the classroom. "X" could mean improved positive achievement-related beliefs, intrinsic motivation to perform a task, or content-specific learning outcomes. Rather, a comprehensive approach that addresses rewards, choice, task structure and complexity, and assessment, among other issues, is needed. PBL gives teachers a test bed where the interrelated effects of these decisions can be considered for motivation and student learning.

A PBL project must remain focused on important knowledge and skills, as many states have adopted Common Core standards and twenty-first century skills, including critical thinking/problem solving, collaboration, and communication. PBL and other forms of inquiry may become essential strategies for students to demonstrate mastery in new assessment tests (Tal, Krajcik, & Blumenfeld, 2006). PBL provides a learning environment where self-direction skills can be developed and provide what some call "deep learning" (Martinez & McGrath, 2014). The key teaching strategy is in-depth inquiry or "problematizing" content by students who define problems and investigate claims and explanations (Barron & Darling-Hammond, 2008). Students engage in a rigorous, extended process of asking questions, using resources, developing answers, and designing options. The first critical activity, the entry event, gives students an opportunity to pose one or more driving question, see the need for further research, and then apply knowledge and skills. PBL requires careful attention to observing how students work and providing practice at learning how to use their time and work effectively with others. Self-regulation skills are embedded in PBL projects as students learn to use feedback to consider revisions on draft work leading to high quality products, and to think about what and how they are learning.

PBL implemented across the school year will ultimately require changes in how the school day is spent. A first step is to give teachers time, resources, and support from the principal. A second step is focused professional development with grade level teachers who pay careful attention to correctly implementing PBL. The approach provides a context for discussing how theories of motivation explain and inform student engagement and achievement. Or said in another way, motivating teachers to better understand the principles extracted from theories of motivation is best accomplished in schools by using an instructional approach, PBL, where student motivation and performance can be directly experienced.

REFERENCES

Bandura, A. (1997). *Self-efficacy: The exercise of control.* New York, NY: W. H. Freeman.

Barron, B., & Darling-Hammond, L. (2008). How can we teach for meaningful learning? In L. Darling-Hammond, B. Barron, P. D. Pearson, A. H. Schoenfeld, E. K. Stage, T. D. Zimmerman, G. N. Cervetti, & J. L. Tilson (Eds.). *Powerful learning: What we know about teaching for understanding* (pp. 11–70). San Francisco, CA: Jossey-Bass.

Bates, J. A. (1979). Extrinsic reward and intrinsic motivation: A review with implications for the classroom. *Review of Educational Research, 49,* 557–576.

Buck Institute for Education (BIE). (2010). *PBL in the elementary grades.* Novato, CA: Bucks Institute for Education.

Driscoll, M. P. (2005). *Psychology of learning for instruction* (3rd ed). Boston, MA: Pearson.

Keller, J. M. (1987). Development and use of the ARCS model of motivational design. *Journal of Instructional Development, 10*(3), 2–10.

Larmer, J. (2009). *PBL starter kit.* Novato, CA: Bucks Institute for Education.

Marchand, G. W., & Schraw, G. (this volume). Finding common ground when teaching motivation: Examples from teaching self-efficacy and self-determination theory. In M C. Smith & N. DeFrates-Densch (Eds.), *Challenges and innovations in teaching and learning educational psychology.* Greenwich, CT: Information Age Publishing.

Martinez, M., & McGrath, D. (2014). *Deeper learning: How eight innovative public schools are transforming education in the twenty-first century.* New York, NY: New Press.

Tal, T., Krajcik, J. S., & Blumenfeld, P. C. (2006). Urban schools' teachers enacting project-based science. *Journal of Research in Science Teaching, 43*(7), 722–745.

Weiner, B. (1992). *Human motivation: Metaphors, theories, and research.* Thousand Oaks, CA: Sage.

White, L., & Smith, D. L. (2010). *Project-based learning (PBL) in West Virginia: Efficacy of professional development delivery mode.* Charleston: West Virginia Department of Education.

Zimmerman, B. J. (1994). Dimensions of academic self-regulation: A conceptual framework for education. In D. H. Schunk & B. J. Zimmerman (Eds.), *Self-regulation of learning and performance: Issues and educational applications* (pp. 3–21). Hillsdale, NJ: Lawrence Erlbaum Associates.

SECTION III

TEACHING HUMAN DEVELOPMENT FOR TEACHERS

CHAPTER 17

TEACHING CHILD DEVELOPMENT TO PROSPECTIVE EDUCATORS

Denise H. Daniels
California Polytechnic State University, San Luis Obispo

"To better understand the connections between developmental theories and research and educational practice" is one lofty objective of courses in child development and educational psychology for undergraduate and graduate students. Many of the students in these courses are prospective or practicing teachers. Our hope is that students who make these connections will value contemporary developmental theories and research as well as advocate for and implement educational practices stemming from this work. In this chapter, I will highlight challenges in moving undergraduate students toward this goal and a few approaches that appear promising.

I encountered some challenges myself as an undergraduate majoring in developmental psychology. I loved my studies and was quite passionate (and idealistic) about applying my learning to improve the lives of children, particularly in early childhood programs where I worked part-time. However, I sensed that what I was learning at the university was disconnected from practices observed in the "real" world. For example, I worked

Challenges and Innovations in Educational Psychology Teaching and Learning, pages 219–231
Copyright © 2016 by Information Age Publishing
All rights of reproduction in any form reserved.

in a preschool/child care program with credentialed teachers who used traditional instructional methods. The children were often listless and bored (and so was I) and sometimes misbehaved during "lesson time" in these classrooms, but demonstrated positive interactions and enthusiasm during playground and free-play periods. One teacher stood out in her ability to engage children in interesting learning experiences throughout the day, using stories, drama, singing, manipulative activities, and field trips; she was considered "gifted" by the other teachers. I found it puzzling that her effectiveness with children was attributed to personal qualities rather than her unique background in child development and education (and Montessori training). I also realized that my background in developmental psychology was critical but insufficient—it had helped me to develop skills for observing and listening to children, and a keen sensitivity to their emotional needs and influences on their behavior, but it did not help me provide valuable learning experiences for them. This insight led me to appreciate the need for connecting developmental science to practice, inspired my pursuit of graduate studies, and paved my professional career (e.g., as a program administrator, researcher, professor, textbook author). Experiences in these diverse roles further supported my conviction that educators need to study, discuss, and observe connections between developmental theories and research and school practices (e.g., Daniels & Clarkson, 2010; Meece & Daniels, 2008).

SIGNIFICANCE

A number of professional organizations have recently called for integrating developmental sciences knowledge in the preparation of educators. For example, the National Council for Accreditation of Teacher Education (NCATE) created a National Expert Panel on *Increasing the Application of Knowledge about Child and Adolescent Development and Learning in Educator Preparation* in 2008. As part of this effort, Pianta, Hitz, and West (2010) argued that educators need access to new knowledge about child and adolescent development, but that little of this knowledge is reflected in educator preparation programs. Similarly, the American Psychological Association's (APA) Coalition for Psychology in Schools and Education (CPSE) called for increased attention to communicating psychological science (including developmental science) in ways that are accessible to teachers (e.g., Rollin, Subotnik, Bassford, & Smulson, 2008).

This call, although louder today, is not new. William James (1899/1916) proposed that fundamental conceptions of psychology were important for the teacher. "Child study enthusiasts," especially, could help teachers understand the developmental processes of their pupils (pp. 11–12). Although James warned that psychological knowledge could not always be used to prescribe specific instructional strategies (because many options would be consistent with psychological principles), it could prevent teachers from selecting "mistaken" or ineffective methods (p. 11). Today, research has confirmed that teachers with a developmental background implement educational practices that support children's academic and social learning and outcomes (NCATE, 2010). And there is a wealth of research on child and adolescent development and schooling available (e.g., Meece & Schaefer, 2010).

A development background includes the study of constructivist and social-constructivist theories of development and learning, originating from Piaget and Vygotsky, and integrating current research on cognitive development (e.g., neo-Vygotskian, neuro-constructivist). A view of learning as a constructive process is one basis for establishing a "developmental philosophy of education" (Elkind, 1991, p. 93). Developmentalists attempt to employ developmentally appropriate practices (DAP) or match learning activities to individuals' emerging mental abilities and understandings of content. Contemporary developmental perspectives also embrace practices suggested by research on motivation, interpersonal relationships, and other areas related to learning and development in educational settings (e.g., Anderson et al., 1995). For example, the American Psychological Association's Learner-Centered Task Force acknowledged research in four major domains as particularly relevant for understanding learning and learners in school: developmental and social, cognitive and metacognitive, motivational and affective, and individual differences (see McCombs, 2010 for a review). Learner-centered practices (LCPs) have been identified and examined within each of these domains, and numerous studies have supported their positive influences on student motivation and learning across grade levels.

A developmental background also includes the study of bio-ecological models of development (e.g., Bronfenbrenner & Morris, 1998). For example, developmental and educational psychologists have adapted Bronfenbrenner's model to explain how children's participation in a dynamic network of relationships (e.g., within home, school, peer groups, neighborhoods) influences their adjustment and learning during major school transitions. From an ecological perspective, teachers are better able to create conditions for meaningful interactions with children if they enjoy positive relationships with their parents and previous teachers. Successful practices and school reform efforts based on these models, such as Comer's (2010) School Development Program, demonstrate the value of embracing and applying developmental or biopsychosocial perspectives. Yet, such applications are not widespread in U.S. schools, partly due to the lack of emphasis on and integration of developmental studies in teacher preparation programs (NCATE, 2010). Like other developmentalists, I believe that solving this problem will eventually reduce the number of students who are disengaged from learning in school (e.g., Meece & Schaefer, 2010) and face mental health and behavioral problems, as well as increase academic performance and well-being. It is not enough, however, to simply require a few additional courses; we must also acknowledge resistance to methods suggested from contemporary developmental or psychological principles in general, before much progress will be made (e.g., McCombs, 2010).

CHALLENGES IN TEACHING CHILD DEVELOPMENT

What are the sources of some "mistaken" methods (using James' term) in today's classrooms? In an earlier *Handbook on Development and Education,* Olson and Bruner (1996) argued that many educational practices are based on teachers' "folk psychologies"—their naïve beliefs about children, learning, and knowledge—rather than developmental research and theory (p. 10). Simply passing a course in child development or developmental psychology may not be sufficient to overcome such beliefs. Dixon (2003) expressed the inherent difficulties in an introduction to a child development textbook, "...students have to overcome the 'common sense' hurdle. Many people come to a child psychology course confident in their expectation the course will confirm what they already know...The obstacle presents itself when many findings in child psychology contradict commonsense beliefs and child-rearing folklore" (p. 2). Too often, when students (e.g., prospective teachers) confront such inconsistencies, they reject developmental science as helpful and return to their own folk psychologies or traditional beliefs about learners and learning that do not take advantage of new knowledge in the field.

For example, in our review of research on teacher beliefs a decade ago, my colleague, Lee Shumow, and I noted that many educators hold fixed views of children's intellectual abilities; some hold extreme maturationist or behaviorist views; and others believe family circumstances ultimately determine children's adjustment and achievement. Each of these views contradicts contemporary psychological perspectives and findings and is associated with use of less optimal educational practices (e.g., hands-off, over-controlling) (Daniels & Shumow, 2003). Furthermore, researchers and teacher educators have found such beliefs to be highly resistant to change, and efforts to help college students develop more sophisticated developmental perspectives often show disappointing results (e.g., McDevitt & Ormond, 2008).

Even when students are open to new insights from contemporary developmental perspectives, they do not always see the relevance for educational practices today. Thus, the second challenge in teaching a course on development and education is determining how to illuminate connections between developmental theory, research, and practice. Helping students to see such connections is difficult for several reasons. One reason is that many developmental theories and studies do not have clear implications for educational practice, or if they do, the connections have not been made explicit. Another reason is that many students have not experienced or observed developmentally appropriate or responsive educational practices (particularly in the upper grades) and have difficulty envisioning how they can be implemented.

This chapter focuses on ways to challenge the underlying beliefs and assumptions that may lead students (especially prospective educators) to disregard the value of developmental theories and research for teaching children. Attention is also given to how to help students see the links between contemporary developmental perspectives and educational practices that promote children's learning and well-being in schools today.

PROMISING PRACTICES

Educational and developmental psychologists have noted several promising practices for fostering learning about development and appropriate educational practices. For example, McCombs and her colleagues (2010) used surveys to encourage teachers to reflect on their beliefs about learners and learning in professional development programs as a strategy to promote learner-centered practices. McDevitt and Ormond (2008) suggested use of disequilibrium-producing experiences and other instructional strategies to foster conceptual change about child development in prospective teachers. My former doctoral students and I advocated for the use of case studies to foster complex developmental understandings (e.g., Daniels, Kalkman, De-Frates-Densch, & Kirchen, 2000). Such practices are consistent with those shared by other developmental educators.

The promising practices described below have been implemented in several sections of an upper-division undergraduate course on development and education required for child development majors and minors.

The Students

Students typically enroll in this course their sophomore or junior year after completing an introductory developmental psychology or child development course. Half or more of the students intend to become teachers at the preschool, elementary, or middle school level; other students are interested in a variety of professional roles related to work with children and youth (e.g., special educators, school counselors, coaches, child psychologists, social workers). Students are mostly young, female, "traditional" college students (entered college immediately after high school), representing a variety of ethnic groups (a majority are Caucasian). Generally, 35–45 students enroll in the course per quarter.

The Course Topics

In general, the course highlights developmental theories and current research pertinent for the schooling of children from preschool through middle school. The course begins (and ends) with a brief overview of ecological models of development, focusing on the connections between school, home, and community. Topics include applications of developmental theories and current research in cognitive and socioemotional domains, with special attention to employing constructivist practices, supporting students' motivation to learn, enhancing positive relationships (teacher-student, teacher-parent, peer), and fostering positive adjustment during school transitions. Students are also introduced to professional organizations, such as the National Association of the Education of Young Children (NAEYC) and the Association for Middle Level Education (AMLE), and school reform models (e.g., Comer's School Development Program) that endorse developmental perspectives and practices.

The General Approach

My general approach to overcoming the obstacles presented above is to first reveal students' beliefs about appropriate educational practices for children and young adolescents (or about learners and learning). The second step is to provide readings, documentaries (cases), discussion activities, and evidence from research throughout the course either intended to challenge students' support of practices considered developmentally inappropriate or instill stronger support for practices based on contemporary developmental perspectives. The third step is to provide opportunities for students to reflect on their thinking about children's development and learning and the implications for education. I will elaborate on each of the three steps in subsequent sections.

It is important to note that creating a classroom climate that encourages respect for different ideas is necessary for students to reconsider their prior assumptions. My hope is that students will make small changes toward endorsing a more complex developmental perspective, and see the relevance of developmental theory and research for educational practices, by the end of the course.

Revealing Students' Views

On the first day of class, before instruction begins, I ask all students to complete surveys of their views of appropriate and inappropriate educational practices for children and youth. I explain that the purpose of completing the surveys is to find out about their current views and that I will return their surveys at the end of class so that they can note any changes in their responses. I assure students that these are informal surveys, not used for research purposes, and that I will not evaluate their responses.

I select items from several surveys for this purpose, such as the Primary Teacher Questionnaire (Smith, 1993) and the Teacher Learner-Centered Beliefs Survey (e.g., McCombs & Miller, 2007). (Other surveys are available.) These surveys include items endorsing DAP and traditional, teacher-centered practices. Students generally complete the items in 10–15 minutes.

I scan the responses briefly at the beginning of the quarter (without attending to students' names). Many students indicate that they are "unsure" about appropriate practices or are inconsistent in their responses (agree with DAP and traditional practices). For example, students might agree with statements such as "children should be allowed to use space flexibly to pursue a variety of learning activities alone or in small groups" and "instruction should consist mainly of reading groups, whole group activities, and seat work" Such inconsistency is not unusual among prospective teachers and other undergraduate students (e.g., Daniels & Shumow, 2003; McDevitt & Ormrod, 2008).

Challenging Students' Views

To challenge some common assumptions about children's development, and encourage reflection on the connection between views of development and education, I ask students to read books and articles and view videotapes on educational practices in other countries. I choose materials that offer some "surprises," make children's experiences in classrooms come alive, and make views of development explicit. For example, I have students read Catherine Lewis's (1995) classic book, *Educating Hearts and Minds*. They also watch videotapes and documentaries that depict different educational practices and developmental perspectives (e.g., *Preschool in Three Cultures, Children Full of Life*). Students engage in small group discussions afterward, responding to questions about how practices reflect different views of development.

Students also read real stories about life in classrooms in the United States. I choose books that describe children's development and experiences from multiple perspectives (children's, teachers, parents). For example,

I recently asked students to read Perlstein's (2003) book, *Not Much Just Chillin'*, which depicts the lives of students in middle school. In the past, I have required one of Vivian Paley's well-known books that depict experiences in kindergarten classrooms. Again, students are given opportunities to discuss their reactions to these stories in small groups. I also use brief cases of children in classrooms to stimulate further discussion, such as those portrayed in Duckworth's (2006) classic, *The Having of Wonderful Ideas and Other Essays on Teaching and Learning*, and in current materials accompanying textbooks on child development and educational psychology.

These stories and cases help students to confront their own assumptions about children's learning and development that often deter them from seeing and/or embracing practices consistent with contemporary developmental perspectives. For example, they often remark on how surprised they are that children (from preschool through the middle grades) are motivated and capable of managing their own learning experiences without constant monitoring, direct instruction, and rewards from teachers. These revelations allow them to see the value of constructivist educational practices based on cognitive developmental theories and research as well as contemporary motivational theories and approaches. Students also recognize the potential role that teachers can play in children's development in general.

Providing Support

Of course, we also want students to be persuaded by empirical research. I present research findings that demonstrate positive effects of educational practices associated with contemporary developmental perspectives on children's learning and well-being in a variety of ways. For example, studies of teacher-student relationships, home-school connections, collaborative learning environments, and other topics commonly included in development and education courses, are introduced in readings and lectures. Students also write a brief research report on one of these topics. In addition, students read about *how* such "evidence-based" practices are implemented in classrooms and schools (e.g., in articles from *Educational Psychology Annual Editions*) and see brief video clips depicting such practices. Sharing current examples is especially important to reduce the skepticism shared by many students concerning real opportunities to implement ideal practices in today's "accountability climate" inspired by the No Child Left Behind Act.

Importantly, students also investigate current examples illustrating how developmentally appropriate practices (DAP) are implemented. Another course assignment requires students to work together in small groups to prepare a brief (20 minutes) whole group presentation/instructional activity on a topic of their choice (listed on the syllabus). As part of the assignment, they are asked to illustrate concepts and ideas from the assigned readings by referring to live examples from interviews with teachers and/or children, video clips of classroom practices, or recommendations from professional organizations or experts in the field.

I provide several suggestions for appropriate sources and approve their plans in advance. For example, students focusing on the topic of teacher-student relations might report practices shared by a local teacher during an interview and show an expert (e.g., Robert Pianta) discussing related research on a video clip (e.g., from YouTube). After the students conduct their presentation/activity, I generally follow with a mini-lecture on developmental research and theory that relates to the topic, making connections to aspects of their presentation. Although the purpose of this assignment is to help *all* students in the class connect the readings on developmental theory and research to practices today, anecdotal evidence suggests (unsurprisingly) that the students who prepare the presentation/activity benefit most. The presenting students often report feeling excited about finding interesting examples that support research findings and helpful resources for practice.

Encouraging Reflection

During the last week of class, I return students' surveys that were completed on the first day. I show how the authors of the surveys characterize each item (as developmentally appropriate/learner-centered or traditional) in a table. Again, I emphasize that this is not research (they do not complete entire surveys), but an exercise to help them think about their responses and how they might have changed over the course of the quarter. I ask them to think about what changes they might make now on the survey and why, and to discuss their reasons with other students in small groups. Then I ask students to write brief reflections (1-page "quick writes") on how, or if, they would change some of their views about appropriate educational practices today.

I briefly examined students' reflections from two course sessions taught within the past two years ($n \sim 80$). The following themes emerged (in order of prevalence):

- *Understanding child and adolescent development is important for teaching.* Many students declared that they felt either "stronger" or "more confident" about their beliefs in the appropriateness of practices consistent with developmental perspectives. Several suggested that although they didn't change many of their responses, they understood better *why* they endorsed certain practices, and that they would be better able to explain or defend such practices (to parents) as well as more likely to implement them.

- A subgroup of students discovered that they were initially inconsistent in their support for DAP for children, but not for young adolescents. They now understood that DAP was equally important for youth and, if implemented, would likely lead to fewer problems with this age group as well as showing greater respect for them in general.

- *Teachers can share management (control) of the class with children.* Students often pointed to how the documentaries and readings on classroom practices in other countries convinced them that children (from the elementary grades on) were capable of directing their own learning at times. In particular, they believed that children could learn as much, or more, from engaging in small group work and project-based learning activities (with some teacher guidance) than in teacher-directed whole group instruction and seatwork. Some expressed that they no longer viewed such child-directed activities in the classroom as "chaotic," and felt more as if they could embrace constructivist educational practices (and hands-on, playful learning activities).

- *Grades and rewards are not always the best motivators.* Many students expressed that they could see how grades, rewards, and performance goals focused children on comparing themselves to others and might undermine mastery motivation, pursuit of challenge, and learning.

- *Children's socioemotional development is just as important as their cognitive development and academic learning in school.* Students noted that they were better able to see how children's academic learning was linked to their feelings about belonging in school (climate), relationships with teachers and peers (classmates), and social and emotional skills.

- *Children's home lives affect their school lives.* Several students stated that they "opened their eyes" to how the circumstances of children's lives at home (particularly those living in poverty) affected their behavior at school—that they should see children as individuals and not judge them (i.e., for misbehavior). Some expressed the importance of getting "troubled" children more involved and communicating with parents.

- *The purpose of school is not just to prepare children for the next grade.* Several students commented that they viewed the purpose of school more broadly (e.g., "teaching life lessons") after examining practices in different countries. This led some to support current school reform efforts in the United States.

- *It is important to question assumptions about development and learning.* A few students revealed that they were more "open-minded" and "flexible" in general after studying diverse educational practices, and were beginning to question some of their own (cultural) assumptions about the ways children learn and develop.

Although not reported in written reflections, some students also voiced in discussions that their responses to the surveys at the beginning of the quarter were inconsistent (e.g., "my answers were all over the place"), and suggested that they could provide a more accurate and coherent description of their beliefs about development and educational practices at the end of the course.

CONCLUSION

Students' self-reports (reflections) provide scanty evidence that use of these promising practices helped to foster greater support for contemporary developmental perspectives and practices. I would have preferred to see more widespread and dramatic shifts in the minds and hearts of students, but am pleased with the progress that they reported in a brief period of time (10 weeks).

Fortunately, I have opportunities to interact with many of these students in a culminating course during their senior year, and witness how their developmental perspectives have become more ingrained or sophisticated (for undergraduates) after additional coursework and internship experiences. This later course focuses on the role that developmental science plays in social policy and prevention programs for children and youth in settings such as schools ("prevention science"). It also includes a look at advocacy campaigns to promote such efforts (to offset students' discouragement when they encounter less-than-ideal programs). I am pleased that students who plan to become teachers have chosen to write papers (applying developmental research and theory to practice) on topics such as fostering parental involvement in school, encouraging collaborative or project-based learning, discouraging grade retention, and promoting engagement in learning. Other students have conducted projects explicitly advocating for DAP in school, and for developmental science courses in teacher preparation programs.

Occasionally, I am rewarded with the most convincing anecdotal evidence that efforts to employ promising practices pays off—when previous students become teachers, and teachers of teachers, who continue to pursue learning and implement practices consistent with contemporary views in the field of developmental and educational psychology.

REFERENCES

Anderson, L., Blumenfeld, P., Pintrich, P., Clark, D., Marx, R., & Peterson, P. (1995). Educational psychology for teachers: Reforming our courses, rethinking our roles. *Educational Psychologist, 30,* 143–157.

Bronfenbrenner, U., & Morris, P. (1998). The ecology of developmental processes. In W. Damon (Gen. Ed.) & R. Lerner (Vol. Ed.), *Handbook of child psychology:*

Vol. 1. Theoretical models of human development (pp. 993–1028). New York, NY: Wiley.

Comer, J. (2010). The Yale Child Study Center School Development Program. In J. Meece & J. Eccles (Eds.), *Handbook of research on schools, schooling, and human development* (pp. 419–433). New York, NY: Routledge.

Daniels, D., & Clarkson, P. (2010). *A developmental approach to educating young children*. Division 15 (Educational Psychology) of the APA and Corwin Press. Washington, DC: American Psychological Association.

Daniels, D., Kalkman, D., DeFrates-Densch, N., & Kirchen, D. (2000). Preservice teachers' explanations of child behavior and beliefs about educational practices: Effects of course experiences. *The Professional Educator, 22,* 27–37.

Daniels, D., & Shumow, L. (2003). Child development and classroom teaching: A review of the literature and implications for educating teachers. *Applied Developmental Psychology, 23,* 495–526.

Dixon, D. (2003). *Twenty studies that revolutionized child psychology.* Upper Saddle River, NJ: Prentice-Hall.

Duckworth, E. (2006). *The having of wonderful ideas and other essays on teaching and learning* (3rd ed.). New York, NY: Teachers College Press.

Elkind, D. (1991). Developmentally appropriate practice: Philosophical and practical implications. In B. Persky & L. H. Bolubchick (Eds.), *Early childhood education.* New York, NY: University Press.

James, W. (1899/1916). *Talks to teachers on psychology: And to students on some of life's ideals.* New York, NY: Holt. (Original work published 1899).

Lewis, C.C. (1995). *Educating hearts and minds: Reflections on Japanese preschool and elementary education.* New York, NY: Cambridge University Press.

McCombs, B. (2010). Learner-centered practices: Providing the context for positive learner development, motivation, and achievement. In J. Meece & J. Eccles (Eds.), *Handbook of research on schools, schooling, and human development* (pp. 60–74). New York, NY: Routledge.

McCombs, B., & Miller, L. (2007). *Learner-centered classroom practices and assessments: Maximizing student motivation, learning, and achievement.* Thousand Oaks, CA: Corwin Press.

McDevitt, T., & Ormrod, J. (2008). Fostering conceptual change about child development in prospective teachers and other college students. *Child Development Perspectives, 2,* 85–91.

Meece, J., & Daniels, D. (2008). *Child and adolescent development for educators* (3rd ed.), New York, NY: McGraw-Hill.

Meece, J., & Schaefer, V. (2010). Schools as a context of human development. In J. Meece & J. Eccles (Eds.), *Handbook of research on schools, schooling, and human development* (pp. 3–5). New York, NY: Routledge.

National Council for Accreditation of Teacher Education. (2010). *The road less traveled: How the developmental sciences can prepare educators to improve student achievement: Policy recommendations.* Washington, DC: Author.

Olson, D., & Bruner, J. (1996). Folk psychology and folk pedagogy. In D. Olson, & N. Torrance (Eds.), *Handbook of education and development: New models of learning, teaching, and schooling* (pp. 1–6). Malden, MA: Blackwell.

Perlstein, L. (2003). *Not much just chillin': The hidden lives of middle schoolers.* New York, NY: Ballantine Books.

Pianta, R., Hitz, R., & West, B. (2010). *Increasing the application of developmental sciences knowledge in educator preparation.* Washington, DC: National Council for Accreditation of Teacher Education (NCATE). Washington, DC: NCATE.

Rollin, S., Subotnik, R., Bassford, M., & Smulson, J. (2008). Bringing psychological science to the forefront of educational policy: Collaborative efforts of the American Psychological Association's Coalition for Psychology in the Schools and Education. *Psychology in the Schools, 45,* 194–205.

Smith, K. (1993). Development of the Primary Grades Teacher Questionnaire. *Journal of Educational Research, 87,* 23–29.

CHAPTER 18

TEACHING COGNITIVE DEVELOPMENT

Catherine M. Bohn-Gettler
College of Saint Benedict–Saint John's University

Imagine that a first grade teacher asks her students to write several paragraphs defining the scientific concept of density and describing how density affects whether objects will sink or float. Prior to this task, students read a textbook chapter providing a definition and several examples. Will the students be successful in completing this task? What challenges will they face? How can the teacher improve the lesson to be developmentally appropriate?

Understanding the development of thinking and reasoning capacities, referred to as cognitive development, is vital for individuals in many professions—especially those in educational settings. In the example, the writing assignment does not align with the cognitive and literacy skills of six- and seven-year-old children and, hence, the students and teacher are likely to become frustrated. First, early primary children are still learning basic reading skills such as decoding. Although they may be able to write a sentence or possibly a short passage, writing several paragraphs of scientific expository text is not a developmentally appropriate task (National Early Literacy Panel, 2008). Second, primary students learn more effectively when utilizing concrete manipulatives. The lesson would better fit the students'

Challenges and Innovations in Educational Psychology Teaching and Learning, pages 233–243
Copyright © 2016 by Information Age Publishing

needs if they constructed an understanding of density by experimenting with whether objects of varying densities float or sink. Third, first graders' mental capacities and reasoning skills are still developing. For example, the amount of information they can mentally process at once is more limited when compared to older children (Munakata, 2006). Teachers may need to provide extra memory supports, such as word walls or breaking tasks down into smaller parts, to help children reason through various problems. This example serves to demonstrate how basic knowledge of cognitive development can assist educators with developing age-appropriate lessons to help students learn and achieve.

The topic of cognitive development is presented to students enrolled in both undergraduate and graduate courses that examine child and lifespan development. It can also be included in coursework focusing on learning theories and strategies, and in introductory psychology classes. The composition of students often includes teacher education and psychology candidates, as well as students from fields such as health professions, social work, and the social sciences. At the graduate level, many candidates are training to become counselors, clinicians, educational and school psychologists, educational leaders, health professionals, and more. The variety of students learning about cognitive development is indicative of its applicability for a wide array of individuals in learning and service settings.

The major topics of cognitive development are often broken down into two or three parts. The first major topic typically covers Piaget's account of the development of children's reasoning skills. The second major topic often focuses on Vygotsky's sociohistorical theory, which describes the social influences of learning and the zone of proximal development (Pressley & McCormick, 2007). Together, Piagetian, neo-Piagetian, and Vygotskian theories provide a well-organized framework for how cognition changes with age. These theories have been taught for decades, and a variety of teaching and learning techniques have been developed to enhance students' learning.

The third major topic typically covered in human development courses, and the focus of this chapter, is information-processing theories (IPTs) of development. IPTs consider the human mind to operate much like a computer: Information is inputted into memory via *encoding*. Once it is *processed*, it has the potential to be *stored* in, and later *retrieved* from, memory. Three general "hardware" components exist in this system: Information is brought into memory through the *sensory register* and then processed in *short-term* or *working memory*, which has a limited capacity. Ultimately, adequately processed information can be stored in *long-term memory*. The storage of this knowledge is represented as a network of concepts linked by semantic associations (Mayer, 2008).

IPTs are not technically developmental theories because they do not describe how humans change over time. However, IPTs have stimulated much developmental research, meriting their inclusion in the study of human development. When teaching how IPTs apply to development, a number of topics are typically covered, including the development of how information is learned, stored, and remembered, and attention and habituation, memory and problem solving strategies, theory of mind, and more. Therefore, IPTs provide a theme for understanding developmental changes in many cognitive capabilities.

SIGNIFICANCE OF TEACHING INFORMATION-PROCESSING THEORIES OF DEVELOPMENT

IPTs of development integrate the psychological concepts of how individuals learn information with how the cognitive system works and, therefore, provide a framework for examining memory, learning, and other aspects of developmental change. IPTs also help students understand their own learning and how to improve it (i.e., metacognition). Finally, because IPTs provide practitioners with an understanding of how students learn and apply cognitive developmental concepts directly to educational settings, they enable practitioners to implement effective, developmentally appropriate practices.

There are two core topics to be learned in IPTs. The first involves the "hardware" components of the information-processing system (i.e., the sensory register, short-term memory, and long-term memory), how information flows through these systems via encoding, processing, storage, and retrieval, and how these processes are guided by executive controls (Mayer, 2008). Long-term memory is conceived of as a semantic network of knowledge, and elaborating upon and making connections between concepts strengthens learning and memory (Pressley & McCormick, 2007).

The hardware and processing components of the information-processing system provide a framework for understanding the second core topic: developmental trends in information processing. A core assumption of many IPTs is that children are active in constructing knowledge and modifying their thinking (Munakata, 2006). Cognitive development is perceived as increases in various skills and capacities related to the information-processing system. Although a wide a wide array of skills are described as improving with age, these developing capacities do not necessarily fit into "neat" stages of growth (e.g., Pressley & McCormick, 2007).

When considering the hardware of the information-processing system, a critical developmental change is that short-term memory capacities increase with age. However, developmental improvements may arise for a number of reasons, such as neurological development, improved processing speed and efficiency, learning more effective rehearsal strategies, ever-increasing prior knowledge, and the development of inhibition skills to ignore irrelevant and interfering information.

Developmental textbooks also cover a range of sub-theories and research regarding how specific information-processing skills develop. These include, but are not limited to, the development of attention and habituation, how children overcome limits in short-term memory capacities, problem solving, and memory strategies to facilitate encoding and retrieval. Several strategies include different rehearsal methods, categorization and classification, elaboration, planning, and monitoring. Children's development of theory of mind and perspective taking skills are also covered. Finally, other executive functioning skills, such as cognitive self-regulation, metacognition, and more, are included.

While there are many topics to be studied, it is important for students to learn about IPTs for at least two reasons. First, those training to work in educational settings will benefit by obtaining a deeper understanding of learning and how it develops, and then can (hopefully) translate this information into effective practice. Second, understanding IPTs and development can help students analyze their own learning strategies and, perhaps, improve their own comprehension and retention.

CHALLENGES IN TEACHING INFORMATION-PROCESSING THEORIES OF DEVELOPMENT

A core challenge in teaching IPTs is finding ways to integrate the numerous theories, sub-theories, and developmental principles. Because of the many theories and perspectives, students struggle to develop a holistic understanding and coherent schema of cognitive development. This is especially problematic when students are expected to translate such knowledge into applied settings. The complexity of this topic leads to at least three other important challenges when teaching, learning, and applying IPTs of development.

The first challenge is that IPTs are not truly developmental theories. Rather, they are general processing theories that provide a framework for understanding age-related changes in how children think and process information, thus deepening our understanding of various stage theories of cognitive development (e.g., Piaget's theory). IPTs present a complex picture of varying developmental findings that address different components of the system. Because so many specific processes are described with little integration, it is challenging for students to connect the various findings and, thereby, understand the development of information-processing skills as a whole. Cognitive theory stipulates that organized knowledge schemas tend to be more coherent and better remembered. Therefore, if students fail to make the necessary connections to build a coherent schema of development, they will struggle when attempting to retain and apply such principles.

This leads to a second challenge: Encouraging students to make connections between concepts is an elaborative process that requires deep thinking. However, many students believe that the development of cognitive processes is simply "common sense." For example, students may think that because they have been in learning situations, and because they participated in their own development, they therefore understand the complexities of learning and cognitive development (Buehl & Fives, 2011). This misconception can lead students to process information in a superficial manner such that they will not think deeply enough to elaborate and make connections.

It is ironic that many students utilize superficial processing when learning about cognitive development because IPTs explicitly advocate for the importance of depth of processing to improve learning. The more deeply a learner processes information (such as through elaboration or organization), the more likely the learner is to encode and retrieve that information. In addition, deep thinking is required for learning complex topics (such as IPTs). To learn complex topics, learners must interpret and organize information (and not simply memorize facts; Resnick, 1984). Thus, students should be encouraged to construct meaning, make connections, and reflect on their knowledge in order to build more coherent mental representations.

The third challenge associated with teaching IPTs relates to transfer of knowledge. A primary goal of educational psychology is to help practitioners utilize evidence-based theory to inform practice. However, because IPTs are so complex, deeper processing is essential for building a coherent understanding of the topic. If the topic is not well understood, then there is little hope of translating theory to practice.

Research suggests that many individuals training to work in educational fields do not necessarily approach practice with knowledge and insights about learning or they struggle with putting their knowledge into practice. One reason for this is that new teachers do not often receive reinforcement when attempting to put theory into practice (Kagan, 1992). It is vital that future educators be able to apply educational psychology principles to real-life settings, whether for lesson planning, developing individualized education or treatment plans, or for other purposes.

PROMISING PRACTICE: INTEGRATING JIGSAW WITH CONCEPTUAL MAPPING

To address the challenges of (1) integrating a complex set of IPTs and sub-theories; (2) encouraging deep thinking (in particular, making connections between concepts); and (3) helping students make explicit links between theory and practice, I developed a combination jigsaw-conceptual mapping lesson containing several interrelated components. The activity is based on cognitive research on enhancing learning. Specifically, it requires students to work in cooperative jigsaw groups to describe, elaborate upon, and identify applications of IPTs. Students also build conceptual maps to make connections. The combination of elaboration, making connections, and cooperative learning helps students construct coherent understandings of the complex topic of IPTs and development.

The activity is embedded within the context of a graduate level course in lifespan development at a Midwestern university (although the activity can be adapted for undergraduate courses). Most students taking this class are pursuing masters' degrees in educational and school psychology, school counseling, and curriculum and instruction (to obtain teacher licensure). However, undergraduates in education, psychology, health professions, and a variety of other majors also enroll in the class. The course is organized thematically and, hence, the lesson on IPTs directly follows learning about constructivist theories of cognitive development (i.e., Piaget, neo-Piagetian theories, and Vygotsky). The lesson spans approximately one week.

Steps in the Jigsaw-Concept Map Activity

Preparation Prior to Class

Prior to attending class, students are assigned to read the text and complete a short online quiz. The students received prior instruction and practice with the principles of effective cooperative learning. These principles include positive interdependence, face-to-face promotive interaction, individual and group accountability, small group and interpersonal skills, and group processing (see Johnson & Johnson, 2007).

Overview of Topic

In the classroom, I provide an overview of the information-processing system's hardware and processing components so students have the baseline knowledge. Then, I describe how the information-processing system provides a framework for understanding a variety of changes in development. For example, there can be developmental progress in the "hardware" (e.g., increases in short-term memory capacities and prior knowledge stored in long-term memory) and processing (e.g., memory strategies, attention and habituation, theory of mind, executive function, and inhibition). I group these developmental trends into four categories: (1) theories regarding development in short-term memory capacity and attention/habituation; (2) development of rehearsal and problem-solving strategies; (3) theories about development in long-term memory and retrieval strategies; and (4) theories addressing behavioral intention, theory of mind, and adolescent egocentrism.

Jigsaw Structure

The next step follows the jigsaw format of cooperative learning (Aronson, Blaney, Stephan, Sikes, & Snapp, 1978). Students divide into "home" groups containing approximately 3–5 members; the number per group should match the number of developmental categories presented in the overview. In their home groups, students self-assign to the different topical categories. This self-assignment is intended to improve motivation by introducing choice (i.e., self-determination theory; Deci & Ryan, 2000).

Next, students leave their home groups and move into "expert" groups based on their self-assigned topic. In their expert groups, students collaborate to learn more about the assigned topic(s), and work together to develop a mini-lesson to present to their home group. Throughout the development of the lesson plan, I move between groups to provide guidance, facilitate effective cooperative work, and ensure the mini-lessons are accurate and of high quality.

When designing their mini-lessons, students are instructed to include four components. First, the lesson should provide an overview of the important points of the theory/topic (including developmental trajectories). Second, students are expected to describe a memory strategy for remembering the important topic information. Third, students must develop a short, interactive activity to deepen their understanding. This activity must require deeper cognitive processing (e.g., enactment, elaboration, organization) on the part of the learner.

The fourth component of the mini-lesson requires students to lead a small-group discussion aimed at elaborating upon concrete applications of the developmental topic(s). When planning this discussion in their expert groups, students brainstorm concrete applications and also develop elaborative questions to guide the discussion with their home groups. Example questions include: how can this be used to help learners? How does this explain developmental differences? How might practice be adapted as a function of this knowledge?

Once students complete their lesson plan, they leave their expert groups and return to their home groups. In their home groups, students take turns presenting their mini-lessons, engaging their group members in the applied activity, and leading discussion so that all group members can elaborate upon any explicit connections that they have made to practice. Thus, each student is responsible for both teaching and learning. Presentations of mini-lessons are limited to 10–15 minutes.

Concept Mapping

After each mini-lesson is presented, the home groups are tasked with developing a conceptual map of all of the theories and topics presented. In concept maps, important concepts and theories are circled and lines are used to depict interrelationships between the concepts. Students may also write words or short phrases next to these lines to help explain the relationships (Nesbit & Adesope, 2006). In this activity, the concept map must contain the major components of IPTs (including the hardware), and each developmental subtopic/theory. Finally, students incorporate some of the major concepts from constructivist theories (e.g., assimilation, accommodation, equilibrium) to achieve a holistic picture of cognitive development. Once the concept maps are developed, each group gives a brief presentation of their concept map to the class.

Evidence Supporting the Jigsaw Concept Map Activity

Research provides consistent evidence for the effectiveness of cooperative learning within the jigsaw framework, as well as for conceptual mapping. Cooperatively working toward a shared goal can improve learning, the development of higher-order and critical thinking skills, and motivation to learn (Johnson & Johnson, 2007). The jigsaw structure contains the benefits of cooperative learning, but improves it by placing responsibility upon each individual to accurately teach particular concepts (Aronson et al., 1978).

A large research base also supports conceptual mapping. Elaborative, meaningful learning occurs when students connect to-be-learned information with concepts already stored in long-term memory. Such elaborative connections help students to construct a coherent schema, which improves comprehension and achievement (Buehl & Fives, 2011). Conceptual mapping also serves as a graphic organizer, which improves comprehension by helping students organize the content (Van Meter, 2001).

Classroom Data

In addition to research documenting the usefulness of both jigsaw and conceptual mapping activities, observational data and student testimonials lend support. Prior to utilizing the jigsaw-concept mapping activity, I asked students to study the material and then come to class for a large-group discussion interspersed with interactive activities (e.g., demonstrations of working memory tasks or re-enactments of the false belief paradigm). While students were moderately engaged (i.e., they asked questions and were on-task), they struggled with higher-order thinking, making connections between concepts, and being able to describe a "big picture" framework of cognitive IPTs. After using the jigsaw-conceptual mapping activity, student engagement increased and they could more readily generate concrete applications, coherently describe the information-processing system and how (and why) it changes with development, and better evaluate IPTs. This led to improved performance on exams, critical analyses of research in assigned papers, making connections between concepts, and applying IPTs to the real world.

Student testimonials also provided evidence for how the jigsaw-conceptual mapping activity influenced perceptions of engagement and learning. Many students commented on the specific applicability of the material (e.g., "Hands-on exercises done in class…represented concepts we learned," "The application activities done in groups were helpful to learn the material. I learned so many things that can be applied to real world situations," and, "I learned so many things to use in the future, and I also applied [them] during the semester").

Students appreciated that the activities were arranged as manageable tasks, and that the tasks aligned to facilitate making connections between concepts. (e.g., "The instructor did a good job creating small steps along the way to help us accomplish major [goals]," "There was a great deal of information to learn…yet [the activity] did a great job of breaking it up into manageable sections," and, "She tried very hard to make [many] connections").

Also, students indicated that the activity increased their retention of content, as one student wrote:

Although this [activity] had many challenging steps, it forced me to work hard. I have never retained information as well as I have with this course. I am able to make connections to theories and understand better how a person develops…cognitively. The real life examples were excellent and are not provided in many other courses.

RECOMMENDATIONS AND CONCLUSIONS

Although the research literature and classroom data align in their support for the effectiveness of the jigsaw-concept map method, a variety of factors should be considered before and during implementation of this activity. First, courses in human development are often organized either thematically or chronologically. The course in which this instructional activity occurred was thematically organized, such that cognitive development was taught in a single unit. In a chronologically organized course, cognitive development would be revisited at each age group throughout the semester (infancy, early childhood, middle childhood, adolescence). There are benefits and challenges to each approach. In a thematically organized course, it is possible to cover all of the information processing content in a single jigsaw-concept map activity, enabling simpler presentation and implementation of the activity. If a course is organized chronologically, the jigsaw-concept map activity could extend throughout the semester and students would receive distributed practice with the content. Groups could add or make revisions to their developing conceptual map at each developmental stage. Even in a thematically organized course, IPTs are often re-visited when learning about perceptual development, moral reasoning, or play behaviors.

The jigsaw-conceptual map activity requires a significant amount of class time to carry out. To maximize efficiency, it is important that students come to class prepared, enabling in-class time to focus on the challenging work of developing and teaching mini-lessons and creating conceptual maps. To verify adequate preparation, I required students to complete an online quiz for the assigned textbook reading prior to class. Also, some of the mini-lesson development was assigned as homework.

The jigsaw-conceptual mapping activity described here was embedded into a course where cooperative learning principles were taught and regularly practiced. However, the activity can be used successfully in courses where this is not the case. For example, the instructor can describe the roles and responsibilities in the jigsaw and cooperative learning groups. The jigsaw requires that every student take ownership and responsibility for their content area, which reduces social loafing. Regardless of the course format, it is important to ensure that all students are providing quality instruction to their peers, and intervene to provide support when necessary. The instructor should actively monitor students' work and encourage deep thinking. The jigsaw method may present unique challenges for online courses. Coordinating times and finding electronic tools for small groups to work collaboratively is essential. Teaching mini-lessons and co-creating concept maps online is challenging but not impossible given appropriate planning. In fact, several tools have been developed for completing jigsaws in online and flipped classrooms (e.g., Dillenbourg & Jermann, 2007).

Overall, the jigsaw-conceptual mapping activity can be useful for teaching and organizing IPTs of cognitive development. However, its usefulness is not limited to this topic; it translates well to other courses within and outside of educational psychology. Like educational psychology, many fields contain an abundance of theories and sub-theories that students may struggle to integrate and apply. The jigsaw-concept map activity could help students organize the information, deepen their understanding, and identify concrete applications to implement in the real world.

REFERENCES

Aronson, E., Blancy, N., Stephan, C., Sikes, J., & Snapp, M. (1978). *The jigsaw classroom*. Beverly Hills, CA: Sage.

Buehl, M. M., & Fives, H. (2011). Best practices in educational psychology: Using evolving concept maps as instructional and assessment tools. *Teaching Educational Psychology, 7*(1), 62–87.

Deci, E. L., & Ryan, R. M. (2000). The "what" and "why" of goal pursuits: Human needs and the self-determination of behavior. *Psychological Inquiry, 11*, 227–268.

Dillenbourg, P., & Jermann, P. (2007). Designing integrative scripts. In F. Fischer, I. Kollar, H. Mandl, & J. M. Haake (Eds.), *Computer-supported collaborative learning: Cognitive, computational, and educational perspectives* (pp. 275–302). New York, NY: Springer.

Johnson, D. W., & Johnson, R. T. (2007). The state of cooperative learning in postsecondary and professional settings. *Educational Psychology Review, 19*(1), 15–29.

Kagan, D. (1992). Professional growth among preservice and beginning teachers. *Review of Educational Research, 62*(2), 129–169.

Mayer, R. E. (2008). Information processing. In T. Good (Ed.), *21st century learning: Vol. 1* (pp. 168–174). Thousand Oaks, CA: Sage.

Munakata, Y. (2006). Information processing approaches to development. In D. Kuhn & R. S. Siegler (Eds.), *Handbook of child psychology: Vol. 2: Cognition, perception, and language* (6th ed., Vol. 2, pp. 426–463). New York, NY: Wiley.

National Early Literacy Panel. (2008). *Developing early literacy: Report of the national early literacy panel.* Washington, DC: National Institute for Literacy.

Nesbit, J., & Adesope, O. (2006). Learning with concept and knowledge maps: A meta-analysis. *Review of Educational Research, 76*(3), 413–448.

Pressley, M., & McCormick, C. B. (2007). Cognitive development: Information-processing theory. *Child and adolescent development for educators* (pp. 92–121). New York, NY: Guilford Press.

Resnick, L. B. (1984). Comprehending and learning: Implications for a cognitive theory of instruction. In H. Mandl, N. L. Stein, & T. Trabasso (Eds.), *Learning and comprehension of text* (pp. 431–443). Hillsdale, NJ: Erlbaum.

Van Meter, P. (2001). Drawing construction as a strategy for learning from text. *Journal of Educational Psychology, 93*(1), 129–140.

CHAPTER 19

TEACHING AN IDENTITY-FOCUSED COURSE IN ADOLESCENT DEVELOPMENT

M Cecil Smith
West Virginia University

Teaching an advanced survey course in adolescent development and behavior to pre-service and in-service teachers, educational psychology students, and other education and social sciences professionals is a rich mixture of challenge and fun. Learning about adolescents' development and behavior is often enjoyable for students because they relate many of the topics and issues that are addressed in the course to their personal experiences during their teenage years. Many adults hold fond memories of their adolescence because of the lifelong friendships formed with schoolmates, the lessons learned from influential teachers and other adult mentors, and the influences of popular culture—movies, music, literature, and fashion—on their attitudes, choices, and sense of personal identity. Further, adolescence is a time when young people begin to develop more equal "adult" relationships with their parents, siblings, and extended family members (De Goede, Branje, & Meeus, 2009).

Challenges and Innovations in Educational Psychology Teaching and Learning, pages 245–258
Copyright © 2016 by Information Age Publishing

However, an adolescent development course can also be challenging for students because survey courses present an array of broad topics and complex issues for students to digest. A typical course in adolescent development addresses aspects of individuals' physical development (including pubertal processes and sexual maturity), cognitive development and intellectual growth, identity formation processes, social and emotional changes with age, the development of moral reasoning and ethical behavior, the roles and impacts of diverse socializing agents in adolescents' lives (e.g., family, peers, schools and other community institutions, and media), as well as the various ways that adolescents' well-being can be derailed by problems such as risky behaviors (including smoking, alcohol and other drug use, and sexual activity), delinquency, emotional problems such as anxiety and depression, social isolation, and interpersonal conflicts with peers, teachers, and parents. These and other developmental challenges can lead to negative outcomes for youth, including dropping out of school, unwanted pregnancy, or involvement in criminal activity. These are all topics about which teachers, academic support personnel (e.g., school counselors), psychologists, and other youth workers need to be informed so that they can understand, relate to, and work more effectively with adolescents. Therefore, these are topics that I address in the graduate course that I teach. I use a variety of whole-class and small-group methods and assignments to achieve the course objectives.

STUDENT PERSPECTIVES

Informal surveys of students in my adolescent development courses over more than 20 years of teaching reveal that many enter the class with negative attitudes and stereotypes about adolescents—stereotypes that are pervasive in the United States regarding adolescents and youth culture (Nichols & Good, 2004). Many of my students believe that adolescents are, by nature, contrary and frequently at odds with their parents; they are "slackers" who are self-centered and unconcerned with the welfare of others; also, teens are obsessed with sex, according to some. These characteristics invariably lead to difficulties with teachers and other adult authorities, according to many of my students. Of course, these beliefs are often fueled by larger cultural perspectives on youth that are presented in popular literature and other media (Chan, McCrae, DeFruyt, Jussim, Löckenhoff, DeBolle et al., 2012). While, like many stereotypes, there is an element of truth to these negative characterizations, the reality of adolescents' development and behavior is much more complex and nuanced and needs to be understood. Of course, many of my students recognize that most adolescents are self-aware, capable, considerate, have healthy attitudes, and close, loving relationships with their parents, among other positive characteristics.

Identity Formation and Adolescent Development

Over time, my approach to teaching adolescent development and behavior has increasingly centered on helping students understand the significance of adolescents' developmental task to establish a sense of individual identity. The writings of Erikson (1968), and many others whose work has been influenced by Erikson (e.g., Marcia, 1980), have shaped much of what we know and understand about adolescents' psychosocial and behavioral development—in particular, identity formation. According to Erikson, forming an identity is the primary developmental task of adolescence. Identity formation is, in Erikson's words, the main quest in life. An identity crisis occurs, according to Erikson, when the adolescent attempts to integrate childhood identifications with his or her ideas about what s/he wants to be(come) as an adult and through validation of one's developing interests, aptitudes, and aspirations, and beliefs and values. Specific aspects of identity formation include gender roles and sexual identity, political beliefs and affiliation, religious and ethical beliefs, and occupational interests and development of one's talents. An individual who has developed an identity has a firm sense of who s/he is, has a purpose in life, and a clear set of personal values, according to Erikson (1968). Further, the identity-achieved person knows what s/he wants out of life, knows where s/he is headed, and has personal goals for the future.

Of course, one's identity is not fully complete by the end of adolescence, but continues to be shaped, changed, and revised as a consequence of adult life experiences. However, the adolescent years are a crucial period for identity issues to arise and be considered and worked through by the individual. Much of this identity work occurs in school, through learning about one's competencies around subject matter (e.g., having an interest in science or art, being a competent writer), through participation in extracurricular activities (e.g., sports and clubs), and by the influences of adult role models (e.g., teachers and counselors) and peers.

During adolescence, teens experience periods of exploration wherein they must choose for themselves—in accordance with their own interests, goals, talents, values, and the standards of their cultural milieu. Adolescents, therefore, need both *support* for their explorations and *affirmation* of their chosen identity commitments. Parents, educators, counselors, and youth workers in various roles can provide the necessary support and affirmation for adolescents. However, first, these persons must understand the importance of adolescent identity formation.

Identity-Focused Instruction

Typically, students in an adolescent development course are exposed to Erikson's ideas (and related work, including Marcia, 1980) and the role of identity formation in adolescence rather briefly—in the form of a single lecture presentation; generously, perhaps two class meetings are devoted to the topic (in large part due to the press to present other important topics and issues in adolescence that are covered within a survey course). Given the core significance of identity formation to adolescent development and well-being, I have infused identity development throughout the whole of my course to bring students' attention back repeatedly to this critical developmental task and its consequences.

Every presentation (lecture) that I lead in class—whether addressing cognitive change during adolescence, the role of peers and family members in shaping adolescents' lives, or health-related issues—also makes connections to identity formation. Here are two brief examples. For my presentation on the biological processes and physical changes associated with puberty, I ask the class to discuss how changes in teens' physical appearance, combined with their awareness of others' responses to these changes, impact the adolescent's sense of self and how this knowledge is incorporated into their identity. For my presentation on the role of media and popular culture in adolescents' lives, we discuss the diverse ways in which modern media—particularly interactive media, such as the Internet—provide avenues for youth to explore multiple *possible selves* (Markus & Nurius, 1986), including both *hoped-for* or positive, and *feared* or negative aspects of the self (e.g., to be a college graduate versus a high school dropout) through role experimentation. Several forms of media enable role experimentation and avenues for teens to express themselves, such as through artistic expression (e.g., creating a video documentary about a topic of interest) or personal views expressed within an online discussion forum. Online social media, for example, connect adolescents to other people, including affinity groups, mentors, and peers. These explicit linkages of the course topics to adolescent identity development lead to rich and engaging class discussions, and students' interests in these topics are heightened.

One of the most important concepts of the course is that teachers, counselors, and youth services professionals are *identity workers* who, through their work, can establish environments and create tasks for teens that support identity formation processes. These educators and youth workers are not—and cannot function effectively as—merely passive observers of adolescents' identity development. Thus, it is important for educators to recognize, for example, the value of teens' role experimentation during adolescence and to convey empathy and understanding, and provide guidance to the adolescents.

We talk frequently in class about what I call "identity-focused instruction." For secondary teachers, such instruction involves creating and offering opportunities for their students to initiate new activities, identify their unique strengths and talents, learn about different views and cultural perspectives, and explore choices for their future. These activities enable identity development. Evidence shows that identity development is strongly related to academic achievement—particularly among students of color and ethnic minorities (Altschul, Oyserman, & Bybee, 2006; Irving & Hudley, 2008). Thus, teachers have a stake in focusing attention on their students' identity formation processes and activities as these relate to learning academic content and skills.

I also make explicit the connections of adolescents' academic motivation, classroom-level and peer group social processes, and individuals' capacities for self-determination and abilities to self-regulate their academic and social behaviors to their identity development, as illustrated in Figure 19.1. These connections have been described in a series of papers

	Internal	**External**
Supporting students' developmental needs	Self-determination	Social goals
Developing students' competencies	Self-regulation and possible selves	Instructional environment

Suggested Instructional Strategies to Support Student Identity Development

In support of students developmental needs

Self-determination
  Allow students opportunities to choose among assignments and activities (*autonomy*)
  Provide direct, explicit, and immediate corrective feedback in response to students' work (*competence*)
  Provide multiple opportunities for students to develop and refine skills (*competence*)
  Create situations and tasks where students can collaborate (*relatedness*)
  Establish warm interpersonal relationships with students (*relatedness*)

Social goals
  Use assignments where students must take another's point of view
  Encourage teamwork and collaboration (cooperative learning)
  Employ peer mediation training and conflict resolution
  Develop service learning assignments
  Use role-playing activities to encourage pro-social reasoning and behavior

In support of developing students' academic competencies

Self-regulation and possible selves
  Teach students how to make appropriate attributions for success and failure
  Help students set goals and develop and enact action plans to achieve these goals

Instructional (classroom) environment
  Nurture and support *situational interest* leading to sustained *personal interest*
  Establish a mastery-oriented classroom
  Emphasize *effort* and *improvement over time*
  Minimize competition and extrinsic rewards for performance
  Avoid making generalization about students' abilities based on gender, race, or other characteristics

Figure 19.1 A model for teacher identity work in secondary grades classrooms.

published in special issues of the *Educational Psychologist* (e.g., LaGuardia, 2009) and *Contemporary Educational Psychology* within the past half-dozen years (Faircloth, 2012).

Course Organization

Given the above considerations, my graduate adolescent development course is organized in the following manner. First, because it is a survey course, I address the essential topics common to all such courses in adolescent development, including: historical and social perspectives on adolescence and youth; scientific methods for studying adolescent development and behavior; physical development and maturation; cognitive and intellectual development; moral development and ethical behavior; social-emotional and personality development; the influences of socialization contexts, including family, peers, schools and communities, and media; and development challenges and problem behaviors during adolescence. At least two class sessions are devoted to many of these topics.

With a few exceptions, all weekly class meetings (which are for 2 hrs., 50 mins.) are organized in the following manner. We begin with a warm-up question and answer activity (10 mins.), and the class then shifts to my presentation of the weekly topic (~50 min). I refer to these as "presentations" rather than lectures because I encourage students to participate in discussions with me, rather than simply listening to me talk at them about the topic. During these presentations, I summarize 6–8 major theoretical concepts or a few relevant research findings, and/or implications for practice. As noted above, I give careful attention to connecting the topic (e.g., moral reasoning) to identity formation tasks and processes, wherever possible. The presentation is interspersed with brief discussion breaks (2–3 minutes) for students to pair up and summarize the information for one another, and devise 1–2 questions to ask in response to the presentation. I address a few questions before proceeding with the presentation. For the latter half of the class meeting (~75 mins.), following a short break, we then move to small-group discussion arrangement.

Structured Group Discussions

Discussion groups are often advocated as a student-centered, social-constructivist approach to learning in university courses (Forsyth, 2003) that can increase students' interest in the subject matter (Cannon, 2006) and boost their classroom performance. Collaborative discussion groups provide a venue for cooperative learning to occur as this has been demonstrated to be an effective instructional model for academic achievement (Thompson, Vermette, & Wisniewski, 2004).

Students in my course are randomly assigned, at the beginning of the semester, to one of five theme-focused groups. The themes relate to the broad topic areas for the course: (1) Genetics, biological processes, and physical development; (2) Cognitive, intellectual, and ethical development; (3) Socialization processes and social development; (4) motivation, achievement, and instructional processes; and (5) developmental challenges and adolescent health. Typically, each group consists of four to six students who are enrolled in different programs, including educational psychology, school counseling, developmental psychology, teacher education, public health, and school leadership. Often, about one-third of students in the class are currently teaching in middle or high schools, so they bring to the class their real-world working experience with adolescents. Having a mix of students in the groups—those who have direct professional experience with adolescents and those who do not—provides a context in which the more experienced students can "mentor" those who are inexperienced. Students remain in their assigned group throughout the semester, and the five groups are assigned, on occasion, to interact and share their learning with one another.

For every weekly topic, each group is presented with up to four discussion questions (they may choose to address any or all of these questions during their group discussion time). All group members preview, prior to class, the discussion questions within their group's folder located on the course site within the online course management system. The week's topic (e.g., cognitive development) is filtered through the discussion group's thematic focus (e.g., motivation, achievement, and instructional processes), and the assigned discussion questions raise issues regarding the interaction of the topic, such as growth in thinking skills, with adolescents' identity formation processes. See Table 19.1 for examples of topics, groups, and discussion questions.

Group members may use any course materials (e.g., textbooks, other assigned readings, notes) as well as the Internet to find information and resources that will inform their discussions. The groups typically rotate leadership responsibilities for their weekly discussion activity; a second group member takes on the role of recorder for the discussion (i.e., they write up and upload a brief summary of the group's discussion to the course management system); a third member gives a brief oral summary of their group's discussion to the entire class during the final 10 minutes of class.

I move around to sit in with each group and listen to the discussions for 10–12 minutes or so. I only participate when asked to do so, or when the group's discussion is clearly flagging or off-topic. I also observe the individual groups from a distance (i.e., when I am sitting with another group). Generally, I have observed that the groups' discussions are lively, serious, focused, and collegial.

TABLE 19.1   Discussion Group Themes, Topics, And Example Discussion Questions

Group Theme	Example Weekly Discussion Topic	Example Discussion Question Re: Identity Development
Genetics, Biological Processes & Physical Development	Physical development and sexual maturation	Consider several ways that pubertal changes can affect adolescents' developing sense of themselves and their personal identity, in terms of their relationships with family members and peers, their physical competencies, and personal academic, social, and occupational goals. (1) What are some ways that schools and teachers can ease the stresses associated with pubertal changes for students? (2) How might instructional content and strategies within given academic domains (math, science, humanities) be employed to assist students?
Cognitive, Intellectual & Ethical Development	Moral development	What is the relationship of moral development to students' identity formation? Consider issues around students' understanding of race, gender, sexual orientation, social class, or disability, and how such understandings might influence students' identities. Topics to consider: – Stereotyping of individuals based on personal characteristics – Beliefs about the "morality" of sexual orientation and sexual behaviors – Immigration and the rights of immigrant students to free public education – Inclusion of students with disabilities in mainstream classrooms – Expressions of faith in public schools – Single gender classrooms Discuss how these issues may influence adolescents' perceptions of themselves and others, identify the moral dimensions of the controversies surrounding these topics, and discuss how schools and teachers can appropriate address such topics with students.
Social Contexts & Socialization Processes	Parents' and family influences	Some experts have argued that parents don't have much influence on their adolescents' behaviors, goals, and values in comparison to peers' influences. Many other experts disagree with this claim and point to evidence that shows parents and peers have somewhat distinct domains in which they are influential. Do you agree or disagree with this claim that peers are more important than parents during adolescence—and why? What evidence can you point to that supports your argument that parents/peers are more/less influential in shaping teens' behaviors, goals, and values?

(continued)

TABLE 19.1 Discussion Group Themes, Topics, And Example Discussion Questions (continued)

Group Theme	Example Weekly Discussion Topic	Example Discussion Question Re: Identity Development
Motivation, Achievement & Instructional Processes	Cognitive development	Each group member must describe a classroom activity, lesson, or project that they would assign to students in their grade level/subject area. Discuss how you would consider individual differences in student motivation and would create the assignment to heighten students' motivation for the task. Describe how you would create the assignment to take into account differences in students' cognitive development (e.g., some students are "concrete" operational, others are in early or full "formal" operations).
Developmental Challenges & Adolescent Health	Physical development and sexual maturation	A 1997 survey of 4,000 young men and women found that body dissatisfaction is increasing. People are discontented with the way they appear. Among adolescent girls, ages 13–19, 62% say they are dissatisfied. More than 75% of young women also say that menstruation (a normal body function) causes them to have negative feelings about their bodies.

- Teasing during childhood or adolescence has a negative effect on women's feelings about their bodies—no matter what shape they are in (i.e., "fit," "unfit," overweight).
- 12% of women reported using diet pills to control their weight. 6% induced vomiting on one or more occasions. Among women with eating disorders, 20% used diet pills, 17% abused laxatives, and 28% induced vomiting to try to lose weight.
- 22% of women report that fashion models influenced their own body images; only 6% of men reported that fashion models influenced them. Men were much more likely to report athletes as body image models.
- 64% of women and 62% of men report that regular exercise makes them feel good about their bodies. 53% of women and 24% of men said that "feeling thin" made them feel good about their bodies. 66% of women and 37% of men said that "gaining weight" made them feel bad about their bodies. 84% of women report ever dieting, but only 58% of men say they ever diet.
- While 54% of men are "extremely" or "somewhat satisfied" with their bodies, only 44% of women are satisfied.
- Using these statistics as a guide, as well as what you know about adolescents' physical development, devise 6–8 strategies that you believe would be useful in altering adolescents' negative body images or, conversely, helpful to them in developing positive body images.

Peer Evaluations

At the end of the semester, each group member is required to complete an evaluation of each member of their assigned discussion group. Students use a scoring rubric that I provide which asks them to rate, along a 5-point scale (5 = "exceptional," 1 = "poor"), the following characteristics of group members: attendance and participation; preparation; leadership; communication; and, collegiality (a copy of the rubric is available from the author). I caution students against colluding with one another to give high ratings when such scores are not deserved, and inform them that their ratings are only advisory, as I will also evaluate each group member independently.

Instructor's Evaluation of Group Participation

I examine the peer evaluations, looking particularly for instances where individuals' peer ratings are at odds with my observations of the student. I use the same rating scale as the students to determine a group discussion score for every student, which is part of each student's overall class participation score.

COURSE ASSIGNMENTS

The major activities for the course include the following three assignments.

Case study papers. A series of three case study papers are assigned in which students select and view a video excerpt from a series of videos that high school students made about themselves (for more information regarding this video project, see Smith & Shumow, 2011). Each of the selected video excerpts (typically, 2–4 mins. in length) that students select must be analyzed from a specific theoretical perspective. The videos have proven to be excellent source materials for introducing adolescents' identity issues to my students because the teen participants were very forthcoming about their struggles and conflicts, desires and ambitions, interpersonal relationships, and needs and values.

To select a theory to use for analysis, interpretation, and understanding of the "case," students read detailed descriptions of several of the 16 different theories of adolescent development in Muuss' (1996) book, *Theories of Adolescence.* They can select different theories for each case study to broaden their understanding of, and to compare and contrast, different theories. The case study papers are then evaluated by the students' peers whom I assign, at random, to evaluate an individual's paper. The peer evaluator (blinded to the writer's identity) must then view the writer's selected case video, read the selected developmental theory chapter in the Muuss textbook, and use the instructor-provided scoring rubric to evaluate the paper. I also read a random selection of the case study papers (but I do not evaluate them unless a student disputes their peer-assigned score; this has occurred in fewer than 10% of all submitted papers over the past decade). The peer evaluation approach increases students' exposure to cases and theories; and, by reading their peers' analyses, they see different interpretations and perspectives regarding adolescent development.

In general, students' chose to use the following theories to analyze and interpret the video cases that they selected, in order of popularity: Erikson's theory of identity development; Marcia's expansion and empirical support for Erikson's theory; Piaget's cognitive theory; Lerner's developmental contextualism; Sullivan's interpersonal theory; and Bandura's social cognitive theory.

Class and small group participation. As described previously, students' participation in class is required and evaluated—both by their peers and me using rubrics—and contributes to a significant portion (25%) of their final course grade.

Student Outcomes

Specific to my students' understanding of the significance of identity development to adolescent well-being, I have gleaned a few representative comments from their papers, small group discussions, and in-class comments to demonstrate how they have benefitted from the course. Their knowledge of adolescent identity better prepares them to teach, counsel, and advise adolescents in school and other settings, as suggested by this student's comment:

> The group discussions have been very helpful. In the group I am in, three people have experience in teaching. I have found their experiences to be valuable... by listening to their perspectives on teaching... broadened my understanding of how I will want to teach. (Mike[1]—teacher certification candidate)

Small group discussions. Students demonstrated understanding of the ways in which identity is fundamental to adolescents' well-being and development, as illustrated by these comments, drawn from group discussions:

> I think that identity is purpose. If you understand your purpose, you are able to set a goal. Then you realize that there are steps to achieving that goal and you can plan or map out a way to achieve that goal. It's also about relevance. If you have purpose and the ability to map out a plan, then you can achieve anything. (Alicia—masters student, psychology)

> When students have their identity figured out, then they are comfortable with who they are. That way, they can spend less time worrying about those other things, like peer pressure, and spend more time focusing in class. (Matt—(8th grade science teacher)

> If [students] are not confident in their identity, then they won't be confident in their academic abilities. Being able to relate to academics is made positive by knowing who you are. (Caryn—middle school media specialist)

In response to several of the posted discussion questions, students frequently discussed different ways that they could, as teachers, counselors, mentors, and parents influence the identity development of adolescents at home, in school, and other developmental contexts. They believed that teachers *can* make their classroom instruction relevant to students' lives and interests. They described a variety of approaches and methods that contribute to students' identity development in school:

> I really try to make lessons in my class relevant to my students and I acknowledge the components of their identity in a positive manner, like using materials related to their ethnicity or culture. (Liz—art education doctoral student)

> I set expectations and expect my students to stick to them... they have to have concrete knowledge of what is expected and appropriate. (Randy—high school physics teacher)

> I know that when I create a safe, group-like atmosphere, my students are more likely to feel as though they belong in the group, and that's really helpful for classroom management. (Becky—6th grade teacher)

Case study papers. Students' responses to the video case studies have been overwhelmingly positive. A number of students have commented that the videos are valuable learning resources because they depict real adolescents' actual circumstances, feelings, and ambitions, and the requirement to apply theory to understand these dimensions of adolescents led to powerful learning for them. A few student comments illustrate their enthusiasm for this work:

> This course... required me to actually apply these theories to real students and situations... the first time I have been asked to apply theories to real people... required me to view student problems in a larger context and use the theories... to help me understand [students]... help guide my actions... (Jan—teacher certification candidate)

> This class has provided useful experience in applying theories to actual people, and has made them [theories] seem much more important in understanding adolescents. (Marcus—counseling student)

> This is where I have found the case study papers most valuable. This was an excellent simulation of how a teacher cannot have all the facts about an adolescent's home and personal life, yet still provide a response based on this information. (Cris—9th grade language arts teacher)

Recommendations and Conclusions

From my decade of experience teaching adolescent development from an identity-focused perspective, it is clear to me that my students have experienced several positive outcomes. First, they have acquired deeper understanding of, and appreciation for, the critical role of identity formation in adolescents' well-being and the contributions of adolescents' identity strivings to their academic achievement. Second, my students are able to apply developmental theories to interpret and explain adolescents' behaviors and developmental processes, and connect identity formation to positive student performance in school. Third, the course increases my students' understanding of their own adolescent experiences and on-going identity strivings. As one student remarked:

> I am getting the sense that maybe I still have some adolescent issues going on inside me which makes me too close to the issues adolescents today face. I am too emotionally involved with my own adolescence and some pain and struggles not resolved back then. (Amber—graduate student, psychology)

This self-knowledge (a part of their identity development) is also valuable in helping students to relate to their adolescent children, students, and clients. Although there is some complexity to the structure of the adolescent development course, given the diverse assignments and group discussion activities, it is a highly enjoyable course to teach. Students' responses to the instructional activities and assignments have been, for the greater part, enthusiastic and their classwork has positively contributed to their professional growth.

NOTE

1. All student names are pseudonyms.

REFERENCES

Altschul, I., Oyserman, D., & Bybee, D. (2006). Racial-ethnic identity in mid-adolescence: Content and change and predictors of academic achievement. *Child Development, 77*(5), 1155–1169.

Cannon, P. (2006). Enhancing understanding and interest through group discussion. *College Teaching, 54*(2), 211.

Chan, W., McCrae, R. R., DeFruyt, F., Jussim, L., Lockenhoff, C. E., DeBolle, M. et al. (2012). Stereotypes of age differences in personality traits: Universal and accurate? *Journal of Personality and Social Psychology, 103*(6), 1050–1066.

De Goede, I. H., Branje, S. J., & Meeus, W. M. (2009). Developmental changes in adolescents' perceptions of relationships with their parents. *Journal of Youth & Adolescence, 38*(1), 75–88.

Erikson, E. H. (1968). *Identity: Youth and crisis.* New York, NY: W.W. Norton.

Faircloth, B. S. (2012). "Wearing a mask" vs. connecting identity with learning. *Contemporary Educational Psychology, 37,* 186–194.

Forsyth, D. R. (2003). *The professor's guide to teaching: Psychological principles and practices* (pp. 87–126). Washington, DC: American Psychological Association. LaGuardia, J. G. (2009). Developing who I am: A self-determination theory approach to the establishment of healthy identities. *Educational Psychologist, 44*(2), 90–104.

Markus, H., & Nurius. P. (1986). Possible selves. *American Psychologist, 41*(9), 954–969.

Muuss, R. E. (1996). *Theories of adolescence* (6th ed.). New York, NY: McGraw-Hill.

Nichols, S. L., & Good, T. L. (2004). *America's teenagers: Myths and realities. Media images, schooling, and the social costs of careless indifference.* Mahwah, NJ: Erlbaum.

Marcia, J. (1980). Identity in adolescence. In J. Adelson (Ed.), *Handbook of Adolescence.* New York, NY: Wiley.

Smith, M C., & Shumow, L. (2011). Improving secondary teachers' knowledge of adolescent development through teens' self-documentaries. *Journal of the International Society for Teacher Education, 15*(2), 45–55.

Thompson, W. B., Vermette, P. J., & Wisniewski, S. A. (2004). Ten cooperative learning activities for the cognitive psychology course. *Teaching of Psychology, 31*(2), 134–136.

CHAPTER 20

HUMAN DEVELOPMENT IN ANNE FRANK

Anne Frank in Human Development

Florian C. Feucht
University of Toledo

WHAT IS HUMAN DEVELOPMENT AND WHO IS LEARNING ABOUT IT?

The interdisciplinary body of knowledge on human development entertains theories and research about the physiological, cognitive, and socio-emotional maturation and growth of human beings from conception to death. Currently, it can be divided into three domains: (1) physiological development, which focuses on the growth and aging of the body, the functioning of its physiological systems, mobility, reproduction and sensory perception; (2) cognitive development, which focuses on the maturation and decline of mental processes and outcomes involving perception, memory and problem-solving, with close ties to learning and language acquisition; and (3) socio-emotional development, which focuses on continuities and changes in intrapersonal aspects like emotions, motivation, and personality traits, as well as interpersonal aspects, such as different role understandings, gender

Challenges and Innovations in Educational Psychology Teaching and Learning, pages 259–271
Copyright © 2016 by Information Age Publishing

stereotypes, and forms of citizenship. Embedded within and cutting across these three domains are additional topical areas that shed light on more specific aspects of human development, such as conception and birth, sensation and perception, cognition and memory, intelligence and creativity, self and personality, gender roles and sexuality, and death and dying, to name a few. The content of human development can be presented in different organizational structures. Textbooks, for example, often have either a chronological structure that follows the actual cycle of life (e.g., Berk, 2012) or a topical structure that maps out the content according to the different knowledge domains (e.g., Siegelman & Rider, 2014).

Human development is typically studied by various education majors and human services professionals at the undergraduate and graduate levels of higher education, ranging, for example, from an undergraduate student teacher to a master's student in educational technology to a doctoral student in the field of educational psychology or school counseling. Often, the course content is part of the core requirements of such programs of study and is tied to licensure requirements of many education professions.

Human development is mainly taught in 3-credit-hour courses by faculty in the areas of psychology, educational psychology, and educational foundations and leadership. The most common type of student enrolled in a human development course seeks a bachelor's degree in education, in conjunction with a teaching license. Often, these bachelor's degree programs are overseen and accredited by associations representing the teaching professions at the state or national level and prepare student teachers for licensure exams mandated by the state departments of education in the United States.

Why is Human Development Important for Educators and Human Services Professionals?

Human development is an area of specialization in the field of educational psychology. Common in the field of teacher education are courses in 'human development and behavior' that cover childhood, adolescence, and adulthood as well as the life span itself. These courses are complemented by courses in applied psychology or educational psychology that emphasize learning theories, cognition and cognitive processes, diversity, and classroom management. Overall, they are meant to inform the everyday practices of classroom teachers and human services professionals from a psychological and developmental perspective.

Most recently, various teaching standards and licensure exams have been focused on student teachers' ability to support their curriculum designs, specifically learning objectives, with theory and research in the field of human development. For example, the *Council for the Accreditation of Educator*

Preparation (CAEP, 2013) articulated 10 standards that describe the expectations for teacher candidates in the area of content and pedagogical knowledge: Human development is recognized as the first standard:

> Standard #1: Learner Development. The teacher understands how learners grow and develop, recognizing that patterns of learning and development vary individually within and across the cognitive, linguistic, social, emotional, and physical areas, and designs and implements developmentally appropriate and challenging learning experiences. (p. 4)

Similarly, the *Ohio Assessments for Educators* (OAE), mandated by the Ohio Department of Education (2013) for licensure, has operationalized 10 standards in its assessment framework of professional knowledge. Again, human development is identified as the first standard:

> 001: Understand processes of human development, variations in student development, and how to apply this knowledge to provide instructional environments and experiences that promote all students' development and learning. (p. 1)

Finally, the nationally accessible *edTPA* assessment system, developed by Stanford University and the American Association of Colleges for Teacher Education (AACTE, 2014), aligns state and national standards to "determine if new teachers are ready to enter the profession with the skills necessary to help all of their students learn." One aim is to measure student teachers' ability to use theory and research to support the feasibility of their learning objectives to cater to the learning of all students in their classrooms. Here, student teachers are expected to apply their content and pedagogical knowledge, generally, and rationalize and operationalize learning objectives based on human development theory and research, specifically. The fact that these three national and state entities concertedly focus on student teachers' ability to apply knowledge of human development, among other standards, demonstrates the importance of teaching human development well in teacher preparation programs.

Important objectives of a human development course are that students understand how developmental theories and research can be used intentionally to describe, explain, and improve the human condition and that students appreciate that this body of knowledge can be an important source for informed decision-making in a teacher's everyday classroom practices.

The *Anne Frank Assignment*, which is the central focus of this chapter, uses the authentic case of a teenage girl for student teachers and other human services professionals to learn to apply human development theory by describing, explaining, and improving the human condition, whether it be a student in a classroom, a patient in a hospital, or a citizen living in a downtown community area. The purpose of the assignment is to offer students the opportunity to develop expertise and professional practices that are informed and driven by the science of human development and its theory and research.

A course in human development can also become important in reminding students that humanity is an essential, yet often forgotten, driving force for science. At times, the appreciation for humanity and human dignity seems to be lost in the broad view of science, even in the field of human development. Do we see and appreciate the human for his or her dignity amidst all the research data, illustrative figures, and calculated tables that amount to abstract theories? Here, the *Anne Frank Assignment* can illustrate how a scientific body of knowledge can be taught in a manner that also contributes to a more tolerant, compassionate, and peaceful world. Therein, teaching human development becomes not only important for professionals to learn about scientific research and theory that informs their expertise and practice, but also lays a foundation in peace education relevant to their civic duty as public servants.

What Challenges are Present When Teaching Human Development?

First, student teachers experience difficulties when trying to apply theory and research to describe, explain, and improve school student behavior, learning, and development. For example, how can a teacher use the concept of adolescent egocentrism to recognize the behavior of adolescent learners, explain and understand related incidents in the classroom, and develop a strategy to overcome the issue and help students feel better about themselves and their peers? In the *Anne Frank Assignment,* students focus on systematically applying the process of *describe, explain, and improve* the human condition, driven by human development theory and research. This competency is required when students begin to articulate, teach, and assess learning objectives as part of their lesson plans. Students are expected to provide rationales for how their learning objectives will be feasibly implemented based on existing theory and research. Students' ability to connect actual student behavior, learning, and development to theory and research is therefore an essential foundation for their professional practice.

Second, a challenge in teaching human development pertains to avoiding the reinforcement of a false understanding of theory-evidence coordination. When student teachers are expected to use theory and research to *describe, explain,* and *improve* school students' learning, behavior, and development as part of their professional practice (AACTE, 2014; CAEP, 2013), they might wrongly assume that the process of matching student data to existing developmental theory and concepts represents the scientific process of establishing a theory. In fact, many adults do not have a sound understanding and habit of coordinating theory and evidence like scientists do (Kuhn, 1989). Hence, Anne Frank's diary can be purposefully used as a case study to distinguish between the use of existing theory and research by teachers to inform their classroom practice and the coordination of theory and evidence by a scientist in the process of scientific inquiry.

Third, students experience difficulties distinguishing and using the different levels of Uri Bronfenbrenner's (1979) eco-system theory (i.e., the micro, meso, exo, macro, and chrono systems). Eco-system theory provides a systematic way to conceptualize and operationalize an individual's learning and living environment and provides an interdisciplinary language for professionals to communicate precisely and effectively about learning outcomes and approaches, for example, in the development of an IEP, treatment plan or resource allocation for an individual. In the *Anne Frank Assignment*, students learn to use Bronfenbrenner's theory to analyze Anne Frank in light of specific human development theories and concepts. They learn to identify examples of data across the different systems, make comparisons across the chrono system, and use the associated terminology to articulate their results in a written essay.

Fourth, students seem to have difficulty understanding the value of human development theory and research for their emerging expertise and professional practice. One reason for the lack of appreciation might be that the content can sometimes be presented at a very abstract level that makes it difficult to connect its relevance to practice without concrete examples. In the *Anne Frank Assignment*, students learn to articulate the abstractness of the textbooks' theories and concepts, formulate definitions in their own words and apply these to an authentic and meaningful case study. These steps allow students to begin to appreciate the value of human development to inform their professional practice.

Anne Frank as a Developmental Case Study

The *Anne Frank Assignment* is a developmental case study with different tasks that extend over the duration of a semester. Students read the book *Anne Frank—Diary of a Young Girl* (Frank, Mooyaart, & Roosevelt, 1993) as supplementary reading material for their human development textbook. They analyze Anne's diary entries from a human development perspective by identifying entries that are data examples of the concepts and theories introduced in the course and textbook. Furthermore, students compare and contrast Anne Frank's case with their own case—their biographical adolescent development and experiences. In this analytical and self-reflective process, they focus on developmental theory and concepts and map them onto the different levels of Bronfenbrenner's (1979) theory. Finally, students discuss how their analyses inform their future classroom practices and role understanding as a teacher or human service professional.

The *Anne Frank Task Assignment* includes two different tasks that build upon each other: (1) The *Anne Frank—Mini Essays* (weekly); and (2) the *Anne Frank—Concept Mapping Papers* (three across the semester). Both tasks are described below in more detail.

Who is Anne Frank?

Anne Frank was a Jewish adolescent born in June, 1929 in Germany. Due to anti-Semitic policies, Anne and her family were forced into hiding to escape deportation and murder during the German occupation of the Netherlands in World War II. Anne's handwritten diary became her imaginary friend, whom she addressed as "Dear Kitty." The diary provides both a chronological documentation of her experiences during her life in the "Secret Annex" in Amsterdam from June 1942 until August 1944 and a biographical reflection on her childhood before that time. Following the betrayal of the hideout, Anne Frank faced deportation and later died in a concentration camp due to a typhus infection in March 1945. Since the publication of her diary in 1947 and its subsequent translation in numerous languages, Anne Frank has been posthumously recognized for documenting her adolescent experiences, beliefs, and feelings during a time of war, terror and genocide. Today, *Anne Frank—The Diary of a Young Girl* is one of the world's most read books.

Why is the Diary an Adequate Data Source for a Case Study?

Anne's diary is a very rare data set for two reasons. From a human development perspective, few published autobiographies and diaries exist that are written by adolescent authors. Most existing accounts of teenage memories have been written by adult authors, based on their fading memories and biased from their now adult perspectives. In a unique way, Anne Frank's diary, with its rich descriptions, is an authentic data source that provides insights into aspects of physiological, cognitive, and socio-emotional development, as all were experienced by this adolescent girl. Second, the diary provides a historical account of a young Jewish person who experienced firsthand what it meant to be a victim of anti-Semitism and genocide. Together, the developmental and historical accounts allow students to study Anne's adolescent development, while considering the contextual influence of living in hiding on her developmental progression (e.g., the role of nutrition, cognitive stimulation, and relationships).

The Anne Frank Mini Essays

Overview

In the first task, the *Anne Frank—Mini Essays*, students gain an understanding of concepts in the field of human development and apply them to an authentic case study. Students read Anne Frank's diary as a case study, searching for example entries that provide some evidence that Anne experienced various developmental concepts typical of adolescence.

More specifically, students are asked to: (1) select a developmental concept within each topic area of the book and to briefly summarize it in their own words; (2) identify a quotation within Anne Frank's diary entries as an example of the selected concept; and (3) explain why the quotation is a good example to illustrate the concept. Each week, students select a new concept from the textbook and submit the completed task online in the form of a mini essay.

Learning Objectives

The learning objectives of this task can be identified at the lower levels of Bloom's (1956) taxonomy of the cognitive domain, focusing on knowledge, comprehension, and application of developmental concepts. The purpose of the task is also to lay a foundation of knowledge and cognitive skills so that students are prepared for the more demanding, higher-order thinking task of writing concept mapping papers (see Task 2). By completing the *Anne Frank—Mini Essay* tasks, students are able to:

- name, explain, and summarize concepts in human development;
- apply developmental concepts to an authentic case by identifying exemplary data of the occurrence and/or delayed occurrence of the concepts; and rationalize theoretically why the exemplary data is appropriate to illustrate identified developmental concepts.

Feedback

When students follow the layout of the task, providing feedback and points becomes an efficient grading assignment. Students receive an equal number of points for each of the three sections and have the opportunity to submit a revised version. If a section demonstrates particular finesse, students can score quality points. Quality points seem to encourage students to put more effort into the task with the first submission, as opposed to submitting a revision, which makes the grading of the task content more enjoyable. Students can use quality points to counter balance lost points in their multiple choice exams. The opportunity for traditional extra credit is not provided in the course. Feedback on how to improve mini essays allows students to refine the foundation of knowledge and skills needed for the more cognitively demanding concept mapping papers.

The Anne Frank Concept Mapping Papers

Overview

The second task, the *Anne Frank Concept Mapping Papers*, requires students to write short essay-style papers about selected developmental concepts and theories in relation to Anne Frank's diary, their own biographies, and their roles as future teachers or human service professionals. Students apply critical thinking by analyzing and evaluating existing information and by creating new information that culminates in their concept mapping papers.

More specifically, students are asked to: (1) identify a developmental concept or topic of their choice from the textbook and to briefly summarize it in their own words; (2) analyze the entries of Anne Frank's diary for representative examples of the selected concept; (3) compare and contrast these examples with examples from their own adolescent years; and (4) generate a concept map with these examples to visually depict the ecological system (Bronfenbrenner, 1979) of Anne Frank and themselves next to each other (see Figure 20.1) to conclude what the analysis and biographical comparison might mean for them as future educators.

Students write three concept mapping papers over the duration of the course and, for each one, select a new developmental concept or topic from the textbook. Students receive timely feedback and have the option to submit a revised version to earn a higher grade, if deemed appropriate. In each round of the assignment, students become more skillful in producing papers of higher quality, and their interest level changes from "no thank you—my brain hurts" to "it's worthwhile putting effort into this paper—I enjoy it, actually."

Critical Thinking

This task requires a broad range of critical thinking skills. In brief, critical thinking can be defined as "the ability to engage in purposeful, self-regulatory judgment" (Abrami et al., 2008, p. 1102). Critical thinking is often described as encompassing interpretation, analysis, evaluation, inference, explanation, and self-regulation, along with several sub-skills and dispositions (Facione, 1990). Most of these skills also align with the higher order-thinking skills in the cognitive domain of Bloom's (1956) revised taxonomy of educational objectives: analyze, evaluate, and create (Anderson & Krathwohl, 2001). Throughout the task of the concept mapping paper, students analyze Anne Frank's diary and their own biography for developmental concepts or theories, compare and contrast these along eco-systemic,

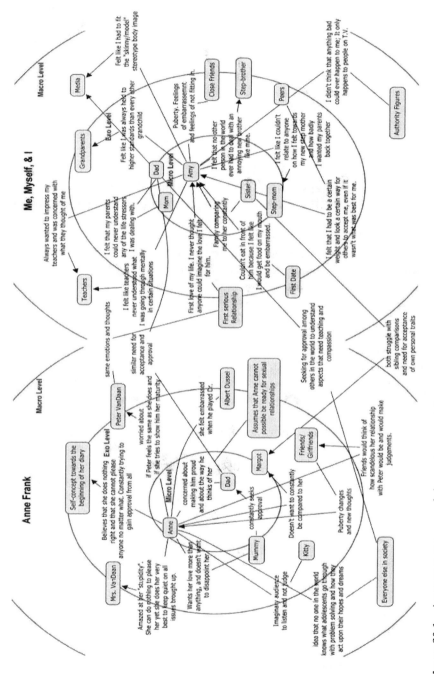

Figure 20.1 A concept map on adolescent egocentrism.

socio-historic, and gender issues, make inferences about the relevance of these concepts for their own teaching, construct concept maps, and write a complete paper. In contrast, the *Anne Frank Mini Essay* task focuses mainly on definitions and examples of concepts of human development and, therefore, requires lower-levels of critical thinking skills as they pertain to knowledge, comprehension, and application (Bloom, 1956; Anderson et al., 2001). From an educational psychology perspective, these weekly *Mini Essays* provide students with knowledge and skills that are needed to execute the higher-order thinking required to complete the *Anne Frank Concept Mapping Papers* successfully.

Concept Mapping

This task also requires some basic concept mapping skills. Concept maps are graphical two-dimensional displays of concepts, connected by links that represent the relationships between pairs of concepts (Cañas et al., 2004). Concept maps are visual representations of information and can be used for instructional and assessment purposes in education (Feucht, Marchand, Obarach, & Olafson, in press). For example, students can use concept maps to identify, organize, and re-construct their own knowledge, illustrate their cognitive models and belief systems, and represent the results of an analysis task (Schraw & Paik, 2013). In the revised version of Bloom's taxonomy, the creation of concept maps would be considered a learning objective that requires the highest level of thinking skills and acts as an extension of evaluation and analysis skills. The concept map functions as a visual representation of the outcomes of their case analyses (Feucht et al., in press). They can be studied and graded effectively by the instructor as a replacement for writing a results section.

During the second week of the course, students learn about concept maps, the process of concept mapping, and the application of simple concept mapping software, IHMC Cmap Tools. Along with the free software, students also receive a graphic file that visually depicts two systems of concentric rings that represent the eco systems of Anne Frank and the student (Me, Myself and I), next to each other (see Figure 20.1). Students can upload the graphic as a background picture into their concept map, which allows them to represent their results effectively, according to the structure of the ecological systems theory. The use of the concept mapping software and background graphic allows students to create, adjust, revise, and print/export their concept maps easily.

Evidence of Students' Learning

The *Anne Frank Assignments* have considerable impact on students' learning, based on the increasing quality of the assignments, students' professional reflections at the end of the concept mapping papers (i.e., "My conclusion as an educator"), and student responses to the open-ended section of the anonymous course evaluations at the end of the semester. Across these different assessment points, students documented that the *Anne Frank Assignments* helped them with respect to the following learning objectives (sorted according to occurrence, highest first):

- better understanding and memorization of different human development theories and concepts;
- connecting different theories and concepts to a real case study;
- applying the learned theories and concepts in their future classroom or workplace;
- taking the perspective of teenage students;
- appreciating a life in freedom and without the direct influence of war;
- learning from history and understanding the Holocaust;
- dealing with their own biographies; and becoming a better parent.

Tips for Instructors

The *Anne Frank* Assignment is applicable for many different professions. The following tips demonstrate its learning outcomes relevant to a broad student audience.

Importance of Task Repetition
Often, students are not used to doing higher-order thinking tasks in their course work; hence, it takes some time for them to acquire and practice the needed competencies. The two-step process of the *Mini Essays* and the *Concept Mapping Paper* scaffolds students towards higher order thinking levels along Bloom's taxonomy. Yet, they still struggle with the cognitive demands of the later assignment to analyze, synthesize, and create knowledge (Anderson et al., 2001) across the domains of scientific theory, biographical memory, and pedagogical practice. Hence, it is important for students to have the opportunity to revise and resubmit their *Concept Mapping Papers*, but also to practice and fine-tune their competencies in reoccurring versions of the assignment. By the third revision, students have greater confidence in completing the assignment and have developed an appreciation for its intellectual merit.

Proficiency of Professional Language
The *Concept Mapping Paper* assignment lends itself to developing and assessing students' use of professional language. Because the learning outcomes of the assignment cut across different knowledge domains, students can demonstrate their ability to use scientific and pedagogical terminology

correctly and effectively in the overlap of theory and application. Proficiency in professional language can be easily added as an assessment criterion to the assignment rubric.

Introduction to Scientific Data Analysis

Both assignments require students to analyze data, present results, and explain their meaning in the context of existing theory. Students gain understanding of how scientific concepts and theory can be used to explain their professional practice from a human development perspective. They also learn how to analyze data from a research oriented perspective, in particular, using a deductive, theory driven coding scheme for data analysis (Feucht, in press). Certainly, as discussed earlier, one needs to ensure that students do not develop a false understanding of theory-evidence coordination when completing these two assignments and when links are made to empirical research as a method of scientific inquiry and discovery. In other words, instructors can use this assignment as a teaching moment to explicitly describe and illustrate the relationship between research, theory, and classroom practice.

CONCLUSION

Dear Kitty, sometimes I wonder what my students would think if I asked them to pick an entry from Anne Frank's diary that is developmentally and biographically meaningful to them and to rewrite the entry from the perspective of a teenager with a different gender, skin color, or sexual orientation, or maybe through the eyes of the "funny looking kid" that they remember from school. Much can be learned from Anne Frank in human development (the science) and from human development in Anne Frank (the humanity).

REFERENCES

Abrami, P. C., Bernard, R. M., Borokhovski, E., Wade, A., Surkes, M. A., Tamim, R., & Zhang, D. (2008). Instructional interventions affecting critical thinking skills and dispositions: A stage 1 meta-analysis. *Review of Educational Research, 78,* 1102–1134.

American Association of Colleges for Teacher Education (2014). *edTPA.* Retrieved from http://edtpa.aacte.org/

Anderson, L. W., & Krathwohl, D. R. (Eds.) (2001). *A taxonomy for learning, teaching, and assessing: A revision of Bloom's taxonomy of educational objectives.* Boston, MA: Allyn and Bacon.

Berk, L. E. (2012). *Child development* (9th ed.). New York, NY: Pearson.

Bloom, B. S., Engelhart, M. D., Furst, E. J., Hill, W. H., & Krathwohl, D. R. (1956). *Taxonomy of educational objectives: The classification of educational goals. Handbook I: Cognitive domain.* New York, NY: David McKay Company.

Bronfenbrenner, U. (1979). *The ecology of human development.* Cambridge, MA: Harvard University Press.

Cañas, A. J., Hill, G., Carff, R., Suri, N., Lott, J., Eskridge, T., . . . Carvajal, R. (2004). In A. J. Cañas, J. D. Novak, & F. M. González (Eds.), *Concept maps: Theory, methodology, technology.* Proceedings of the First International Conference on Concept Mapping (pp. 125–133). Pamplona, Spain: Universidad Pública de Navarra.

Council for the Accreditation of Educator Preparation (CAEP) (2013). *CAEP Accreditation Standards.* Retrieved from http://caepnet.org/standards/

Facione, P. A. (1990). *Critical thinking: A statement of expert consensus for purposes of educational assessment and instruction. Research findings and recommendations.* Newark, DE: American Philosophical Association. (ERIC Document Reproduction Service No. ED315423)

Feucht, F. C., Marchand, G., Obarah. D., & Olafson, L. (2015). Instructional use of concept maps in teaching research and measurement courses. In M. McCrudden, G. Schraw, & C. Buckendahl (Eds.), *Use of visual displays in research and testing: Coding, interpreting, and reporting data* (pp. 207–235). Charlotte, NC: Information Age.

Frank, A., Mooyaart, B. M., & Roosevelt, E. (1993). *Anne Frank. Diary of a young girl.* New York, NY: Bantam.

Kuhn, D. (1989). Children and adults as intuitive scientists. *Psychological Review, 96*(4), 674–689.

Ohio Department of Education (2013). *Ohio Assessments for Educators (OAE). Fields 001 to 004: Assessment of professional knowledge: Assessment framework.* Retrieved from http://www.oh.nesinc.com/

Schraw, G., & Paik, E. (2013). Toward a typology of instructional visual displays (pp. 97–129). In G. Schraw, M. McCrudden, & D. Robinson (Eds.), *Learning through visual displays.* Charlotte, NC: Information Age.

Siegelman, C. K, & Rider, E. A. (2014). *Life span human development* (8th ed.). Boston, MA: Cengage Learning.

CHAPTER 21

TEACHING ABOUT FAMILY, NEIGHBORHOOD, AND COMMUNITY EFFECTS ON CHILD AND ADOLESCENT DEVELOPMENT

Lee Shumow
Northern Illinois University

OVERVIEW

Families and communities can be studied in classes from many academic disciplines. In educational psychology classes, the topic generally pertains to understanding how families contribute to students' academic adjustment, which includes students' learning, development, behavior, motivation, and performance. Learning about the ways that families, communities, and schools interact to influence student learning and development is essential in many educational psychology classes. Further, because so many students in our classes will be or are practicing educators, it is important for them to learn how to apply that knowledge in practice so that they can partner with parents to foster students' well-being.

Challenges and Innovations in Educational Psychology Teaching and Learning, pages 273–285
Copyright © 2016 by Information Age Publishing
All rights of reproduction in any form reserved.

In this chapter, I describe two different approaches that I have used to teach about families and communities. First, with support from an initiative managed by the American Association of Colleges of Education and funded by the MetLife Foundation, I designed and, with colleagues, implemented a model for preparing future teachers to work with families in fostering their students' learning and development. That model entailed embedding content and learning activities about families in six different classes taken by pre-service teachers that were required for teacher certification at Northern Illinois University. Those courses were: Educational Psychology; Development of the Elementary School Child; Philosophy of Education; Developmental Reading Programs in Elementary Schools; Organizing Effective Elementary Reading Instruction; and Tests and Measurements in Elementary School Student Assessment. I use an activity in my adolescent development class, which is required for teacher certification that is similar to the activity in the child development class.

Second, I designed a graduate class for teachers and other educators about working with families and communities. The class focuses on understanding how relationships among educators, families, and communities impacts student learning and adjustment and on understanding the educator's role in facilitating positive relationships that support student learning and development.

Student Characteristics

Units on Families for Initial Teacher Certification

As is the case across the United States, the vast majority of the elementary education pre-service teacher certification candidates who participated in the classes with embedded units were female, White, middle class, and of traditional college age. Students in my adolescent development classes who participate in a case study are also predominately White and middle class; there are generally more male and returning students enrolled in the secondary certification classes than the elementary certification program classes.

Graduate Class on Family and Community

The graduate course on family and community has been offered both on campus to a diverse group of students who came from various schools and off campus in school districts that contracted with the College of Education to offer the class for their employees. The course was offered under the auspices of the university's external programs office. Human service professionals like counselors and social workers also registered for the course as did school department heads and vice principals. The College of Education educational leadership faculty subsequently approached me to teach the class to cohorts of students who were pursuing administrative certification. The course meets one of the Interstate School Leadership Licensure Consortium Policy Standards (ISLLC) standards and I subsequently taught several cohorts of school leaders. Recently, the educational leadership area designed a new program to certify school principals in the state of Illinois and adopted the course for that program. The proposed teacher leadership graduate program has also included the families and communities course as a required class.

Currently, that graduate course is taught to cohorts of students who have been accepted into the principal certification program. The standards for that program are high. Applicants must hold a valid license in either teaching or in a school support professional area and they must have passed a basic skills test. Students also must have a letter of commitment from an internship mentor and the superintendent of the district in which they will complete an internship. Before admission, candidates must successfully complete the initial course in the program with a grade of B or higher. During the prerequisite course, candidates are interviewed by two full-time faculty members, respond to a scenario in writing, and submit a portfolio of their professional achievements. The stringent admission requirements have resulted in having highly motivated, committed, and academically able students enrolled in the course. Men and women from varied ethnic backgrounds who live and work in a wide range of communities are enrolled in the course.

Significance of Teaching Educators About Families

Relevance of Teaching About Families and Communities in Educational Psychology

Educational psychologists are concerned with understanding student learning and development. We build and test theories about learning and we translate implications and insights from theory and research for practitioners. On one hand, parents can be conceptualized as important influences on student's learning and development. On the other hand, parents can be thought of as adult learners who, along with educators, are partners in learning about children. Studies of families and communities have been framed in theoretical perspectives that are very familiar to educational psychologists such as ecological systems, sociocultural, and social cognitive theories. These theories take into account the bidirectional influences between parents, educators, and students.

Why Educators Need to Know About This Topic

Researchers have repeatedly demonstrated that families play an important role in their children's school adjustment and that strong teacher-parent relationships are beneficial for children (Shumow, 2014). Educators who have the knowledge, skill, and support to work with families are better prepared than those who do not to build strong relationships with families and positively impact student adjustment (Caspe, Lopez, Chu, & Weiss, 2011). Unfortunately, many educators report that they receive little preparation for understanding or engaging families during their professional education. Importantly, they further report that there is little support or information provided for engaging families after they enter their professions (MetLife, 2006).

Essential Knowledge About Families and Communities for Educators

There is some essential knowledge that, in my experience, generally leads educators to work well with families and communities. First, it is important to recognize and respect the roles that educators, parents, and communities play in student learning and in relation to one another. Educators need to understand the contributions that families and communities make to students' school adjustment and they need to understand their role as professionals to invite family and community participation. Second, it is critically important to understand that parents are likely to have different knowledge and perspectives about their children than does the teacher. Thus, it is imperative that educators learn how to obtain the knowledge and perspective of the parents. Third, educators need to understand why, in what ways, and with what consequences parents are involved in their children's education and schooling. Fourth, it is essential for educators to understand that parenting practices, beliefs, and expectations differ between cultural groups and communities. Fifth, it is valuable for educators to understand how to find and utilize community resources for students and their families. Finally, educators need an array of skills including trust, relationship, and partnership-building skills, communication skills, and advocacy skills.

Over the years as I have worked as a classroom teacher, parent educator, parent volunteer (in my own children's schools), and a professor teaching about families and communities, I have come to believe that a few dispositions are essential for successful home school relations. Those dispositions include open mindedness, optimism, and a willingness to collaborate. To some extent, knowledge helps facilitate the development of these dispositions, but I have found that promoting perspective taking has been very helpful in supporting the development of these dispositions

Challenges of Teaching Educators About Family and Community

As is the case with most other topics that educators have to learn, a number of common challenges can be identified. First, many students have preconceived beliefs and expectations, based on their own background experiences. Second, educators are faced with many competing and complex demands in their work. Third, novice teachers tend to have limited knowledge coupled with high confidence. Finally, many educators lack knowledge about or immersion experiences with diverse families.

Educators bring their personal history and experience with them to our courses. Given the traditional (i.e., one way communication from school to the home and parents invited as volunteers rather than partners) nature of most family involvement practices in schools, it does not come as a surprise that our students come to teacher education and professional development programs with ideas that such traditional practices are how they define their role and what they expect to do as teachers (Patte, 2013). Many of those ideas come from what pre-service teachers observed as K–12 students themselves. Those traditional beliefs and expectations about the nature of family involvement are likely exacerbated by the fact that practicing teachers obtain most of the preparation for interacting with families during their student teaching (Chavkin, 2005). Thus, they are likely to see and gain experience with traditional forms of school-family interaction. The prior knowledge and experience is often a challenge that must be overcome if educators are to welcome families as partners.

Another challenge is limited time. Learning about families and developing expertise in how to interact with them requires a great deal of time on the part of educators who have to play many roles and take on many responsibilities in their daily work (Chavkin, 2005). Pre-service teachers almost universally (95%) describe limited time on their part and on the part of parents more frequently than any other barrier to developing family school partnerships (Patte, 2013). Being an educator is tremendously demanding and multifaceted. It takes time to develop knowledge about something as complex as working with families and communities and there is a great deal of competition for that time.

Walker and Dotger (2012) found that, as with many other aspects of teaching, pre-service teachers reported high efficacy and evinced limited knowledge and skill in responding to parents and in meeting professional standards related to parent engagement. In the absence of experiences during teacher education designed to help those prospective teachers develop the knowledge and skills they will need, their overconfidence results in limited motivation on their part to rectify their lack of knowledge and skill which, in turn, sets them up for failure in their first job. Many of the practicing educators I encounter have low efficacy in terms of working with parents and tend to avoid parents in general and blame individual parents for any problems that arise.

Yet, another challenge is related to the demographic characteristics of teachers at both the pre-service and in-service levels. According to the National Center for Educational Statistics, 83.5% of the public school teaching force in the United States is non-Hispanic White, but only 52% of the students are and that percentage is expected to fall to 45% by the year 2023. In general, the students in my classes lack experience with and knowledge about diverse families and, because so few of these students come from diverse backgrounds, it is rarely possible to broaden their perspectives by having them listen to and learn from each other. Numerous studies have found that both parenting practices and communication patterns differ by social class, culture, ethnicity, and immigration status. It is challenging to negotiate a path that avoids stereotyping and that provides the educators with tools that will enable them to learn from and about various cultures in one activity or even one class.

There are several specific populations of students that either receive or need particular attention in coursework. Special educators have typically received far more preparation to work with families than have other types of educators. In my graduate classes, the special education teachers are often tremendously helpful in that they can articulate the reasons that families are important and they generally have well-organized systems and a tool kit of strategies that they share. Those systems are often efficient and help overcome the time challenge. Early childhood educators are another group that has usually focused on families. On the other hand, teachers who are either preparing to work with adolescents or who currently work with adolescents often resist the idea that families should be involved with adolescent students. They often espouse the common misconception that adolescents are only oriented to their peers and are seeking independence and therefore do not want or need family involvement in their lives.

Promising Practices

Undergraduate Course Activities

The undergraduate model was unique in that a different activity was embedded in each class on both practical and reasonable grounds. A central reason that a course on family involvement was not offered in the teacher certification program at my university and many other colleges and universities is that students have a difficult time fulfilling all the requirements for a degree and certification. Thus, programs have been reticent to require additional coursework. Faculty do perceive that it is important to prepare future teachers to work with families and they were amendable to including some instruction and an activity about families in six different education courses in the certification sequence. Theoretically, I believed that embedding information and practice in these courses sent the message that working with parents was an integral part of teaching and not a stand-alone and separate practice.

Pre-service teachers were engaged in an array of activities to prepare them to understand and work with parents. Some textbook reading related to each topic was assigned in each class. In the Child Development course, students wrote a comparative case study of two children which entailed observing the children and interviewing their parents about their children's learning and development, experiences at home, and about the parents' relationship and interactions with educators. In the Educational Psychology course, students studied various communications that educators could send to parents, rated them, and recommended the best ones to practicing teachers in a partnership school. Students in the Philosophy of Education course read different perspectives on what family involvement could be and discussed the readings in class; each student subsequently interviewed a teacher to ascertain his/her beliefs and practices regarding family roles and relations with schools. Two literacy classes (Methods 1 and Methods 2) also participated. In the first class, students created brochures and displays about supporting literacy at home. The students installed the displays for and distributed the brochures during parent teacher conferences in a partnership elementary school. Students in the second methods class designed homework assignments and accompanying guides for families to use in helping their children successfully complete the assigned homework. Finally, students in the assessment course role-played four different types of communication with parents regarding assessments. Those interactions included: Explaining standards to be met during the school year at an initial open house; responding to a parent complaint about a child's grade; discussing a child's behavioral change and classroom expectations with a parent; and, interpreting a child's standardized test results for parents during a formal conference

Graduate Course

One unique aspect of the graduate course stems from the fact that it is usually taught to cohorts of students. As a result, although the basic topics remain the same, a number of the required readings change to reflect the specific context in which I am teaching (i.e., school district, local community). This allows me to make the subject matter more relevant to the students. For example, when I taught the class to educators who work in an urban setting with families who are predominately minorities with low-income, we read articles about such families and about programs and practices that have been successful in that context. On the other hand, when I taught the course in a high school district located in an upper middle-income suburban area, I assigned readings about the academic, social, and emotional well-being of adolescents from affluent families.

The course is conducted in a format that blends typical college instructional practices with a workshop. Part of the course entails discussions, readings, and case studies, such as those found in a book developed by several experts on involving families (Weiss, Lopez, Kreider, & Chatman-Nelson, 2013), participating in small cooperative group learning activities, student presentations, and viewing video examples. The video examples come from commercial films, You Tube videos, and a series of interviews I conducted with parents of children in various communities. The children of these parents ranged from early elementary school through high school and the videos were filmed and edited by media professionals on campus. There is some evidence that video promotes perspective taking among both practicing and pre-service educators (Smith & Shumow, 2011).

Assignments include participation in planning one class period (during the second half of the semester) with a small group and creating an individual project. Approximately an hour of each three hour session is devoted to "work time" during which teachers work on their individual projects either alone or plan with other students in their group. I provide some resources to help them with their projects, assist them in their searches for resources, and answer individual questions or concerns pertaining to the project.

The planning assignment involves having the students identify their personal and professional interests pertaining to family and community. The interest is usually related to their individual project (to be described subsequently). I identify common themes across these interests (e.g., racial or ethnic diversity, special needs, social-emotional adjustment, literacy) and place students in groups. Students individually read approximately 100 pages of materials on their topic and submit an annotated bibliography on the reading. They are each asked to recommend one of these readings that will be beneficial for their colleagues to read. They then work in groups to select assigned readings and to plan class activities for students during their group's class period. I work with them to facilitate their planning.

The individual project is a comprehensive assignment in which students design an applied project on family involvement and community connections related to their professional responsibilities. In completing this assignment, they are expected to apply the knowledge and skills they have gained during the course. Most projects address parent and community involvement pertaining to one group of students within the school (e.g., first graders) and parents within the community (e.g., parents of ELL students). The project focuses on: (a) an area of student learning/curriculum (e.g., biology: genetics; language arts: writing expository essays); (b) a type of student development (e.g., attendance, conflict resolution, graduation); or (c) a school or community issue/need (transition to high school, safety, bullying).

There are five components to Part One of the project, which is due at mid-semester. First, the educators identify, explain, and justify the focus of the project using data about the need and importance for the school community. For example, they present evidence that students scored below expectations in an academic area or evidence of an increase in fights in the locker rooms. They are expected to provide some background information about the context and history of the issues and explain why it is important for their school community to focus on the topic. Second, drawing upon extant data, they describe the group of students and parents that the project will involve (e.g., number, demographic characteristics, current involvement).

Third, they gather information through interviews, questionnaires, and/ or focus groups about the perspectives of: (1) a representative sample of parents; (2) a school representative such as a social worker, counselor, or administrator (e.g., curriculum coordinator, department chair, dean of students) who has responsibility for the topic selected for the project; and (3) representatives from at least one group impacted by or involved in the topic of the project such as administrators, faculty, students, or community members. Perspectives are to be sought on the: (a) knowledge, attitudes, beliefs about parent and community involvement relative to the issue and about the types, amount, and success of parental involvement or community connections as they exist now or are needed; and (b) the importance of/commitment to the particular area of student learning, development, or need that is addressed.

Fourth, students identify their project's goals. Fifth, they identify resources available in their community and among their families that will promote the particular area of learning and development or the issue/ need they are addressing. For example, how many families have Internet access at home and what resources does the public library own to support the goals of the project?

There are also five components to Part Two of the project, which entails plans for implementation and is due at the end of the semester. Although the project goes hand in hand with school based curricula or procedures which might be in development in the district, the project focuses specifically on the family community links. Each planned component must be annotated. The annotation entails using comment or footnote functions to cite and briefly explain why the practice is justified based on texts from the class. The plans (components) are, first, to clearly identify and describe utilization of a resource present in families or the community to help students learn the selected topic, contribute to their development, or address the identified need. Evidence must be presented that the resource has been investigated and is available.

Second, a fun or motivating family activity or event to support project goals must be planned. The event/activity can be held at school, in the community, or completed independently by families and can be an educational opportunity for families and/or communities on the topic or it can entail showcasing students' work. Third, homework assignment(s) or home-based preparatory or follow-up activities must be developed to support project goals.

Fourth, three types of communications need to be designed: (1) inform-ing parents about the project activities; (2) informing parents about stu-dent learning, development, and progress related to project goals; and (3) preparing a formal press release for the local media. Finally, an evaluation must be designed that ascertains how educators will know whether their goals were met.

One class reading and class "work time" is devoted to having pairs of students read and provide feedback to each other on their project the week before it is due. During the final class period of the semester students share of their projects with each other so that they can each benefit from the ideas and resources identified and developed by their colleagues.

Student Benefits

Undergraduate Course Activities

Table 21.1 summarizes the results reported in Shumow (2004). As can be seen in the table, the pre-service teachers who participated in the activities reported increased knowledge and skill about: how to solicit the perspective of parents, how to communicate with and provide information to parents, and ways that parents promote student learning. Students also reported increased confidence in their ability to exchange information with parents. Extensive analysis was done of the products that students produced during their role playing experiences in the assessment class (Mehlig & Shumow, 2013). The evidence suggested that, overall, these students demonstrated

TABLE 21.1   Evidence That Preservice Teachers Benefitted from Class Activities

Course and Activity	Compared to Students in Control Group Classes
Child Development: Case study observation and interview	Increased knowledge about how to interview parents
	Increased knowledge about how to learn about families
	Grew in confidence about how to interview parents
Reading Methods I	Increased knowledge about how to inform parents about learning expectations
	Increased knowledge of specific ways parents can help children learn to read
Assessment	Increased knowledge about how to implement presentation and workshops for parents
	Increased knowledge about how to inform parents about results of student assessments
Philosophy of Education	Increased knowledge about how to communicate with parents
	Increased confidence in ability to involve parents

Note: Educational Psychology and Reading Methods II students did not participate.

knowledge and skills about how to establish a positive relationship, communicate effectively, and exchange information with parents as well as how to promote parent understanding of assessment practices used in school and their children's progress in school. Students in the assessment class further reported that the role-playing activities were very important in their learning and that they intended to practice what they had learned when they became teachers. Others also have found that simulations are effective means of preparing teachers (Dotger, Harris, & Hansel, 2008)

Graduate Course

Student learning in my graduate course has not been formally studied. Nevertheless, evidence from evaluations conducted both immediately following the course and at the conclusion of the cohort suggests that at least some of the practicing educators find the class to be extremely valuable in their work. The class evaluations immediately following those classes that were conducted in the school districts tend to result in a bimodal distribution. There have been highly positive ratings from half or more of the educators and negative evaluations from the others. Many educators who rate the course highly report that it is transformative for their thinking and practice. Those who rate the course negatively object either to the work (which they deem too taxing because they do not intend to follow through on it) or to the idea of partnering with parents. The evaluation conducted immediately following the first course offered to educators pursuing the principal certificate was overwhelmingly positive. Those students perceived the course content as central to the role of a principal and as very practical and novel.

Interestingly, and to my surprise, in the two cohorts in which I received the most resistance and the most immediate negative feedback following the course, later evaluations indicated that, upon reflection, the educators changed their minds. In one case, a formal evaluation was conducted of a large professional development grant under which one of these course was offered about two years after the class ended. The cohort had taken ten classes during a three-year period. I was stunned to read in the evaluation report that my family and community class was identified as extremely helpful and useful and as the most important course that these educators had taken! In the other case, one of the class members (who had been among the most resistant and negative educators that I had ever taught in that class) became the director of professional development in the same school district. Much to my amazement, one day my department chair invited me into his office to ask me if I would teach the course in that school district for a new cohort of teachers. In fact, he explained, the director of the district's professional development insisted that the course be included, that I had to be the instructor of it, and admitted that he did "not get it at the time," but later realized that what he learned in the course was essential to his practice. The knowledge put into practice had contributed substantially to the success of the school improvement plan that had been undertaken by many of the educators in the cohort.

Recommendations and Conclusions

Based upon my experiences in teaching both undergraduate and graduate students, I have several recommendations for others who wish to teach pre-service or prospective teachers about parents and families. As noted in the beginning of the chapter, there are a number of disciplines in which learning about parents is appropriate. Given the multifaceted nature of the topic, it would behoove educational psychologists involved in pre-service teacher education to advocate for including the topic in multiple classes required for teacher certification and for the knowledge and skill development to increase in complexity as students advance in their programs. Chavkin (2005) refers to this as horizontal (activities in numerous classes) and vertical (increasing complexity) in her recommendations for practice. Recommendations for educational psychology courses include: (1) engaging students in authentic learning activities; (2) promoting student perspective taking abilities; and (3) and arming students with practical strategies together with theoretically and empirically grounded reasons for using them.

REFERENCES

Caspe, M., Lopez, M., Chu, A., & Weiss, H.B. (2011). *Teaching the teachers: Preparing educators to engage families for student achievement* (Issue Brief). http://www.hfrp.org/publications-resources/browse-our-publications/teaching-the-teachers-preparing-educators-to-engage-families-for-student-achievement

Chavkin, N. F. (2005). Preparing educators for school-family partnerships: Challenges and opportunities. In E. Patrikakou, R. Weissberg, S. Redding, H. Walberg, & A. R. Anderson (Eds.), *School–family partnership for children's success* (pp. 164–180). New York, NY: Teachers College Press.

Dotger B., Harris S., & Hansel A. (2008). Emerging authenticity: The crafting of simulated parent–teacher candidate conferences. *Teaching Education, 19*(4), 335–347.

Mehlig, L. M., & Shumow, L. (2013). How is my child doing?: Preparing pre-service teachers to engage parents through assessment. *Teaching Education, 24*(2), 181–194.

MetLife, Inc. (2006). *The MetLife survey of the American teacher: A survey of teachers, principals, and leaders of college education programs.* New York, NY: Author.

Patte, M. M. (2011). Examining pre-service teacher knowledge and competencies in establishing family–school partnerships. *School Community Journal, 21*(2), 143–159.

Shumow, L. (2004). Northern Illinois University partnerships for parent engagement. *Thresholds in Education, 30*(2), 11–18.

Shumow, L. (2014). Is the compass broken or did the navigators err? *School Community Journal, 24*(1).

Smith, M C., & Shumow, L. (2011). Improving secondary teachers' knowledge of adolescent development through teens' self-documentaries. *Journal of the International Society for Teacher Education, 15*(2), 45–55.

Walker, J. M., & Dotger, B. H. (2012). Because wisdom can't be told using comparison of simulated parent–teacher conferences to assess teacher candidates' readiness for family-school partnership. *Journal of Teacher Education, 63*(1), 62–75.

Weiss, H. B., Lopez, M. E., Kreider, H., & Chatman-Nelson, C. (Eds.). (2013). *Preparing educators to engage families: Case studies using an ecological systems framework.* Thousand Oaks CA: Sage.

CHAPTER 22

TEACHING MORAL DEVELOPMENT

Daniel Lapsley
University of Notre Dame

Anyone who takes up the profession of teaching, at any level, is taking up
the cause of moral-character education. Indeed, there is universal consensus that education is value-laden and that moral education is inescap-
able in classrooms and schools. Moral values are implicated in the topics
chosen or excluded for instruction; in the respect accorded for truth and
the demand for excellence, good effort, and mastery. It is evident in the
way groups are formed, relationships encouraged or discipline enforced.
Values are intrinsic to what it means to develop, set goals, and aspire to
achieve them. Indeed, Stengle and Tom (2006) insist that the language
of morality is heard in schools every time issues of *right relation* and *what
is worth doing* emerge in instructional lessons or within the interactions of
students, teachers, and colleagues.

This is worth noting if only to counter the charge that morality has been
expunged from schools. In fact, values are immanent to the life of classrooms and inevitable in any instance of teaching and learning. But there is
legitimate concern that the moral work of teaching is too often remanded
to the school's hidden curriculum where it cannot be properly tended as an

Challenges and Innovations in Educational Psychology Teaching and Learning, pages 287–302
Copyright © 2016 by Information Age Publishing

intentional curricular objective (Lapsley, Holter, & Narvaez, 2013; Sanger & Osguthorpe, 2013). Moreover, teachers receive almost no pre-service training in moral-character education unless a required course in educational psychology includes a brief module on moral stage or social domain theory. Unfortunately, such scant attention will hardly prepare teachers for moral-character education; and it all but assures that recent innovations in theory and research will find no place in the curriculum.

In this chapter, I outline a syllabus of topics that I use to teach moral development in a course that targets in-service, but novice, teachers. For at least a generation it was de rigueur to teach moral development by slogging through Kohlberg's moral stage theory. I suspect this is still the drill if extant textbooks are any guide. Although I still teach Kohlberg's theory and the cognitive developmental tradition more generally, I try to place these topics within a broader intellectual context that has resonance with instructional practice (at least this is my hope). There is not much current interest in the details of Kohlberg's specific claims about moral development; and, indeed there is reason enough to think of it as a degenerating research program (Lapsley, 2011, 2005). But the cognitive-developmental tradition can still contribute to a vibrant pedagogy of moral-character education that will be found useful for the moral work of teaching.

The Hook

I admire Doug Lemov's *Teach Like a Champion* (2010) because, while it is written for the practitioner, many of the teaching techniques that it touts are nonetheless vouchsafed by well-attested educational psychology literatures. One technique ("The Hook") is to start a class or unit with an engaging exercise that inspires and excites students "to take the first step willingly" (p. 75). My hook for the moral development unit begins with a display of Breughel's masterpiece *Landscape with the Fall of Icarus*. I ask students to report what they see in the painting. Students readily report obvious figures in the foreground—the ploughman tending his field, the shepherd looking away from the sea upwards towards the clouds. There is a ship sailing briskly off the shore and then—barely noticed: a boy's white legs are about to disappear into the sea.

This painting inspired W. H. Auden to write one of his iconic poems, *Musee des Beaux Arts*, which is recited for class consideration. It begins "*About suffering they were never wrong/the old Masters: how well they understood/Its human position: how it takes place/While someone else is eating or opening a window or just walking dully along.*" The final lines of the poem come to the point:

In Breughel's *Icarus*, for instance, how everything turns away
Quite leisurely from the disaster; the ploughman may
Have heard the splash, the forsaken cry,
But for him it was not an important failure; the sun shone
As it had to on the white legs disappearing into the green
Water, and the expensive delicate ship that must have seen
Something amazing, a boy falling out of the sky,
Had somewhere to get to and sailed calmly on.

The hook of this exercise is to reflect on how anyone can turn away leisurely from disasters that do not concern us. How is it we do not see the moral dimensions of our experience? How is it that we can "walk dully along" and take little notice of suffering and other dilemmatic features of our moral landscape? Which of us is like the ploughman in the painting, or the shepherd looking away, or the ship that takes notice of a "boy falling out of the sky" but sails calmly on?

The old Masters may have been on to something. One point to underscore is that what we *see* depends upon who *we are*. Individuals with well-developed moral faculties, or moral schemas chronically accessible, are likely to view the world through the prism of morality; to detect the "near occasions of sin" that are likely to put virtue to the test. To be a moral person, to be in trait possession of the virtues, is to be a person of a certain kind; and such a person appraises the social landscape differently than others who are morally obtuse, or whose virtues are less readily accessible. Some individuals never notice the moral features of their experience, or do not see them as readily as do others (while others see morality or virtue at stake in everything—which might be another problem).

What we see depends on who we are, but *who we are* can be understood in at least two ways relevant to the moral development unit: first, in terms of moral stage theory and the cognitive developmental tradition; and second, in terms of the literatures on character education. Put differently, moral perception depends upon structures of *moral cognition* and upon the structure of *character*. For a long time these two traditions have elided the common ground that exists between them; and the unit unfolds in the direction of an integrative perspective. But it is instructive to unpack the key claims of the two traditions.

Two Paradigms: Moral Development and Character Education

Moral development and character development arose out of two very different intellectual traditions whose core assumptions and beliefs seemed difficult to reconcile. Indeed, whether one was a moral or character educator was often revealing of paradigmatic commitments across a range of issues. The two paradigms can be usefully compared on three dimensions: orienting ethical theory; tradition of liberal education; and, preferred pedagogy (Lapsley & Yeager, 2014).

Ethical Theory

The moral development and character education paradigms align with different ethical theories. For example, the moral development paradigm is concerned with deontological aspects of morality, that is, with decisions about moral obligation and what one *ought to do* given the requirements of the moral law. It asks, "By what moral decision-making calculus can I resolve a dilemma and discern the proper course of action"? In this paradigm moral evaluation falls upon conduct—did I do the right thing? Was my behavior justified by the requirements of a moral principle, say, by Kant's Categorical Imperative? Kohlberg's moral stage theory illustrates this approach. It describes a sequence of moral reasoning that reveals increasing appreciation of the deontic requirements of the moral law as one approaches the final stage. Consequently, the aim of education is the development of deliberative competence to discern the moral point of view when faced with competing demands on justice.

If moral development aligns with Kantian ethical theory then traditional character education invokes Aristotle and has other priorities. The basic issue is not so much the qualities of moral reasoning but rather the qualities of *agents*. The goal is to become a person of a certain kind, a person whose behavior habitually displays the moral virtues. Hence, virtue ethics is the guiding ethical theory rather than Kantian deontology. Instead of asking "what should I do?" character education asks "what sort of person should I become?" Not surprisingly, the target of character education is the cultivation of habits, traits and virtues.

Traditions of Liberal Education

According to Kimball (1986), the idea of liberal education from antiquity to the modern era can be described by reference to two traditions that he terms *philosophical* and *oratorical*. Indeed, Kimball (1986) argues that the history of educational reform, including the reform initiatives of the twentieth century, oscillates between these two traditions. The same reforms are simply recycled as first one then the other tradition becomes ascendant. I argue that moral development reflects the philosophical tradition of liberal education; while traditional character education reflects imperatives of the oratorical tradition.

In the philosophical tradition truth is unsettled and elusive; we see through the glass darkly, as it were. And so, the search for truth is an act of discovery. Therefore, one must equip learners with philosophical dispositions to reason, to think critically, judge fairly, and to keep an open mind. In contrast, the oratorical tradition locates truth in great texts and traditional wisdom; and so the search for truth is an act of recovery. The truth must be imparted by oratorical transmission, by exhortation and enjoinder, so that learners are well equipped with the certain verities of the past. The oratorical tradition knows exactly what it wants to transmit and how. Thus, it is strong on content but weak on method (no one would mistake it for best practice). In turn, the philosophical tradition seems stronger on method but is weak on content. It encourages philosophical dispositions of inquiry but is agnostic about committing to anything in particular. As we will see, one source of tension between moral development and traditional character education was precisely on the content of moral-character formation and the pedagogy for making it come alive and stick.

Preferred Pedagogy

Not surprisingly, moral development and traditional character education prefer different approaches to instruction. The pedagogy of moral development is more indirect in the sense that it encourages children to actively construct moral meaning by means of transactive discussion of moral issues and dilemmas. Following Dewey, it wants to give children authentic opportunity to experience democratic participation and a sense of community. It encourages class meetings and cooperative groupings.

In contrast, traditional character educators are suspicious of indirect methods (Wynn & Ryan, 1997). Our common experience has already sorted out the required and acceptable schedule of virtues. The wisdom of generations has already identified desirable features of character—why should we let children debate and discuss them as if character were up for grabs? Hence, traditional character education more often favors direct didactic instruction, exhortation and "telling" for passing along the "Great Tradition" to students. The oratorical sympathies of traditional character education could not be clearer (Lapsley & Narvaez, 2006).

Moral Stages and Just Communities

A Biographical Introduction

There is no getting around a consideration of Kohlberg's moral stage theory. Although I dislike slogging through stages, there is value in considering the rhythm of moral development, and students often warm to the task. I introduce moral stage theory by placing it in the context of Kohlberg's biography. I draw attention to three early formative experiences that formed the basis of his life's work.

During the Second World War, and just out of high school, Kohlberg enlisted in the merchant marines where he was assigned to an escort ship in the Atlantic theater. When Nazi Germany was defeated Kohlberg took up another cause. He got involved in the movement to smuggle European Jews, who were remnant of the Holocaust, to Palestine. This was contrary to Allied policy and Britain set up a blockade to prevent wholesale immigration to Palestine. The boat on which Kohlberg served was stopped by the British Royal Navy and the crew was remanded to a British internment camp on Cyprus. Some months later Kohlberg and others were sprung by the Haganah, a Jewish paramilitary defense force, and spirited to an Israeli kibbutz where he stayed for about six months. Kohlberg made his way back to the United States, where he eventually earned a doctoral degree in clinical psychology at the University of Chicago. Doctoral dissertations typically draw no attention, but Kohlberg's dissertation provided preliminary evidence for a stage sequence of moral reasoning that would come to dominate developmental psychology for over five decades.

The Anti-Relativism Project

This biographical sketch is meant to introduce students to Kohlberg's motivation for proposing a theory of moral development. By the time he was their age he had undergone three profound moral experiences: as an enlisted soldier he fought against the Nazi ethos; his humanitarian work on behalf of European Jews collided with allied policy he thought unjust; and then there was his experience of communal egalitarian life on a kibbutzim. These experiences motivated important ethical questions: How is one to justify the moral decisions that one makes? How are we to determine the adequacy of our moral commitments?

When he took up his doctoral studies these questions of justice were ever present. Which of the extant psychological systems of his time (behaviorism, psychoanalysis) could provide the intellectual resources to make sense of his struggle against Nazism and injustice? As it turned out, none of them could. Neither psychoanalysis nor behaviorism took a stand on how to determine the legitimacy of moral systems or else actively embraced ethical relativism. Kohlberg's life's work was to be a corrective to this. His moral stage theory was an attempt to devise the psychological resources to defeat ethical relativism, and along the way Kohlberg became one of the most famous developmental psychologists of the twentieth century.

Jean Piaget's genetic epistemology was crucial to Kohlberg's understanding of moral development; and it is hard to understand Kohlberg's project without making this point. In the cognitive developmental framework each forward movement in stages yields reasoning that is qualitatively better that predecessor stages. It is better because it is capable of more complex adaptations. The final stage in the sequence describes a mode of perfected operations that serves as the basis for evaluating the progressive nature of developmental change. To say that the goal of development is to attain a particular endpoint is to make not only an empirical claim about the natural course of development, but also an evaluative or normative claim. One is making implicit reference to a standard that allows one to distinguish progressive development from mere change, and the standard is instantiated in one's conceptualization of the end point. Developmental change, if it is to count as an instance of development, is evaluated in terms of how closely it approximates the "ideal equilibrium" represented by the final stage of the developmental process. So much depends, then, on the coherence of the final stage of a sequence because the final stage makes developmental explanation possible.

Thus, one can view movement through Kohlberg's stages as the dawning awareness that some moral perspectives are errant and inadequate, that others are preferred, and that there is a way to know the difference. It is the growing realization, as one approaches the moral ideal, as one closes in on the final stage, that moral dilemmas are not insolvable, that moral conflict is not intractable, and that consensus is possible if disputants are motivated by the moral point of view captured by the final stage of moral development. Put differently, ethical relativism is defeated by the attainment of the principled stages of moral reasoning (Lapsley, 2005).

Educational Implications

It is now clear that Kohlberg's theory is on the margins and no longer dominates social cognitive development (Lapsley, 2005). Indeed, Piaget's theory no longer drives the research agenda either, and there seems little interest among contemporary researchers to map developmental change around a conception of stage. Although there is notable longitudinal evidence in favor of Kohlberg's theory, the pace of stage change is turgid and there is little evidence of principled reasoning. Indeed, the final stage was dropped from the scoring manuals, which undermines developmental explanation of stage change. Moreover, there was prima facie refutation of two foundational claims: invariant sequence and the structured whole assumption. Attempts to repair the theory now have the look of ad hoc adjustments that reduced the scope of the theory to something cramped and narrow (e.g., to judgments of fairness derived from oral interviews). The theory now seems incapable of anticipating novel facts in the moral domain and, on this basis, it is a degenerating research program (Lapsley, 2011).

That said, Kohlberg's project has important educational implications. It underscores the importance of discussing moral dilemmas as they arise in lessons. Inducing cognitive disequilibrium by confronting students with higher stage arguments (within the limits of one stage) is still a valuable implication of the cognitive developmental tradition. Moreover, it would be a mistake to limit the educational implications to dilemma discussion. Indeed, Kohlberg's approach to moral education seemed less interested in moving students through the moral stages than in developing a school culture that is experienced by students as a just community (Power, Higgins, & Kohlberg, 1989).

Just Communities

In a just community, students value the institution (e.g., the school is valued for its own stake and can obligate members to uphold group norms and responsibilities) and they value the school as a community (e.g., the sense of community is considered an entity apart from specific relationships). Moreover a school's moral community can be revealed by the development of its collective norms. Are collective norms held out as an expectation of conduct that is enforced by the group? How willing are members to uphold collective norms, defend them and to confront violators, and take responsibility for enacting the norm within the life of the school? Are the norms of the school "theirs" or "ours?"

To reach this level of community requires a change in school culture. It requires, for example, class meetings, moral discussion, giving students "voice-and-choice," and a stake in devising and enforcing norms. Although no one is organizing schools in quite the way the Kohlberg team envisioned (e.g., with democratic decision-making and whole-school meetings to establish and defend norms), its insistence on developing community is well-grounded by contemporary educational science. Finding ways to give adolescents more autonomy, for example, or more "voice-and-choice," is one way to improve the stage-environment fit of adolescents and schools. Effective schools with strong student achievement are marked by communal organization (and academic press) where school culture is experienced as a caring community. Kohlberg's research program deserves some credit in getting us to that conclusion.

Domain Theory and Implications

If moral stage theory has been pushed to the margins then social domain theory has certainly stepped in to replace it. Domain theory's central claim is that Kohlberg got it wrong when he suggested that conventional reasoning must be supplanted in a sequence of moral development. Instead, conventional reasoning is a domain distinct from moral reasoning (Turiel, 1983). Social reasoning about morality and conventions is bounded by domain because understanding of these issues arises out of different kinds of experience. Morality is bound up with issues of harm, rights, and the welfare of others. Convention is bound up with issues of social order. Children build up different ways of understanding the requirements of rights-and-welfare and the requirements of effective social organization, and can readily understand this domain distinction even as toddlers (Smetana, 1983).

Each domain comes to different understanding of rules and transgressions. Moral rules are universally applicable and unalterable by consensus. Conventional rules are arbitrary and binding but can be changed by consensus. It is a moral rule not to visit harm upon another, but a conventional violation to address teachers by their first name or to go up-the-down-staircase. Violation of moral rules is held to be more serious than conventional violations. Moreover, a third, personal domain has also been identified (Nucci, 1981) that includes private aspects of one's life and behavior, such as what books to read, what friends to choose, how to dress and groom, what music to like, whether to masturbate or not, or whom to vote for. These are choices that resist social regulation and the demands of deontic moral obligation. It is a useful and engaging exercise to ask students to generate examples of social conventional rules in both families and schools.

It is not always noticed just how Piagetian domain theory is. The boundaries of domains are partial structures that are constructed on the basis of certain behavioral experiences. This is precisely the way Piaget described the emergence of domains of conservation. Cognitive groupings are based on overt actions that have become interiorized, made part of mental cognitive activity—but groupings always retain an element of content specificity just because they are based on different kinds of overt actions. Each grouping of operations is adaptive for its particular content, and some actions are easier to group than others.

I have always understood the construction of social domains to follow the logic of the construction of conservation domains. Piaget was also a domain theorist, and it was Turiel's inspiration to push this Piagetian cognitive developmental insight into social cognitive development. Domains arise as interiorized cognitive constructions of behavioral experiences of certain kinds. But if I am right about this, then social domain theory is just about the last Piagetian theory still standing.

Implications for Education

One implication of social domain theory is that teachers should be sensitive to domain distinctions and calibrate discipline accordingly. Even young children are aware that rules fall into different domains, and that rule violations should not be treated identically. In other words, do not "moralize" about conventional violations. It diminishes the force of moral argument when it is sent chasing after matters of convention; but it also misses opportunities to engage student thinking about legitimate issues of classroom or school convention. Indeed, teachers can increase their influence as socialization agents when they are sensitive to domain distinctions in their disciplinary practices (Nucci, 2001).

A second implication is to recognize that many issues are a mixture of moral, conventional, and personal considerations, and it would be a mistake to treat complex issues solely from the standpoint of morality. Take the matter of peer inclusion and exclusion as an example. Wrapping this complicated issue solely in the discourse of morality will be ineffective because it taps into multiple social reasoning domains (Horn, Daddis, & Killen, 2008). It taps into moral concerns about fairness, harm, and discrimination ("It's not fair to exclude him just because he is gay"), student conventions about group membership and functioning ("The group won't work well with someone different in it"), and personal concerns about friendship selection ("I can be friends with whomever I want").

A useful rule of thumb is to hold fast and advocate for moral considerations, negotiate social (household, school) conventions, and give wide latitude to the personal domain. Of course, rules of thumb will not resolve all conflicts. I suspect parents and teachers will want to park more issues under the moral domain than children find reasonable or fair; and children will have a more expansive view of the personal domain than adults can tolerate.

Modern Character Education

I noted earlier that moral development and character education seemed to spin out of two very different paradigms. Of the two paradigms, character education does not command as much attention as moral development in standard developmental and educational psychology coursework. It is also strangely absent from the curriculum of pre-service teacher education programs. Interestingly, the language of character and character education is loudly heard in a popular education press that otherwise pays scant attention to moral development.

But character education has moved beyond its traditional paradigmatic formulation and is hardly a uniform educational movement. In fact, modern character education is characterized by four rather different approaches that I group under three headings: *Best Practice, Broad Character Education* and *Intentional Moral-Character Education*. The first approach places no additional burden on teacher education programs; the second approach requires teachers to deliver curricula or programs in addition to best practice instruction; and the third approach addresses virtues and morality directly and asserts that moral self-identity is the aim of moral-character education.

Best Practice

On this view, character education is just good education. Teachers attend to the moral formation of pupils when they engage in teacher practices that maximize opportunities for student learning and build a classroom and school culture that is caring and communal. Students who attend schools like this typically show a range of positive outcomes that are of interest to traditional character educators. If character education is just good education, then pre-service teachers and school leaders who are trained in these matters are also learning how to direct students' behavioral outcomes towards desirable ends; and these ends will be deemed marks of good character.

The best practice approach aligns with principles of effective character education as promulgated by the Character Education Partnership (CEP, Character Education Partnership, 2010). For example, CEP Principle 6 insists that effective character education *"includes a meaningful and challenging academic curriculum that respects all learners."* It calls for differentiated instruction, the development of thinking strategies and the minimization of external rewards to sustain motivation. In other words, CEP Principle 6 affirms that character education requires academic press. CEP Principle 2 (*"defines character comprehensively to include thinking, feeling and doing"*) endorses the cognitive-mediational perspective of constructivist learning. CEP Principle 3 (*"Uses a comprehensive, intentional, proactive and effective approach to character development"*) encourages teachers to have high expectations, to develop a sense of community by giving students "voice-and-choice" and a chance to shape group norms. CEP Principle 4 (*"Creates a caring school community"*) explicitly addresses the communitarian ethos that characterizes good schools. CEP 7 (*"strives to foster students' self-motivation"*) endorses fostering intrinsic motivation to do well on academic tasks by encouraging growth and learning mindsets; and intrinsic motivation to do the right thing by building a climate of trust and respect, encouraging autonomy, and building shared norms through class meetings and shared decision-making.

In short, principles of effective character education endorse a set of well-attested pedagogical strategies that are considered best practice for teachers and school leaders. Moreover, it has the added virtue of requiring no significant alteration of pre-service teacher training (provided that training is already of high quality). Indeed, Narvaez and Lapsley (2008, p. 158) suggested that the "knowledge base that supports best practice instruction is coterminous with what is known to influence the moral formation of students." Hence it is neither necessary nor desirable to treat general education and character education as two separate instructional objectives if indeed character formation is a precipitate of best practice education.

Broad Character Education

The second category requires something more than good teachers engaging in best practice instruction. Broad character education requires teachers to deliver special programs as an intervention or curriculum. Two options are evident. One adopts a public health prevention model and the language of developmental psychopathology to advocate for programs that drive down risk factors and mobilize protective mechanisms. Many traditional character educators point to troubling epidemiological trends of youth disorder, for example, adolescent delinquency, dropping out of school, precocious sexual behavior, teen pregnancy, violence and substance use, and so on, as evidence that young people lack moral character (and that schools have ceased to teach it). Consequently, intervention and prevention programs that drive down these trends could reasonably be considered instance of character education if the outcome is *good conduct*. Similarly, anything that strengthens protective mechanisms for children exposed to psychosocial hazards would also count for moral-character education if the outcome minimizes risk behavior.

However, these programs are designed without recourse to the language of moral valuation, without reference to virtues, values or morality. It is difficult to credit moral-character education for outcomes driven by models of risk, resilience, and protection. In addition, the positive youth development movement has objected to over-reliance on risk behavior, deficits, and problems. In the view of this movement, *problem-free is not fully-prepared*, and so there is more work to do after reducing risk exposure and mobilizing protective mechanisms. Thus, a second approach to Broad Character Education focuses on the positive development of all students and on "performance" (vs. moral) character traits that underwrite success in school.

It is now impossible to teach moral development and character education without reference to the positive psychology of character. Peterson and Seligman (2004) identified 24 character strengths that are assigned to one of six universal virtues in their Values in Action classification. The virtues are *Wisdom* (creativity, curiosity, judgment, love of learning, perspective), *Courage* (bravery, perseverance, honesty, zest), *Humanity* (love, kindness, social intelligence), *Justice* (teamwork, fairness, leadership), *Temperance* (forgiveness, humility, prudence, self-respect), and *Transcendence* (appreciation of beauty and excellence, gratitude, hope, humor, spirituality). Character strengths are said to buffer stress and enable behaviors that maintain adaptation and positive youth development.

Grit is a character strength that has attracted the interest of educators (Duckworth & Quinn, 2009). It is defined as trait-level perseverance and passion for long-term goals in spite of challenges and setbacks. There is an emerging empirical profile that attests to the importance of grit for a variety of educational outcomes. Moreover, the literatures on grit and character strengths have led many educators to elevate the importance of "performance character" or "non-cognitive" factors in curricular planning. The KIPP charter school network has taken the lead in developing a character report card for each student that includes the following character strengths: *grit, zest, optimism, gratitude, social intelligence* and *curiosity*. These traits are the target of explicit socialization and instruction, which is evident upon any visit to a KIPP school. Providing opportunities for children to develop and practice these strengths is an important instantiation of KIPP's credo "Work hard, be nice." Curricular programs that emphasize growth mindsets and social-emotional learning would also fall under this heading.

Of course, performance character is not the same as moral character and so programs that tout gains in performance traits and character strengths should not be counted for what works in *moral* education. Indeed, character strengths could just as well be used for nefarious as for moral ends. Whether grit, for example, is good or bad depends upon the ends for which it is deployed. Therefore, a third approach has an explicit, intentional aim to develop the avowedly moral capacities of students.

Intentional Moral-Character Education

What if character education is defined not in terms of outcomes but in terms of *treatment*—what would that look like? In addition to commitments to constructivist best practice and academic press, in addition to teacher practices that support social belonging and character strengths, Intentional Moral-Character Education would be infused with the language of moral valuation. It would have an explicit theory of action whose objective is to influence the moral formation of children. It would amend the motto of positive youth development *problem free is not fully prepared* to say "*but fully prepared is not morally adept*" (Lapsley & Narvaez, 2006, p.162). It would acknowledge that there is still more work to do by way of moral formation after reducing risk behavior, developing competencies, and building character strengths.

We all want children and adolescents to be free of significant problems and to be learned, competent students. But we also want them to have a moral compass, to be conversant with ethical issues and to become persons who *care about morality* and who desire to have moral considerations govern their behaviors and aspirations. And insofar as all learning is specific, the language of values, morality, and virtue would have to be heard in classrooms; appeals to moral principles would have to be extracted from lessons. Schools would have to stand explicitly for core values, articulate and defend them, and animate them in all things in the life of the school.

Two additional CEP principles bring the values implications of character education out of the shadows. CEP principle 1 ("*The school community promotes core ethical and performance values as the foundation of good character*") asserts that schools must come to consensus about core values that "affirm human dignity, promote the development and welfare of the individual, serve the common good, define our rights and responsibilities in a democratic society, and meet the classical tests of *universality* (i.e., Would you want all persons to act this way in a similar situation?) and *reversibility* (i.e., Would you want to be treated this way?)." The CEP nominates *caring, honesty, fairness, responsibility* and *respect for self and others* as core ethical values; and *diligence, effort, perseverance, critical thinking,* and *positive attitude* as core performance values.

But the major point is not *which* values are selected but that some are, and that the selected values serve as the touchstone for everything that goes on in the school. Effective schools are those that are infused with a clear moral purpose that is out in the open, not hidden but transparent in the practice of teaching and learning, in the way relational trust, social belonging and a sense of community is cultivated, in the disciplinary practices of the school and the way it reaches out to families and communities. Importantly, effective schools also give students an opportunity to engage in moral action. The call-to-action is reflected in CEP Principle 5 (*"The school provides students with opportunities for moral action"*). The insistence that education include a commitment to moral action makes the CEP principles something more than a mere catalogue of instructional best practice, although they are certainly that as well.

CONCLUSION

I have presented three possible responses to the challenge of preparing preservice teachers and aspiring school leaders for the moral work of teaching and of school leadership. Best Practice mobilizes the educational psychology literatures of constructivist learning, academic press and communal organization of schools to guide the formation of "good learners." Broad Character education reduces the exposure of good learners to psychosocial hazards, reduces risk behavior, builds competencies, and fortifies the good learner with character strengths. Finally, Intentional Moral-Character Education transforms the Fortified Good Learner into a Moral Self.

These three responses should be considered moments in the moral formation of students and the moral work of teaching. The challenge for the educational sciences, and for schools of education, is to connect the bolts so that these three moments are a seamless weave in the training of teachers and school leaders. The effective moral educator must first be an effective teacher who brings powerful lessons alive with pedagogical techniques that maximize student interest, engagement, and learning; and so the effective teacher will be skilled in the best practice attested by the learning sciences. But teachers skilled in the mechanics of best practice also need to count on the relational trust of colleagues and school leaders. It is the school leader who sets the tone and puts into place the school-wide structures and policies that build the communitarian ethos and sense of belonging so crucial to student success.

But, increasingly, the tools of effective teaching include the mobilization of character strengths and motivational orientations that sustain good effort in the face of academic challenges. The literatures on social-emotional learning, grit, and mindsets are particularly promising ways to fortify learning, and it is imperative that the instructional strategies that devolve from these literatures are folded into teacher training. But moral education requires pedagogical content knowledge in its own right, like any other instructional objective. Effective instruction will yield good outcomes across a range of outcomes of interest to educators, and such an effect would be catalyzed when fortified best practice is yoked to intentional commitment morality, virtues, and values (Lapsley et al., 2014).

REFERENCES

Character Education Partnership (2010). *Eleven principles of effective character education* Washington, DC: Author.

Duckworth, A. L., & Quinn, P. D. (2009). Development and validation of the Short Grit Scale (Grit-S). *Journal of Personality Assessment, 91,*166–174.

Horn, S. S., Daddis, C., & Killen, M. (2008). Peer relationships and social groups: Implications for moral education. In L. Nucci & D. Narvaez (Eds.), *Handbook on moral and character Education* (pp. 267–287). New York, NY: Routledge.

Kimball, B. A. (1986). *Orators and philosophers: A history of the idea of liberal education.* New York, NY: Teachers College Press.

Lapsley, D. (2005). Moral stage theory. In M. Killen & J. Smetana (Eds.), *Handbook of moral development* (pp. 37–66). Mahwah, NJ: Lawrence Erlbaum Associates

Lapsley, D., Holter, A. C., & Narvaez, D. (2014). Teaching for character: Three alternatives for teacher education. In M. N. Sanger & R. D. Osguthorpe, R. D. (Eds.), *The moral work of teaching: Preparing and supporting practitioners* (pp. 115–128). New York, NY: Teachers College Press.

Lapsley, D., & Yeager, D.S. (2014). Moral-character education. In I. Weiner (Ed.), *Handbook of psychology* (Vol. 7, Educational Psychology; W. Reynolds & G. Miller, Vol. Eds., (pp. 147–177), New York, NY: Wiley.

Lapsley, D. (2011). Developing and framing meaningful problems. In C. Conrad & R.C. Serlin (Eds.), *SAGE handbook for research in education* (2nd ed). Newbury Park, CA: SAGE.

Lapsley, D. K., & Narvaez, D. (2006). Character education. In W. Damon & R. Lerner (Series Eds.), A. Renninger & I. Siegel (Vol. Eds.), *Handbook of child psychology: Vol. 4. Child psychology in practice* (6th ed., pp. 248–296). New York, NY: Wiley.

Lemov, D. (2010) *Teach like a champion: 49 techniques that put students on the path to college.* San Francisco, CA: Jossey-Bass.

Nucci, L. (2001). *Education in the moral domain.* New York, NY: Cambridge University Press.

Nucci, L. (1981). Conceptions of personal issues: A domain distinct from moral or societal concepts. *Child Development, 52,* 114–121.

Peterson, C., & Seligman, M. E. P. (2004). *Character strengths and virtues: A handbook and classification.* Washington, DC: American Psychological Association.

Power, F. C., Higgins, A., & Kohlberg L. (1989). *Lawrence Kohlberg's approach to moral education.* New York, NY: Columbia University Press.

Sanger, M. N., & Osguthorpe, R. D. (Eds.). (2013). *The moral work of teaching: Preparing and supporting practitioners.* New York, NY: Teachers College Press.

Smetana, J. (1983). Social-cognitive development: Domain distinctions and coordinations. *Developmental Review, 3*, 131–147.

Stengel, B. S. & Tom, A. R. (2006). *Moral matters: Five ways to develop the moral life of schools.* New York, NY: Teachers College Press.

Turiel, E. (1983). *The development of social knowledge: Morality and convention.* Cambridge, MA: Cambridge University Press.

Wynne, E. & Ryan, K. (1997). *Reclaiming our schools: Teaching character, academics, and discipline* (2nd ed.). Upper Saddle River, NJ: Prentice Hall.

SECTION IV

TEACHING RESEARCH METHODS, STATISTICS
AND ASSESSMENT FOR THE NEXT GENERATION
OF EDUCATIONAL PSYCHOLOGISTS

CHAPTER 23

TEACHING INTRODUCTORY STATISTICS

Challenges and Strategies

Gregory Schraw and Matthew L. Bernacki
University of Nevada, Las Vegas

This chapter examines a variety of curriculum and pedagogy issues related to teaching introductory statistics at the college level (hereafter *statistics*). Statistics is a challenging class for students due to their lack of background knowledge, common math concepts and procedures they have forgotten since high school, anxiety, and lack of relevance (Conners, McCown, & Roslos-Ewoldsen, 1998). Most students take the class late in their programs, typically because they are required to complete it to graduate.

We believe that statistics does not need to be a stressful experience if taught properly with instructional scaffolding for the "big concepts" and data-analysis procedures. We propose that students face at least four major challenges, including a new technical vocabulary, many new concepts that are not connected adequately across chapters (e.g., different error terms for different inferential procedures), manual calculations, and learning statistical software which can easily stress one's cognitive limits. Some of these

Challenges and Innovations in Educational Psychology Teaching and Learning, pages 305–319
Copyright © 2016 by Information Age Publishing
305

activities, such as manual calculations, may be eliminated from the class and added to optional workshops facilitated by the instructor or a tutor, or incorporated into electronic tutoring systems (MacDougall, 2008). We believe it is better to use instructional strategies that help minimize as many of these four challenges as possible; thus, the first author no longer requires students to perform manual calculations and has made a concerted effort to reduce the cognitive load involved in language to use new software such as SPSS or SAS.

The remainder of this chapter includes eight sections. The first addresses the role of academic standards of competence for introductory statistics. The second summarizes seven common uses of statistics discussed in the literature. The third discusses the importance of beliefs and attitudes. The fourth section considers the content and sequence of the big ideas taught in statistics, while the fifth section provides an overview of the most important classroom support strategies, including class assistance and embedded strategy instruction. Section six considers how to best teach critical thinking skills in statistics, and section seven considers how to teach better conceptual integration. We conclude in section eight with 16 principles for more effective instruction.

Academic Guidelines

Academic guidelines for statistics provided by the American Psychological Association and American Educational Research Association's respective websites make excellent instruction guides (APA, 2011). Other organizations, such as the National Council of Teachers of Mathematics (NCTM, 2000) and the American Statistical Association (ASA, 2005) have also produced content standards for K–12 instruction (i.e., GAISE standards). The ASA and GAISE K–12 guidelines based on NCTM standards provide additional guidance regarding post-secondary instruction in statistics at the introductory and advanced undergraduate levels (see Table 23.1), which focus on the instructional principles by which statistics educators might ensure that students attain these goals. These guidelines have been adapted for the contemporary statistics curriculum (Everson, Zieffler & Garfield, 2008). Goals include dispositional (e.g., "data beat anecdotes"), factual (e.g., operational definitions of "random" and "normal"), procedural (e.g., "how to graph data"), conceptual (e.g., p-values), and interpretive (e.g., "interpret statistical results in context") levels of knowledge. Their recommendations for achieving these standards include: (1) a balanced focus on statistical thinking and literacy; (2) the use of real data; (3) a focus on conceptual understanding; and (4) using active learning, technology, and assessment to improve and evaluate learning. Ideally, each big concept is taught and assessed at multiple levels of understanding (Webb, 2007),

---

TABLE 23.1   Standards and Goals Guiding Statistics Instruction

NCTM (2000) Standards for Data Analysis and Probability [subgoals omitted]

- Formulate questions that can be addressed with data and collect, organize, and display relevant data to answer them.
- Develop and evaluate inferences and predictions that are based on data.
- Understand and apply basic concepts of probability.

American Statistical Association's Guidelines for Assessment and Instruction in Statistical Education (GAISE; 2005) K–12 Standards–Level C

- Formulate Questions
  - Students can make the statistics question distinction
  - Students pose their own questions of interest
  - Questions seek generalization
- Collect Data
  - Students make design for differences
  - Sampling designs with random selection
  - Experimental designs with randomization
- Analyze Data
  - Understand and use distributions in analysis as a global concept
  - Measure variability within a group; measure variability between groups
  - Compare group-to-group using displays and measures of variability
  - Describe and quantify sampling error
  - Quantification of association & fitting of models for association

ASA GAISE (2005) College Goals [with sample subgoals]

- Students should believe and understand why [Data beat anecdotes]
- Students should recognize [That words such as "normal," "random," and "correlation" have specific meanings in statistics that may differ from common usage]
- Students should understand the parts of the process through which statistics works to answer questions, namely: [How to obtain or generate data]
- Students should understand the basic ideas of statistical inference, including [The concept of statistical significance, including significance levels and p-values]
- [S]tudents should know [How to interpret statistical results in context]

---

ranging from factual recall to a conceptual synthesis of the course's big ideas. Much of the present chapter is geared toward moving beyond recall to thoughtful application of principles and procedures as well as conceptual synthesis.

The Uses of Statistics

We suggest instructors begin by reviewing the uses of statistics, including summarizing data, making population estimates, defining range and shape of a distribution of scores, posing and testing hypotheses, measuring the correlation between variables, computing one variable in terms of other variables (e.g., regression), and testing the significance of the difference within or between groups. Other important concepts may be highlighted as well, such as estimating the effect size of a treatment, calculating the power of a statistical test in advance, and statistical modeling beyond the case of simple regression. Highlighting these activities is useful as an advance organizer for main concepts as well as illustrating the practical importance of statistics in everyday life.

The Role of Beliefs and Attitudes

One of the main obstacles students face are their beliefs and attitudes about their ability to succeed in statistics. Research shows that debilitative anxiety is higher and self-efficacy for statistics is lower in statistics than for other education courses (see Curtis & Georgieva, this volume). Factors contributing to statistics anxiety include math phobia, lack of connection to daily life, pace of instruction, and instructor's attitude. In contrast, prior course work in statistics and math reduces anxiety and increases expectations (Leech, 2008). A variety of instructional strategies reduce anxiety and increase self-efficacy, including flexible in-class and out-of-class assistances (e.g., tutors, instructor availability), the use (and instruction) of active learning strategies, and focusing on the big ideas (Finney & Schraw, 2003). In addition, an emphasis on learning goals that focus on improvement rather than comparative achievement significantly reduce anxiety and increase statistics students' self-efficacy (Bandalos, Finney & Geske, 2003).

Teaching the Big Ideas

The most important choice that instructors make in statistics is what concepts to teach and in what order they teach them. We are proponents of teaching the *big ideas*, meaning that the bulk of instruction is focused on previewing the core concepts, teaching these concepts in an applications-based manner with real-world data sets and embedded statistical procedures, and reviewing the big ideas regularly to promote an integrated conceptual understanding of how the big ideas fit together into a cohesive picture. We stress the importance of both *previewing* and *reviewing* because many students lack relevant math skills and knowledge. Those with higher levels of prior knowledge experience less anxiety and learn more than those without knowledge (Leppink, Broers, Imbos, van der Vleuten, & Berger, 2012). In addition, previewing and reviewing helps to integrate important concepts across chapters and build an integrated conceptual understanding of statistical principles (Jones, Jones &

Vermette, 2011). We focus on teaching the big ideas to reduce cognitive over-load attributable to a steady stream of new vocabulary, concepts, and computational procedures. To do so, we focus on both content and embedded computational procedures using statistical software as a module tied directly to the concept. We emphasize regular preview, review, and across-chapter connections to strengthen the big ideas and promote conceptual understanding through distributed rather than massed practice (Marson, 2007).

So what are the big ideas? In Table 23.2, we list the core big ideas and embedded computational procedures for each big idea in a statistics class that span the material covered in a typical 13-week semester.

Most statistics textbooks address these topics in a similar order; thus, instruction progression is embedded within the curriculum itself. Regardless

---

TABLE 23.2   Core Ideas in Introductory Statistics Course

1. Central tendency
   A. Mean
   B. Median
   C. Mode
2. Distributions
   A. Normality
   B. Variation and range
      i. Sample and population standard deviation
      ii. Standard error of estimate
      iii. Standard error of the mean
      iv. Standard deviation of differences between samples
   D. Skewness
   E. Kurtosis
3. Correlation (measures of association)
   A. Magnitude of association
   B. Valence of association
4. Prediction (regression techniques)
   A. One predictor
   B. Two or more predictors
5. Hypothesis testing
   A. Type I and II errors; power
   B. p values
   C. Confidence intervals
6. Univariate group comparisons
   A. Testing effect size
   B. Two-group comparisons
   C. Three or more group comparisons
   D. Multi-way comparisons
   E. Within group comparisons
7. Non-parametric analogs

---

of content sequencing differences (Barron & Apple, 2014), most texts do not return to core concepts in later chapters to link conceptually similar and often confusing concepts, such as the distinction between the *sampling error of the mean* and the *sampling error of the difference between means.*

Classroom Support Strategies

Effective instructors not only teach and illustrate statistical principles, but provide strategic support to students through a variety of self-regulated learning strategies. Research shows that ongoing professional development for teachers of statistics is a very effective way to improve instruction and student learning (MacGillivray, 2009). Research also suggests that a wide variety of strategies complement learning and, collectively, enable students who persist to succeed in statistics. We recommend the following strategies based on a review of the literature.

In- and Out-of-Class Assistance

There are many ways to provide assistance to students that complements in-class instruction. For example, a recent project by the mathematical learning sciences unit at Queensland University of Technology provides a comprehensive list of learning support strategies (MacGillivray, 2009). The purpose of these assistance strategies is to increase statistics enjoyment and achievement, provide hands-on practice, use real-world problem solving skills, and introduce relevant support technology. The full list is as follows: drop-in assistance; sessions or classes on specific topics or supporting specific subjects or courses; appointments for one-on-one assistance; support facilities in paper or electronic form; diagnostic testing with associated support assistance on specific topics; designated space for support; enabling or remedial programs; support for postgraduates; programs with no associated credit towards the student's course; professional development for support staff; and, programs of relevant research or scholarship for students (p. 459).

Embedded Strategy Instruction

One of the most common activities is to embed scaffolded strategy instruction into the statistics class. Research suggests that embedded strategy instruction with feedback is far more useful than stand-alone programs outside of the classroom context (Pressley & Harris, 2006). Strategies discussed in the literature include problem-based learning, worked real-life examples based on surveys and vignettes, simulations using web-based applications, self-explanation designed to make procedures explicit, tutors, collaborative groups, ongoing formative feedback, use of diagrams and visual displays to summarize information and illustrate principles, and supportive technology.

TABLE 23.3 Instructional Sequence for Problem-Based Learning in Statistics

1. Teacher presents PBL scenario and the evaluation rubric to students
2. Teacher describes steps students should follow to solve the scenario
3. Student groups work on assigned scenario
4. Students do individual research on scenario-related topics
5. Students share with their group the research they have done; they establish problems to solve
6. Students work collaboratively with team members to propose solutions to problems
7. Students present their work to classmates and distribute their report
8. Teacher comments on similarities/differences among the groups' work
9. Teacher pulls out of the presentations the main concepts involved in the problems / solutions
10. Teacher evaluates reports using PBL rubric

Problem-based learning (PBL) requires the learner to construct and test solutions to real-world problems through collaboration with peers and help from the teacher when necessary (Canturk-Gunhan, Bukova-Guzel & Özgür, 2012). PBL is designed to help students construct an extensive, flexible knowledge base and develop effective problem solving skills. Problems with multiple solution paths are especially helpful because they require the group to construct multiple solution paths and compare them in terms of their overall effectiveness. See Table 23.3 for a typical PBL instructional sequence.

Worked examples include these from the text or course learning materials as well as those based on first-hand student experience (Marson, 2007). For example, the authors use student data based on self-efficacy, expected grade, prior math classes, gender, and a pre-test collected electronically the first week of class. This is the primary data set used to conduct statistical analysis for each chapter in the text. Providing data themselves helps students to better understand the interpretation and limits of data. Simulations come in many shapes and sizes. We have used web-based apps so students can construct a sampling distribution of the means using samples of 5, 10, 25, 50, 100, 250, and 1,000 cases, respectively. We have found that simulations illustrate nicely the conceptual and computational advantages of large data sets.

Self-explanation helps students working alone or in dyads to construct an explicit procedural script for solving problems. One feature to this method is that its effectiveness increases as prior knowledge increases; thus, high-knowledge students work well alone while low-knowledge students benefit from worked examples of tutors during the early stages of problem solving (Leppink et al., 2012). In general, tutors and small collaborative groups help other learners construct and share strategies for solving problems. Tutors are more helpful for low-knowledge students while small groups are especially useful when high-knowledge students work together. Both advanced tutors and small-group activities have positive effects on students' factual, conceptual, and procedural learning. A recent meta-analysis (Kalaian & Kasim, 2014) of small group learning in statistic classes provides an excellent overview of methods for setting up and using groups to increase learning and engagement.

Ongoing formative feedback is a crucial component of statistics instruction in order to enable students to check understanding, ask for strategic help when performance is poor, and build confidence (Marson, 2007). Feedback should be timely (e.g., within 24 hours) and cognitive in nature, meaning students are provided with information that explains the rationale and strategies used by experts to reach the correct answer. In addition, assessment and feedback should be geared toward multiple levels of understanding, including factual, conceptual, and procedural levels (Sebastianelli & Tamimi, 2011).

We have found visual displays to be extremely useful for helping students summarize and compare important concepts across chapters and understanding important processes such as hypothesis testing and causality. We feel that including diagrams and displays promotes far better conceptual and procedural understanding than do lectures or demonstrations alone. The research literature supports this conclusion, suggesting there are three general types of displays that help students learn (Brase, 2009). The first type summarizes and contrasts related concepts. Table 23.4 shows different types of estimated variance scores that appear in introductory statistics, their purpose, calculation, and how they differ from one another. We have found that Table 23.4 helps students to reduce much of their confusion regarding different types of scores and why these scores vary across significance testing contexts. Another example is in Table 23.5; it provides a real-world courtroom analog to hypothesis testing. In this case, students are introduced to key concepts such as Type I and II errors, power, and p values in the context of a familiar activity.

The second type focuses on decision-making (Calderwood, 2012). One type is a decision tree that appears in the statistics text that helps novices to choose the correct statistical test based on the number and scale of the independent and dependent variables. For example, a variable measured on an interval or ratio scale can be tested across two groups using a t-test or three or more groups using an F test. Another type of display is the summary matrix that helps students to select from among a variety of post-hoc comparison tests after an analysis of variance is conducted. These summaries compare the tests in terms of rigor when controlling alpha rates and assumptions about the data that the test must meet.

A third type of display illustrates relationships or processes. Structural equation models (SEM) typically include a variety of variables that are

TABLE 23.4 A Comparison of Different Variance Scores

Error Estimate	Description	Formula
Sample Standard Deviation	This is the square root of the sum of squared deviation scores divided by $(n-1)$. The standard deviation tells us *the average deviation from the mean* in a set of scores.	$SD = \sqrt{\left[\sum(X_i - \bar{X})^2\right]/(n-1)}$
Standard Error of the Estimate	This is the sum of squared errors between estimated Y values and the regression line. The SEE tells us *the average deviation in our estimated values* in regression analysis.	$SEE = \sqrt{\sum e^2/(n-2)}$ (where e^2 is squared deviation from the regression line for a score).
Standard Error of the Mean	The SEM is *the standard deviation of the sampling distribution of the means.* If you drew a sample of 100 cases and computed a mean for this sample, and repeated this n number of times, you would have the sampling distribution of the n means. The SEM would be the average deviation of a mean from the center of that the distribution of means.	$SEM = s/\sqrt{n}$ (where s is the sample standard deviation of a sample).
Sampling Error of the Difference between Means	The SEDM is the standard deviation of a distribution based on the difference between two means. For example, the difference between the mean of a treatment versus control group.	$SEF = \sqrt{s^2(1/n_1 + 1/n_2)}$

TABLE 23.5 Courtroom Decision-Making Scenario

Imagine a courtroom scenario in which a man is accused of premeditated murder. The jury must decide based on the collective *weight of the evidence* whether the man is guilty or not guilty. This creates a situation in which one of four mutually exclusive outcomes might occur:

True status of defendant:	Did not commit crime	Committed crime
Jury's Decision:		
Innocent	Correct rejection of guilt	Type II error (β)
Guilty	Type I error (α)	Power ($1 - \beta$)

Notes: The weight of evidence corresponds to the amount and quality of data in a statistical analysis. Type I error occurs when a null effect is judged as a true effect (e.g., a non-criminal is convicted of the crime); Type II error occurs when a true effect is judged as a non-effect (e.g., a criminal is judged as innocent); power occurs when a true effect is judges as a true effect (e.g., a criminal is convicted). The *p*-value associated with a particular value of α is the *minimum value* that can be obtained without (incorrectly) rejecting the null.

related directly or indirectly to one or more criterion variables of choice. SEM models usually provide graphic information about the process of modeling as well as the hypothesized relationship among variables. A different example is that of a three-dimensional plot of factors in an exploratory factor analysis. This type of diagram helps students to understand the multiple dimensions, whether or not the dimensions are assumed to be independent, and how the factors are situated within the plot.

Online technology can be used successfully in both face-to-face (F2F) and online classes. All of the activities described above can be implemented using student discussion groups, online whiteboards, use of visual displays, and reflection journals and diaries to promote strategy use (Basturk, 2005). In addition, Bush, Menzies, and Thorp (2009) provide a detailed compendium of applets for most of the core topics in introductory statistics, including using Excel spreadsheets and generating data tables and graphic representations. Another possibility is to use computer-assisted instruction (CAI) within a F2F context. For instance, this format enables instructors to respond more quickly to students in a class that meets once weekly. In addition, CAI makes it easier for instructions to field questions from individual students that they share with the entire class electronically (Bush et al., 2009).

Summary

There are many ways to promote in and out of class assistance. F2F out of class interactions remain one of the most important constraints on statistics achievement (MacGillivray & Croft, 2011). We recommend that all instructors consider ways to meet with students to increase their motivation. Also, utilize tutors whenever possible. Using cognitive strategies is an important technique to promote learning (Pressley & Harris, 2006). We encourage instructors to identify the strategies they use, provide a brief written summary of them for students (e.g., the strategy evaluation matrix described by Schraw, 1998), and model them whenever possible. Similarly, tutors may model strategies for students in or out of class. Using visual representations to summarize and illustrate complex processes is an excellent way to scaffold learning. It is also important to consider how to leverage instructional strategies in online statitics courses using CAI. Online courses may benefit from the use of tutorials and short learning modules, faster and more detailed feedback, and video chats (Bush et al., 2009).

Teaching Critical Thinking Skills

Ultimately, the art of statistics boils down to thinking critically about data. Like the strategies described above, critical thinking skills are learned best when they are embedded within a specific context and are used to solve real-world problems (Abrami et al., 2008). For example, David and Brown (2012) describe a revamped statistics class for non-statistics majors; it focuses on the role of small, collaborative groups using class-based skills to solve real-world problems. To do so, students use several scripted guidelines to scaffold critical thinking such as stating the problem, identifying relevant information and data, weighing and evaluating the data, selecting a data analysis strategy, and evaluating conclusions. Using real-world application problems also improves transfer of skills to new problems and self-efficacy for statistics skills compared to students who do not solve application problems (MacDougall, 2008).

Garfield and Ben-Zvi (2009) developed a six-component statistical reasoning intervention they referred to as the *Statistical Reasoning Learning Environment* (SRLE) model based on constructivist pedagogy, including: (1) focusing on developing central statistical ideas rather than on presenting sets of tools and procedures; (2) using real and motivating data sets to engage students in making and testing conjectures; (3) using classroom activities to support the development of students' reasoning; (4) integrating the use of appropriate technological tools that allow students to test their conjectures, explore and analyze data, and develop their statistical reasoning; (5) promoting classroom discourse that includes statistical arguments and sustained exchanges that focus on significant statistical ideas; and (6) using assessment to learn what students know and to monitor the development of their statistical learning, as well as to evaluate instructional plans and progress. Garfield and Ben-Zvi argue that the SRLE model promotes statistical reasoning that transfers to new problems and domains beyond statistics.

Teaching for Conceptual Integration

One of the most challenging aspects of teaching statistics is promoting an integrated conceptual understanding of the relationships among concepts. Probably the three most important reasons are the sheer number of new concepts, the subtlety of some concepts such as understanding p values, and failure on the part of textbooks (and sometimes classroom instructors) to promote conceptual understanding across chapters. Ironically, the topic of conceptual understanding often is left unaddressed in the statistics literature. We believe that several of the techniques and strategies discussed are especially important ways to increase conceptual understanding (Leppink et al., 2012), such as: providing relevant background knowledge; previewing and reviewing concepts in order to emphasize their cross-chapter connections; using summary tables to compare and contrast related concepts; and using concept maps and diagrams that grow and expand over the course to illustrate how the big ideas are related.

Principles of Effective Statistics Instruction

We close with a brief summary of effective instructional principles described in this chapter. These principles are an extension of those described by Everson et al., (2008) and Jones et al. (2011), as well as the GAISE standards in Table 23.1. We provide a variety of principles that complement one another. We list them in order as they would occur in a real-time classroom, but make no assumptions about their overall importance relative to the remaining principles listed below.

1. Address the role of student anxiety, self-efficacy, and goal orientations (Bandalos et al., 2003; Finney & Schraw, 2003).
2. Provide relevant background knowledge and skills in class or use out-of-class tutorials (Leppink et al., 2012).
3. Use data from students generated early in the course as the basis for real-life problems (Davies, 2011).
4. Focus on big ideas and concepts (Leech, 2008).
5. Balance the roles of factual, conceptual and procedural knowledge (Jones et al., 2011).
6. Review and preview important concepts periodically and link explicitly to new concepts (David & Brown, 2012; MacGillivray, 2009), and strive to build conceptual bridges across chapters (Leppink et al., 2012).
7. Use visual displays (e.g., concept maps) to build conceptual understanding (Brase, 2009; Calderwood, 2012).
8. Embed statistical software such as Excel, SAS and SPSS (Basturk, 2005).
9. Embed statistical software procedures and utilize tutorials, simulations, and applets (Hodgson & Burke, 2000).
10. Embed cognitive strategy instruction to improve self-regulation (Pressley & Harris, 2006).
11. Practice solving real-life worked problems using hand calculations or software; provide opportunities for students to discuss practice and receive formative feedback from peers and the instructor.
12. Use collaborative groups and tutors in or out of class or in small online discussion groups.
13. Help students develop essential critical thinking skills via teacher modeling in which students make generalizations through compar-

ing, analyzing, and drawing conclusions from examples (Garfield & Ben-Zvi, 2009; Jones et al., 2011).

14. Use ongoing formative assessment to provide self-regulatory feedback (Sebastianelli & Tamimi, 2011).

15. Engage in ongoing professional development through colloquia and or relevant journals such as the *Journal of Statistics Education, Teaching Statistics,* and *Teaching Psychology* (Foley et al., 2012).

16. Provide out of class access to instructors and tutors (Kalaian & Kasim, 2014).

REFERENCES

Abrami, P. C., Bernard, R. M., Borokhovski, E., Wade, A., Surkes, M. A., Tamim, R., & Zhang, D. (2008). Instructional interventions affecting critical thinking skills and dispositions: A stage 1 meta-analysis. *Review of Educational Research, 78,* 1102–1134.

American Psychological Association. (2011). Principles for quality undergraduate education in psychology. Washington, DC. Retrieved from http://www.apa.org/education/undergrad/principles.aspx

American Statistical Association. (2005). Guidelines for assessment and instruction in statistics education: College report. Retrieved from www.amstat.org/education/gaise/GAISECollege.htm.

Bandalos, D. L., Finney, S., & Geske, J. A. (2003). A model of statistics performance based on achievement goal theory. *Journal of Educational Psychology, 95,* 604–616.

Barron, K. E., & Apple, K. J. (2014). Debating curricular strategies for teaching statistics and research methods: What does the current evidence suggest? *Teaching of Psychology, 41,* 187–194. doi:10.1177/0098628314537967

Basturk, R. (2005). The effectiveness of computer-assisted instruction in teaching introductory statistics. *Educational Technology & Society, 8,* 170–178.

Brase, G. L. (2009). Pictorial representations in statistical reasoning. *Applied Cognitive Psychology, 23,* 369–381.

Bush, S., Menzies, G., & Thorp, S. (2009). An array of online teaching tools. *Teaching Statistics, 31,* 17–20.

Calderwood, K. A. (2012). Teaching inferential statistics to social work students: A decision-making flow chart. *Journal of Teaching in the Social Sciences, 32,* 133–147.

Canturk-Gunhan, B., Bukova-Guzel, E., & Özgür, Z. (2012). The prospective mathematics teachers' thought processes and views about using problem-based learning in statistics education. *International Journal of Mathematical Education in Science and Technology, 43,* 145–165.

Conners, F. A., McCown, S. M., & Roslos-Ewoldsen, B. (1998). Unique challenges in teaching undergraduate statistics. *Teaching of Psychology, 25,* 40–42.

Curtis, R., & Georgieva, Z. (this volume). Leveraging statistical anxiety and other promising practices. In M C. Smith & N. DeFrates-Densch (Eds.), *Challenges and innovations in teaching and learning educational psychology.* Charlotte, NC: Information Age.

David, I., & Brown, J. A. (2012). Beyond statistical methods: Teaching critical thinking to first-year university students. *International Journal of Mathematical Education in Science and Technology, 43,* 1057–1065.

Davies, N. (2011). Developments of *AtSchool* projects for improving collaborative teaching and learning in statistics. *Statistical Journal of the IAOS, 27,* 205–227.

Everson, M., Zieffler, A., & Garfield, J. (2008). Implementing new reform guidelines in teaching introductory college statistics courses. *Teaching Statistics, 30,* 66–79.

Finney, S., & Schraw, G. (2003). Self-efficacy beliefs in college statistics courses. *Contemporary Educational Psychology, 28,* 161–186.

Foley, G. D., Khoshaim, H. B., Alsaeed, M., & Er, S. N. (2012). Professional development in statistics, technology, and cognitively demanding tasks: Classroom implementation and obstacles. *International Journal of Mathematical Education in Science and Technology, 43,* 177196. doi:10.1080/0020739X.2011.592616

Garfield, J., & Ben-Zvi, D. (2009). Helping students develop statistical reasoning: Implementing a statistical reasoning learning environment. *Teaching Statistics, 31,* 72–77.

Hodgson, T., & Burke, M. (2000). On simulation and the teaching of statistics. *Teaching Statistics, 22,* 91–96.

Jones, J. L., Jones, K. A., & Vermette, P. J. (2011). Putting cognitive science behind a statics teacher's intuitions. *Teaching Statistics, 33,* 85–90.

Kalaian, S., & Kasim, R. M. (2014). A meta-analytic review of studies of the effectiveness of small-group learning methods on statistics achievement. *Journal of Statistics Education, 22,* 1–20.

Leech, L. N. (2008). Statistics poker: Reinforcing basic statistical concepts. *Teaching Statistics, 30,* 26–28.

Leppink, J., Broers, N. J., Imbos, T., van der Vleuten, C. P., & Berger, M. P. (2012). Self-explanation in the domain of statistics: an expertise reversal effect. *Higher Education, 63,* 771–785.

MacDougall, M. (2008). Ten tips for promoting autonomous learning and effective engagement in the teaching of statistics to undergraduate medical students involved in short-term research projects. *Journal of Applied Quantitative Methods, 3,* 223–240.

MacGillivray, H. (2009). Learning support and students studying mathematics and statistics. *International Journal of Mathematical Education in Science and Technology, 40,* 455–472.

MacGillivray, H., & Croft, T. (2011).Understanding evaluation of learning support in mathematics and statistics. *International Journal of Mathematical Education in Science and Technology, 42,* 189–212.

Marson, S. M. (2007). Three empirical strategies for teaching statistics. *Journal of Teaching in Social Work, 27,* 199–212.

National Council of Teachers of Mathematics. (2000). *Principles and standards for school mathematics.* Reston, VA: The Council

Pressley, M., & Harris, K. R. (2006). Cognitive strategy instruction: From basic research to classroom instruction. In P. Alexander & P. Winne (Eds.), *Handbook of educational psychology* (2nd ed., pp. 265–286). San Diego, CA: Academic Press.

Sebastianelli, R., & Tamimi, N. (2011). Business statistics and management science online: Teaching strategies and assessment of student learning. *Journal of Education for Business, 86,* 317–325.

Schraw, G. (1998). Promoting general metacognitive awareness. *Instructional Science, 26,* 113–125.

Webb, N. L. (2007). Issues related to judging the alignment of curriculum standards and assessments. *Applied Measurement in Education, 20,* 7–25.

CHAPTER 24

TEACHING INTRODUCTORY STATISTICS

Incorporating Motivational Principles

Jennifer G. Cromley and Tony Perez
University of Illinois at Urbana-Champaign

Ting Dai
Old Dominion University

OVERVIEW: TEACHING INTRODUCTORY STATISTICS

Educational statistics is a subject that students in educational psychology and other education disciplines do not typically look forward to taking. They may have heard that the subject is difficult, irrelevant, or the courses are taught in ways that are confusing to them. They may have anxiety about mathematical subjects or, more specifically, about statistics. Over the course of 11 collective years of teaching introductory statistics in educational psychology, we have introduced a number of features to educational statistics courses that are built on principles from research in academic achievement motivation. These course features are designed to help students see the relevance of introductory statistics, feel capable of handling the tasks in

Challenges and Innovations in Educational Psychology Teaching and Learning, pages 321–331
Copyright © 2016 by Information Age Publishing
All rights of reproduction in any form reserved.

the course, and lessen their anxiety about reading and using statistics in educational research.

An introductory statistics course typically covers how to calculate and report measures of central tendency and variability, the sampling distribution of the mean, the normal distribution, principles of hypothesis testing, measures of association such as correlation and chi squared, an introduction to hypothesis testing/inferential statistics via the independent samples *t* test, and the concept of statistical power. Such a course covers topics that range from somewhat familiar concepts (e.g., "averages") to quite unfamiliar procedures (e.g., calculating a correlation). While some mathematical calculations are included in such a course, the calculations tend to be ones that are easily carried out on a simple calculator. APA manuscript style for reporting these statistics and analyses is also typically taught. Other topics are sometimes included, such as using SPSS or other data analysis software programs.

One goal of an introductory course is for students to not simply know the individual facts (i.e., a statistic is significant when the obtained value is greater than the critical value; the standard error will decrease as sample size increases, all else being equal), but to begin to connect these facts into an integrated conceptual understanding (i.e., we have more power with larger sample sizes because when the standard error (SE) decreases, the obtained test statistic increases). To the extent that statistics explanations and applied exercises focus on a series of disconnected facts, it will be difficult for students to form such an integrated conceptual understanding of the topic. Furthermore, research on transfer (e.g., to further coursework on ANOVA, regression, multilevel modeling, etc.) suggests that without such an integrated conceptual understanding, students will not apply what they have learned in such an introductory course to additional coursework in statistics (Nokes-Malach & Mestre. 2013).

Students in a graduate-level introductory educational statistics course can come from many disciplines within and outside of a college of education. Our students have come from educational psychology, language arts/science/math education, TESOL, urban education, educational leadership, and school counseling, to name just a few. Across these disciplines, students tend to come from one of three groups: (1) beginning researchers who will use the statistics in a lab and in their own research and are preparing for advanced statistics and measurement courses; (2) students pursuing technical master's degrees who will not take advanced statistics but will need to use these techniques in their jobs; and, (3) students who—whether they know it or not—will need to be able to read, comprehend, and summarize for others the findings from new research discoveries in their field. Thus, developing a meaningful understanding of the content is important for all students in our course. We address the significance of teaching each of these categories of students below.

The Significance of Teaching Statistics

The significance of introductory statistics is rooted in preparing educational psychology graduate students (and other education graduate students) to conduct and report on research, as well as to understand published reports. For students wishing to pursue their own research and those seeking job skills at the master's level (categories 1 and 2), the significance of teaching statistics is to learn how to accurately carry out the techniques. The former group may more often have to interpret the meaning of the results in light of prior research, whereas the latter group may simply write up results in APA style and leave the interpretation to others. The first group also needs to develop a solid conceptual foundation in order to learn more advanced statistical techniques; an understanding of two-way ANOVA is very difficult if the basic concepts of variance and dependent variable are not understood. Likewise, faculty count on instructors of introductory statistics to prepare advisees and graduate research assistants to write up results accurately for conference and journal submissions. For all students, such a course is significant for learning how to read research reports and identify major flaws in the design or analyses (e.g., a severely underpowered study). The third group tends to be mainly focused on this aspect of learning statistics because their future work is likely to involve reading articles for their own professional development, and perhaps summarizing or critiquing an article for peers or supervisors.

Challenges Present in Teaching Introductory Statistics

Why do students struggle with introductory statistics? Typical problems include weak basic math skills, poor conceptual understanding of math, math anxiety, a fixation on math procedures rather than concepts, poor graph comprehension, some features of statistical terminology, and a clash between American individualism and the notion of drawing conclusions from groups.

Some master's degree programs have low or no requirements for math proficiency. Students from these programs may have very weak math skills: They may not know what to do with parentheses, how to read decimal fractions or understand their magnitude, what an exponent or square root means, or how to calculate them. Some students are returning to school after decades in the workplace and have not used math much since their undergraduate years.

Even if students have good calculation skills, many have a poor conceptual understanding of math. They may be able to carry out simple algebra, but do not understand the tasks they are carrying out. Likewise, they may not understand what happens in a statistic when the numerator is increased or the denominator is decreased. Often associated with poor skills and poor conceptual understanding is students' anxiety about mathematics, which translates into resentment about taking a course that uses mathematics. Students tend to think of mathematics as consisting of a set of procedures, rather than consisting of interrelated concepts. Students can be surprised to the point of being caught off guard when they are expected to demonstrate conceptual understanding of a mathematical topic (e.g., to explain why certain conclusions follow, such as why poor reliability of a measure increases risk of Type I error).

Introductory statistics can use more visual displays than more advanced courses: the histogram, bar graph, scatterplot, and normal curves are all used; sometimes the t distribution, pie charts, and Venn diagrams are also introduced. Research on graph comprehension typically finds low levels of graph reading skills among Americans (Okan, Garcia-Retamero, Galesic, & Cokely, 2012), and students often ignore issues of scale and labeling when constructing graphs. Furthermore, these visual representations sometimes have to be combined, such as a scatterplot with distributions shown along the axes, multiple overlapping histograms combined with a formula, and so on.

Statistical terminology can map poorly onto everyday vocabulary; terms such as average, correlate, distribution, error, hypothesis, mean, power, prove, significant, theory, and variable have different meanings in statistics than in daily conversation. Learning and using the statistics-specific meanings takes extensive practice. The number of new terms that students must master each week is also large—in the first week of many courses students learn dependent and independent variables, scale, interval, ordinal, mean, median, mode, average, central tendency, standard deviation, variance, descriptive, and statistics as well as terminology related to a data analysis software package such as SPSS, Excel, or a programming-intensive application such as SAS or R. These statistical terms are also quite abstract, and research on vocabulary learning shows that abstract terms are harder to learn than concrete, imageable terms (Schwanenflugel, Stahl, & McFalls, 1997).

For some students there is a "culture clash" between the notion of an individual proving that he or she has some ability versus inability to prove (only to disprove) in the group-centered approach of statistics. Such a student will have enormous difficulty grasping the logic of null and research hypotheses and the logic of hypothesis testing.

In addition to difficulties with math skills and statistics concepts, some students—even those in educational psychology PhD programs—fail to see the relevance of learning statistics for their education. Many more students have low levels of interest in learning statistics and perceive statistics as dry or boring. Statistics courses are often thought of as courses that are required to complete a degree, rather than courses that are anticipated as exciting or interesting. Indeed, when informally surveying students in our classes about their reasons for taking a statistics course, "because I have to" is a common response. Students' low intrinsic motivation and lack of interest in taking statistics courses may often be rooted in low self-confidence for learning statistics due to the challenges cited above. This low motivation for statistics may also be rooted in perceptions of how statistics is typically taught. Therefore, we highlight several of the strategies we use, which are based in research and theory on academic achievement motivation, to mitigate the many challenges that come with teaching introductory statistics.

Innovations and Promising Practices

Inspired by our own graduate school instructors and based on various theories of academic achievement motivation, we have deployed a suite of approaches in our introductory statistics course to address the challenges above.

Gentle Re-Instruction in Basic Math

Our PowerPoints and web-based handouts include re-instruction in basic math and the conceptual mathematical underpinnings (e.g., a smaller denominator yields a bigger test statistic) without embarrassing students who lack these skills. We often humorously point out that some students may not have used this math in decades; we emphasize re-learning and de-emphasize any shame about not knowing the basic math. Also, we provide handouts that students can download without anyone knowing. We videotape the class meetings as well and make them available on the course website for re-play at any time.

Ample Feedback With Opportunities to Revise

Students complete SPSS assignments that include analyzing and interpreting data to solve problems, and creating various types of graphs and tables to present analysis results. These assignments can be revised within one week of receiving instructor feedback, putting an emphasis on eventual mastery rather than perfection the first time.

Emphasis on Conceptual Understanding and Application

Students create a personal "crib sheet" with key formulas, output, principles, and examples (the terms "cheat sheet" or "formula sheet" are used in some courses). Quiz and exam questions are never low-level factual questions; they ask students to calculate, apply, interpret, and report just as we do in our own research. We state explicitly that we will not test factual knowledge of specific, small pieces of information and remind students that these should be on the crib sheet for ready reference. Students often note on final course evaluations that the process of making the crib sheet was an important learning experience itself; some even reflect that they did not use the crib sheet much on an exam because the process of identifying important information, organizing it, and writing it down led to such robust learning.

To give one example of our emphasis on conceptual understanding on assessments, we show students histograms of various (imaginary) data sets, showing a relatively rectangular distribution, a more normal distribution, and a highly kurtotic distribution (a very large peak at the mean). Assuming that other parameters are the same across the distributions (M, Min, Max, N), we ask students which distribution would have a larger standard deviation. This requires students to understand that conceptually the SD is the extent to which the set of scores is spread out about the mean; it requires no calculation, though an understanding of the formula for the SD from a crib sheet might help the student get insight into the problem. As another example, we ask students to look for indications of a violated assumption from descriptives and results of an independent samples t test; in our example we have unequal variances, but other such problems could be compiled that show, for example, the df for a dependent samples t test. The critical features of these problems are that they require students to apply their knowledge, not simply regurgitate facts. Writing these kinds of problems is only possible because we allow students to have a crib sheet and it simultaneously encourages the development of a good crib sheet, which students are encouraged to save and use as a reference when working with statistics in other settings.

Opportunities for Practice to Build Fluency and Automaticity

At the same time, we provide optional opportunities for practice to help build fluency and automaticity. Although students might not need to memorize the formula for calculating a correlation, they should understand that, conceptually, it includes deviations from the X and Y means as well as the standard deviations of the X and Y variables. Calculating a correlation a few times until the process is relatively fluent can lead to faster retrieval of this information from memory. We provide opportunities for repeated practice calculating the standard deviation and mean from small datasets in "optional calculation homeworks" and on exam reviews. Likewise, we provide opportunities for repeated practice calculating the independent samples t statistics from published means and standard deviations in similar assignments. Students have the chance to fill in missing numbers from F tables for various ANOVA models and to fill in "missing" coefficients (b given beta, or vice versa) for regression.

Humor

We sing, dance, put on accents for Abraham de Moivre (a statistician and consultant to gamblers), Sir Ronald Fisher (famous for ANOVA), and Geoff

Cumming (for confidence intervals). We ask students to "let go" of everyday meanings of terms with "a deep cleansing breath." We create a class-wide shoe-size-by-height scatterplot on the whiteboard. We use a martini glass icon in PowerPoints for information that might impress someone at a cocktail party but is not required for the class, and a skull and crossbones for statistics that are not that relevant. We use mnemonics to make novel terms memorable (e.g., "t" for two). We poke fun at mistakes that we have made in our own analyses as we have learned new techniques. Anecdotally, math anxious students say that this use of humor puts them at ease. Possibly, the novelty of these techniques helps to make the information more memorable.

Giving Choices and Demonstrating Relevance

Students have periodic article critique assignments where they find an article from their own topic of study that uses the statistic that we are learning (e.g., correlations in a counseling psychology article). We also provide examples from our own research of when we have used a statistic, as well as segments of published articles. Providing choice is associated with building intrinsic motivation (Ryan & Deci, 2000) and showing relevance increases perceived task value for a subject (Eccles & Wigfield, 2002), both of which are associated with more effort and better achievement.

Student-Constructed Practice Questions

Our exam reviews begin with a question-and-answer period, but the bulk of the review is spent by students making up practice exam questions. We ask them to "think like me" and write questions that apply what they have learned within and across topics, further emphasizing applications and conceptual integration. We typically work about 10% of the questions during review, and post answers a few days later. This is a chance to reflect on questions that are too simple, ones that represent the kind of easy questions we might ask, ones that represent the hardest kind of question we might ask, and ones that represent a question that is too hard.

A sample of actual student-generated questions is shown in Table 24.1 with our suggested answers and the comments that we provide with these answers. The review sessions are also a chance for students to compare and improve their crib sheets (e.g., adding some output, correcting how they report results in APA manuscript style) or to confirm that they correctly understand a concept.

Impact of the Innovations

We have only a little evidence regarding the impact of these innovations. We did, however, find a statistically significant increase in midterm exam

scores from the semester before offering the homework revision opportunity to the semester after offering the homework revision opportunity
(t[42] = 2.04, p = .02, d = .63). There was also a statistically significant increase in final exam scores (t[42] = 1.93, p = .03, d = .60). We cannot control for incoming student characteristics in these analyses but the exams
and syllabi were identical, other than the opportunity to revise.

Anecdotally, we have found that students experience reductions in their
anxiety about learning statistics by the end of the course. We also find that
students appreciate the approach we take to teaching statistics as evidenced
in the course feedback we receive. For example, on a final course evaluation, one student wrote:

> I thought you did a great job of teaching the material. I haven't taken a math
> course since my first year of college probably close to 8 years ago but I felt

**TABLE 24.1   Sample Student-Generated Questions, Suggested
Answers, and Comments—With Our Suggested Answers**

Student-generated question	Our suggested answer	Our comments provided to class with answer
When we work hard to avoid Type I error, we increase the likelihood of _____ .	Type II error	This question is too simple, the answer could be read from a crib sheet
Why does a one-tailed test give more power than a two-tailed test?	A one-tailed test has a lower critical value (check the *t* or *r* table), and a lower critical value is easier to reach, in the sense that the difference between means does not have to be as large (or the correlation does not have to be as large) as with a two-tailed test.	This is a typical medium-difficulty exam question
What is the significance of the 5% rule	[None]	We only use *significance* to mean *statistically significant*. It is unclear what this question is asking.
Why do we have to square our "deviation from the mean" scores when calculating SS?	[None]	Too difficult for this course: Answering this question requires calculus.
Explain the assumption of multivariate normality and why it is necessary for 2-way ANOVA.	Each variable is normally distributed and the pair of distributions forms a cone shape in space.	We never discussed why this assumption is necessary.

you helped us every step of the way. I also felt this course was challenging and rigorous, but in a very manageable way if we stayed on top of studying, the reading, and picking out where we got stuck in the material.... I loved the final project. When I was working on it I remember thinking, 'Wow. I feel like I'm pretty cool being able to answer these questions about how to analyze a real data set. If I get these questions right, I really think I could make it as a researcher in the future.' ... This class was a real joy going to. I actually looked forward to it every week.

RECOMMENDATIONS AND CONCLUSIONS

Introductory educational statistics courses are often a gateway course for graduate students in educational psychology and other education disciplines for understanding the application of statistical methods in educational research. It is of great importance that students in educational psychology master the variety of topics taught in introductory statistics and develop a solid conceptual understanding of basic statistical methods. We as instructors of introductory statistics, however, have found challenges in teaching this course. The challenges are largely due to: (a) the wide range of degree programs and disciplines students come from; (b) the various levels of math proficiency students bring; (c) students' anxiety about mathematics and their lack of math conceptual understanding; (d) difficulty in comprehension of graphic representations and counterintuitive statistical terminology; and (e) low interest in and enjoyment of learning statistics.

In an attempt to address these challenges, we have recommended a number of instructional approaches, including gentle instruction of underpinning math concepts, providing constructive feedback and ample opportunities to revise assignments, emphasizing conceptual understanding and applications, using humor to alleviate math anxiety and shame, promoting student autonomy, and making statistics learning relevant to students' degree programs, research interests, or purposes for learning statistics.

An important caveat regarding our suggestions is that these approaches are recommended mostly based on theories of learning and motivation, our personal experience of teaching introductory statistics courses, and anecdotal evidence such as student evaluation and feedback about the course. We have not conducted empirical research on teaching and learning introductory statistics to support the use of these pedagogical approaches for teaching statistics, although some of the approaches are supported in research by other scholars and teachers who have taught introductory statistics (e.g., Stalder & Olson, 2011).

More research is needed to develop a systemic understanding of the challenges in teaching introductory statistics and to develop more informed solutions to the issues that impede student learning in this course. There are a number of scholarly journals that contribute to addressing pedagogical issues in statistics education, which may be of great help for instructors of introductory statistics and similar statistics courses. These journals are *Teaching Statistics, Statistics Education Research Journal, Journal of Statistics Education,* and *Technology Innovations in Statistics Education,* to name a few. These journals cover the teaching of topics that are particularly difficult for students. A number of these topics (e.g., the meaning of *p* value, probability and distributions, the notion of randomness, and statistical power) are covered in introductory statistics courses. The journals have articles dedicated to discussing effective teaching of these difficult topics and abstract statistical concepts. In addition, journals that address pedagogical issues in psychology, educational psychology, and sociology also occasionally publish articles that discuss the teaching of applied statistics in social sciences and education, such as past issues of *Teaching Educational Psychology, Psychology Teaching Review,* and *Teaching of Psychology.* We recommend referring to these resources for teaching specific topics, and for advice on pedagogy and instructional strategies that are relevant to introductory statistics.

Each class at each university is different in terms of the student skill set and the beliefs about statistics that the students bring. However, we believe our techniques are useful for anyone teaching statistics. Reviewing basic mathematical skills and concepts will likely be useful for even the most confident statistics students. Creating a context of mastery is critical for students' success, especially for students who will be applying their statistics skills as future researchers. Allowing students to have choices and helping them create relevance can help them all to enjoy their learning experience and increase their motivation for statistics. Finally, helping students to construct their own understanding (e.g., by creating test questions) can help them deepen their understanding of the concepts and application of statistical methods. While we have not studied these techniques empirically in our own graduate-level statistics courses, the techniques are supported by decades of research on learning and motivation and they have worked well in our 11 plus years of combined experience in teaching statistics.

REFERENCES

Eccles, J. S., & Wigfield, A. (2002). Motivational beliefs, values, and goals. *Annual Review of Psychology, 53*(1), 109–132.

Nokes-Malach, T. J., & Mestre, J. P. (2013). Toward a model of transfer as sense-making. *Educational Psychologist, 48*(3), 184–207.

Okan, Y., Garcia-Retamero, R., Galesic, M., & Cokely, E. T. (2012). When higher bars are not larger quantities: On individual differences in the use of spatial information in graph comprehension. *Spatial Cognition & Computation, 12*(2–3), 195–218.

Ryan, R. M., & Deci, E. L. (2000). Self-determination theory and the facilitation of intrinsic motivation, social development, and well-being. *American Psychologist, 55*(1), 68–78.

Schwanenflugel, P. J., Stahl, S. A., & Mcfalls, E. L. (1997). Partial word knowledge and vocabulary growth during reading comprehension. *Journal of Literacy Research, 29*(4), 531–553.

Stalder, D. R., & Olson, E. A. (2011). "t" for two: Using mnemonics to teach statistics. *Teaching of Psychology, 38*(4), 247–250.

CHAPTER 25

LEVERAGING STATISTICS ANXIETY AND OTHER PROMISING PRACTICES

Reagan Curtis and Zornitsa Georgieva
West Virginia University

Literature on teaching statistics and research can be summarized nicely with this quote from the preface to *Best Practices for Teaching Statistics and Research Methods in the Behavioral Sciences* (Dunn, Smith, & Beins, 2007).

> Statistics and research methods courses are arguably the mortar that holds the behavioral sciences curriculum together. Pedagogically, the material taught in statistics and methods bridges the broad expanse of introductory offerings and the depth and necessarily narrower focus of advanced topics... Unfortunately, some students approach these courses with fear and trepidation, if not outright dread. Instead of thinking about the content of statistics and methods as helpful for conducting or interpreting research, all too often students view the courses as something to be endured and passed. (p. xv)

When teaching graduate students in colleges of education, we have found this problem to be particularly pronounced. Our students include pre- and in-service teachers, counselors-in-training, nascent educational researchers,

Challenges and Innovations in Educational Psychology Teaching and Learning, pages 333–343
Copyright © 2016 by Information Age Publishing
All rights of reproduction in any form reserved.

and the next generation of educational psychologists. Not merely "some" students, but most of our students report "fear and trepidation" at the outset in response to research methodology and statistics, and the mathematics involved. Our goal as instructors is to overcome that fear to allow students to experience success with these difficult concepts. We do this, not by lowering the bar, but by addressing issues of anxiety head-on while holding high expectations for our students and providing high levels of support as they learn to apply concepts from lectures and textbooks into real world research and evaluation projects. It is through real world application, while directly confronting anxiety, that students develop deep and rich understandings of the material in our courses.

In this chapter, we first describe our approach to identifying and confronting statistics anxiety: leveraging student anxiety profiles to tailor instruction. Following that, we describe several instructional practices we use to support students' learning of statistics and research methods content. These practices include:

- realistic data simulation for analysis;
- juxtaposition of textbook versus real-world data;
- manuscript style write-ups and peer feedback;
- screen capture video tutorials; and
- audio commenting feedback on assignments.

We conclude with a strong recommendation to combine practices such as these and embed them in supportive learning communities where anxiety is confronted and leveraged to tailor instructional practices to meet students' needs.

WHY DOES STATISTICS ANXIETY MATTER?

Statistics anxiety is an essential factor that impacts students' learning and performance in research methodology related courses (Onwuegbuzie & Wilson, 2003). DeCesare (2007) reported about 60% of undergraduate students enrolled in a statistics course experienced anxiety relative to the course. Onwuegbuzie (1998) described similar trends in graduate student populations, and statistics anxiety associations with course performance have been documented (e.g., Onwuegbuzie, Slate, Paterson, Watson, & Schwartz, 2000). While some anxiety may be unavoidable, it must not be allowed to turn into a long-term impediment to student learning and participation in research activities. In fact, anxiety is considered "one of the most significant barriers that instructors encounter while teaching statistics" (Bessant, 1992, p.143). Baloğlu (2004) emphasized that one of the main goals of teaching statistics should be to address and reduce the statistics anxiety that students experience.

Statistics anxiety is not a phenomenon limited to statistics courses. Onwuegbuzie (1997) reported that one area impacted by statistics anxiety was reading and fully understanding research articles, which are critical for writing research proposals and conducting literature reviews. Knowledge of statistics is often utilized in the interpretation of data analyses and journal article reviews in research methodology courses and in other courses covering research literature in specific fields. In fact, statistics anxiety was found to be the best predictor for student achievement in research methodology courses (Onwuegbuzie et al., 2000).

In addition to immediate lower performance associated with high anxiety, long-term impacts are likely. Students dreading statistics courses postpone them as long as possible; sometimes until the very end of their degree programs (Onwuegbuzie, 1998; Roberts & Bilderbeck, 1980). Academic programs are designed with course sequences meant to maximize student learning, and delaying completing statistics courses to the end of the program may impact student learning and choice of field (Rodarte-Luna & Sherry, 2008). In the context of statistics anxiety, higher levels of anxiety have been associated with lower willingness to study statistics (Birenbaum & Eylath, 1994). An additional consideration for long-term impacts specific to graduate education is the requirement to complete a thesis or dissertation project that may require statistical expertise. There is some literature linking statistics anxiety with constructs such as perceived scholastic competence, perceived intellectual ability, and perceived creativity (Onwuegbuzie, 2000). If students develop such negative self-concepts as a result of bad experiences in statistics and research methodology courses, this may alter their degree paths and post-graduation careers. High levels of anxiety may shift student trajectories to careers that require minimal utilization of quantitative techniques as "[m]any students view statistics courses as a major threat to the attainment of a degree" (Onwuegbuzie & Seaman, 1995, p. 115).

One factor that impacts students' statistics anxiety is the structure and content of statistics courses and other courses that assume statistical content knowledge. Some researchers have suggested examining differences in anxiety levels across courses with different student requirements, content, and organization (e.g., DeCesare, 2007). For example, Bessant (1992) recommended that "the lecture method needs to be combined with carefully planned training sequences" (p. 144) as a way to battle student anxiety. Other recommendations for effective teaching include encouragement and positive reinforcement, emphasis on application of statistical knowledge in specific contexts, practice exams, and administering untimed exams (Onwuegbuzie, 1998, 1999). From student accounts, the examination of case studies in class contributed more to student learning than students had originally expected (Zanakis & Valenzi, 1997). Even though these recommendations appear in the literature, there is little empirical examination of how these teaching approaches impact student learning and anxiety levels. With few exceptions, researchers have tended to examine statistics anxiety as a static phenomenon, capturing anxiety levels at a single time.

INNOVATIONS AND PROMISING PRACTICES

Confronting and Leveraging Statistics Anxiety Over Time

We use the Statistical Anxiety Rating Scale (STARS; Baloğlu, 2004) and a brief statistics content knowledge test to understand our students' statistical anxiety profiles across six subscales: Test and Class Anxiety, Interpretation Anxiety, Fear of Asking for Help, Worth of Statistics, Computational Self Concept, and Fear of Statistics Teachers. Administering these measures at the start of the semester in introductory statistics, educational research, and educational psychology courses gives us unique opportunities to explicitly confront anxiety issues that might otherwise remain outside of classroom discourse, tailor our instruction to our students' needs, and have real data that is personally relevant to students with which to demonstrate and understand statistical techniques.

STARS data collected at the outset and midterm of the semester informs both whole-class and individual student-instructor interactions. For the whole class, we demonstrate how real world data collection and analysis can be conducted and presented. As the semester progresses we contextualize teaching and learning of statistical content such as descriptive statistics (e.g., mean, median, standard deviation), box plots (e.g., showing quartiles, medians, and outliers), internal consistency (e.g., Cronbach's α for total and subscales), and correlations within the context of an actual ongoing research project with data specifically relevant to the students themselves. Research methods issues such as sampling, instrumentation, longitudinal versus cross-sectional designs, and many others can be discussed in this context, as can more advanced statistical topics covered in later coursework.

We also engage students in discussions around their class-level anxiety profile, which prefaces later discussions with individual students about their personal anxiety profiles. We focus on differences across subscales, often finding that "Test and Class Anxiety" and "Computational Self Concept" are most problematic. We have found that Computational Self Concept is most strongly correlated with statistical content knowledge. We use this as an opportunity and rationale for students to spend time strengthening computational skills. It has been common that we find the correlation between "Interpretation Anxiety" and statistical content knowledge to strengthen by the midterm, and we spend additional time at that point focused on interpreting each component of statistical analyses and questioning students to reveal which aspects of interpreting statistical findings are most worrisome to them.

Individual student anxiety profiles often follow class-level trends, but some do not. We meet with individual students during office hours to discuss their profile and the practices they can engage in to reduce their anxiety and build competence in weak areas. For example, students having high anxiety relative to computational self-concept are encouraged to work multiple problems with small datasets and to check their work against Excel spreadsheets we provide that have embedded formula to calculate each component of complicated formulae. Students with high interpretation anxiety are encouraged to utilize peer feedback and share early drafts of their work for feedback from instructors prior to submission for grading. These practices complement and support whole class activities and alleviate aspects of anxiety common to the classroom STARS profile.

Realistic Data Simulation for Analysis

We often require students to conduct data analyses within realistic, meaningful research contexts. This is a purposeful choice that differs from a common practice where instructors have students collect actual data on trivial topics (e.g., counting number of cars of different colors at a particular intersection or at different times of day). Our assignments involve identifying a research topic (perhaps a potential thesis or dissertation topic), conducting a literature review to identify variables of interest and their interrelationships, generating realistic data on those variables, conducting appropriate analyses, and writing up a brief research report. We believe the authentic nature of the topic and associated tasks, and potential to further pursue the topic beyond the course, give this kind of assignment richness and depth.

We focus here on realistic data simulation, which we have not written about elsewhere but our students routinely describe as highly valuable for their understanding. Students are required to come individually to office hours prepared by having reviewed the literature to identify their research question, variables of interest, instruments to operationalize the identified variables, and hypothesized relations among the variables. The instructor prompts the student to identify elements of data structure (e.g., scales of measurement, range of scores, sample size) that make it appropriate for the type of analysis (e.g., ANOVA, regression) to be done. We then use SPSS, using compute and random variable functions, to create a dataset that conforms to the specifications, including hypothesized relations among variables.

Here is an example. A student is interested in whether gender, locus of control, and past trauma have predictive relations to depression. The student identifies specific instruments related to each variable to determine the potential range of scores. The student describes what the literature says about each variable's relation to depression and then predicts both the direction and general strength of that relationship for each variable. If the student asserts that higher levels of trauma, indicated by a specific measure, are moderately and positively related to higher levels of depression (as indicated by another specific measure), then that relation can be modeled. The instructor then works through the process of generating data in SPSS while the student watches.

There are many points in this process when the student and instructor stop and discuss relevant statistical content knowledge integration. The process often proceeds as follows. The instructor opens SPSS and defines the appropriate variables: Depress, Gender, Locus, and Trauma. A sample size is identified after the instructor and student discuss power, effect size, and the number of predictors in a regression framework. In SPSS, the instructor types any numerical digit into the otherwise blank data file on the line corresponding to the final case. This has the effect of defining the sample size when data are later generated with the Compute command (found on the Transform menu). The following SPSS syntax creates the outcome variable (Depress), generated randomly following a normal distribution with a mean of 50 and a standard deviation of 10 (the "RND" function rounds each score to a whole number, which is appropriate if that is how the measure is scored):

COMPUTE Depress=RND(RV.NORMAL(50,10)).

We then query the student about how to create a second variable that has a specified relation to this outcome. To generate a second Trauma variable that is positively and moderately correlated with Depress, the following syntax can be created through the compute command:

IF (depress >= 50) Trauma=RV.NORMAL(4.5,.75).
IF (depress < 50) Trauma=RV.NORMAL(3.5,.75).

This syntax assumes the Trauma measure is on a 7-point Likert type scale where multiple items are averaged so there is no need for the RND command used previously. Two random sets of scores are generated: The set for those above the mean in Depress is centered on a higher mean than is the set for those with below average depression scores. The syntax can be modified, changing the mean and standard deviation values, and the resulting correlation and frequency tables are then examined to see how they change in relation to those modifications. This is an excellent opportunity to discuss and model the implications of centrality and spread for relations among variables. This approach helps the student to develop deeper understanding of how the involved statistical concepts connect in a larger integrative conceptual model.

Juxtaposition of Textbook Versus Real-World Data

Instructors should give the messiness of real-world data more attention than do quantitative methodology textbooks. We find that students often get an unrealistic view of research and statistics from textbooks. While some texts allude to the "messiness" of real-world research, we have not found any that treat this topic thoroughly. The various typologies generally read as if instances in reality will fit neatly into one category or another and the datasets generally have no missing values, no out-of-range data entry errors, and follow predictable patterns. Thorough treatments of how to structure data for entry, how to clean messy data, or how to identify and handle missing data are difficult to find for early career graduate students. All of this leaves students at a loss when they are engaged in their first research projects. The messiness of educational research data is something that students have not been adequately trained to deal with and work out.

We, therefore, expose students to data across a continuum from sample datasets, from data that have been thoroughly cleaned and curated, on one hand, to "messy" data files, on the other hand, that are taken from previous research projects. We vary the assignments utilizing these datasets across the semester. Initially, we introduce statistical concepts and exercises with clean data sets but, subsequently, introduce the messy data sets and teach our students how to address the problems with the sorts of data that invariably are obtained when conducting an actual research project.

Manuscript-Style Write-Ups and Peer Feedback

Consistent with our assertion that students should be exposed to the messiness of real-world data acquisition, we also believe that students should learn to write up statistical and research findings in the forms they will employ as full-fledged scholars. This is another area where students that are exposed to one or two statistics textbooks may get inaccurate views. Each textbook author tends to use somewhat idiosyncratic notations, and instructors, too, often impose their own idiosyncratic formatting and style requirements on their students. We suggest, instead, that students be directed to existing published research and an appropriate style manual (e.g., Publication Manual of the American Psychological Association) for information about statistical notation and manuscript formatting. This exposes students to diverse notation systems and a variety of acceptable formats. We require students to use notation that is consistent with the articles they are reading.

We also have found that peer influence is invaluable. We have draft versions of homework assignments brought to class before they are due for a grade, and we ask students to spend a few minutes evaluating each other's work to determine if all the components of the assignment have been addressed. This has several benefits, including allowing students to develop their skills at giving constructive criticism to colleagues, supporting development of a classroom learning community, exposing students to the diversity of work products generated by their peers, and shaping students' initial work on an assignment toward mastery before review by the instructors.

Screen Capture Video Tutorials and Audio Commenting Feedback

We believe it is critical to provide high levels of support, along with the high expectations that we hold for our students. In addition to class meetings, required attendance in office hours, and substantial supplemental online materials, we focus here on two types of support: screen capture video tutorials and audio commenting feedback.

We create screen capture video tutorials for many statistical procedures that are conducted utilizing software (e.g., SPSS, Excel). There are a variety of software tools available for creating these videos, but we have found http://www.screencast-o-matic.com/ to be very user-friendly. These videos allow us to show students the steps required to carry out statistical analyses while also talking them through analysis and interpretation. Because the videos are posted online, students can view them on their own schedule— and repeatedly, if necessary. Student feedback in response to the videos has been consistently strong and positive; students ask us to create more videos for additional topics. We, therefore, suggest that instructors periodically poll students about the topics that are well suited for tutorial videos that can benefit students' learning.

For all written assignments in our courses, we provide formative audio feedback to each student.[1] Ice, Curtis, Phillips, and Wells (2007) found that students strongly preferred audio commenting, and applied their knowledge more often (and at a higher level on Bloom's Taxonomy) when they had received audio commenting on their assignments. Instructors spent 75% as much time giving comments while providing 255% more feedback! They noted that "[w]hile increases in quantity of feedback delivered with less demand on instructors' time is a strong reason to use the technique, evidence that it also increased retention and understanding of content at deeper levels makes it hard to argue *against* using audio commenting..." (p. 19). We initially saw audio commenting as a way to increase online teaching presence in our asynchronous courses, but we also have found it almost universally appreciated in our face-to-face classes, with student feedback similar to that described by Ice et al. (2007).

While there are many ways to produce and distribute audio feedback, the process we have found the easiest is with Adobe Acrobat Pro. Our students submit their assignments through our online learning management system. We then convert their papers into Adobe PDF format. In some cases, we employ "track changes" in Microsoft Word prior to PDF conversion. Students cannot then "Accept All" changes to their document without actually making the changes themselves, and this forces deeper cognitive processing on their part, which should lead to greater retention and learning. Adobe Acrobat Pro allows us to insert audio comments throughout the PDF document. Generally, we read through the document and insert comments on format, notation, and analytic and interpretation content where these issues occur before we return to the beginning of the document and leave an overall summative comment. We then post the PDF file on our learning management system for students to access. Students can view the file and listen to our feedback using the freeware version of Adobe Acrobat Reader.

RECOMMENDATIONS AND CONCLUSION

We have described approaches that we find beneficial in our practice as instructors of graduate level statistics and research methodology courses. These practices include:

- identifying, confronting and leveraging student anxiety profiles to tailor instruction;
- using realistic data simulation for analysis;
- juxtaposing textbooks and real-world data;
- requiring manuscript style write-ups and peer feedback;
- using screen capture video tutorials; and
- providing audio commenting feedback on assignments.

We adopt a proactive strategy each semester to learn from our students about their greatest fears and anxiety-generating aspects of the research methods and statistics courses. We can then provide the necessary supports for learning and embed them in the course structure so that even those students who are most fearful can be successful. A single supporting mechanism cannot address the complexity and multidimensionality of statistics anxiety. For that reason, combinations of learning scaffolds must be tailored to individual students and to each new group of students each semester.

We have found it essential to establish close connections between course content and students' personal academic interest. The application of statistical concepts in specific contexts has been suggested by others as a way to alleviate high statistics anxiety and enhance learning (Onwuegbuzie, 1999). Such practical experiences become key levers for student motivation and success as statistics and research design move away from the hypothetical and abstract and turn into tangible work to which students can relate. Along with multiple practice opportunities through which students correct and learn from their mistakes, we create authentic data analytic learning experiences. Such experiences result in products (e.g., initial research reports, result section drafts, literature review drafts) that students can build upon and further develop in their subsequent coursework.

NOTE

1. We provide written feedback for any student who is deaf, hard of hearing, or who has an auditory processing exceptionality.

REFERENCES

Baloğlu, M. (2004). Statistics anxiety and mathematics anxiety: Some interesting differences I. *Educational Research Quarterly, 27*(3), 38–48.

Bessant, K. C. (1992). Instructional design and the development of statistical literacy. *Teaching Sociology, 20,* 143–149.

Birenbaum, M., & Eylath, S. (1994). Who is afraid of statistics? Correlates of statistics anxiety among students of educational sciences. *Educational Research, 36*(1), 93–98.

DeCesare, M. (2007). Statistics anxiety among sociology majors: A first diagnosis and some treatment options. *Teaching Sociology, 35,* 360–367.

Dunn, D. S., Smith, R. A., & Beins, B. C. (Eds.). (2012). *Best practices in teaching statistics and research methods in the behavioral sciences.* Mahwah, NJ: Erlbaum.

Ice, P., Curtis, R., Wells, J., & Phillips, P. (2007). Using asynchronous audio feedback to enhance teaching presence and student sense of community. *Journal of Asynchronous Learning Networks, 11*(2), 3–25.

Michaelsen, L., Sweet, M., & Parmalee, D. (2009). Team-based learning: Small group learning's next big step. *New Directions in Teaching and Learning,* 7–27.

Onwuegbuzie, A. J. (1997). Writing a research proposal: The role of library anxiety, statistics anxiety, and composition anxiety. *Library & Information Science Research, 19*(1), 5–33.

Onwuegbuzie, A. J. (1998). The dimensions of statistics anxiety: A comparison of prevalence rates among mid-southern university students. *Louisiana Educational Research Journal, 23*(2), 23–40.

Onwuegbuzie, A. J. (1999). Statistics anxiety among African American graduate students: An affective filter? *Journal of Black Psychology, 25*(2), 189–209.

Onwuegbuzie, A. J. (2000). Statistics anxiety and the role of self-perceptions. *The Journal of Educational Research, 93*(5), 323–330.

Onwuegbuzie, A. J., & Seaman, M. (1995) The effect of time and anxiety on statistics achievement. *Journal of Experimental Psychology, 63,* 115–124.

Onwuegbuzie, A. J., Slate, J., Paterson, F., Watson, M., & Schwartz, R. (2000). Factors associated with underachievement in educational research courses. *Research in the Schools, 7,* 53–65.

Onwuegbuzie, A. J., & Wilson, V. A. (2003). Statistics anxiety: Nature, etiology, antecedents, effects, and treatments—a comprehensive review of the literature. *Teaching in Higher Education, 8*(2), 195–209.

Roberts, D. M., & Bilderback, E. W. (1980). Reliability and validity of a statistics attitude survey. *Educational and Psychological Measurement, 40*(1), 235–238.

Rodarte-Luna, B., & Sherry, A. (2008). Sex differences in the relation between statistics anxiety and cognitive/learning strategies. *Contemporary Educational Psychology, 33*(2), 327–344.

Zanakis, S. H., & Valenzi, E. R. (1997). Student anxiety and attitudes in business statistics. *Journal of Education for Business, 73*(1), 10–16.

CHAPTER 26

TEACHING STATISTICS THROUGH TEAM-BASED LEARNING

Daniel H. Robinson and James Folkestad
Colorado State University

Teaching introductory statistics is one of the most challenging courses, pedagogically speaking. The reason is that there is such a wide range of student ability, preparation, and motivation in each class. Some undergraduates simply take statistics to satisfy an easy core requirement, whereas others similarly take it as a core requirement—but fear that the math will be too difficult. Several graduate students in educational psychology also enter the course with fear, as their introductory statistics course represents a major hurdle that will (supposedly) determine whether they are cut out for graduate coursework.

Because statistics can serve an important weeding-out function, similar to introductory chemistry, physics, and calculus courses, some educational psychology departments appear to be at ease with the high drop/withdrawal/failure rates associated with the course. For those of us who embrace the pedagogical challenge, however, we constantly search for ways to allow more students to successfully clear this infamous hurdle. We have been

Challenges and Innovations in Educational Psychology Teaching and Learning, pages 345–355
Copyright © 2016 by Information Age Publishing
All rights of reproduction in any form reserved.

using team-based learning (TBL) for the past eight years in our introductory statistics courses. We firmly believe that TBL has allowed many students to "get" statistics that they otherwise would not had they been exposed to it via traditional instruction.

TEAM-BASED LEARNING BACKGROUND

TBL has been around for over 20 years and is the brainchild of Larry Michaelsen, who conceived the idea when he taught large business courses at the University of Oklahoma. He was disappointed in the lack of student involvement and interaction in the large lecture sections. So, he devised an instructional system that proponents claim harnesses the power of student learning teams to enhance individual student learning (see Michaelsen & Sweet, 2009, for an explanation of how TBL works). Although the version of TBL we use for statistics is based on Michaelsen's original work, it has evolved over the years based simply on our learning what seems to work best. Thus, what we describe in this chapter is not "pure" TBL in the sense of what is described elsewhere. Nonetheless, the TBL we describe contains the four basic components described by Michaelsen. First, strategically formed, heterogeneous teams of five to seven students are permanent for the entire course to build trust and communication. Second, students take multiple-choice, readiness assurance tests (RATs) to prepare them for instruction. These tests are first taken individually, without feedback, and then again in teams where they answer quiz items until correct. The RAT is followed by instruction that focuses on areas where students are weak, as revealed by their performances. Third, teams are required to apply the content by tackling the same problem, making a specific choice, and revealing their choices simultaneously. Teams may then challenge each other's choices. Finally, team members provide feedback to one another often to promote team development and coherence.

TBL was, at first, yet another highly-proclaimed instructional intervention with little empirical support. Early studies promoting TBL were nonexperimental (e.g., Carmichael, 2009; Vasan, DeFouw, & Compton, 2011; Vasan, DeFouw, & Holland, 2008; Wiener, Plass, & Marz, 2009; Zgheib, Simaan, & Sabra, 2010; Zingone et al., 2010). However, more rigorous studies have followed. Koles, Stolfi, Borges, Nelson, and Parmelee (2010) compared TBL to case-based instruction with pharmacology students using a crossover design. TBL students performed better on a comprehensive examination than did the case-based instruction students. Also using a crossover design, Thomas and Bowen (2011) compared TBL to small-group lecture with medical students. Again, TBL compared favorably on content knowledge questions. In a randomized study using eighth-grade history students, Vaughn, Swanson, Roberts, Wanzek, Stillman-Spisak et al. (2013) found TBL students performed higher on tests of content knowledge and reading comprehension than did traditional students. In a similar randomized study using eleventh-grade social studies students, Wanzek, Vaughn, Kent, Swanson, Roberts et al. (2014) also found advantages for TBL that supported learning content knowledge.

Statistics tests and quizzes are some of the more stressful events in the life of an educational psychology student. Consider the typical testing experience: Students shuffle in and are seated in a crowded classroom. The instructor distributes the test and the students proceed to sweat blood and take years off their lives for the next hour. When finished, the students turn in their tests and leave. A few students might discuss the test afterwards by recalling certain items, what they answered etc. But, for the most part, the emotional energy students generated for the test is wasted. A week later, the instructor has graded the tests and students learn how well they performed and what they missed. Anger and resentment are the common student emotions at this stage and these feelings are directed solely at the instructor.

TBL attempts to capture this energy and these emotions and put them to good use. In a TBL testing experience, students first take the test or quiz individually—exactly as they would in a traditional class setting. They turn in their answer sheets but are allowed to keep the test with the questions. Students then assemble in their teams and take the same test again. This time, they must reach consensus for each item. It is in the process of reaching consensus where students will hopefully reveal their individual choices, their rationale for why they answered that way, and their level of confidence in their choice. For the first few tests, students tend to be more concerned about being polite than right. They may quickly accept a classmate's reasoning and several team errors are made. As the semester progresses, students shift toward greater concern for being right than polite. It is not uncommon to see students serving as gatekeepers for an overbearing classmate, while at the same time serving as solicitors for a shy classmate who tends to be right but rarely speaks up. It is truly a joy to witness this transformation in the student teams where students really "get into" the material—much more than we have ever witnessed in a traditional setting. In fact, our favorite episodes occur after the last test of the semester when we see students shaking each other's hands and high-fiving. Ask yourself, in what classes you have taught where students have done this?

We both decided to try TBL for similar reasons that Michaelsen developed it. We were growing tired of the "chalk and talk" approach and the level of student enthusiasm. To be honest, it was also our level of enthusiasm that was waning. TBL, for those of you who may dare to give it a try, can be considered a form of Extreme Makeover: Teaching Edition. It has truly been a transformative experience for us. In the following, we describe the five primary components of TBL that we have implemented: (a) readiness assurance quizzes; (b) team games; (c) examinations; (d) appeals; and (e) teammate feedback.

Readiness Assurance Quizzes

To walk you through the TBL approach to teaching statistics, we will begin by simply showing how the syllabus differs from a traditional one. Here is a section on quizzes:

> There will be six 15-point multiple-choice, readiness assurance quizzes. Each quiz will cover conceptual material presented in the assigned readings. Quizzes will first be taken individually (without the help of others) and then again in teams. You will take the individual quizzes for 20 minutes. Upon completion of the individual quiz, students will assemble in their teams and take the same quiz again as a team. The team quiz will also last for 20 minutes. Students may receive bonus points if their team takes fewer attempts to answer all items correctly than other teams. For example, if a team takes fewer attempts than all other teams, individuals from that team will receive two points added to their individual score. So, if a student scores 13 and their team performs better than all other teams, then that student receives a 15 for the overall score; second place teams receive one point. If teams tie, they get equal points. Thus, a student may receive up to 12 extra credit points on quizzes.

Perhaps the biggest objection you will get from students when you implement TBL is the same reaction one would get when implementing a flipped classroom. Students are responsible for learning some of the content before the instructor covers it in class. This can be quite daunting. However, we quickly assure them that they are not responsible for learning statistical computation absent instruction. Rather, they are responsible for the conceptual understanding of important concepts covered in the textbook chapters that are prerequisite to receiving instruction in computation. An example item from one of the quizzes follows:

> Dr. Jeffreys is interested in whether a snack incentive could help boost attendance in early morning statistics classes. She decides to conduct an experiment and randomly selects eight introductory statistics courses from the spring catalog which meet from 8 to 9 a.m. Half of the instructors are instructed to provide donuts to their students during class the other half are not.
>
> In this study, the four no-donut courses represent
>
> a. the independent variable
> b. the dependent variable
> c. the control condition

d. the experimental condition
e. a confounding variable

This quiz format requires that students receive a quiz and an answer sheet. Answer sheets are collected after the individual quiz portion. Students then receive a new answer sheet for their team and use their quizzes to see how they answered each item. When teams are ready to have their quiz graded, the instructor simply marks the items they missed. Teams then get a second attempt on these items. Teams keep doing this until all items are answered correctly. There are several advantages to this system. First, students leave the classroom knowing the answer to each question and how well they and their team performed. Second, they are able to expend their emotional energy in a constructive way. We have witnessed students literally running to their teammates when it is time for the team quiz. They want, no, *demand* to know what their teammates put for, say, question #7.

Discussion ensues and if they answered questions differently, students want to know why their answer was incorrect. Rather than the instructor providing these explanations and having anger directed toward them, students receive explanations from their teammates (who are not the *enemy*). Moreover, if you agree with Vygotsky, these more-knowledgeable peers are better equipped to provide these explanations than the instructor. Finally, students receive feedback much faster than the typical one week delay with traditional quiz practices. Lecture then follows this readiness assurance process, and we have found that students also *demand* explanations concerning items their team struggled to answer. We find that we are energized by this provision of such explanations during lectures, which is much preferable to the typical reaction students have to lectures (i.e., trying to stay awake).

This "just-in-time" instruction provided after students have read the chapters and "gotten into" the material just might be the cure for instructors who struggle with their enthusiasm for teaching. One last thing about lectures: We find it helpful to record our lectures and then make them available online for students following the class. Statistics is one of those courses where many students find it useful to go back and view the lecture again at their own pace.

TEAM GAMES

After the quiz and lecture, students have opportunities to further practice their newly acquired computational skills by participating in team games— what Michaelsen would call application-oriented activities. Students are given difficult problems and asked to solve them in their teams. An example of one of these difficult team games problems follows:

A number of studies have used animals to examine possible relationships between neuroticism and alcoholism. Here is a typical study of this type. Two cats were randomly selected from each of 12 litters. One cat from each litter was offered milk spiked with 5% alcohol. Its littermate was first subjected to a procedure designed to induce experimental neurosis and then offered the spiked milk. The amount consumed in three minutes was measured in cubic centimeters. Does neuroticism increase the tendency to consume alcohol?

Control	Neurosis
250	244
217	210
226	218
253	255
242	230
221	198
230	235
220	230
227	213
254	222
237	232
225	218

What is the observed test statistic?

  a. 2.43   b. 2.10   c. 1.46   d. 2.76   e. 1.37

Which of the following conclusions is appropriate?

  a. Neurotic cats drank less alcohol.
  b. Neurotic cats drank more alcohol.
  c.. It is not possible to experimentally induce neurosis.
  d. Not enough information to draw a conclusion at this time.
  e. Neurotic cats drank the same amount of alcohol as the controls.

What is the 95% confidence interval around the population parameter?

  a. −0.16 to 16.36
  b. −2.16 to 18.36
  c. −4.16 to 20.36
  d. 1.26 to 14.9
  e. 0.76 to 15.4

What is Cohen's d effect size?

  a. .54
  b. .70
  c. .38
  d. .45
  e. .23

Teams are given the same problem and report their answers simultaneously. The instructor then displays each team's work to the other teams and they critique the work of all of the teams. The discussions that ensue provide further evidence that students are engaging the material at a level that rarely occurs in typical lecture classrooms. By the way, in the example above, spirited discussion typically ensues concerning whether one should use an independent or dependent t-test.

EXAMINATIONS

Finally, after having read the chapters, taken a quiz to demonstrate their readiness for instruction, participated in a lecture, and practiced several problems, students are given a unit exam that involves similar statistical analyses. An example examination question follows:

> A school psychologist investigates the relationship of preschool background to emotional adjustment during the first grade. A teacher within the system is asked to test her students on relative adjustment based on some carefully designed criteria. Is preschool background related to emotional adjustment?
>
> Home with parent: 35, 39, 50, 45, 48
> Home with babysitter: 37, 40, 32, 33, 42
> Nursery school: 48, 55, 44, 46, 51
> Home with friend or relative: 31, 44, 38, 36, 43
>
> Which of the following conclusions is appropriate, based on the data?
> a. Preschool background is related to emotional adjustment, $F(3, 16) = 5.59$, $p < .05$. A Tukey HSD follow-up test indicated that first graders who went to nursery school are better adjusted than those who stayed at home with a babysitter and those who stayed home with a friend or relative.
> b. Preschool background is not related to emotional adjustment, $F(3, 16) = 3.15$, $p > .05$.
> c. Preschool background is related to emotional adjustment, $F(3, 16) = 4.15$, $p > .05$. A Tukey HSD follow-up test indicated that first graders who stayed home with a parent and students who stayed home with a friend or relative are better adjusted than those who stayed at home with a babysitter.
> d. Preschool background is related to emotional adjustment, $H = 5.53$, $p > .05$. A Mann-Whitney U-test follow-up indicated that first graders who went to nursery school are better adjusted than those who stayed at home with a babysitter.
> e. Preschool background is related to emotional adjustment, $H = 3.28$, $p > .05$.

Appeals

An important part of the TBL approach is allowing students to appeal quiz and exam questions. Perhaps we have all experienced what we thought was an unfair, poorly worded, or incorrectly keyed question. The syllabus section on appeals is as follows:

> If your team feels strongly about the correctness of an item that it missed, the team may submit a written appeal to the instructor. This appeal process must occur immediately following a readiness quiz or problem-solving test. Only teams, not individuals, may write appeals. Only teams that write successful appeals get points for that appeal, even if another team missed the same question(s). Appeals are not simply an opportunity to dig for more points. Rather, they are an opportunity for teams to make scholarly arguments for their collective positions. All arguments must be supported by evidence from the text or lecture notes. If the appeal is based on an ambiguously phrased question, the team must suggest wording that is less ambiguous. The decision to grant or refuse an appeal will be made by the instructor after class via e-mail. The following is an example of a successful appeal:
>
> **Argument:** "We feel that A, rather than B, should be the correct answer to question 15."
>
> **Evidence:** "According to Table B.6, the critical r for 10 degrees of freedom, two-tailed test, and an alpha of .05 is .576, which is larger than the calculated r of .570. This would lead us to conclude that there is no relationship between shoe size and intelligence."

In our experience, the appeal process is yet another way for students to dig deeply into the material. They use whatever emotions were elicited from missing a question and turn them into useful energy that has them diving into their notes, textbook, and even lecture videos to get to the bottom of the contested issue. To discourage gratuitous appeals, we limit teams to one appeal per quiz or test. This requires consensus in deciding which question to appeal. Sometimes many team members miss a question, but they decide that it is not the best question to appeal as the answer is now obvious. As instructors, rather than feeling bad about weakly written items, we instead feel good about the level of learning that has occurred because of a weak item.

Teammate Feedback

In TBL, according to Michaelsen, three things determine students' grades: individual student performance, team performance, and peer evaluations. We started using TBL by following Michaelsen's suggestion of allowing students to determine how much each of these three components was weighted in determining the final grade. After a few semesters, we abandoned this system as it usually led to students voting to place the most weight on the latter two and the least weight on individual performance. If you allow peer evaluations to heavily influence student grades, we have found that students will do their best to make sure their teammates agree on a plan where everyone receives the highest possible ratings. Even if you require different ratings for each team member, students will find a way to make things fair. What we have found to work best is simply to ensure that individual performance is by far the most influential grade determinant. Students can earn bonus points if their teams do well, but they NEVER lose points based on team performance. In fact, if a student feels strongly about not wanting to be on a team, we give them the option to take every quiz and test individually only. We have never yet had a student take us up on this offer. As for peer evaluations, we have devised a system where they only affect a student's grade when they are within a few points of a desired grade. Below is the section on teammate feedback:

In this class, professionalism is very important. In the professional world, your life is influenced by three things: your own effort, the effort of the people you depend upon, and the way you work together, which is why I have chosen the Team-Based Learning system which values all three of those things. Twice during the course you will provide teammate feedback to each member of your team. The feedback should reflect your judgment of such things as:

Preparation: Were they prepared when they came to class?

Contribution: Did they contribute productively to the team discussion and work?

Respect for others' ideas: Did they encourage others to contribute their ideas?

Flexibility: Were they flexible when disagreements occurred?

Feedback will consist of two statements for each person:

Something you appreciate about this teammate is . . .
Something you would like to request of this teammate is . . .

Your comments will be anonymous in the sense that neither your teammates nor I will know who made the comments. The TA will email all blinded comments from team members to the individual. It is important to provide positive feedback to people who truly worked hard for the good of the team and to also make suggestions to those you perceived not to be working as effectively on team tasks. I will refer to the feedback a student has received from team members in those situations where the student is a few points short of a letter grade. Improvement as a team member and/or sustained good work may convince me to give a few points to students who barely miss the cutoffs.

CONCLUSION

In conclusion, we have found using TBL to teach introductory statistics has transformed us as instructors. TBL creates energy and enthusiasm by allowing students to engage as part of highly effective learning teams. Inter-team competition fosters intra-team cohesion. Students tend to sit with their teammates during lectures. As for teammate feedback, common requests of teammates include, "I wish you came to class more often," or "I wish you would speak up more as you tend to know the right answer." In how many classes have you taught where Student A is concerned about Student B's attendance? On one occasion, we had a student who had an emergency and asked to take the final exam early. She did so and had enough points to earn an A in the course without participating in the team version of the exam. However, she decided to come back to campus and join her teammates so that she could help them earn bonus points. Again, is this type of altruistic behavior common in traditional instruction classrooms?

REFERENCES

Carmichael, J. (2009). Team-based learning enhances performance in introductory biology. *Journal of College Science Teaching, 38,* 54–61.

Koles, P., Stolfi, A., Borges, N. J., Nelson, S., & Parmelee, D. X. (2010). The impact of team-based learning on medical students' academic performance. *Academic Medicine, 85,* 1739–1745. doi: 10.1097/ACM.0b013e3181f52bed

Michaelsen, L., Sweet, M., & Parmalee, D. (2009). Team-based learning: Small group learning's next big step. *New Directions in Teaching and Learning,* 7–27.

Thomas, P. A., & Bowen, C. W. (2011). A controlled trial of team-based learning in an ambulatory medicine clerkship for medical students. *Teaching and Learning in Medicine, 23,* 31–36. doi:10.1080/10401334.2011.536888

Vasan, N. S., DeFouw, D. O., & Compton, S. (2011). Team-based learning in anatomy: An efficient, effective, and economical strategy. *Anatomical Sciences Education, 4,* 333–339. doi: 10.1002/ase.257

Vasan, N. S., DeFouw, D. O., & Holland, B. K. (2008). Modified use of team-based learning for effective delivery of medical gross anatomy and embryology. *Anatomical Sciences Education, 1,* 3–9. doi: 10.1002/ase.5

Vaughn, S., Swanson, E. A., Roberts, G., Wanzek, J., Stillman-Spisak, S. J., Solis, M., & Simmons, D. (2013). Improving reading comprehension and social studies knowledge in middle school. *Reading Research Quarterly, 48,* 77–93. doi: 10.1002/rrq.039

Wanzek, J., Vaughn, S., Kent, S. C., Swanson, E. A., Roberts, G. Haynes, M., . . . Solis, M. (2014). The effects of team-based learning on social studies knowledge acquisition in high school. *Journal of Research on Educational Effectiveness, 7*(2), 183–204. doi: 10.1080/19345747.2013.836765

Wiener, H. H., Plass, H. H., & Marz, R. R. (2009). Team-based learning in intensive course format for first-year medical students. *Croatian Medical Journal, 50,* 69–76. doi: 10.3325/cmj.2009.50.69

Zgheib, N. K., Simaan, J. A., & Sabra, R. (2010). Using team-based learning to teach pharmacology to second-year medical students improves student performance. *Medical Teacher, 32,* 130–135. doi: 10.3109/01421590903548521

Zingone, M. M., Franks, A. S., Guirguis, A. B., George, C. M., Howard-Thompson, A., & Heidel, R. E. (2010). Comparing team-based and mixed active-learning methods in an ambulatory care elective course. *American Journal of Pharmaceutical Education, 74,* 160–160. doi: 10.5688/aj7409160

CHAPTER 27

TEACHING LARGE SCALE DATA ANALYSIS

James B. Schreiber and Misook Heo
Duquesne University

HISTORY

Around 1660 A.D., statistics and social science were known as political arithmetic. Most of the work dealt with the calculation of annuity rates and, sometimes, state policy. But, the foundation for large scale data analysis was being set. This can be seen in Cassini's 1740 examination of years of data on the inclination of the earth's equator to its orbit about the sun using linear interpolation. This work led to the "astronomer's error" law, which we commonly call the bell shaped curve. One must also not forget Bayes and Laplace's work on posteriori probabilities in the 1700s. The work of Legendre in 1805 for the method of least squares moved us again forward to larger and larger analyses. You can also see the birth of modeling and large-scale data analysis in Bachelier's (1900) random walk work on stock prices. Then comes the work of Sir Ronald Fisher in statistics, which most of us were indoctrinated into during graduate school, if not earlier.

Large scale data analysis through graphic representation also has a long history. Charles Minard's (1845) map of Napolean's Russian campaign is one of the best, and according to Edward Tufte (2003), the best graphical

Challenges and Innovations in Educational Psychology Teaching and Learning, pages 357–368
Copyright © 2016 by Information Age Publishing
All rights of reproduction in any form reserved.

representation of a large amount of data for the time period. It displays the losses, troop movements, and temperature across time. Thus, statistics and large scale data analysis are old topics. The history of statistical thinking is important and we embed little bits of this history into our course. Plus, many of the people involved (for example, Fisher) were very interesting characters.

The topic of large scale data analysis has always been important, but a seeming renewal of interest is currently underway due to the massive amounts of data that are now collected and housed electronically. For example, the U.S. government collects 45,000 different economic indicators. As Silver (2013) noted, this represents over a billion comparisons that can be analyzed.

Significance of Topic

Large scale data analysis is relevant to educational psychology, both historically and currently. Educational psychology has been a leader in the development and use of statistical models and many educational statistics programs are housed in educational psychology programs and departments. In addition, the field utilizes large scale analysis techniques to answer more nuanced research questions within many applied social science subfields. We are particularly happy with the increasing use of Bayesian analyses in educational psychology and, although that topic is not discussed here, it does come up in our course.

With the rise of extremely large data sets, analyses of these data have become more important for students. This is because the expected analytical techniques are more complicated, the analyses that are published in research journals are more sophisticated, and many of these studies use large scale data analysis techniques. These techniques allow researchers to develop and test more nuanced hypotheses, which deepen our understanding of social science phenomena. Students without this knowledge are at a competitive disadvantage as professionals who must read and use the literature in their post-graduate work. We also personally believe that it is important because many persons trained in educational psychology do not enter academe, but leave for industry where they conduct incredible research—most of which we never see due to proprietary reasons (and only learn about it through word of mouth). Therefore, training educational psychologists at the highest level of statistical analyses helps them to be the knowledge creators in a variety of fields.

Key Course Content

For the students we typically have, our large scale data analysis course is organized as a foundations course with literacy, design, and analysis as three focal areas. We cannot cover all of the topics we want, but we can provide foundational experiences so that students can move forward on their own or in other professional development situations. Thus, the course is focused on core content knowledge and interpretation (e.g., content standards). The students' assigned projects and activities tend to focus on technical and procedural knowledge (e.g., performance standards). The core areas of focus for the course, along with assigned textbooks (see References), are shown in Table 27.1.

Visualization

Visualization, the graphical display of numeric and non-numeric data, is new to the course, but the first author (JS) has had a few students use visualization in portions of their dissertations. As the access to large scale data has grown, students and faculty members have become more interested in the topic, and the need to add course content on data visualization has become impossible to ignore. The essential content for visualization focuses on three components: (1) obtaining data; (2) organizing data; and (3) planning for and executing data visualization. To obtain data, students search databases such as Google's public data, the U.S. Census Bureau, or the U.S. Bureau of Labor Statistics. Typically, students need a bit of direction about where to look, but once they get going, they become accomplished at locating data.

During their search, students can also be mashing the data for further analysis. Mashing data is the combining of data sets from different, multiple sources. For example, the Pennsylvania Department of Education has a new

---

TABLE 27.1 Large Scale Data Analysis Course Topics and Assigned Textbooks

Multivariate data choices and presentation

   E. Tufte's (1983, 2003, 2006) books

Color

   A. Loomis' (1947) book

   R. L. Blaszczyk (2012) book (www.e-corpus.org/notices/102464/gallery/)

Graphic representation

   E. Tufte et al.'s (1983, 2003, 2006) books

   N. Yau's (2011) book

   C. Mulbrandon's website (visualizingeconomics.com)

   D. Smith's website (chartporn.org)

Understanding storytelling

   J. Heinrich's (2013) book

---

performance scoring system for each public school in the state (paschool-performance.org). There is a data link in the right-hand corner of the web page from which all of the reported data for each school can be downloaded. Public use data can also be downloaded from other websites, such as the U.S. Census or Internal Revenue Service data. One of us (JS) has mashed together median family income and school data with zip codes and linking variables; a graduate student is now adding data from the National Center for Educational Statistics. The purpose is to obtain a more stable estimate of the relationship between income and school performance, based on standardized tests. A great deal of data cleaning is required during this process because the data sets do not always link together easily. We use Excel, Access, SPSS, and JMP for basic data mashing.

Once the data are mashed and cleaned, the data must be organized for visualization. How the data are prepared for analysis depends on the program being used for visualization. When using Tableau, the data can be put in an Excel file that has a proper heading for each column variable. Tableau is expensive software but, fortunately, there is a free public version available, and it works well for basic course projects. If R is used for data analyses, then the data must be specifically formatted for this software. R is available for free, but students will need help to learn how to use this statistical analysis program. We suggest that instructors also teach students how to use Adobe Illustrator so that their graphics have a polished, professional appearance. Once the data are ready to be used, students will need a little background and help to design graphical displays. We have students look at Mulbrandon's and Smith's websites at the beginning of the course as examples of data visualization. The websites help them to generate ideas about what they might want to do for their assigned projects.

Modeling: The Family of SEM and Other Techniques

Instead of trying to discuss all of the core content that we feel is essential for the course and each type of analysis (e.g., confirmatory factor analysis, structural equation modeling, path analysis, life cycle assessment, growth modeling), we provide a general checklist (see Table 27.2). Using this checklist as an overarching scheme helps students to see the same topics over multiple occasions, and it provides them with an analytic rubric for reading manuscripts and writing up their own work. We introduce the checklist in the third week of the course.

If we were to rank the topics in terms of most important, our top choice is error and understanding error. We spend a great amount of time and effort explaining error, both measurement and model (i.e., specification). We do not offer a formal psychometric course, so this topic (i.e., $X = T + E$) is introduced in our course.

TABLE 27.2   Data Analysis Checklist

1. **Nonanalytic reporting**
   Well-developed theoretical framework
   Theorized model display
   Operational definitions

2. **Analytic reporting**
   Sample size
     Original and final
   Missing data
     How was missing handled (listwise deletion, imputed means…) and is it justified?
   Specification/identification
     Normality
     Outliers
     Linearity/multicollinearity: are variables correlated >0.90?
   Software and estimation method stated: Is it justified?
   Power
   Assessment of fit
     Model Chi-square
     Multiple fit indices justified
     Parameters estimated and significant tests: Low estimations good fit high estimations bad fit paradox.
   Squared multiple correlation (e.g., CFA) variance accounted for (e.g., SEM)
     Standardized and unstandardized estimates
     Residual/Error analysis: predicted and actual covariance matrix examination
   Correlation and means tables
   Modifications
     Theoretical and statistical rationale for modification
     Lagrange test for adding paths
     Wald test for dropping paths
   Correlation between estimated parameters (hypothesized & final models)
     Equivalent models

3. **Diagram of final model**

Particular Populations

The course is taught as the last one of the statistics sequence in our doctoral program. Many graduate students in other academic units also enroll in the course. Almost all of the students enrolled in the advanced statistics courses that we teach are in doctoral programs, although there are a handful of masters' students. Of the doctoral students, almost all are going on to work as professionals (i.e., counseling and school psychologists) rather than as academics and research-focused faculty. Thus, statistics literacy is their main focus in the course. In addition, the majority of faculty members that the students work with have no experience with large scale data analysis. Therefore, students' level of excitement is similar to that of eating broccoli: I do it because it is good for me, but not because it is desirable! But, this attitude is changing, especially when we teach large scale data analysis through visualization.

The students that we encourage to enroll in the course are those who will go on to a research career and will use this type of research and data analyses in their work. More recently, we have started recruiting students outside of our academic unit, particularly those students who might want to go into a policy-based career where they also need the skills for making policy decisions based on data analyses.

Challenges

We identify challenges in five areas. The first is for student to learn (or re-learn) the basics of matrices and mathematics. In our programs, very few students have a STEM background and most have not mastered previous statistical analysis procedures. Also, they lack sufficient experience with statistical analysis and statistical thinking. The gaps in their knowledge and understanding must be bridged throughout the semester. We, therefore, do a great deal of revisiting of previous material (e.g., the spiral curriculum method). Even students' understanding of Greek letters has been an obstacle to learning statistics for them.

The second challenge is for students to learn to write the code necessary to run the statistical software programs. Most of the time, they need to diagnose why the program will not run. Students have become accustomed to simple "point-and-click," efforts and, if this doesn't work, they are reluctant to try another approach. Over time, they realize how much control over their analyses they have given up when they do not write their own code—and how much better they can test their hypotheses when they do so. Also, when a program does not run, it is nearly always a typographical error in the code, but students may not be good line editors of their own work. Therefore, we have to teach good coding behavior (e.g., writing a non-code statement to indicate what each line of code does or means).

The third challenge is that required psychometric courses—classic and IRT—are lacking in students' programs of study, so their understanding of psychometric issues is very limited. Recently, we have developed a reading list for the topics that are not covered in our course, and we emphasize that reading these materials outside of class is very important to ensuring deeper understanding of large scale data analysis.

The fourth challenge is that students tend to be very compliant, but not inquisitive. This is a challenge we are still working to address. We find that our students will do what is asked of them, but they will not try to do additional work on their own. If something does not work the first time, they do not go the extra mile to try and figure out how to solve the problem on their own. Web-based discussion boards have exacerbated this problem: students hope that someone else (i.e., a classmate, Researchgate.net) will solve their problem.

The fifth challenge is that the large scale data analysis course is difficult. We are honest with the students about this condition. Each time we teach the course, we are never certain about how much content we will be able to cover because of the wide variability in students' knowledge of statistics. Students' prior knowledge and experience with statistics, as well as their future career plans, drives the amount of material that we cover in the course. We accept this challenge as a way to improve what we are doing in the course, but it can also hamper students' motivation.

THE COURSE

Design

We admit that nothing we do in our course is particularly innovative. What we do is to follow core educational psychology and instructional design principles in the design, development, and execution of the course—although we do have moments of mini-c creativity! (Beghetto & Kauffman, 2007).

The class is designed with the targets we want students to meet. These targets fall along four knowledge dimensions: (1) declarative; (2) procedural; (3) schematic; and (4) strategic. Working within these dimensions, task demands, cognitive demands, task openness, and additional factors are then considered. For example, we explain that Comparative Fit Index is a fit index that uses chi-square values for the unconditional and test model. This is declarative knowledge and, therefore, a relatively easy definition task for students

The checklist (Table 27.2) is a tangible schematic for students, and the course and the assigned projects are designed to allow students' autonomy to develop their procedural competence. The presentation of content is logically ordered to help students make connections to prior declarative knowledge. We also focus on "models" rather than statistical significance. Through their sequence of statistics courses, students often forget that the analyses and results from previous courses are all based on mathematical and statistical models. Or more simply, this knowledge was never encoded! Finally, students are given a heavy dose of formative feedback before their assigned work is evaluated.

Delivery of the Class: Old to New

During the first two weeks of the course, we start with basic statistical analyses and work up through multivariate analyses, covering key features of each. For example, we address distributions, t-tests to ANOVA, ANOVA to MANOVA, regression to multivariable regression, and how these analyses fit the general linear model. This is similar to how Richard Feynman taught mathematics and physics and is similar to how one of us (JS) taught Advanced Placement calculus. For example, Feynman would start with addition, subtraction, and so on, moving through the content and illuminating key features of each change, and what comes next. His students would then complete several tasks to determine what they understood about the past material and could accomplish independently.

One example task is a basic linear regression analysis that we have students complete by hand. That is, we mean that a data set with an outcome variable and a predictor variable is provided to students in an Excel file. A tutorial is then provided about how to use Excel and also an online line matrix calculator to obtain the beta estimate. This process was implemented a few years ago when JS realized the students were misinterpreting the parameter estimates and could not explain how these estimates were determined. They could run the point-and-click software but could not accomplish much else. With their regression results in hand, we have them try to answer the question, "Why is $p < .05$?" With large data sets, this is typically not a principal concern, but it is important to connect to students' prior declarative knowledge to get at their schematic knowledge (i.e., knowing *that* versus knowing *why*). Many students have been told that the rule of thumb is $p < .05$ for statistical significance (declarative knowledge), but they have no understanding of why this is the rule, or where that decision about using $p < .05$ came from (schematic knowledge).

In addition, another course activity is related to variables in space (for exploratory factor analysis) to determine what students understand mathematically (i.e., the actual mathematical meaning of correlated factors). None of our students have had high dimensional geometry and they do not understand what Pearson's formula looks like in geometric language (i.e., a correlation between factors is the cosine of the angle between).

Essentially, we are scaffolding from old to new knowledge although, at times, it looks like Skinnerian shaping! Scaffolding is the assistance provided through expertise guidance or activity structure to assist students in learning and using the material. Skinnerian shaping is the external reinforcement of systematically designed behaviors combined to create a complex behavior. For example, we state, without shame, that we are not varimax rotation supporters. Typically, we show students mathematically the difference and have them work on understanding the difference. Next, the students analyze some data to see the difference in the analysis results. Finally, we then discuss the interpretation of their results. Finally, correlations from the Thurstone box problem are used to show varimax and direct oblimin examples (and, later, we use this again in Confirmatory Factor Analysis). This activity functions as a recurring theme and distributed practice, scaffolding experience, throughout the semester. Only after this work do we start moving into traditional structural equation modeling (SEM) material.

Software and Programming

We typically use the student version of LISREL because it is accessible to all. We provide instructions on both the original programming language and Simplis programming language for LISREL. Also, we run the same analyses in EQS and MPlus so that students see basic programming differences but also come to understand that both programs yield the same answers. One issue is that many students do not have the LISREL software after they finish the course so we are migrating to R (and RStudio) using the LAVAAN package. We feel this approach will better serve our students in the long run, although it is time consuming, initially.

New Material Activities

We receive a lot of positive feedback from students about an article quest activity that we assign. This assignment requires students to find a statistical modeling article on a topic far from their academic focus or disciplinary background. For example, students enjoy reading an article about the pricing of wines (Ashenfelter, 2008). We also ask students to find articles that contain a covariance matrix or, alternatively, to email the lead author of the article and request the matrix. The students are assigned to re-run the original model and, then, to run alternative models. Finally, they must search for (mathematically) equivalent models. This is somewhat of a game, but it is a great deal of fun and helps students learn both the content of and procedures for using the statistical packages.

For a data visualization activity, we have students search the literature for what they consider the best and worst visualizations before we discuss the topic. They are required to make lists of what counts as "good" and "bad" about the specific visualization components (e.g., color, layout, ease of understanding) from each list. Once the lists are completed students pair up, and then report their findings and the instructors act as recorders. Once we have all of the information that the students have obtained, we present material on design issues (e.g., structure, font type and size) from the books and websites listed in Table 27.1.

Long Term Projects

Students complete multiple projects throughout the course. The first involves a universal data set that everyone uses. This represents the lowest level of cognitive demand among the required projects because it is designed so that everyone obtains the same results when they run the same model. We typically use a confirmatory factory analysis that must be run first with a covariance matrix and then with the raw data. Students are also required to write up a "results" section to understand the core reporting practices for the SEM family and for general multivariate analyses.

The main project assignment requires students to use path, CFA and SEM analyses with the data they obtain. This project is announced early on because students need time to obtain data from one of the many available datasets (e.g., NCES, BLS, Census, NAEP) or from a faculty member in their program of study. As with the universal dataset project, students are required to create a narrative for the analyses. This narrative includes: (a) method; (b) results; and (c) limitations. We do not focus on the theoretical rationale for the study in the course, but the tested models have to make both logical and theoretical sense.

Visualizing Project

The visualization project is new to our statistics course and, truly, should be a separate course in itself. The first step in the project is for students to determine a topic, and then identify a related data set that they want to visualize. As with the main course project described above, we do this to support students' autonomy in the course and give them experience in making decisions about their data and graphical display. They need to be autonomous about their visualization decisions (e.g., color, layout) because, once they make a choice, several other choices will be affected. We cannot tell them every possible path or option, so students must work independently. If the data are easily downloadable then students can move ahead; if not, then we have them learn how to scrape data. By "scraping data," we refer to using a program that takes individual data elements from a webpage and saves it into a .dat file or text file for later analyses. The data scraping activity is for all of the students and we believe it is a skill that every student needs; however, this activity is primarily for those that do not have an existing data set.

For scraping, we use as a starting point Yau's (2011) weather scraping example. We have to make adjustments to his discussion about how to scrape the data for it to work for our students. The main programming language we use is Python, along with a package called Beautiful Soup. Weather data are scraped for each day, over many years, from Buffalo, New York. The key task for students is to learn that they can get any data they want with a few lines of code. Once the basic program is written, it is easy to change the target website and the data desired.

Evidence for Students' Learning

We use rubrics for all of the assigned projects. We give some tests, but these are short-term, formative assessments. Primarily, we want to know what the students understand about large scale data analyses. We also use a pre-post testing scenario, which has demonstrated significant changes in students' knowledge about large-scale data analyses. Of course, students should not know the material on the pre-test so the change we observe is expected. Our best evidence for student growth is in their abilities to use the course material in their dissertation work or when they, subsequently, email or call us to discuss a specific issue or idea for a large scale data analysis project that they are working on, independently, for the classes they are teaching or in other professional work. It is on these occasions when we know that they have learned and valued what we assigned them to do in our course.

RECOMMENDATIONS

Based on our experiences, we recommend the development of multiple versions of the large scale data analysis course and its assigned activities and projects. Essentially, we have created a differentiated instruction model, and we have developed a series of 2–3 minute videos that explain a variety of concepts, methods, and data analytic techniques to support our differentiated instruction approach. We experimented with making a set of Khan Academy style videos, but found that it is easier to make different videos for each group of students; we keep an archive of videos to use in class, as we need them. We highly recommend this approach. The model and tactics that we have described in this chapter are those we have used in all of our classes. The large-scale data analysis course was originally a face-to-face course, but all of our courses are now either completely online or are hybrid courses. So, the videos are invaluable for these courses and delivery formats. Finally, we would like to say that this course is one that truly keeps us "on our toes" because we never know what background experiences students bring to the course that are relevant to its content and purpose.

REFERENCES

Ashenfelter, O. (2008). Predicting the quality and prices of Bordeaux wine. *The Economic Journal, 118*(529), F174–F184.

Bachelier, L. (1900a), Théorie de la spéculation. *Annales Scientifiques de l'École Normale Supérieure, 3*(17), 21–86.

Beghetto, R. A., & Kaufman, J. C. (2007). Toward a broader conception of creativity: A case for "mini-c" creativity. *Psychology of Aesthetics, Creativity, and the Arts, 1*(2), 73.

Blaszczyk, R. L. (2012). *The color revolution: Lemelson Center studies in invention and innovation.* Cambridge, MA. MIT Press.

Loomis, A. (1947). *Creative illustration.* New York, NY: Viking Press.

Mulbrandon, C. (n.d.). *Visualizing economics.* http://visualizingeconomics.com.

Silver, N. (2012). *The signal and the noise: Why so many predictions fail-but some don't.* New York, NY: Penguin Press.

Smith, D. (n.d.). *Chart porn: Data visualizations you just gotta love.* http://chartporn .org.

Tufte, E. R., & Graves-Morris, P. R. (1983). *The visual display of quantitative information* (Vol. 2). Cheshire, CT: Graphics press.

Tufte, E. R. (2003). *The cognitive style of PowerPoint* (Vol. 2006). Cheshire, CT: Graphics Press.

Tufte, E. R. (2006). *Beautiful evidence* (Vol. 1). Cheshire, CT: Graphics Press.

Yau, N. (2011). *Visualize this: The flowing data guild to design, visualization, and statistics.* Indianapolis, IN, Wiley Publishing, Inc. (http://flowingdata.com)

CHAPTER 28

TEACHING MULTILEVEL MODELING

Janet K. Holt
Southern Illinois University Edwardsville

Diana J. Zaleski
Illinois State Board of Education

Multilevel models (MM) constitute a class of statistical models, which are the preferred analytic tool for analyzing hierarchically nested or clustered data (e.g., when a set of students are randomly selected from randomly selected classrooms then the students are "nested" within classrooms).

Multilevel models are known by several names, including hierarchical linear models (HLM), linear mixed-effects, random coefficients regression models, and covariance components models (Scientific Software International, 2014). When analyzing longitudinal data, multilevel models are often referred to as multilevel growth models. MMs are also known as multilevel regression analyses because the method builds on the regression framework and, conceptually, can be thought of developing regression lines for each higher-level cluster (e.g., schools, neighborhoods, employee teams). MM allows for the study of such hierarchical data in a single analysis

Challenges and Innovations in Educational Psychology Teaching and Learning, pages 369–382
Copyright © 2016 by Information Age Publishing
All rights of reproduction in any form reserved.

while simultaneously accounting for the variability associated with each level of the hierarchy (Raudenbush, & Bryk, 2002).

Hierarchies prevail in education data. Educational professionals engaged in research, teaching, and policy making frequently encounter data that are hierarchical in nature. For example, in a school setting, students are often arranged in hierarchical groups (e.g., students nested within classrooms, and classrooms nested within schools within school districts). Further, large-scale government surveys of educational data are frequently collected by some form of cluster random sampling in which schools are randomly selected and then classrooms or students within the schools are randomly selected; it is much more cost effective to conduct a national survey with a select group of schools than to randomly sample all schools across a state or the country. Even longitudinal data can be construed as a hierarchy, with multiple observations nested within individuals.

Analyses of hierarchical data result in underestimation (i.e., negative bias) of regression coefficient standard errors when the cluster level is ignored in traditional regression analysis. That is, if the randomly selected classrooms are not accounted for, and students are the unit of analysis in a traditional regression analysis, the classroom effects—which may be large—are ignored. Multilevel modeling yields more accurate estimates of regression effects than traditional regression analysis and allows more analytic flexibility in the investigator's ability to capture variation due to cluster characteristics when data are nested.

MULTILEVEL MODELING VERSUS REGRESSION METHODS

The following scenario is an example in which multilevel modeling is more appropriate than ordinary least squares regression methods, hereafter referred to as linear regression. In this example, a researcher wants to examine the influence of a specific instructional intervention program meant to increase third grade students' reading proficiency on the state's standardized assessment. However, the researcher knows that the characteristics of students and schools can have a significant effect on student achievement as well. Therefore, the researcher plans to conduct a study that examines which characteristics of students, programs, and schools predict students' reading proficiency scores.

When conducting the study, the researcher must consider the possibility of statistical dependency among students who attend the same school— while also including school characteristics to accurately account for the differences between students' reading proficiency scores. A primary assumption of linear regression is that each independent variable is unrelated to the other independent variables included in the model. However, students who attend the same school are often more similar than those students who attend other schools, and the nesting of students within programs within schools also leads to correlated observations. Therefore, when using education data, it is often difficult to meet this assumption.

Multilevel modeling provides a solution by allowing the researcher to analyze statistically dependent data. Unlike linear regression, MM produces unbiased estimates of the standard errors associated with the regression coefficients when the data are nested and allows group characteristics to be included in models of individual outcomes such as reading proficiency scores. Therefore, the researcher in our example uses MM to analyze data from 600 third grade students in 30 different elementary schools across the state. After running the unconditional model, the researcher calculates the intraclass correlation coefficient and determines that 25% of the variability in students' reading proficiency scores is due to differences between schools (e.g., instructional interventions) and 75% is due to differences between students (e.g., socioeconomic status). If the researcher had used linear regression approaches to analyze student scores, she would have ignored the 25% of the variability that is between schools—possibly leading to biased results.

The use of MM in education is likely to increase due to two major phenomena. First, there is a nationwide push to develop statewide longitudinal data systems (SLDS) for education data. These SLDS will be spanning the education continuum, linking preschool, K–12, higher education, and workforce data. Statistical methods that are appropriate for large-scale nested data, modeling change over time, and across educational transitions are needed. Second, there is a trend toward collecting "big data." The recent explosion of online learning in higher education and the increase in virtual K–12 schools provides a plethora of data on student performance, and student and instructor online behavior. Making sense of all these data will require advanced predictive modeling tools such as MM.

MULTILEVEL MODELING FERVOR

In 1986, Goldstein introduced the mathematical basis for the multilevel mixed linear model and provided an example of its use utilizing a longitudinal study of educational attainment (Goldstein, 1986). Goldstein also developed the MLwiN program which was the first dedicated statistical package for analyzing multilevel data (Rasbash, Charlton, Browne, Healy, & Cameron, 2005). In the United States, this technique was brought to the forefront with the original publication of *Hierarchical Linear Models: Applications and Data Analysis Methods* (Bryk & Raudenbush, 1992) and the development of the HLM software package (Bryk, Raudenbush, & Congdon,

1996). With the availability of user-friendly software, training opportunities, and access to large-scale education survey data that requires methods for handling clustered data, MM use has grown. The current edition of *Hierarchical Linear Models: Applications and Data Analysis Methods* (Raudenbush & Bryk, 2002) expands on new frontiers of multilevel modeling, including categorical data analysis, Bayesian inference, modeling latent variables, and cross-classified effects. In addition, HLM Version 7 (Raudenbush, Bryk, & Cheong, 2011) provides users with the ability to model four levels of nested and cross-classified data.

Within the last decade, there has been a substantial increase in the prevalence of published research using MM (e.g., Reise & Duan, 2001). Most education journals publishing quantitative research regularly include articles that use MM. The rapid growth of MM in education can also be attributed to strong professional development efforts led by the American Educational Research Association's Institute on Statistical Analysis, the National Center for Education Statistics, and the HLM software publisher, Scientific Software International. In addition, many universities offer short courses or workshops on MM analysis methods.

Today, universities that offer graduate-level social science and statistical coursework include courses in which MM is the primary focus or is embedded within a regression or multivariate course. Given the broad applications of MM, often these types of courses are co-listed between schools or departments of educational research, educational psychology, psychology, sociology, and statistics or attract students from these varied fields into one course. For example, the University of Illinois at Champaign-Urbana offers an HLM course that is cross listed in the educational psychology, psychology, and statistics departments. The course is described as an overview of MM where students learn techniques and theory of hierarchical linear models and apply the methods in the social sciences (University of Illinois, 2014).

THE LANDSCAPE OF THE
MULTILEVEL MODELING COURSE

Multilevel modeling coursework is typically offered as an elective for graduate level students who have a strong interest in quantitative methodology in the social sciences (e.g., educational psychology, educational research, psychology, and sociology). For example, before enrolling in MM coursework, most universities require the successful completion of basic statistical coursework that includes descriptive statistics, correlation and linear regression, variance and covariance, and perhaps even multivariate analysis and nonparametric methods. Because students come to MM with prerequisite courses such as linear regression, we might assume that students are ready to understand the nuances of interpreting regression coefficients within a multilevel context. However, understanding multilevel models works best if students have thoroughly internalized linear regression and other statistical concepts such as regression coefficients and error variance. For example, interpreting the nuances of coefficients from a multilevel model may involve learning how each school can have a different regression slope and how to use the slope variance to describe how relationships differ across schools or learning how the interpretation of the intercept changes depending on the type of centering of the predictor variables. To do so, learners must first have a strong understanding of how to interpret regression coefficients within a multiple regression context. For these reasons, linear regression and a general statistical review are worthwhile activities for the first few class sessions. Even those students who have recently taken a linear regression class seem to benefit from one or more review sessions.

ESSENTIAL KNOWLEDGE

Students in an MM course must learn to move from a linear regression model to a multilevel model that estimates separate regression coefficients for each level of analysis (e.g., classroom, school, neighborhood), and how to think in terms of models that combine different units of analysis into a single analysis as the term multilevel implies. The level-1 equation is not dissimilar from a linear regression equation, although the terms contain an additional subscript, j, indicating the level-2 cluster unit (e.g., school). The level-2 equations predict the level-1 regression coefficients from cluster-level variables (e.g., schools). So, although MM builds upon the linear regression model, learners must relearn how to write, conceptualize, and interpret the coefficients. Therefore, multilevel models offer the benefit of allowing for more nuanced relationships, but with it comes added complexity that students need to absorb. Additionally, students need to learn new software that is specific to multilevel modeling (e.g., HLM), or learn different procedures from those used for linear regression analyses in SPSS (e.g., Mixed Models, or SAS, e.g., PROC MIXED) for conducting the analyses.

As with all statistical methods, students also need to understand when multilevel modeling is appropriate to use. This involves delving into the assumptions of linear regression—particularly the assumption of independent and identically distributed observations. Students must move from a mindset of either meeting or not meeting assumptions, to one in which they learn to determine *how much* this assumption is violated and the potential advantage of using MM when the assumption is violated *to a large degree*. Other essential course knowledge includes: (a) how to formulate MM equations addressing particular research questions; (b) distinguishing between fixed and random coefficients; (c) how to conduct MM using various computer software programs; (d) how to interpret the results of multilevel analyses within the context of the research questions; and (e) familiarity with how MM is used in the educational literature.

SPECIFIC APPLICATIONS

Moving beyond essential knowledge, there are many variants of MM for specific purposes including using MM for: (a) meta-analysis (Kalaian & Kasim, 2008); (b) cross-classification models for partially nested data (Beretvas, 2008); (c) non-linear multilevel models for non-continuous outcomes (O'Connell, Goldsten, Rogers, & Peng, 2008); and (d) modeling of longitudinal data or growth modeling (Holt, 2008a; Holt, 2008b; Singer & Willett, 2003). Recently, these types of MMs have become popular with the collection of repeated measures data obtained through the Experience Sampling Method (ESM; see Hektner, Schmidt, Csikszentmihalyi, 2007).

Moreover, MMs are particularly well suited for analyzing longitudinal data. In this special case of multilevel models, multiple observations are viewed as nested within the person. Using this unique framework, each individual is not required to have the same number of observations or the same spacing of observations, a restriction that is present when using repeated measures analysis. In multilevel growth models, growth curves are modeled at level 1 and person-level characteristics are added at level 2. This results in a growth model that can be modeled as a function of student-level characteristics. As an example of the power and versatility of growth modeling, Hadley, Rispoli and Holt have used this approach to model early sentence production as children begin to use tense and agreement morphemes (around two years of age) and have studied child and parent input characteristics related to language growth. This approach allows: (a) testing and theory modification related to the development of grammatical encoding in young children (Rispoli, Hadley, & Holt, 2012); (b) examination of the difference in growth patterns between children with typical and atypical language development (Hadley & Holt, 2006; Rispoli, Hadley, & Holt, 2009); and (c) determination of how parent input can be modified to accelerate a child's early sentence growth (Hadley, Rispoli, Holt, Papastratakos, & Hsu, 2015).

A strong foundation in the essential knowledge of MM modeling is critical to successfully transitioning to each of these more specialized topics. In addition, as the use of MM rapidly increases, these more specialized applications are becoming commonplace in the literature. Therefore, an introductory course on MM should expose students to these advanced applications and how they are used in the education and social science literature.

WHICH STUDENTS BENEFIT?

MM coursework is typically offered as an elective for graduate students who have a strong interest in quantitative methodology. Knowledge of MM allows students to analyze an array of data due to its hierarchical structure, such as K–12 education data or data from other types of organizations. Multilevel modeling provides many opportunities for social scientists to study the complex data structures found in schools, workplaces, and social settings. In addition, those interested in administration and policy analysis should be familiar with MM as it is becoming prevalent in both practitioner and policy-related journals.

Because graduate students take MM coursework to use these methods in their theses or dissertations, it is important to support their unique interests, motivations, and capabilities. Students can learn MM by working on their own data sets and applying MM in a personally meaningful context.

CHALLENGES WHEN TEACHING AND LEARNING MULTILEVEL MODELING

Many students struggle to learn MM because they do not have a solid understanding of linear regression. If students do not understand the assumptions of linear regression, its advantages, or how to interpret regression coefficients, it will be difficult for them to fully internalize multilevel modeling methods. Multilevel modeling requires students to think about quantitative analyses in a new way that many struggle to comprehend. Therefore, students must have a strong foundation in linear regression before they are able to comprehend and apply MM concepts. For this reason, it is recommended to have a linear regression prerequisite for a multilevel modeling course.

Before addressing essential MM knowledge, instructors often find themselves having to revisit linear regression concepts. This is an important first step to ensure student success. Key concepts to review include the interpretation of intercepts and regression coefficients in models with multiple predictors and how centering the predictors changes the interpretation. Ideally, MM should be offered during the second of a two-semester course sequence that focuses on regression and MM methods. This structure will help students master basic regression concepts before being introduced to MM. Also, students will benefit from examples that are tailored to their specific area of study; for example, students in industrial/organizational psychology might be interested in small groups nested within the workplace, whereas educational psychology students are more likely to be interested in examples with students nested within schools.

Students' interest, motivation, and prior experiences varies in statistics classes and instructors often find themselves teaching classes with different types of students. Some have a strong foundation and high motivation to learn difficult concepts; others appear less interested and are intimidated by statistical content. Such situations are challenging to the instructor and pose dilemma: "Do I teach to the more confident and engaged students, which is a disadvantage for the less confident and less engaged students?" or "Do I provide a lot of review for the more intimidated students and risk boring the more motivated students?" Peer mentoring can be one solution for such situations.

PROMISING PRACTICES

Visual presentations of the difference between linear regression and MM are helpful for introducing MM while building on students' existing knowledge of regression. For instance, I (JKH) visually represent the difference between what is commonly done in linear regression analysis, total regression (see Figure 28.1a), what happens if the data are aggregated to the cluster level with between-groups regression (see Figure 28.1b), and what occurs in MM when both the student-level and the school-level units of analysis are taken into account (see Figure 28.1c). This approach has been helpful for introducing the concept of within-groups regression in MM. Graphs are also helpful to illustrate individual variability in intercepts and slopes, such as differences in average reading proficiency across schools (i.e., intercept variance) and between-school differences in the relationship between socioeconomic status and reading proficiency (i.e., slope variance).

To learn and apply MM techniques effectively, students must be engaged in an instructional process that supports the construction, rather than the simple communication, of knowledge. Many students struggle to grasp MM when it is taught solely through lecture presentations. Students learn MM more quickly and deeply when they are actively engaged in scaffolded lab activities throughout the MM course, in which the instructor is present to answer questions and provide support to students.

Students in multilevel modeling courses want to apply what they are learning in different ways. It is important for the instructor to provide a learning environment that supports students' unique interests, motivations, and capabilities, and allows them to engage with data that is relevant and timely. One way to do this is to allow students to have a database that has several variables at their disposal so that they can formulate research questions that are of most interest to them. In some cases, students may have their own multilevel datasets. These datasets can be incorporated into class exercises or projects to facilitate students' learning and they enable

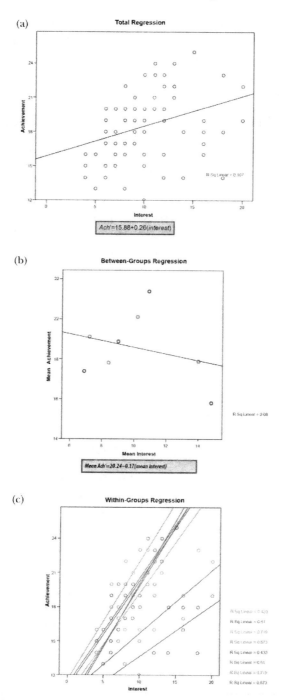

Figure 28.1 Illustrations used to introduce multilevel modeling.

students to pose personally meaningful research questions. The key is to retain enough structure so that the instructor can be sure that learners encounter concepts that they will need to gradually build their knowledge of MM. The course structure should be flexible so that students can link their new learning to their existing knowledge and schema.

When teaching a group of students that vary in background knowledge and abilities, it is helpful to assign peer mentoring activities. Peer mentoring contributes to collaborative relationships, allows those who are ahead in the course to practice explaining the concepts to others, thereby solidifying their understanding and providing a resource to students who are struggling.

THE INSTRUCTOR'S PERSPECTIVE

My method (JKH) to facilitate students' learning of multilevel modeling is to begin with structured in-class activities in which all students use the same dataset and explore the same problems. I give them assignments that transfer the demonstration problems in class to other contexts and, at the same time, ensure that they are learning the complexities of multilevel modeling in a series of stage progressions. Once students have completed the lab activities, I assign a larger project activity in which they must formulate their own research questions and select variables, tailoring the project to their unique interests.

Students are scaffolded in several ways. I address their questions in real time as they practice in the lab. They complete some data analysis activities in small groups or with partners, which promotes peer interaction and collaborative problem solving. When students have difficulty with a data analysis problem, their computer monitors' images are transferred to the classroom projection screen so that all students can see the problem and the whole class can discuss and problem solve together, with my guidance. Another scaffold that students find to be helpful is when I provide annotated printouts (see Figure 28.2) from a multilevel growth model analysis and result. Students can refer to the example and compare their MM outputs from their projects.

Technology enables multiple approaches to support students' learning. Screen capture and screen recording software enable me to provide step-by-step MM software tutorials and data analysis simulations and I can create screencasts and podcasts, adding audio and/or animation to a slide deck or other types of presentations. These tools allow students to review and check their understanding and bolster their independence for analysis and interpretation of MM data outside of the classroom. I also provide detailed illustrations for interpreting coefficients and examples of exemplary projects from previous MM courses.

```
The outcome variable is MATH_ACH

Final estimation of fixed effects
(with robust standard errors)
-------------------------------------------------------------------
                                    Standard           Approx.
    Fixed Effect        Coefficient Error     T-ratio  d.f.    P-value
-------------------------------------------------------------------
For         INTRCPT1, P0
    INTRCPT2, B00        56.573741  0.492757  114.811    509   0.000
      SES3, B01           5.454772  0.674909    8.082    509   0.000
For GRADEAVG slope, P1
    INTRCPT2, B10         1.649127  0.145769   11.313    509   0.000
      SES3, B11           0.646738  0.197440    3.276    509   0.002
For GR_AV_SQ slope, P2
    INTRCPT2, B20        -0.600787  0.092784   -6.475    509   0.000
      SES3, B21           0.081580  0.127783    0.638    509   0.523

-------------------------------------------------------------------
B00 Average Math Ach in 9th grade
B01 A one unit increase in SES is associated with 5.45 increase in math
    achievement score.
B10 Instantaneous linear growth rate at grade 9, positive slope
B11 Relationship of SES and linear growth rate at grade 9, a 1-unit increase
    in SES is associated with a .65 increase in linear growth rate at grade 9.
B20 Average quadratic growth rate in grades 7 - 11, negative curvature,
    a 1- grade increase is associated with a .60 decrease in growth rate.
G21 Average relationship between SES and quadratic growth rate - not
    significant.
```

Figure 28.2 Excerpt of an annotated print-out of a multilevel growth model output.

A STUDENT'S PERSPECTIVE

As a former graduate student, I (DJZ) was terrified of taking a first statistics course. I had no experience in statistics and had very negative experiences in prior math courses. However, after taking my first course, I realized how much I enjoyed the work and how applicable statistical data analysis methods were to my program of study. The three key instructional methods that I found most helpful in my statistics courses, including courses on MM, were: (1) reviewing applicable content at the beginning of each course; (2) engaging in project-based learning; and (3) reviewing analytic content using annotated output and screencasts.

Review of the foundational concepts and skills at the beginning of each new statistics course was vital to my success. In addition, the instructors who used project-based learning framed the course contents within challenging real-world problems and they engaged me and my fellow students in collaborative lab activities. These in-class lab activities allowed us to apply content and skills and receive immediate feedback from our peers and the instructor. The resources that were most beneficial were the instructor-annotated outputs that provided detailed interpretations of coefficients and the annotated screencasts that supported the use of different software programs (e.g., SPSS, SAS, HLM).

I was first introduced to MM during a workshop and subsequently enrolled in an MM course and, then, an independent study using MM methods. My instructor encouraged me to utilize data that was applicable to my research interests, and this bolstered my confidence to apply MM for my thesis and subsequent dissertation. By engaging deeply with meaningful data, I could explore advanced MM topics such as multilevel mediation modeling—which cemented my understanding of MM.

RECOMMENDATIONS AND CONCLUSIONS

We have four recommendations for instructors of MM courses. First, MM should be sequenced after a linear regression course and, ideally, in the semester following the regression course. Instructors should plan to spend instructional time reviewing linear regression, particularly the interpretation of coefficients, to ensure that all students have the appropriate foundational knowledge to comprehend and apply MM concepts.

Second, students do not have much difficulty executing the analyses correctly, but they have problems interpreting their output. Therefore, it is best to allow for a lot of class time for students to practice, discuss, and problem solve—particularly for the interpretation of fixed and random coefficients. Visual displays of outputs are powerful instructional tools that aid understanding of what the coefficients and different variance measures assess.

Third, students will experience the most success in grasping MM concepts if instructors scaffold meaningful and structured in-class activities, such as labs and small group discussions. Students learn best when information is presented in small chunks followed by collaborative in-class activities that allow them to immediately apply and review their new knowledge. This approach builds confidence and scaffolds students' learning. As students develop competence in multilevel modeling, instructors can add more complexity to in-class activities (e.g., allowing random coefficients, adding cross-level interactions, contrasting different ways of centering coefficients). While students are building their MM skills repertoire, instructors can allow students to choose their data analysis. During this phase of learning, it is optimal to provide students with different supports, as needed (e.g., annotated printouts, video clips or demonstration examples).

Statistics instructors should establish learning environments that support students' unique interests, motivations, and capabilities. Project-based learning is a constructivist approach that contextualizes MM skills and engages students in the active construction of knowledge of MM as they apply the data analysis methods to actual data. Students' interpretations of MM output are also improved when they have a good grasp of the research questions that they want to address, and such questions are best derived in authentic situations.

This instructional blueprint for teaching MM is applicable to many data analysis courses. Reviewing prior relevant content is a foundation for the beginning of the course. Identifying the course content areas that are stumbling blocks for students and having multiple practice exercises in these areas will help students master the content and skills. Through these efforts, students can overcome the challenges of learning MM and will enjoy using multilevel modeling in new and interesting ways that will answer important research questions in education.

REFERENCES

Beretvas, S. N. (2008). Cross-classified random effects models (pp. 161–197). In A. A. O'Connell & D. B. McCoach (Eds.), *Multilevel analysis of educational data*. Quantitative Methods in Education and the Behavioral Sciences: Issues, Research and Teaching Series (Volume 3). Charlotte, NC: Information Age.

Bryk, A. S., & Raudenbush, S. W. (1992). *Hierarchical linear models: Applications and data analysis methods*. Newbury Park, CA: Sage.

Bryk, A. S, Raudenbush, S. W., & Congdon, R. (1996). *HLM 4 for Windows* [Computer software]. Chicago, IL: Scientific Software International, Inc.

Goldstein, H. (1986). Multilevel mixed linear model analysis using iterative generalised least squares. *Biometrika, 73*(1), 43–56.

Hadley, P. A., & Holt, J. K. (2006). Individual differences in the onset of tense marking: A growth curve analysis. *Journal of Speech, Language, and Hearing Research, 51*, 953–961.

Hadley, P. A., Rispoli, M., Holt, J. K., Papastratakos, T., & Hsu, N. (2015, June). *Parent input subject diversity accelerates children's early sentence growth*. Presented at the annual meeting of the Symposium on Research in Child Language Disorders, Madison, WI.

Hektner, J. M., Schmidt, J. A., & Csikszentmihalyi, M. (2007). *Experience sampling method: Measuring the quality of everyday life*. Thousand Oaks, CA: Sage Publications.

Holt, J. K. (2008a). Analyzing change in adulthood with multilevel growth models: Selected measurement, design, and analysis issues. In M C. Smith (Ed.), *Handbook of research on adult learning and development* (pp. 137–161). New York, NY: Routledge.

Holt, J. K. (2008b). Modeling growth using multilevel and alternative approaches (pp. 111–159). In A. A. O'Connell & D. B. McCoach (Eds.), *Multilevel analysis of educational data*. Quantitative Methods in Education and the Behavioral Sciences: Issues, Research and Teaching Series (Volume 3). Charlotte, NC: Information Age.

Kalaian, S. A., & Kasim, R. M. (2008). Multilevel models for meta-analysis (pp. 315–343). In A. A. O'Connell & D. B. McCoach (Eds.), *Multilevel analysis of educational data*. Quantitative Methods in Education and the Behavioral Sciences: Issues, Research and Teaching Series (Volume 3). Charlotte, NC: Information Age.

O'Connell, A. A., Goldstein, J., Rogers, H. J., & Peng, C. Y. J. (2008). Multilevel logistic models for dichotomous and ordinal data (pp. 199–242). In A. A. O'Connell & D. B. McCoach (Eds.), *Multilevel analysis of educational data*. Quantitative Methods in Education and the Behavioral Sciences: Issues, Research and Teaching Series (Volume 3). Charlotte, NC: Information Age.

Raudenbush, S. W., & Bryk, A. S. (2002). *Hierarchical linear models: Applications and data analysis methods* (2nd ed.). Newbury Park, CA: Sage.

Raudenbush, S. W., Bryk, A. S., & Congdon, R. (2011). *HLM7 for Windows* [Computer software]. Skokie, IL: Scientific Software International, Inc.

Rasbash, J., Charlton, C., Browne, W. J., Healy, M., & Cameron, B. (2005). *MLwiN Version 2.02*. Bristol, England: Centre for Multilevel Modelling, University of Bristol.

Reise, S. P., & Duan, N. (2001). Multilevel models [Special issue]. *Multivariate Behavioral Research*. Mahwah, NJ: Erlbaum.

Rispoli, M., Hadley, P. A., & Holt, J. K. (2009). The growth of tense productivity. *Journal of Speech, Language, and Hearing Research, 52,* 930–944.

Rispoli, M., Hadley, P., & Holt, J. (2012). Sequence and system in the development of tense and agreement. *Journal of Speech, Language and Hearing Research, 55,* 1007–1021.

Scientific Software International. (2014). *History of multilevel models*. Retrieved from http://www.ssicentral.com/hlm/history.html

Singer, J. D., & Willett, J. B. (2003). *Applied longitudinal data analysis: Modeling change and event occurrence*. New York, NY: Oxford.

University of Illinois (2014). *Course catalog*. Retrieved from http://education.illinois.edu/edpsy/courses/587

CHAPTER 29

ASSESSMENT FOR TEACHERS

Designing a Practice-Based Learning Path

Diane Salmon and Shaunti Knauth
National-Louis University

OVERVIEW

The topic of assessment in teacher preparation has recently grown in terms of both stature and scope (Popham, 2011; Shepard, Hammerness, Darling-Hammond, & Rust, 2005). In its most basic sense, assessment refers to the process of using students' responses on tasks that are either designed or naturally occurring to make inferences about their knowledge and skill (Popham, 2000). While essentially a process of reasoning from evidence, assessment in practice becomes quite complicated as it can serve a variety of purposes and audiences (Pellegrino, Chudowsky, & Glaser, 2001). Pellegrino and colleagues cite three key educational assessment purposes: (1) to make formative decisions about how students are learning and shape immediate feedback to assist their progress; (2) to make summative decisions regarding the level of success students achieve in a particular unit or program of study; and (3) to make evaluation decisions about the effectiveness of particular programs and/or teachers. With these levels of purpose,

Challenges and Innovations in Educational Psychology Teaching and Learning, pages 383–395
Copyright © 2016 by Information Age Publishing
All rights of reproduction in any form reserved.

the topic of assessment in teacher education intersects with a variety of issues of vital importance to teachers including instruction, grading, learning standards, standardized testing, and teacher evaluation, to name only a few. What, then, is most important for teachers to know and be able to do? How can teacher educators and educational psychologists design optimal learning experiences for teacher candidates to develop assessment literacy?

In this chapter, we describe how we responded to these questions within a course for teachers entitled, Frameworks for Data-Informed Instruction. We focused on formative assessment because teachers engage in this practice regularly in their classrooms and it has strong potential to positively impact student learning. We highlight challenges in facilitating teacher learning of formative assessment in the structure of traditional teacher education programs. We describe a set of learning activities we designed and used in the context of the course. The learning pathways we designed linked candidate learning to a subsequent course on Cognition and Instruction which focuses on developing pedagogical content knowledge and investigating student learning progressions. For us, planning for linkages between these two courses helped ensure that assessment was presented in the context of deep questions about student learning. This must be the basis of any effective course on assessment.

Critical to informing the course learning activities was the program context. Candidates in the data course were enrolled in a master's degree program in Urban Teaching while simultaneously completing a teaching residency in a high need urban school. This allowed for a practice-based approach to the course where the learning activities linked directly to our candidates' simultaneous experience in schools.

A Knowledge Base for Formative Assessment

Formative assessment is fundamental to the daily practice of teachers as it occurs during the learning process and is intended to foster, rather than evaluate, student learning (Pelligrino, Chudowsky, & Glaser, 2001). A growing body of research shows that teachers' regular use of evidence of learning to adjust instruction has a strong positive impact on student learning and achievement (Hattie, 2009). Further, syntheses of the research on learning indicate that formative assessment is an essential dimension of effective learning environments, forming the bridge between learning and teaching (Bransford, Brown, & Cocking, 2000). Formative assessment can actually be viewed as a system of feedback that involves cycles of eliciting student responses, interpreting these responses, and taking action based upon them (Heritage, 2010).

The Nature of Feedback

To effectively use formative assessment in their classroom, teachers can benefit from reviewing research on the nature of feedback in learning. Hattie and Timberley (2007) conducted a meta-analysis on the research on the effects of different types of feedback provided in classroom learning environments. They found that feedback is more effective when students receive specific information about how they performed on a task and what they need to do to improve, rather than when they simply receive praise, rewards, or punishment. Feedback is more effective when focused on correct rather than incorrect responses, and builds on improvements from previous performances. Feedback is also more impactful when the learning goals for students are clear, specific, and challenging.

Using findings from their meta-analysis, Hattie and Timberley developed a model of feedback to enhance learning. They differentiated four levels of feedback including the task, the process, self-regulation, and the self and three key questions that can be addressed at each level: Where am I going? How am I going? Where to next? These questions prompt teachers to provide the types of feedback that have been found to be most impactful in the learning process. In addressing the question 'where am I going,' teachers need to specify the learning goal for an activity. With this question, they need to be clear about the success criteria and the evidence of student learning they anticipate. In providing feedback on the 'how am I going' question, teachers identify how they will use the evidence of learning to interpret students' progress toward the learning goal. In providing feedback on the 'where to next' question, teachers identify the specific actions students need to undertake in order to continue to advance their learning. Overall, the model provides a structure to reduce the discrepancy between students' current performance and the learning goal and offers a framework for designing and implementing formative assessments.

Student Learning Progressions

Well-designed formative assessments can capture and represent students' understandings or skill competencies to reveal if learning is happening in the expected ways. To make sense of the evidence provided in any formative assessment process, teachers need to know what they are looking for. They need a model for student progress or a student learning progression (Heritage, 2008). A student learning progression is a descriptive continuum of how students typically gain more sophisticated understandings in a topic or content area over time (Hess, 2010).

Research efforts are underway to document student learning progressions in a variety of content areas (Heritage, 2008). In the absence of research documenting a student learning progression, Popham (2011) outlines a process for unpacking the curriculum to identify key building blocks in a learning progression. Such learning progressions can inform the design of effective formative assessments and provide a model for instructional decision-making. The more teachers understand the nature of student learning progressions, the more confident and skillful they can become in eliciting evidence of student progress to help students interpret and direct their own learning performances.

Formative Assessment and Teacher Learning

In addition to advancing student learning, formative assessment can be a powerful means of advancing teachers' professional knowledge and skill. Wiliam (2011) argues that improving teachers' use of formative assessment data in their classrooms is probably the most effective approach to increasing teacher quality. Since formative assessment is a complex skill that requires many years to master, learning to assess student progress formatively needs to start in pre-service teacher preparation. The highly contextual nature of this practice further suggests that it may be best learned in the context of field learning experiences. Most importantly, by practicing effective formative assessment in initial teacher preparation, teacher candidates acquire critical habits of thinking and decision-making that can enable them to continue to learn from teaching beyond the life of their preparation program (Hiebert, Morris, Berk, & Jansen, 2007). As teachers seek evidence of student learning from a particular lesson structure, they can simultaneously update their knowledge schema for diverse student learning trajectories within a domain of study and draw upon this knowledge in planning future lessons.

Challenges in Learning the Practice of Formative Assessment

Helping teacher candidates learn effective formative assessment is challenging for several interrelated reasons. As suggested, the practice itself is complex, demanding that novice teachers integrate their knowledge of teaching, student learning, and a particular subject matter. This very complexity is what makes it worthy of prioritizing within the teacher education curriculum. Indeed, the richness of formative assessment, its high positive impact on student learning, and its frequency of occurrence combine to make formative assessment a high leverage practice.

However, the structure of higher education and the delivery of the teacher preparation curriculum create a second challenge for teachers to learn this practice. Courses that can contribute to teachers' understandings of assessment in general and formative assessment in particular are often taught in different departments. For example, instructional method courses are typically offered in teacher education departments, while assessment and measurement courses and cognition/learning courses are taught in educational psychology departments. The instructors teach from different discipline bases and likely introduce a variety of assessment frameworks, concepts, and tools that teacher candidates experience as widely divergent and perhaps a bit confusing. While additional assessment courses seem to help teacher candidates to feel more confident about the practice of assessment, they do not seem to have commensurate impact on teacher candidates' assessment competence. Similar to other teaching practices, teacher candidates struggle to see connections between theory and practice and, hence, have difficulty putting the assessment knowledge they do have into practice in their classrooms (Hammerness, Darling-Hammond, & Bransford, 2005).

Exacerbating the challenge is the unprecedented focus on assessment for accountability in schools. Standards defining education competencies in assessment developed in the 1990s lack attention to the knowledge and skill teachers need for formative assessment (Brookhart, 2011). The accountability emphasis is no doubt shaping teacher assessment practices, perhaps prompting them to privilege summative assessments that will impact teacher evaluation and curtail attention to developing and refining formative assessment practices. Without helping teachers to distinguish and relate formative and summative assessment practices in meaningful ways, the potential of both types of assessment will be diminished.

Effective preparation of teachers to understand and engage in assessment is a specific example of a larger challenge in teacher education, the gap between theory and practice (Darling-Hammond, 2010). Teacher candidates often gain theoretical knowledge in isolation from opportunities to put it into practice. This gap results in beginning teachers struggling to enact in their classrooms the knowledge they gained in preparation programs (Hammerness et al., 2005). Researchers are calling for practice-centered approaches to teacher education that can better prepare teacher candidates to overcome these problems of enactment (Hammerness et. al., 2005). Practice-based approaches aim for a tighter integration between theory and classroom practice and align well with research on how people learn (Bransford et al., 2005). Specifically, practice-centered approaches focus more in-depth on a smaller number of core concepts and practices and a careful sequencing of these concepts and practices to enable adaptive learning.

DESIGNING PRACTICE-BASED LEARNING PATHWAYS TO ASSESSMENT EXPERTISE

Residency Context: Academy of Urban School Leaders

Our design of the data course for teachers took place in the context of an urban teacher residency (UTR) program. In a UTR, teacher candidates combine a year-long apprenticeship in a high need urban school classroom with a master's level university program. The classroom apprenticeship takes place with a mentor teacher who is selected and trained by the UTR. Over the course of the year, the residents carry out sessions of acting as lead teacher in the classroom, with the mentor continuing to coach and give feedback on their work. With the year-long provision of deep hands-on experience in the classroom and simultaneous university coursework, UTR's enact the opportunities and challenges of the practice-centered approach described above.

Research to Inform Course Design: Characterizing Local Assessment Expertise

To inform the course design, we engaged in a *faculty research residency*—a vehicle to improve teacher preparation courses that was supported by our institution and required faculty to investigate teacher practices and challenges in partner schools (Gardiner & Salmon, 2014). Our research residency involved an investigation of the assessment practices of three mentor teachers who were regarded as experts in the formative assessment within the school network. To surface their thinking around formative assessment, interviews involved a think aloud protocol with specific sets of student assessment data that the teachers typically used to plan for instruction.

Through cross case comparisons of these three teachers' assessment practices, we identified four themes:

- These "assessment experts" had the big picture of assessment in their schools. They were able to make direct linkages between specific teacher designed classroom assessments and standardized tests used to determine student and classroom progress.
- They exhibited a strong growth oriented mindset that was informed by a vision of student learning trajectories, including knowledge of necessary prior knowledge and typical gaps students brought to their classrooms.
- They used deep pedagogical content knowledge to carefully observe students, question, interpret, and take instructional actions.

- They all recognized the value of assessment tools as feedback and a source for their own professional learning.

We saw implications of these four themes for our graduate courses for the candidate teachers in training. Candidates needed to understand the larger assessment context in their schools. These expert cases also helped us to recognize the need for more coordinated practice in collecting different types of assessment data and triangulating that data to identify student learning needs and to make instructional decisions.

THREE PRACTICE-BASED LEARNING PATHS

We designed three practice-based learning activities for the course: Investigating the Assessment Environment, Systematic Observation of Students, and Using Formative Data. Through these learning activities we emphasized assessment as part of the learning process. We attempted to address the complexities of formative assessment by first prompting candidates to get an overall picture of assessment at their school and then to practice specific data collection and analysis skills that could advance their understanding and use of formative data in their classrooms.

Investigating the Assessment Environment

Purpose

For candidates to develop a systematic understanding of assessment in their schools, and to consider a definition of sound assessment practices. Through this learning path, we wanted to address the complex use of assessment in schools today.

Activities

Candidates inventoried the assessment frameworks and tools at their school, and considered their findings through a definition of sound assessment processes and components. Key readings included chapters in *Driven by Data* (Bambrick-Santoyo, 2010) and additional articles, particularly *The Role of Assessment in a Learning Culture* (Shepard et al., 2005). We emphasized four assessment concepts in course lecture/discussions: practicality, reliability, validity, and consequential validity in the use and interpretation of assessment data.

We provided two tools for the activity. The *School and Classroom Data Inventory Investigation* suggested types of assessments to look for, and provided questions candidates could use in interviewing their mentors and other educators in their building involved with student assessment. Candidates summarized the results of their investigation in a data table that we provided. As part of the data summary, candidates wrote a short analysis describing the patterns they saw and used the definition in their text to describe the *core drivers of assessment data use* in their school and classroom. The criteria for evaluation and feedback on this learning activity included:

- Clear identification of assessments at the school and classroom level;
- At least two content areas fully addressed at both levels of the Inventory Summary;
- Thorough description of the patterns of assessment use evident in the Inventory Summary;
- Full description of the core drivers of assessment;
- Explicit linkages between assessment practices and concepts in the text; and
- Assessment practices critiqued based on course readings and discussion.

Systematically Observing Students during Learning

Purpose

The purpose of this learning path is for *candidates to practice systematic observations of their students, and to integrate the results with other forms of data.* Our case studies showed that highly expert data use involved observation. While observation of students may be a ubiquitous activity for teachers, little time is devoted to learn and practice systematic observation of student learning in the teacher education curriculum.

Activities

The candidates carried out two sessions of systematic observations and wrote a five-page report on the results. To support them in this process, we provided three behavior observations categories relevant to successful learning across content areas: Students' *persistence in problem solving*, student *communication skills*, and behavior that demonstrated *pre-requisite knowledge* for the task being observed. These behavior categories were highlighted by the experienced teachers we studied and are recognized in the literature as important to informing differentiated instruction (Coyne, Kame'enui, & Carnine, 2011) of their students. We identified two systematic observation procedures, time sampling and event sampling, and provided sample observation protocols for each type of observation sampling method. The candidates were free to use these samples, adapt them, or develop their own. In class, we examined examples of each behavior sampling method and practiced each approach using online teaching videos. For their actual observations, the candidates observed for approximately 20 minutes using one of the observation sampling methods; they also videotaped this observation, and carried out the second observation sampling method using the videotape.

Through small group discussions, candidates clarified patterns in their observation data and discussed the evidence for their students' skills in problem solving and communication. They wrote short summary reports in which they were expected to articulate patterns in their observations, differentiate what they learned from each observation format, and develop implications for instruction.

A key course assessment prompted candidates to integrate their learning from their data inventory investigation and their student learning observation.[1] Specifically, the paper provided an opportunity for candidates to triangulate data from a key interim assessment and their observations of student learning. The intention was for candidates to have practice in approximating the more fluent formative assessment practices of experienced teachers.

Formative Data Analysis, Representation, and Dialogue

Purpose

To build candidates' capacity to represent and analyze formative data, and to apply the results to their instruction. This practice-based learning path focused directly on developing our candidates' capacity to use weekly formative assessments to inform their instruction.

Activities

We used structured, in-class data workshops in a consistent format over four class sessions. The components were:

Data Representations

Each week, each candidate prepared a representation of formative assessment data gathered in his or her classroom. These data were often weekly quizzes or key exit slips. The representations could be in a chart, graph or table format. The candidates needed to summarize data for the whole class as well as show data on individuals. We suggested that they use Excel or Google charts tools, and also asked candidates to report on useful charting tools from their own experience. To prepare candidates for the representation process, we looked together at examples of data summaries. We discussed what patterns were visible in the representations, and whether the information that could be used to inform instruction.

Data Workshops

The candidates brought their representations to class sessions, usually in digital format on their own laptops or tablets, and discussed them with each other in a format we termed data workshops. We formed the candidates into groups of three to five persons based on similarity in grade level and content they were teaching. We provided, modeled, and required a specific protocol for discussion, the Tuning Protocol, which we adapted from Easton (2009). In the steps of the Tuning Protocol, a presenter first explains a set of data and poses questions about its implications. The other participants briefly ask clarifying questions, and then reflect on and discuss the data. During the discussion, the presenter listens, but does not take part, and in fact may turn away while listening. The presenter then reflects back to the group on what s/he has heard, and what s/he finds the implications to be. The process is designed to be relatively brief, lasting approximately 20 minutes, depending on the size of the group. Two to four candidates presented in each group during the workshops.

The assessments for this learning path included three individual formative data representations and a final paper synthesizing student performance across the three assessments.[2] In analyzing patterns across the three formative data representations, candidates developed implications for their instruction and developed insights and questions regarding the nature of student learning progression in the topic area.

CONCLUSIONS AND RECOMMENDATIONS

What did candidates learn through this set of practice-based learning paths? In their analyses of the assessment inventory and the observations of student learning, candidates developed the capacity to examine standard practice in their schools in terms of the effect on student learning. In the analyses of the assessment inventory, for example, most candidates recognized that the key assessment drivers, in terms of instructional decisions, occurred in the classroom. Many candidates were critical of the school level benchmark assessments for the students in primary grades. They observed that these assessments frequently failed to measure what students really knew or were able to do, and instead captured their lack of experience with formal assessment procedures, especially computerized assessments. Most candidates observed that their mentors supplemented formal required assessments for young children with more relevant informal observations of their performance.

Through their observations, many candidates came away with insights into the factors—some subtle and some not so subtle—that can enhance or inhibit student learning. The most salient theme centered on the quality and the distribution of talk in the classroom. Most residents were chagrined to find a much higher proportion of teacher talk than student talk. Many noted that student talk involved simply answering or repeating information with few opportunities to ask questions or explain. They observed that students' persistence decreased over time as the lesson progressed. Not surprisingly, they also found that student engagement increased when teacher talk decreased. The residents observed that student engagement was also associated with opportunities to communicate with their peers; however, they noted the quality of these peer conversations varied greatly. Through the observation exercise, many became very aware of communication skills their students lacked, and identified this as an important avenue for future instruction. Interestingly, several residents questioned the value of "rug time." They now recognized this instructional context as ripe with all the factors that degrade student engagement. Several residents pledged to experiment with alternative formats. These themes were reflective of the literature on effective learning environments and instruction, but were very compelling to the candidates since they identified them in their own classrooms rather than in a textbook summary.

The data representations produced for the workshops showed candidates moving from summary statistics, in the early weeks, to detailed views of patterns in students' learning individually and in the class aggregate. Some candidates began to incorporate data specifically linked to next steps in instruction. Overall, in the workshops the candidates had focused discussions on the instructional implications of the data. A comment by one candidate highlighted her growth in understanding the use of systematic evidence. She commented that because she knew her own students so well, she could not at first see the value of having others interpret formative data from her classroom. In the workshops, however, she found that the discussions gave her new perspectives on her students' learning, and new ideas for instruction. In their final papers, the candidates often wrote about having a new understanding of how assessment data could inform their instruction. This understanding was evidenced through the extent to which the candidates described their use of assessment as a continuous cycle of feedback on their students' and their own learning. They often described experimenting with assessment, such as adding new questions to existing forms; they posed the next set of questions they wanted to explore about their students.

While we saw an increased understanding of assessment systems and use across our own assessments, we also have questions about the translation of the candidates' learning to their practice as teachers of record. In papers and classroom discussions, many residents talked about the time-consuming nature of the systematic observations, and of preparing data representations, and questioned their capacity to continue those practices as teachers of record. We spoke to this regularly in our materials and discussions by emphasizing that the goal was to develop habits of mind that would guide the candidates' continued development of sustainable assessment practices. The case studies of the exemplars served as examples of such practices. However, it is important to note that the challenge of translating pre-service learning to ongoing teacher practice continues to emerge in a practice-based approach. The challenges to teachers in learning how to carry out effective assessment—and the complexities of the task and of the environment—cannot be met through pre-service training alone. Teacher learning must, therefore, be viewed as a continuous process. Activities such as the data workshops can prepare teachers to engage in inquiry teams using meaningful classroom assessment data to investigate student learning and relate findings to other assessment; school environments can provide those continued learning opportunities.

The three practice-based learning paths hold promise for promoting candidates' learning about assessment as well as enabling their skill to use formative assessment in their classrooms. The approach we took is consistent with other practice-based approaches to teacher education, and involved several key steps. We identified a core practice that teachers use regularly and that has high impact on student learning. Formative assessment clearly fit these criteria. Using research on formative assessment and our own case studies of expertise, we decomposed the practice into component knowledge and skill reflective of the practice as a whole and designed activities to provide candidates opportunities to construct the knowledge and practice the skills. For our candidates, learning formative assessment included developing a schema for the big picture of assessment in their schools—including the feedback system provided by both key school-wide and classroom assessments. It also entailed practice in analyzing feedback from different data sources to interpret student learning and derive implications for instruction. While the three learning practices described in this chapter resided in the assessment course for teachers, the concepts and practices within the learning paths were intentionally designed to intersect with learning activities in a second course on cognition and learning. In these design efforts, we were conscious of the challenges in negotiating boundaries within teacher education and between teacher education and classroom practice. Further practice-centered research needs to investigate how candidates build on these practices to continue to improve through their first years of teaching.

NOTES

1. Final paper guidelines may be obtained by emailing the first author.
2. Final paper guidelines may be obtained by emailing the first author.

REFERENCES

Bambrick-Santoyo, P. (2010). *Driven by data. A practical guide to improve instruction.* San Francisco, CA: Jossey-Bass.

Bransford, J. D., Brown, A. L., & Cocking, R. R. (Eds.). (2000). *How people learn: Brain, mind, experience, and school.* Washington, D.C.: National Academy of Science.

Bransford, J., Derry, S., Berliner, D., Hammerness, K., & Beckett, K. L. (2005). Theories of learning and their roles in teaching. In L. Darling-Hammond, J. Bransford, P. LePage, K. Hammerness, & H. Duffy (Eds.), *Preparing teachers for a changing world: What teachers should learn and be able to do* (pp. 40–87). San Francisco, CA: Jossey-Bass.

Brookhart S., (2011). Educational assessment knowledge and skills for teachers. *Educational Measurement: Research and Practice, 30,* 3–12.

Coyne, M. D., Kame'enui, E., & Carnine, D. (2011). *Effective teaching strategies that accommodate diverse learners* (4th ed.). Boston, MA: Pearson.

Darling-Hammond, L. (2010). Teacher education and the American future. *Journal of Teacher Education, 61*(1–2), 35–47.

Easton, L. (2009) *Protocols for professional learning.* Washington, DC: Association for Supervision & Curriculum Development.

Gardiner, W., & Salmon, D. (2014). Faculty research residencies: A response to problems of enactment. *The Professional Educator, 38*(1).

Hammerness, K., Darling-Hammond, L., & Bransford, J. (2005). How teachers learn and develop. In L. Darling-Hammond, J. Bransford, P. LePage, K. Hammerness, & H. Duffy (Eds.), *Preparing teachers for a changing world: What teachers should learn and be able to do* (pp. 358–389). San Francisco, CA: Jossey-Bass.

Hattie, J. (2009). *Visible learning: A synthesis of over 800 meta-analyses relating to achievement.* London, England: Routledge.

Hattie, J., & Timperley, H. (2007). The power of feedback. *Review of Educational Research, 77*(1), 81–112. doi:10.3102/003465430298487

Heritage, M. (2010). *Formative assessment: Making it happen in the classroom.* Thousand Oaks, CA: Corwin.

Heritage, M. (2008). *Learning progressions: Supporting instruction and formative assessment.* Report prepared for the Council of Chief State School Officers. Washington, DC.

Hess, K. K. (2010, December). Using learning progressions to monitor progress across grades: A science-inquiry learning profile for preK–4 students. *Science and Children, 47*(6), 57.

Hiebert, J., Morris, A., Berk, D., & Jansen, A. (2007). Preparing teachers to learn from teaching. *Journal of Teacher Education, 58,* 47–61.

Pellegrino, J. Chudowsky, N., & Glaser, R. (2001). *Knowing what students know.* Washington, DC: National Academies Press.

Popham, W. (2000). *Modern educational measurement: Practical guidelines for educational leaders.* Needham, MA: Allyn and Bacon.

Popham, W. (2011). Assessment literacy overlooked. A teacher educator's confession. *The Teacher Educator, 46,* 265–273.

Shepard, L., Hammerness, K., Darling-Hammond, L., & Rust, F. (2005) Assessment. In L. Darling-Hammond, J. Bransford, P. LePage, K. Hammerness, & H. Duffy (Eds.), *Preparing teachers for a changing world: What teachers should learn and be able to do* (pp. 275–326). San Francisco, CA: Jossey-Bass.

Wiliam, D. (2011). *Embedded formative assessment.* Bloomington, IN: Solution Tree.

CHAPTER 30

FROM IDEA TO PUBLICATION

Course Embedded Authentic Research Experiences

Louis S. Nadelson
Utah State University

In this chapter, I describe the process of taking graduate students in educational psychology from idea to publication using course embedded research projects. Course embedded research provides opportunities for using an authentic context for teaching educational psychology course content, but also gives graduate students chances to gain experience with conducting and reporting research. Embedded research experiences can also improve the speed and quality of their individual projects, such as dissertations. I provide a timeline and details of the process and justifications for why I made the choices in my approach for each step in the process. I also describe some of the challenges I have encountered through my multiple years and seven embedded research projects associated with the graduate courses I have taught. While I have focused on graduate students in educational psychology, the ideas I present can be applied to an array of graduate programs in the social sciences.

Challenges and Innovations in Educational Psychology Teaching and Learning, pages 397–410
Copyright © 2016 by Information Age Publishing
All rights of reproduction in any form reserved.

JUSTIFICATION FOR COURSE EMBEDDED
RESEARCH EXPERIENCES

Engaging educational psychology graduate students in an authentic research project can provide them with invaluable experience that can be readily transferred to their short-term and long-term success. In the short term, the research experience provides students with a model for how to conduct academic research, but perhaps from a more pragmatic position, the process provides graduate students with a model for doing research that they can rely on as they conduct their thesis or dissertation research. Understanding how to form research questions, examine the literature for relevant studies, determine a methodology for data collection, collect data, analyze data for results, discuss findings, propose implications, recognize limitations, and draw conclusions—all of these are daunting activities for the rookie researcher (Chen & Anderson, 2008; Kiewra, 2008; Mayer, 2008). However, if the first exposure to these research processes take place within a group of graduate students and is effectively scaffolded and mentored by the instructor, then students are more likely to achieve a high level of success. They can develop the knowledge necessary for more independent research, including the dissertation. Of tremendous benefit to my colleagues is that students refine their writing skills, learn APA formatting, and how to use citations, quotes, and professional language effectively. Thus, students are better prepared to engage in their dissertation projects, which decreases the demands on chairpersons and committee members.

The long-term benefits to graduate students include understanding: (1) how to collaborate with colleagues to conduct research; (2) how to work within university and perhaps school systems to gain authorization to conduct research; (3) how the peer review process takes place; and (4) how to produce a referenced peer-reviewed publication. Many students are not employed as graduate research assistants; for these students, experience with authentic research must be acquired through their degree programs and coursework. Yet, I have found that embedding authentic research experiences in courses for educational psychology graduate students is uncommon in the field. But, the long-term benefit of these course embedded authentic research experiences is particularly valuable for those students seeking to pursue academic careers that will necessitate conducting and publishing research.

Some Considerations

Embedding authentic research experiences within a course is challenging. There are several issues that faculty members should consider before embedding such research experiences for students. First, given a rather well established curriculum for most graduate programs, there may be little flexibility within many courses to include such a labor-intensive activity as research. Second, students should experience research when it makes sense—both in their professional development and their course sequence. If the research experience takes place too early in the degree program, then students may not have the knowledge or understanding of the fundamentals of research. If the research takes place too late in the program, then students may be consumed with their own research projects and, therefore, less able or motivated to work on, for example, a group research project. Also, if the activity occurs too late in the program, then the students may not benefit from the research experience as a model for thesis or dissertation projects. Third, not all courses align well with an authentic research project, as some may be more theoretical and less applied, making the inclusion of a research activity a poor fit. Fourth, class size is an important consideration because there needs to be a reasonable number of students per project, and a manageable number of projects per course. While I have found a solution that addresses these major issues, there are likely to be other configurations that faculty members can implement that will engage their students in authentic research.

My Solutions

I have taught two courses in two different doctoral programs that proved to be ideal for authentic research experiences. The first is a quantitative research methods course. The objective of the course is to increase students' knowledge of quantitative research design and measurement. Thus, an embedded research project is well aligned with the course objective. Further, the course typically enrolls 10–15 students, most of whom are about a year from beginning their dissertation research.

The second course in which I have successfully embedded authentic research experiences is research design and analysis. The objective of this course is that students will acquire deeper understanding of statistics and associated analyses. Again, the course enrolls about 10–15 students, most of whom are in their last year of coursework prior to their dissertation. For both courses, the research project provides an ideal context for teaching research design and quantitative methods content. Further, the students are well positioned to both engage in and benefit from the research projects.

The Structure of the Project

The course-embedded research experience provides students with an authentic research activity that extends from conception of a research idea or topic to the publication of the reporting product. Given the limited research knowledge of the students, I act as the primary author, guiding all aspects of their research, from brainstorming ideas to submitting the research report for peer review. I mentor the students as co-authors throughout the report writing process. I typically form teams of four or five students for each project and, therefore, may have three or four active projects through a given semester. I have the teams devote both in- and out-of-class time to their projects, and I delegate greater and greater responsibility for the research to the students as we progress through the projects. I have outlined the steps and time line for projects in Table 30.1.

Research Focus

During the first class meeting, I introduce the idea of the research project to students and we brainstorm possible topics and ideas for research. I record all ideas for consideration. After about an hour of brainstorming, we then look for common or complementary topics. I also share my knowledge and describe the support that I can provide to these topics, as some may be very distal to my experiences and, therefore, require more work from me to provide adequate support. My goal is to have five or six potential research topics for the students to ponder. I assign students to conduct a preliminary literature search on these topics to determine what, if any, extant research exists, and identify gaps in the literature.

During the following class meeting, we further discuss the list of possible topics and, based on students' preliminary literature searches, we determine which ideas are the most viable topics for research and publication. We also refine the topics based on the preliminary literature search, settling on the

TABLE 30.1 Major Steps and Time Line for Course Embedded Group Research Projects

Time	Research Group Activity
Week 1	Brainstorm ideas
Week 2	Select topics and form groups
Week 3	Preliminary literature search, create research questions and form hypotheses
Week 4	More literature search and develop/select a methodology
Week 5	Submit to IRB a protocol seeking authorization to conduct research
Week 6–7–8	Collect data; outline manuscript and assign responsibilities; begin writing
Week 9–10	Compile and condition data; conduct analyses
Week 10–11	Report results
Week 12–13	Draft discussion, implications, limitations, and conclusion
Week 13–14	Route full working draft of the manuscript for editing
Week 15–16	Submit for review and consideration of publication
Subsequent	Editor decisions, revisions, acceptance letter, contact information

population of interest and construct(s) to be measured. This process assures that we can conduct an investigation that is meaningful and of interest to the larger academic community. The students indicate their topic of choice and research groups are then formed. While I find that the most effective groups have three or four members, I have worked with a group that consisted of 11 students. Group size is important in terms of the time available from the instructor to lead the projects, balanced with the desire for the research project to be meaningful for the students. Thus, a class of 15 students is well-suited to three groups of five students, assuming that the instructor has the capacity to lead and manage three research projects over the semester.

Because Institutional Review Board (IRB) approval is needed prior to conducting much of the research that is of interest to the students and myself, I emphasize to students that working with adult participants is much easier and quicker than is working with children. For example, gaining access to teachers in K–12 schools for data collection is likely to require an exempt or expedited protocol, while working with K–12 students will require an expedited or full board protocol. Further, collecting data from students in K–12 schools is likely to also require administrators' and parents' permissions—both of which can be challenging obstacles that consume precious time.

Research Questions and Hypotheses

Once we have brainstormed ideas, selected topics, and determined the students' research groups, the next step is to conduct a more complete review of the literature to determine viable and optimal directions for the research. I assign each student to find at least three relevant research articles or reports associated with the topic and have them share the reports with their group. Based on the retrieved articles, we then refine our research questions to address observed gaps in the literature. We also develop associated hypotheses or predictions to help guide the research. Development of the research questions is followed by another round of searching and reviewing the literature to determine gaps in the research. We use this iterative process to refine the research question(s) and directions for our investigations.

Methodology

Because the group research projects I have led have been embedded in quantitative research courses, I require that the data collection be quantitative in nature—with the possibility of conducting a mixed methods (i.e., quantitative and qualitative data) study, if there is adequate justification for doing so. Thus, most of our projects involve data collection using surveys, requiring us to either locate an existing survey or develop a new one. There are advantages and disadvantages to each approach. Using an existing survey has required us to locate valid and reliable tools that align well with our research question, which is sometimes difficult to accomplish. Selecting an existing tool that has been validated and has acceptable reliability saves time. Developing a new survey is time consuming, and much effort must be put into using appropriate language and aligning the tool to our research question to assure construct and content validity. Establishing the reliability and validity of an instrument increases the complexity of the research project. Validation requires input from experts in the field to justify instrument validity. Also, field testing is necessary to establish the reliability of the tool. Field testing requires research participants. These participants are then ineligible to be in the study sample, thereby reducing the pool of potential participants for the final data collection. Nonetheless, developing an instrument is a valuable learning experience for students. They learn that, through validation and reliability testing, there is greater assurance that the instrument aligns with their research question(s) and is, therefore, more likely to be useful for gathering the desired data.

Following the selection or development of an appropriate instrument for data collection, we then focus on the data collection process. The process of determining the sampling procedure may occur in tandem with instrument selection or development. However, I have found that there are advantages to securing an instrument first because our research questions may shift as we delve deeper into the literature. In general, our populations have been college students or in-service teachers. We have also focused on specific subgroups within these populations for our research (e.g., first year students, pre-service teachers, and in-service teachers engaged in professional learning communities).

After we have decided what tools we will use to collect data, and from whom we will collect the data, we then determine how we will collect the data. We have used both face-to-face surveys (paper forms) and online surveys, and use email to solicit participants. Both approaches have been equally successful for the projects I have led. While we have used our research questions to guide us, other aspects of the data collection need to be considered as well, including access to participants. The students have been invaluable resources in gaining access to groups such as in-service teachers and K–12 school administrators, which has enhanced our data collection and participation in the research projects. By leveraging my students' access to these populations, the student co-authors have been highly involved in the research and they have assumed greater ownership of the research process and outcomes.

Once we have determined what, how, when, and from whom we will collect data, I write an initial draft of the methodology for the respective research papers, creating a model for the students. I have found that it is most effective if I take the lead in developing the methods section, but I also walk the students through the intellectual and behavioral processes that I use to write this section, thereby modeling this activity for them.

IRB Protocol

Because of the need to submit an accurate description of our research methods in the IRB applications, I take the lead in writing the method sections to assure a quick approval from the IRB so that we can get started collecting the data. The first step I take to develop our IRB applications is to verify that all of my students can be part of an IRB protocol. In many cases this involves completing the online Collaborative Institutional Training Initiative (CITI) courses. I approach the IRB application process as another important learning opportunity for students, and I ask individuals or pairs of team members to take the lead to complete parts of the application. Because I have to sign off before any application can be submitted, I review the applications and make any needed corrections. Because most of my students have never completed an IRB application, having them complete the application as a group activity gives them valuable experience in this critical task prior to their dissertation projects. IRB applications can be submitted electronically or in paper form; regardless of format, the elements are essentially the same, and include submitting the research description, instruments, and participant informed consent documents.

Data Collection

Collecting the data is one of the most exciting aspects of the research project for students. Data gathering has tangible rewards as the data are essential to answering our research questions. When we gather data face-to-face, we go to classes or events and distribute paper copies of surveys (along with the informed consent documents) and share information about what we are doing, and why, and we invite people to participate. We then remain on site and collect all completed surveys. Next, the surveys are distributed to the research team members for data entry, using an agreed upon template to ease merging of the data.

When we collect data online, we use a SurveyMonkey account or the university's Qualtrics survey account. We distribute emails that contain a link to the survey to potential participants and invite them to participate. We typically email reminders after the first and second week of data collection, and then terminate data collection after three weeks. Once completed, we download the data and prepare it for analysis.

All students in each research group contribute to the data collection process, and they leverage their knowledge and resources to seek out and encourage individuals to participate in our studies. As with other aspects of the projects, my students benefit by learning about the challenges and pitfalls associated with data collection. They also learn how to resolve data collection problems (e.g., lack of participation; inability to get access to participants) so that they can obtain the data needed to answer their research questions.

Outline the Manuscript, Assign Responsibilities, and Begin Writing

During data collection, I work with the students to develop an outline of the manuscript, from introduction to conclusion. Typically, there is enough material in the review of literature to divide the sections among the students, assigning each some portion of the review to write. I then review APA formatting and provide students with examples of both good and poor writing, and I reinforce the importance of taking the time and making the extra effort to develop a quality manuscript. The manuscript writing task is very demanding for both the students and myself. Students have limited experience with academic writing for publication and, therefore, must put forth great effort to produce a quality project. This writing is also demanding for me because I devote a lot of time to editing and commenting on drafts to help the students develop their writing skills. Most students—though not all—are pleased with the feedback that I provide them.

My leadership is important for both mentoring the students and developing a common voice for the manuscript. As students complete their assigned writing, I have them send their drafts to me for comments and editing. Three common writing pitfalls characterize my students' writing. These are: (1) being overly verbose; (2) overstepping the bounds of their research and data into other areas of the literature; and (3) and making bold statements that are not framed as argument or supported by the literature. Thus, as I edit their drafts, I focus on clarity and continuity and make comments such as, "did we measure this?" "does this provide justification for our research?," and "does that statement need support from the literature?" While editing is time consuming, the return on investment is large because the students develop significantly as academic writers. As a consequence, their dissertation writing is much improved. Students frequently state that my feedback on their writing is the first time in their doctoral program that their writing has received such careful scrutiny.

Compile and Condition the Data

After we have completed the data collection, we either import the data from an online survey system into a spreadsheet or enter the data by hand from paper versions of surveys into spreadsheet. The data transfer is very important for helping students learn how to handle incomplete survey responses or unexpected responses, or to make corrections to any errors in data entry. I spend time leading students through this process and discuss the "art and science of research" that is associated with assuring that data sets are accurate, representative, and useable. For example, we examine our data sets for outliers, discuss the plausibility and implications of the observed values, and explore the possibility that extreme observed/reported values are likely due to either errors in responses or to data entry. Effort and time spent on data conditioning depends on the sample size, the nature of the data, and the methods of analysis. Data conditioning typically involves tasks such as assuring that data are recognized as quantitative values (e.g., years of age is a numeric value, such as "35," and not a string: "35 years").

Once the data are entered and conditioned, we import the data into SPSS and again check for possible problems (e.g., qualitative values appear as string variables indicating that text was entered someplace for the variable, or formatting was retained from the spreadsheet). I frequently hear from my students how they benefitted from experiencing the process of conditioning, transferring, and formatting data. Students then create a number of graphical displays of data (e.g., box plots, histograms, and scatter plots), to determine if data are plagued by outliers, skewness, or unexpected relationships. The graphs help students to understand how visual displays can be used to gain deeper knowledge of their data and the relevant associations.

Conduct the Analyses

Because all of the group research projects have involved collection of demographic data, we begin with relevant descriptive data analyses. These analyses support our review of the basics of statistics: frequencies, measures of variation and central tendency, normal distributions, and other descriptive statistics. Analyses of data depends on our research questions and the methods used to gather the data. Generally, because of my students' limited knowledge of statistical analyses, data analyses are often restricted to descriptives (e.g., means, standard deviations), correlations, t-tests, ANOVAs and chi-square tests. For example, in research examining relationships between or among groups, we typically conduct t-tests, ANOVA, correlation, or regression. In other studies, our analyses have included making simple descriptive comparisons. Through this approach, my students can participate, learn, and comprehend statistical analysis, and their ownership of the research and its outcomes is increased.

Reporting the Results

I use descriptive data analyses to teach or review APA data and statistical reporting. Reporting descriptive data analysis is an ideal context for teaching my students how to write in a concise manner. Many students claim that they have done similar writing in other coursework, but it is apparent that their understanding of how to report data is not aligned with what is found in most peer-reviewed publications. I have each group member perform the same task of describing their research participants by using the available demographic data that their group obtained. As a group, we then critique each student's work to determine and select the best language and representation of the data to use in the manuscript.

I typically take the lead on drafting the report of the research question analyses. The need for a common voice, succinct reporting, and accurate representation have led me to realize that students benefit from my modeling of the manuscript writing process. Although we share in the analysis, I have observed that the students are significantly challenged as they try to write the report. By modeling the writing process for students, they develop an understanding of how to think about results and report the findings in ways that align with their group's literature review and research questions.

Drafting the Discussion, Implications, and Directions for Future Research, Limitations, and Conclusion

Next, students must discuss, interpret, and explore the meaning of their research results. This is difficult for most students because they tend to want to review the results of their analyses, rather than to speculate about possible explanations for the results. Thus, I meet with students in their research groups and lead their conversation about their results. I prompt the discussions with questions about why we have found what we did, what questions they can ask that arise from their explanation of the obtained results, and what results may be interesting to further examine in future research. I focus on helping them align the literature review, research questions, results, and discussion. Here again, I take the lead in writing the discussion but, by now, the ideas and organization have been well established and all students have participated in writing portions of the manuscript.

For the limitations section of the manuscript, we discuss what we could have done in our research if we had more time and resources, what we simply could not do, and what would be good to know and recognize as fruitful areas for future research. Students tend to see the description of the limitations of their study as pitfalls rather than as an effort to be transparent about the research project. Here, I want them to recognize that all research has limitations, and that these limitations can frequently be considered as opportunities for future research.

Editing the Working Draft of the Manuscript

Although we typically draft and edit for several weeks, there is a delightful feeling of having a full working version of our manuscript circulating for each member of the groups to edit and comment upon. I emphasize the importance of a common voice and language in the manuscript, encouraging students to think as a unified team about the message and look for writing that might convey the views of an individual rather than the whole group. We do not parallel edit, as version control is an issue. I manage the editing process of routing by sending the paper out to the team and asking a volunteer to take the first pass, and then instruct the other students to wait until I send the paper out again for additional comments and editing. After students complete their edits, they return the paper to me. I then review the edits and comments, accept appropriate changes (as we "track changes"), and send it out to the group again for the next author to provide a round of editing. We continue until all group members have reviewed and edited the report.

While editing, I instruct students to look for statements that may need support from the literature, and to consider adding references that strengthen the case for our research. Students cross reference the citations and references. As frequently happens with multiple author manuscripts, citations are added or removed without adequate attention to the reference list. Thus, I then align the citations and references—often not knowing where some citations were found by the students. Maintaining vigilance regarding the citations and references saves time and helps students learn about the importance of attention to these details when writing.

Submit for Publication Review

Once we are satisfied with the state of the manuscript we again consider an appropriate outlet for our work. I have the students identify where the work that we have cited was published as these sources can serve as possible outlets for our work. Students also examine and consider other related journals. At this time, we discuss acceptance rates of different journals, their impact factor scores, the fees associated with open access publications, and the typical length of time from submission to review and publication, as well as the different formats for article publication (i.e., print or online).

Occasionally, I write to the journal editor and share the abstract of our work, asking if the work aligns with the current direction the editor is taking with the journal. I include the student co-authors on these emails and encourage them to communicate with journal editors prior to submitting their future work. I demonstrate how to submit a manuscript to a journal—by electronic means (i.e., uploading to the journal's manuscript management system, or via email to the editor). This takes the mystery out of the manuscript submission process and prepares students to submit their own manuscripts independently.

Editors' Decisions and Requests for Revisions

It is critical for students to learn how to respond to editors' decisions (i.e., accept, reject) and requests for revisions, resubmission, or a new submission. Once I receive the reviews, I send out the original manuscript, along with the editor's decision letter and the reviewer's comments to all contributing student coauthors. With reviews coming back as much as one year after submission, it is not always possible to keep all of the contributing students involved until their group research paper is published because some have graduated or left their programs. Others are, by now, immersed in their own thesis or dissertation research and are not able to devote time to revising the manuscript. Thus, the sustained involvement of student co-authors varies widely across these projects. I work with the students that I can readily contact to assist with the revisions needed for resubmission.

I take the lead role to revise and resubmit our work and model this process for the students. I begin by constructing a three-column table; one column contains the reviewers' comments; a second column contains our responses to the reviewers; and the final column indicates to the editor where in the manuscript we have made revisions. I edit and revise, using "track changes," according to the reviews. Once completed, I share the manuscript with the student coauthors and ask them to review and consider additional changes. For some projects I have had considerable input on the final version of the work. At other times, my input has been minimal, leaving the students to take a larger role in addressing the reviewer comments. Regardless, the students have indicated that the revise-and-resubmit process is a valuable part of their research project experience.

Once a manuscript is accepted for publication, I share the notification with the students, thank them for their work, and request their current contact information (in a few cases, I have needed their signature to release copyright ownership to the publisher).

For several publications, I have received complementary authors' copies of the journal issue and, in these cases, I give a copy to each member of the research team, along with a note that reads: "This is for you, our work is published in here. Thank you for being my colleague!"

Examples of Successful Group Projects

I have integrated authentic research experiences into my research methods several times and have led seven groups of doctoral students from idea to publication. In my first attempt, I worked with 11 graduate students in my quantitative research methods course. Given my limited experience doing this kind of collaborative work with students, we went through the steps I have described in this chapter. We focused on research efforts on multicultural efficacy (Nadelson et al., 2012), using a validated instrument (Guyton & Wesche, 2005) that, at the time, had not been used for any other published research. We used the instrument to gather data from a sample of undergraduate pre-service teachers. Some of the graduate students were working with the pre-service teachers as teaching assistants or adjunct faculty, which gave them quick and easy access to our participants. Following an exempt IRB approval, we were able to gather data and rapidly move to analysis, allowing me to use both the process and data for teaching analysis and reporting research. Further, because of the timing, I was able to achieve the goal: Achieving a successful learning experience for the graduate student enrolled in the course. We submitted the paper for peer review shortly after the end of the semester. Students were listed alphabetically as co-authors. The paper was published almost two years after submission.

My second example is my most recent success, and the project involved ten doctoral students who were enrolled in my quantitative research methods course. I split the class into two groups and assigned each group the task of coming up with some possible research topics while I circulated between the groups. I guided their discussions, based on my interest, knowledge, and capacity to support their ideas. Because the students discussed and decided on possible topics in the first meeting of the course, we were able to rapidly progress to making decisions about methods and students' individual roles in their group projects. However, both of the selected topics—teachers' perceptions of common core and pre-service teachers' experience, use, and perceptions of instructional technology—required the development of new research tools. While the students gained valuable experience with instrument development, data collection and analyses were delayed, and this limited my ability to use the described collaborative research processes while teaching the course.

The delay in our data collection resulted in postponement of the development of our manuscript until after the course ended. Also, completing the manuscript after the conclusion of the course was complicated by the limited amount of time that the students were able to commit to writing and editing. Thus, to bring the project to completion, I took responsibility for a greater part of the data analyses, writing, and editing than I had intended. A few students from each group remained engaged and they each contributed to the development of their respective group's reports. As a result, the research teams decided to change our alphabetical-ordering convention for authors and, instead, recognize the contributions of these coauthors by listing them as first authors. Both groups' papers were subsequently published (Nadelson, Bennett, Gwilliam, Howlett, Oswalt, & Sand, 2013; Nadelson, Pluska, Moorcroft, Jeffery, & Woodard, 2014).

IMPLICATIONS FOR INSTRUCTORS

Instructors attempting to embed authentic research experiences in their courses should keep in mind that the process is a learning experience for both themselves and their students. While the research process may be familiar to the faculty member, effective project management is essential to assuring successful project outcomes for the students' research. Thus, the faculty members must attend to the timing and pacing of the work over the semester, define each group member's role, communicate clearly the expectations for the work to be done by each group member, and monitor and evaluate students' efforts and contributions. The authentic research project is an important learning activity for graduate students, and it can be used to enhance course goals and curricular objectives in graduate programs within a variety of applied social science courses.

My final piece of advice is to start with a small project, if possible. A single project for the course is best, as you are likely to learn about how to organize and manage such collaborative projects. Set realistic goals for the research project and the research report so that the students (and you) will not be disappointed if the research results are not compelling or the research manuscript is rejected by an editor. Embedding an authentic research experience into a course contributes to aligning curriculum and instruction with the expectations of high quality graduate programs. It is an efficient and effective way to contribute to the preparation and development of students as education and applied social science researchers.

REFERENCES

Chen, X., & Anderson, R. C. (2008). Reflections on becoming a successful researcher. *Educational Psychology Review, 20*(1), 65–70.

Guyton, E. M., & Wesche, M. V. (2005). The multicultural efficacy scale: Development, item selection, and reliability. *Multicultural Perspectives, 7*(4), 21–29.

Kiewra, K. A. (2008). Advice for developing scholars. *Educational Psychology Review, 20*(1), 79–86.

Mayer, R. E. (2008). Old advice for new researchers. *Educational Psychology Review, 20*(1), 19–28.

Nadelson, L., Boham, M. D., Conlon-Khan, L., Fuenteabla, M. J., Hall, C. J., Hoetker, G. A. et al. (2012). A shifting paradigm: Preservice teachers' multicultural attitudes and efficacy. *Urban Education, 47*(6), 1190–1205.

Nadelson, L. S., Bennett, D., Gwilliam, E., Howlett, C., Oswalt, S., & Sand, J. (2013). The intersection of preservice teachers' confidence, perceptions, and ideas for using instructional technology for learning. *International Journal of Higher Education, 2*(4), 77–90.

Nadelson, L. S., Pluska, H., Moorcroft, S. Jeffery, A., & Woodard, S. (2014). Educators perceptions and knowledge of the Common Core State Standards. *Issues in Teacher Education. 23*(2), 47–66.

CHAPTER 31

DEVELOPING CODING SCHEMES

From Cognitive Principles to Best Practices

Florian C. Feucht
University of Toledo

CODING SCHEMES IN QUALITATIVE RESEARCH

In the field of qualitative research, not much guidance is provided to students in the process of developing coding schemes to analyze qualitative data. Method books and graduate course work focus more on qualitative research methods and designs than on explaining the concrete steps needed to create coding schemes to capture meaningful evidence in qualitative data sets such as, for example, expert interviews, family photographs, or among existing cases files. This lack of guidance is surprising because coding schemes are the essence of data analysis, establishing the structure and content of the research results. More specifically, coding schemes are cognitive tools that qualitative researchers develop in an explicated and deliberate process to enable data analyses that warrant meaningful scientific

Challenges and Innovations in Educational Psychology Teaching and Learning, pages 411–423

inquiries and discoveries. To fulfill this purpose, coding schemes need to be methodologically sound and cognitively viable. For students to become successful qualitative researchers, they need to acquire the knowledge, skills, and tenacity to create effective coding schemes for the qualitative studies they set out to accomplish in their professional careers.

In general, a coding scheme is a research tool used to identify, capture, and triangulate evidence in data to corroborate an emerging or existing theory to answer the research questions of a qualitative study. A coding scheme facilitates the coordination of theory and evidence in the process of scientific inquiry in a valid, reliable, and objective manner. Typically, a coding scheme has a hierarchical structure with the purpose of organizing evidence and claims by the means of more concrete, specific, and applied codes at the bottom and moving toward more abstract, general, and theoretical codes at the top of the hierarchy (see Figure 31.1). Distinct organizing principles are used as sorting criteria to determine what quotation (the evidence-bearing data snippet) should be assigned to which code. The organizing principles may emerge from the data, be informed by existing theory or be a combination of both and, as such, define the coding scheme as inductive, deductive, or abductive in nature. Similar to a tree, codes form organizational units ranging from neighboring codes to code branches to analytical levels within the coding scheme (see Figure 31.1 and Principle 3 for an example).

The development of a coding scheme is an iterative process that negotiates the best architecture to account for different data formats, data sources, and data collection procedures. Therein, a coding scheme is often determined by the research design of the study, such as ethnography, narrative research, phenomenology, or case study (e.g., Creswell, 2013). Often researchers and students who are new to and unfamiliar with qualitative research underestimate the level of higher-order thinking required to design a precise and multi-faceted coding scheme and the cognitive demands its application has on working memory during the data analysis process. Software and technology may support the human mind in the development and application of a coding scheme, but do not replace it.

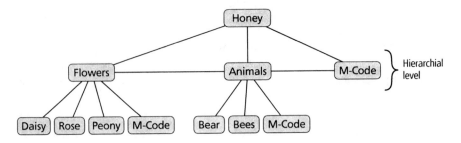

Figure 31.1 Hierarchical structure and organizing units of a coding scheme.

In this chapter, I describe my approach to teaching the development of coding schemes in the context of a qualitative research course that focuses on data analysis and the use of software (Atlas.ti) in this process. Based on learning theory in the field of educational psychology, I introduce eight cognitive principles as starting points for the development of methodologically sound and cognitively viable coding schemes, as well as the transition into best practices of modeling a research team, using theory to inform practice, and analyzing authentic data sets.

Students who enroll in advanced qualitative research courses are predominately doctoral students dedicated to completing a qualitative or mixed-method research study for their dissertations. Data analysis courses are often placed at the end of a course sequence and are elective in nature. Hence, most enrolled students are highly motivated, close to the end of their program of studies, and interested in pursuing an academic career utilizing qualitative and mixed-method approaches. While these are characteristics of advanced students, the approaches described in this chapter are also suitable for preparing novice undergraduate and graduate students to become qualitative researchers.

SIGNIFICANCE OF TEACHING QUALITATIVE CODING SCHEMES

From a career perspective, graduate students who choose an academic career utilizing qualitative research and mixed-method approaches are well advised to acquire a solid foundation of the methodological knowledge, practice, and culture during their program of studies. These competencies are also relevant for qualitative researchers and methodologists outside of academia who are hired by industry and organizations to conduct program evaluation, policy research, and educational measurement and testing.

From a proficiency perspective, the knowledge, skills and attitudes to develop and apply coding schemes are instrumental to all professionals who conduct serious qualitative research. Therefore, students need to acquire an understanding of methodologically sound and cognitive viable coding schemes and apply this know-how in their professional practices. Methodological competence allows students to deploy strategies to create coding schemes that strengthen the validity, reliability, and objectivity of a research study and, therefore, have the potential to contribute to meaningful basic and applied research. Knowledge about cognitive principles derived from theories of human learning enables students to employ strategies to optimize the structure and operationalization of coding schemes to make them less taxing for the mind. Thus, students (and researchers alike) will be less prone to making mistakes with respect to the processes of coding and theory-evidence coordination. For example, a coding scheme that is built on a structure that accounts for the limited capacity of working memory (7 ± 2 items at a time; Miller, 1956) can decrease the cognitive load of the researcher and, therein, decrease the number of mistakes that might otherwise occur during the coding activity. Fewer mistakes, in turn, safeguard the analytical precision of the coding scheme, ensure transparency in the corroboration of the emerging or existing theory, and strengthen the methodological merit of the research.

From a collaborator and consumer perspective, the methodological soundness and the cognitive viability are of relevance for a research study beyond the work of an individual researcher. Research team members, who account for the cognitive demand of a coding scheme, benefit from fewer coding errors and more analytical precision when establishing inter-rater reliability. Reviewers and readers of a qualitative research article or grant proposal benefit from an intelligible coding scheme (and results section) and can focus on the scientific merit of the overall project. In the end, the competency to develop and apply effective coding schemes has an encompassing impact on the current work and future success for qualitative researchers.

LACK OF STUDENT READINESS TO EXECUTE QUALITATIVE DATA ANALYSES

Students lack the knowledge and practice to conduct qualitative data analysis. The main problem for students to become proficient is manifest in their ability to understand, develop, and apply qualitative coding schemes successfully. Too often, students ask pragmatic questions such as: How should I structure my coding scheme? Do I need to code all of the data? How extensive or detailed should the coding scheme be? These questions are indicators of a conceptual struggle with methodological knowledge underlying the development of coding schemes. Further, students also need to understand:

- the importance of coordinating theory and evidence when handling evidence, claims, and arguments to corroborate emerging or existing theories;
- the purpose of structure and organizing principles to identify, code, and triangulate meaningful evidence in the data;
- the need for rigor and transparency to accomplish a valid, reliable, and objective research study according to a field's expectations; and
- the relationship between the structure and operationalization of a coding scheme and the layout and findings of a results section.

Explaining to students the nature and purpose of a coding scheme from a cognitive learning perspective can complement their emerging methodological understanding and also help to teach students about the importance of considering cognitive components when designing coding schemes. In the next section, eight organizational principles are introduced that can function as starting points and scaffolds in the development of coding schemes. The rationale for the usefulness of cognitive principles to leverage methodological competence is based on the understanding that scientific inquiry is a form of knowledge acquisition in its most fundamental principles.

USING COGNITIVE PRINCIPLES TO UNDERSTAND, DEVELOP, AND IMPROVE CODING SCHEMES

Links between Research Methodology and Cognitive Learning Theory

Eight principles derived from cognitive learning theory in the field of educational psychology provide a foundation for the development and application of coding schemes in qualitative research. The rationale for why learning theories can inform and optimize research methodologies is based on their common goal to describe components and processes that lead to the exploration and acquisition of new knowledge. In other words, the method of scientific inquiry is an explicated and deliberate method of learning (e.g., Bruner 1961; Dewey, 1910). While one should be careful not to make sweeping generalizations in this comparison, "cognitive schemas" in cognitive learning theory and "coding schemes" in qualitative research methodology can be considered as parallel constructs. Both represent knowledge structures that (a) obtain and store information from the environment or in the data; and (b) use an iterative process to organize and update the knowledge stored within them.

In Piaget's (1952) theory of cognitive development, schemas are described as mental networks or structures of organized information. Once schemas are developed, they can be used to identify and understand new information based on existing information. Schemas can differ in size, differentiation, and complexity. The cognitive processes that develop and organize schemas over time are referred to as assimilation and accommodation. Equilibrium is the tendency to find consistency between the incoming information and the already stored information by adding and revising organizational principles. Coding schemes have a similar purpose of organizing and storing evidence (i.e., information). They are revised in an iterative process to better account for newly identified evidence. That is, the organizing principles of codes and code branches are changed by revisions and additions that impact the size, differentiation, and complexity of the coding scheme. The data analysis (i.e., knowledge acquisition) is completed when the coding scheme has captured and triangulated all meaningful evidence in the data to corroborate an emerging or existing theory (i.e., equilibrium).

Coding schemes are cognitive tools because they represent knowledge structures like schemas, require higher-order thinking in their development, and strain the capacity of working memory during data analyses. In fact, it is the capacity of working memory that sets limits on the effectiveness of a coding scheme as it controls the overall processing power, when comparing it to the information processing model of a computer (Atkinson & Schiffrin, 1968). Limited to processing 7 ± 2 information items at a time (Miller, 1956), working memory restricts the number of organizing principles a researcher can pay attention to when navigating the mental structure of a coding scheme. More specifically, a coding scheme that requires a researcher to compare and contrast more than 7 ± 2 organizing principles at a time when coding data—for example, assigning a quotation to 12 potential codes on one branch—can lead to unnecessary coding errors. An increasing number of such errors will compromise the analytical precision of the coding scheme. Hence, it makes sense, from a cognitive perspective, to limit the organizing principles within an organizing unit to no more than 7 ± 2 items at a time. To follow the cognitive principle, a coding scheme should have no more than 7 ± 2 codes per branch, no more than 7 ± 2 branches per hierarchy level, and no more than 7 ± 2 hierarchy levels, overall. Despite the organization limit of 7 ± 2 items per unit, the level of analytical differentiation of a coding scheme is still ensured using an unlimited number of codes (or organizing principles).

Cognitive Principles

The eight cognitive principles are derived from the components and processes of cognitive learning theories discussed above. They are starting points for the development and application of coding schemes. These principles provide an additional perspective to existing methodological practices and information to optimize coding schemes from a cognitive perspective. The principles are written as instructions for students.

1. **Theory and evidence coordination.** Develop and use a coding scheme to identify, capture, and triangulate evidence in the data to corroborate an emerging or existing theory in response to the research question of the study.

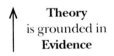

Theory
is grounded in
Evidence

The goal of the coding scheme is to facilitate the coordination of theory and evidence transparently and systematically in the scientific inquiry of a qualitative research study. A common mistake is to consider only evidence that supports a pre-existing theory (or hypothesis) and to disregard evidence that does not support the theory (data selection bias). *Note:* Researchers who aim to answer theory-driven research questions are more at risk of "cherry picking" evidence.

2. **Hierarchical structure.** Use a hierarchical structure to facilitate the coordination of evidence (bottom) to theory (top). A coding scheme can have several levels with different branches of codes (see Figure 31.1). Codes at the bottom are used to capture the evidence in the data. They are more concrete, specific, and applied in nature. Codes towards the top are used to compile evidence and to corroborate theory. They are more abstract, general, and theoretical in nature. Also, it should be noted that concept maps can be used to visually and effectively represent the changing structure of an emerging coding scheme.

3. **Organizing principles.** Use distinct and comparable organizing principles to create and differentiate codes (e.g., characteristics, sorting criteria). The organizing principles of "neighboring codes" must be conceptually different from one other (e.g., "rose" versus "daisy"), yet share the same overarching principle of the overall coding branch (e.g., "flowers"; Figure 31.1). Then, quotations that entail similar evidence can be assigned to a distinct and dedicated code. The organizing principles may emerge from the data (inductive coding scheme), be informed by existing theories (deductive coding scheme), or consolidate both data and theory (an abductive coding scheme). Also, a commitment to distinct yet comparable organizing principles increases the analytical precision of the coding scheme.

4. **7 ± 2 items limitation.** Limit the structure of the coding scheme to no more than 7 ± 2 items per organizational unit. The 7 + 2 items principle protects the investigator from making unnecessary coding errors arising from cognitive overload while navigating the coding scheme during the analysis process. This limit applies to the number of codes per branch, the number of branches per hierarchy level, and the number of hierarchy levels in the coding scheme (but not the overall amount of codes). The 7 ± 2 items limitation per unit safeguards the analytical precision of the coding scheme.

5. **Operationalization.** Operationalize the organizing principles of codes. The operationalization of a code should be documented in writing and should include: (a) a code label to identify the code by a name; (b) a code definition to pinpoint its organizing principles; (c) a code description to compile and summarize the evidence within its

assigned quotations and data context; and (d) two "exemplary" quotations to illustrate the code with authentic sample evidence. A clear, detailed, and comprehensive operationalizing of the coding scheme increases the credibility, reliability, and objectivity of the study. Also, a thoroughly operationalized coding scheme translates well into a written draft of the results section of the research manuscript.

6. **M-codes.** Create an M-code as part of each code branch in the coding scheme (Figure 31.1). The purpose of an M-code is to capture miscellaneous quotations ("sunflower") that appear to be associated with the organizing principle of a branch ("flowers"), but do not match the specific operationalization of the existing codes ("rose" and "daisy"). M-codes are a good strategy for: (a) safeguarding the analytical precision of existing codes; (b) avoiding premature revisions of the coding scheme; and (c) alleviating working and long-term memory processing demands. A new code might emerge from an M-Code, if a distinct organizing principle can be identified in the evidence of the assigned quotations.

7. **Grounding of evidence.** Consider the number of quotations assigned and the evidence that is captured by a code. The investigator should maintain codes that are sufficiently grounded in the data. Codes that do not have enough or have too many quotations assigned to them should be merged or split into new codes. The amount of evidence sufficient to corroborate a theory is determined by the scientific community and is often reflected in the expectations of dissertation committees and journal manuscript review panels. Double-checking the grounding of codes is a good strategy to clean up the coding scheme at the end of the analysis.

8. **Collaboration.** Improve the quality of the coding scheme by collaborating with other researchers. Different perspectives help the investigator to develop a more comprehensive and less subjective coding scheme. The level of agreement among researchers when coding data can be used as an indicator of the reliability of the coding scheme and the objectivity among the team members: The higher the agreement, the higher the overall quality of the coding scheme. Remember: Great minds think alike—idiots never disagree!

These eight principles are interrelated and influence each other. Thus, the modifications made to a coding scheme based on one principle might require additional adjustments based on other principles.

From Starting Points to Best Practices

The above principles are communicated in a brief in-class lecture during the general research methods course. They are a good starting point for students to understand and begin their data analyses. However, the best practice for students to learn these principles is within the authentic setting of a research team that has original and complex data, and which uses theory to inform decision making. This form of apprenticeship learning allows students to observe and acquire the necessary data analytic competencies within the context of "whole task" experiences; that is, tasks that are neither reduced in complexity nor compartmentalized into isolated sub tasks (van Merriënboer & Kirshner, 2007). A variation of this approach is to simulate a research team within a graduate research methods course, including the use of assignments that help develop appropriate research practices and culture.

SUGGESTIONS FOR BEST PRACTICES IN TEACHING CODING SCHEMES

In my advanced course for qualitative analysis, graduate students learn to develop and apply coding schemes using a best practices approach. The goal is for them to acquire the cognitive and methodological competencies necessary by participating in professional research practices throughout the course and, over time, they will use these competencies in their everyday routines in their careers as researchers and research team leaders. Three components provide the foundation of the course: (1) simulating a research team; (2) using theory to inform practice; and (3) analyzing authentic data sets.

To fully activate and integrate students' learning through these components, they analyze three existing data sets for the main activity of the course. The data sets serve as the main course materials, increase in their complexity throughout the course, and inform the organization and schedule of the course. The processes and products of students' data analyses constitute the graded assignments. In sum, the course establishes a learning environment for best practices, guiding students through three complete data analyses. They acquire, exercise, and fine-tune their competencies in developing and applying coding schemes with increasing levels of task complexity, thoroughness, and sophistication.

Simulating a Research Team

During the majority of the course, the students and I, as the expert in qualitative research, form a research team to analyze different data sets. Although a qualitative research team is often comprised of 3–5 core members, modeling the tasks, habits, and culture of a team is feasible in a group of 9 to 12 students. This larger group size, on the one hand, permits students to progress through the developmental and analytical steps in a timely fashion. On the other hand, it provides ample opportunities and time for students to learn from one another and acquire an overall understanding of the research processes.

Developing a Coding Scheme

Students read through the data and create an initial coding scheme depicted in the form of a concept map (see Figure 31.1). As a group, we note the proposed codes on a white board, discuss similarities and differences between the code proposals, and listen to the various rationales for organizing principles that are reflected in the proposed structures of their coding schemes (Feucht, Marchand, & Olafson, 2015). As the research team leader, I moderate this iterative process, introduce methodological concepts and the aforementioned cognitive principles, and map the emerging coding scheme on the whiteboard. In this process, I model the development of the coding schemes using think-alouds, sharing with students my thinking and decision making as a qualitative researcher. My modeling strategy allows students to observe and internalize the relevant steps and underlying decision making at the initial stages of coding. Students become increasingly able to verbalize and enact these competencies independently by the end of the course.

Applying a Coding Scheme

Next, using the new coding scheme to analyze the data, we model similar processes as a research team. We project the data onto the whiteboard and take turns analyzing small segments of the data at a time. Again, as research team leader, I moderate the decision making with the goal of finding consensus among the members and addressing emerging issues (e.g., code operationalization, quotation size, etc.). This process simulates the training of researchers for establishing inter-rater reliability. Throughout the course, students become more and more competent in using coding schemes. Students may work in small groups or independently to carry out the coding procedures.

Using Theory to Inform Practice

I do not dedicate time for formal class lectures on qualitative research methodologies. Rather, I use mini-lectures and classroom activities in the moments when teaching is most relevant to infuse the work of the research team with knowledge about methodology (e.g., inductive coding schemes, data triangulation), cognitive principles (e.g., working memory, cognitive schemas), and overlapping concerns (e.g., coordination of theory and evidence). This experience of conducting data analyses, grounded in methodological knowledge, and making theory-driven decisions models the processes of best practices.

Analyzing Authentic Data Sets

The goal of this component is to engage students in the authentic task of analyzing qualitative data. Modeling a research team and infusing theory to inform practice are important components, but they only reach their full potential when students can use authentic data sets to complete data analyses genuinely—from the initial task of preparing the raw data for analysis to the writing up of a results section. This component constitutes a reality check for students about what it means to deal with complex data, triangulate multiple data sources, and cope with ambiguity and difficulty of finding methodologically sound solutions. In doing so, they must adopt a best practices approach and collaborate as a team. Students complete the data analyses and the associated assignments as whole tasks rather than compartmentalized tasks which would, otherwise, artificially reduce the complexity of the analysis and authenticity of the data.

Sequencing the three data sets allows students to repeatedly practice and consistently improve their competencies. The associated assignments also become more complex and demanding in association with the different data sets. Three core assignments are repeated throughout the course. For each data set, students are required to: (1) develop and operationalize a coding scheme, including code labels, definitions, descriptions, and two exemplary codes; (2) analyze all data and triangulate the data sources; and (3) write a report of the findings. The first two assignments increase in difficulty and comprehensiveness as the data sets' complexity increases. Writing the research report is more demanding with each assignment: writing an abstract (Assignment 1); writing a summary with illustrative quotations (Assignment 2); and, writing a succinct results section based on the coding scheme's operationalization (Assignment 3).

The focus of the course also shifts from discussions among research team members to the generation of reports that are written by individual team members. From a higher-order thinking perspective, this shift allows the assessment of students thinking both during group discourse and, later, based on their individual writing assignments. Thus, these three components are instrumental to developing the thinking skills of future researchers towards best practices in qualitative research.

Evidence of Student Learning

Indicators based on these repeated course activities and assignments provide descriptive evidence of student learning. First, students' abilities to rationalize and develop arguments based on methodological knowledge and cognitive principles increase over the duration of the course. This is evident in the fluency and conceptual depth of their thinking and talk during group discussions and in their individual written work. Second, students become more skillful and effective in developing coding schemes and using them for data analyses. This is evident in the increased quality of their assignments and the decreased time that is spent on tasks. Finally, students enjoy the rigorous learning environment and they take ownership of their work during the data analyses. This is evident in the quality of their individual and collective contributions, active in-class and research group participation, and positive course evaluations at the end of the terms.

RECOMMENDATIONS AND CONCLUSION

The success of the best practices approach in a qualitative research methods course depends on the expertise of the instructor regarding analyses of qualitative data and the instructor's dedication to structuring the course in the guise of a research team. A simulated research team approach requires constant higher-order thinking and decision-making, and cognitive modeling (on the part of the instructor), and development and use of coding schemes (on the part of students). The instructional effort contributes to developing motivated students who feel empowered by their engagement in data analysis decision-making processes, and ownership of the analyzed data. As a consequence, they become more knowledgeable and skilled qualitative researchers. Personally, I find it intellectually rewarding, as an educational psychologist, to teach graduate students how to develop and use coding schemes from a qualitative methodological perspective, but also to explain to students the underlying mechanisms of scientific inquiry and discovery based on principles of human cognition and learning.

REFERENCES

Atkinson, R. C., & Shiffrin, R. M. (1968). Human memory: A proposed system and its control processes. In K. W. Spence & J. T. Spence (Eds.), *The psychology of learning and motivation* (Vol. 2, pp. 89–195). New York, NY: Academic Press.

Bruner, J. S. (1961). The act of discovery. *Harvard Educational Review, 31*(1), 21–32.

Creswell, J. (2013). *Qualitative inquiry and research design: Choosing among five approaches* (3rd ed.). Los Angeles, CA: Sage.

Dewey, J. (1910). *How we think.* Washington DC: Heath & Company.

Feucht, F. C., Marchand, G., & Olafson, L. (2015). Use of concept maps to facilitate student learning in research and measurement courses. In M. McCrudden, G. Schraw, & C. Buckendahl (Eds.), *Use of visual displays in research and testing: Coding, interpreting, and reporting data.* Charlotte, NC: Information Age.

Miller, G. A. (1956). The magical number seven, plus or minus two: Some limits on our capacity for processing information. *Psychological Review 63*(2), 81–97. doi:10.1037/h0043158.

Piaget, J. (1952). *The origins of intelligence in children.* New York, NY: Norton.

van Merriënboer, J. J. G., & Kirshner, P. (2007). *Ten steps to complex learning.* Mahwah, NJ: Erlbaum.

CHAPTER 32

TEACHING PROGRAM EVALUATION

David M. Shannon and Jessica Cooper
Auburn University

Program evaluation is fundamental to professional preparation in educational psychology. Students who will work as educational psychologists will rely
on assessments, measurement, and evaluation to improve their knowledge of
issues related to teaching and learning. An important aspect of developing
this knowledge lies in evaluating the impact and outcomes of interventions,
teaching methods, classroom environments, student behavior, and other factors. Program evaluations are especially important because they provide opportunities for empirically based discussions of essential elements of an educational program, curriculum, or intervention. While there is high demand
for program evaluation experts, education programs specializing in program
evaluation training are limited (Christie, Quinones, & Fierro, 2013). Often,
educational programs that identify themselves as having an emphasis in program evaluation are housed within a larger discipline—typically, educational
psychology (Dewey, Montrose, Schroter, Sullins, & Mattox, 2008). The goal
of this chapter is to describe: (1) essential evaluation competencies; (2) challenges of preparing students to carry out program evaluation studies; and
(3) several promising classroom practices and practical experiences that will
assist those faculty who prepare students for careers as evaluators.

Challenges and Innovations in Educational Psychology Teaching and Learning, pages 425–437
Copyright © 2016 by Information Age Publishing
All rights of reproduction in any form reserved.

EVALUATION COMPETENCIES
AND PREPARATION OF STUDENTS

As described by Fitzpatrick, Sanders, and Worthen (2011), evaluators are responsible for describing the program in question, designing the evaluation procedures, collecting and analyzing data, and providing feedback and recommendations based on the evaluation results. Because entry into program evaluation practice is mostly uncontrolled (i.e., no certification or licensure is needed), Stevahn, King, Ghere, and Minnema, (2005), suggest that training should focus on developing six specific competencies among students. These competencies are: (a) systematic inquiry; (b) situational analysis; (c) interpersonal competence; (d) project management; (e) professional practice; and (f) reflective practice (see Table 32.1). The competencies serve as an "anchor" in structuring training and they provide some degree of consistency across diverse preparation programs. When conducting evaluations, each of these competencies comprise the foundation upon which program evaluators should derive their knowledge, skills, and attitudes. These competencies also provide a consistent set of qualifications for all evaluators, a focus for evaluation training, and a guiding model for effective practice (Stevahn et al., 2005). In the sections below, we describe each of these competencies.

Systematic Inquiry: Theoretical and Methodological Knowledge

Skills associated with systematic inquiry relate directly to the technical aspects of program evaluation, such as design, data collection, analysis, and reporting. This competency requires theoretical and methodological knowledge of how to pose questions, develop a sound plan to fully answer the questions, properly identify data sources, support the validity and reliability of the data, and gather and analyze data. While most graduate students complete a research methods sequence in which they learn research design, data collection and data analysis procedures, specific knowledge pertaining to evaluation theory and evaluation approaches requires specialty coursework in evaluation (Christie et al., 2013; Davies & MacKay, 2014; Dillman, 2012).

Situational Analysis: Contextual Considerations

Evaluators also need to understand the context of the program and determine its readiness for evaluation. Situational analysis provides a comprehensive description of contextual factors, including the needs of a program,

TABLE 32.1   Evaluation Competencies, Course and Practical Experiences

Competency	Course Experience and Assignments	Practical Experiences*
Systematic Inquiry Design, data collection, analysis, interpretation, and reporting	*Course Experiences:* Research methods coursework, specialized evaluation coursework, review of evaluation reports, case studies and discussions with invited program directors and clients *Assignment(s):* Evaluation and Sampling Plan	*Field Experiences:* Work with an experienced evaluator to develop evaluation design and reporting plan for a real project.
Situational analysis Attending to and addressing unique interests, issues, and circumstances	*Course Experiences:* Discussion with invited clients, role play and case studies *Assignment(s):* Needs assessment proposal	*Field Experiences:* Shadow or observe an experienced evaluator when meeting with clients to discuss various phases of evaluation. Provides opportunity to develop communication skills related to working with various stakeholders and explaining the complexities of an evaluation while maintaining integrity of results.
Interpersonal Competence Communication, negotiation, conflict, collaboration, and cross-cultural skills	*Course Experiences:* Discussion with invited clients and role play different roles (e.g., client, stakeholder, evaluator) *Assignment(s):* Interviews with evaluation professionals and stakeholders	
Project management Budgeting, coordinating resources, supervision	*Course Experiences:* Review/critique of grant RFP's, project management plans, and evaluation reports; class discussion and case studies *Assignment(s):* Logic Model, Project Management Plan, Budget and Budget narrative	*Advanced Students:* Seek out independent consulting opportunities to develop skills related to negotiating contracts, budgets, timelines, and deliverables. *Mentorship:* Develop relationship(s) with experienced evaluators. Mentors will be a valuable resource when understanding the intricacies of each individual evaluation.
Professional practice Adherence to evaluation standards and ethics	*Course Experiences:* Cases (and discussions) pertain to ethics in evaluation situations *Assignment(s):* Small scale evaluation (e.g., workshop or summer camp)	
Reflective practice Setting goals for improvement; seeking appropriate professional development	*Course Experiences:* Online resources (e.g., AEA webinars); blogs and community interest groups online *Assignment(s):* Journal reflections on professional interactions and engagement in evaluation.	*Field and Professional Experience:* Join professional organizations such as AEA and AERA. Present, network, and participate at conferences as a tool to continually develop as an evaluator.

* Please note that practical experiences related to program evaluation are best gained through working with longer-term projects (i.e., assistantships, internships, practica, etc.) that provide on-going hands-on experience related to each of the six critical evaluator competencies.

its strengths and weaknesses, available resources, and the political issues that can influence a program's reach and impact. Each evaluation project will present unique challenges for the evaluator. Therefore, involving others in the evaluation from its beginning stage will facilitate cooperation, or buy-in, from stakeholders. Learning more about the program, including how individuals within the organization interact and who has (or is perceived to have) more influence will produce more meaningful results. While these issues are discussed in class and explored in course projects, students need to participate in real evaluation situations (i.e., fieldwork) that allow practice and feedback from experienced evaluators and mentors (Dillman, 2012).

Project Management

Evaluators must be focused on the overall purpose of the evaluation while supervising the evaluation project's personnel and managing its budgets. Being able to develop written plans for personnel tasks, data collection, budgets, timelines, and formal agreements aids in identifying potential obstacles to carrying out the evaluation. Expertise related to planning, organizing, and coordinating resources is needed to determine how, when, and where to conduct the evaluation. Students typically engage in the planning stages of evaluation while in their coursework, but rarely have the chance to implement such plans. It is not until they serve as project directors in actual evaluations that they are in a position to manage resources and supervise personnel.

Interpersonal Competence

Good interpersonal skills are essential to the success of an evaluation. Evaluators must communicate well (both in speech and writing) with key stakeholders. Clearly communicating program goals, processes, and projected outcomes of the evaluation is critical to implementing the evaluation. Before evaluators are able to conduct an evaluation, they must negotiate the boundaries and budget of the evaluation. Communication is essential throughout all phases of evaluation: Evaluators conduct interviews and direct focus groups, request information, prepare evaluation reports, and discuss the evaluation's findings. While communication skills can be developed in coursework, fieldwork and mentorship are also necessary for students to practice and refine these skills.

Professional Practice

There is often a large gap between the technical and practical aspects of evaluation practice. While students may get classroom experience with the technical aspects of evaluation planning and implementation (i.e., analyzing data with statistical tools or theoretical knowledge), the real world application of these skills is often lacking (American Evaluation Association, 1995; Stevahn et al., 2005). Professional practice relates to evaluators' abilities to work ethically and professionally (adhering to evaluation norms and standards) while considering potential impacts from the evaluation outcomes (Stevahn et al., 2005). Again, hands-on learning through fieldwork experiences and mentorship is essential.

Reflective Practice

The practice of program evaluation is constantly evolving. As an evaluator, it is important to think critically about one's self as a practitioner and to consider areas for one's knowledge growth and skill improvement. These areas can be addressed through professional developments activities. Journaling, collaborating with peers, and reflecting on completed projects are examples. While initial training begins with coursework, evaluators must continue to learn and refine their knowledge and skills through field experiences and in professional development programs offered by organizations such as the American Evaluation Association (AEA) and the American Educational Research Association (AERA).

CHALLENGES IN TEACHING PROGRAM EVALUATION

Many challenges are present when preparing students to become evaluators. These challenges primarily pertain to students' limited field experiences in conducting evaluations and in the graduate education curricula for program evaluation coursework.

Students' Backgrounds and Experiences

In general, students' prior knowledge of program evaluation (i.e., what it is, why it is done) is limited. Even students who have taken research methods courses may be unfamiliar with program evaluation, as it is rarely taught as part of an education research methods course. Most often, student experiences with evaluation are limited to end-of-semester assessments of their courses; less likely, they may have experience with institutional assessments of academic programs (i.e., the accreditation process), challenging faculty to broaden students' evaluation experiences. More specifically, instructors must address program evaluation as applied in diverse settings, not only in schools, but also community outreach programs, health care sites, businesses and industries, and for funded research projects.

Instructors need to get students involved in a range of evaluation activities—working with potential clients, developing and revising evaluation plans, and communicating evaluation findings to stakeholders. Such tasks will increase students' knowledge for carrying out program evaluations independently, and will serve to improve their skills and build confidence.

Curriculum Challenges

While most experienced evaluators have completed multiple courses in both program evaluation and advanced research methods (Christie et al., 2013), a typical evaluation preparation degree program offers two or three evaluation courses (Engle, Altschuld, & Kim, 2006). But, by far, most students who learn about program evaluation take just one course in evaluation (Davies & MacKay, 2014). Students are, therefore, unlikely to acquire the full range of skills needed to conduct evaluations competently (Morris, 1994).

The content that can be adequately addressed in a single course typically includes only an overview of evaluation approaches, and some attention to the practical issues involved in planning an evaluation project (Davies & MacKay, 2014). While methodological and theoretical knowledge is often acquired through other, supporting research methods courses, skill-oriented competencies require additional fieldwork experiences and mentorship (Dillman, 2012). While such arrangements help students learn and refine their evaluation skills, the limited curriculum in place within many graduate education programs precludes prolonged practical experiences such as year-long courses and multi-course sequences Thus, faculty must integrate field experience components and other authentic evaluation activities into their courses. Next, we describe the practices that we use to provide our students with the needed educational and professional opportunities to become knowledgeable and competent evaluators.

PROMISING PRACTICES

We have integrated three essential experiences into our program evaluation coursework in order to develop students' evaluation competencies. These are: (1) case-based discussions; (2) meetings and discussions with evaluators and evaluation stakeholders; and (3) project-based assignments that require students to apply the knowledge and evaluation skills that they are developing in the course.

Using Cases and Vignettes for Class Discussion

Cases have been used effectively in teacher education and educational psychology to help generate discussion of critical issues and possible solutions (Sudzina, 1997, 1999). We have found the use of brief cases and vignettes to be a valuable pedagogical tool as class discussions are more rich and meaningful when based on real evaluation cases. In a program evaluation course, case studies help students connect theory to data that require analysis, interpretation, and recommendations for action (Patton, 2005).

During class meetings, we have found the use of briefer vignettes (just a few paragraphs) to be very effective. We have used vignettes that pertain to requests for evaluations, planning of evaluation projects, design and sampling issues, and political and ethical dilemmas. These vignettes provide enough context and information for students but are vague enough not to disclose the source and so that students are required to explore the issues and next steps. Students review and discuss the brief vignettes in class. These discussions must be carefully facilitated by the instructor in order to protect the identity of the individuals and programs upon which the cases were constructed.

In addition to brief vignettes, we have used more detailed cases with supporting artifacts. Typically, these detailed cases and artifacts are distributed to students in advance so that they will have time to review and analyze the materials and prepare for class discussion. Materials have included published program resources (i.e., brochures, reports, and web pages) for students to review to determine the purpose for the evaluation, the program's activities, and the intended and actual outcomes. These resources provide the basis for students to establish an initial evaluation plan that consists of program objectives, evaluation questions, and logic models. We also have students read requests for proposals (RFPs) from funding agencies to understand guidelines for submitting proposals to conduct project evaluations. Finally, students have critiqued evaluation reports in regards to appropriateness of the evaluation design, methods used, and consideration of alternative approaches. We want students to: (a) learn about a variety of situations for which evaluation is applied; (b) interact with stakeholders who have real evaluation needs; and (c) engage in authentic evaluations to develop their evaluation skills.

Meetings and Discussions With Evaluation Stakeholders

When searching for experienced evaluators and potential stakeholders to invite to class, you need not look far. There are likely numerous ongoing evaluation activities within your department, college, university, and local community, including academic program reviews, faculty research, and outreach and extension programs. Having students meet with individuals (e.g., evaluators, clients, other stakeholders) who are actively involved in evaluation projects is essential to their learning about the scope and complexity of evaluations. Student feedback obtained on course evaluations has consistently supported these experiences as one of the most valuable components of the course.

When we work with evaluation clients (e.g., program directors), students prepare a list of questions (or concerns) before the class work session that is submitted to the client(s). When meeting with the client(s), our class sessions focus on clarifying the purpose of the program and the role that an evaluation will play (or has already played) in determining the outcomes or success of the program, identifying methods that can be used to gather valuable data, and developing data collection strategies. In some cases, students assist in gathering and examining data and help prepare reports of findings for the client.

Most graduate students are unfamiliar with the purposes and outcomes of academic program reviews that determine the viability and continuation of university degree programs. We invite university administrators (e.g., provost, vice-president for academic affairs, director of institutional research), college administrators (e.g., dean, associate dean), department and program leaders (e.g., department head, graduate program officer, program coordinator), and faculty reviewers to participate in our class discussions on the purposes of program reviews and the role that program evaluation plays in the success of such reviews.

Invited stakeholders are asked to present such issues and challenges to the class in advance, as this arrangement allows time for students to think about the issues prior to class. In the context of academic program reviews, class discussions have focused on the evaluation approaches used to gather information, what data serve as evidence of program quality, how decisions are made based on the academic reviews, and how evaluation results are subsequently used to improve programs. Students also participate in role playing activities to explore issues from multiple perspectives (e.g., faculty member, department head, external reviewer), and reflect on these activities. Students gain valuable insights from the class discussions, and they learn about other perspectives on the "value" of academic program reviews beyond their limited experiences.

The discussions with evaluation stakeholders have contributed to expanding students' experiences and roles in evaluations. Working directly with clients from diverse situations has also afforded them the opportunity to work on their interpersonal competence, situational analysis, project management skills, and systematic inquiry skills.

Faculty members are expected to produce research and secure funding to support their research activities. As such, their externally funded research frequently requires evaluations of their progress and outcomes. Therefore, we have students meet with principal investigators (PIs) to discuss the contributions of these evaluations to advancing their funded research. These conversations broaden students' understanding of research processes, college and program-level expectations for faculty members' grant writing and scholarly productivity, and gives students insights into how to best prepare for careers in academia.

Finally, many community and statewide programs require evaluations of their efficacy and impacts. The program evaluation leader at the Alabama Cooperative Extension System (ACES) at Auburn University—a graduate of our educational psychology doctoral program—has met with our students to describe how s/he has used evaluations to determine if ACES-sponsored programs have had intended impacts. We have also had our program evaluation classes either review existing ACES program evaluation plans or develop new ones.

Project-Based Assignments

These assignments are sequenced and culminate in a final evaluation product. The assignments (Table 32.1) require students to: (a) investigate an existing program and determine the purpose for the evaluation (including a review of program materials and interviews with key stakeholders); (b) develop evaluation questions that support learning about the program and refining the evaluation plan; (c) construct a logic model for the evaluation; and (d) develop a budget and write a budget justification. The written evaluation plan must describe the evaluation design, sampling plan, data collection procedures, data analysis and reporting processes, and project timelines.

Thus, by the completion of the course, students have developed an initial evaluation plan and begun to build an evaluation portfolio. As an example, students in the counselor education and teacher education programs in our college must submit a portfolio for their comprehensive examinations. In doing so, they can draw from their evaluation portfolio to meet this requirement.

While students gain valuable experiences in coursework, they must also have experiences beyond the classroom to continue to practice and refine their evaluation skills. Due to logistical constraints faced by many programs, gaining longer-term practical experience in evaluation is often left to the student. In the next section, we share the perspective of one student (co-author Jessica Cooper) who has sought opportunities and experienced success in several program evaluation experiences.

A STUDENT'S PERSPECTIVE
ON PROGRAM EVALUATION PREPARATION

As a graduate research assistant, I have worked on two evaluation projects. The project work cemented my understanding of how evaluations are typically conducted. I learned the importance of relationship building when conducting evaluations. I also was encouraged to join professional organizations so that I could present findings from the evaluation projects, network with other evaluators, and continue to learn about program evaluations methods and procedures. Most important, these work experiences enabled me to directly apply the skills and knowledge I learned in my program evaluation courses.

I did not enter the Educational Psychology program at Auburn intending to become a program evaluator. However, my exposure to, training, and experience in the program evaluation curriculum has resulted in presentations of my evaluation projects at local and national conferences, independent consultations on small program evaluation projects, and a network of potential employers. Based on my experiences, I offer the following advice to graduate students in education who are interested in studying program evaluation.

Build relationships and get involved. Develop relationships with those who conduct evaluations. These relationships can lead to work on program evaluation projects which can, in turn, lead to thesis and dissertation research ideas. Because opportunities are limited for students to conduct research independently and get their work published, developing a network of colleagues and clients is essential. These persons can address questions that arise for the novice evaluators, such as: What happens when you are the sole evaluator on a project? What if there is no experienced colleague you can turn to in order to help you troubleshoot? So, having a professional relationship with an experienced evaluator and mentor who can advise you is invaluable. Mentors also model appropriate dispositions and ethical practices and demonstrate how to communicate with clients and stakeholders. Thus, students should seek out-of-class opportunities to work with experienced evaluators to gain the extended practical training experiences not afforded to them in coursework. These experiences are essential for students to learn and refine the skills necessary to become an evaluator.

Understand each part of the evaluation process. In our program evaluation course, we developed an evaluation plan based on a real program (one in which we were involved in or planned to start). We developed the evaluation plan from the ground up by focusing on a different activity each week: identifying stakeholders; discerning between types of data needed; planning data analyses; and, communicating results to stakeholders. I was able to subsequently use the evaluation plan that I developed to evaluate a large federal program in Alabama. When implementing this plan, I learned about the importance of communicating with and understanding the needs of stakeholders. In formal research methods training, students learn about the importance of control and not deviating away from the originally stated methods and questions. However, evaluators must adjust their methods to meet the evolving needs of stakeholders and changing conditions of programs.

No matter if you are meeting a client, conducting an observation, or writing a report, good communication skills are vital to your success as an evaluator. You have to learn how to effectively and clearly communicate the evaluation purpose, plan, and results to stakeholders in a way that is appropriate and useful for them. Research skills are important to an evaluator, but communication and negotiation skills are equally essential to becoming an effective evaluator.

Participate in professional organizations. Students who want to learn more about program evaluation and identify themselves as a program evaluation professional will be well-served to join an organization such as the American Evaluation Association (AEA) or American Educational Research Association (AERA). Not only do these groups support one's professional identity, they also sponsor meetings that give students venues in which to network with other evaluators, attend training sessions, and present the results of their evaluation studies for peer review. This exposure has provided me with the opportunity to develop as a more competent evaluator and researcher through dialogue and networking with both novice and experienced evaluators.

SUMMARY AND RECOMMENDATIONS

Conducting successful program evaluation work requires a mix of methodological knowledge and interpersonal skills. The knowledge and skills needed can be developed through courses, fieldwork, mentorship, and reflective practice (Dillman, 2012). Too often, however, evaluation training is limited to a single course and students have few opportunities to become involved in authentic program evaluation projects to further develop their evaluative skills and knowledge.

A significant challenge for program evaluation faculty is finding space within the curriculum to give students the necessary experiences to learn and apply critical evaluation skills in authentic situations. We have described, in this chapter, activities that involve students in such situations and which will help them develop, use, and refine their evaluation skills. Based upon our experiences, we make the following two essential recommendations for those teaching program evaluation courses.

Focus coursework activities and assignments on authentic, meaningful evaluation situations. Employ realistic evaluation scenarios, vignettes, case studies and, whenever possible, actual evaluation projects as pedagogical tools. Require students to review, analyze, discuss, and plan further action steps in these situations. Develop a sequence of inter-connected assignments in which students must demonstrate required evaluation knowledge and skills. Invite evaluation stakeholders from your department or other departments on campus to describe their needs for evaluations of their programs and practices. Encourage students to work with these clients. These experiences will help students develop valuable professional contacts that can lead to assistantships and future employment.

Connect students to practical evaluation experiences. Practical experience is a critical component of evaluator preparation. Through coursework and strategic assignments, students can develop foundational evaluation skills. However, these skills can be refined through hands-on, real world experience. Therefore, faculty should develop opportunities for graduate students to work on research and evaluation projects. Also, students should submit proposals to present at professional conferences. Becoming involved in these organizations leads to networking with other professionals where students learn about future career opportunities in the evaluation profession.

Informative program evaluation requires a comprehensive approach to planning, design, data gathering and analysis, and communication of findings to stakeholders. Thus, evaluation training should emphasize to students the connections between theory and practice, purpose and methodology, and the need for strong communication skills when working with clients. Through course work, practical field experiences, and mentorship, students can gain the necessary foundational skills to become competent evaluators.

REFERENCES

American Evaluation Association, Task Force on Guiding Principles for Evaluators. (1995). Guiding principles for evaluators. *New Directions for Program Evaluation, 66,* 19–26.

Christie, C. A., Quinones, P., & Fierro, L. (2013). Informing the discussion on evaluation Training: A look at evaluators' course taking and professional practice. *American Journal of Evaluation,* online version (Oct 4, 2013). doi: 10.1177/1098214013503697

Davies, R., & MacKay, K. (2014). Evaluator training: Content and topic validation in university evaluation courses. *American Journal of Evaluation*—online version (Feb 12, 2014). doi: 10:1177/1098214013520066.

Dillman, L. M. (2012). Evaluator skill acquisition: Linking educational experiences to competencies. *American Journal of Evaluation, 34*(2), 270–285.

Dewey, J. D., Montrose, B. E., Schroter, D. C., Sullins, C. D., & Mattox, J. R. (2008). Evaluator competencies: What's taught versus what's sought. *American Journal of Evaluation, 29*(3), 268–287.

Engle, M., Altschuid, J. W., & Kim, Y. (2006). 2002 Survey of evaluation preparation programs in universities: An update of the 1992 American Evaluation Association sponsored study. *American Journal of Evaluation, 27*(3), 353–359.

Fitzpatrick, J. L., Sanders, J. R., & Worthen, B. R. (2011). *Program evaluation: Alternative approaches and practical guidelines.* Boston, MA: Pearson.

Morris, M. (1994). The role of single evaluation courses in evaluation training. *New Directions in Program Evaluation, 62,* 51–59.

Patton, M. Q. (2005). Diverse and creative uses of cases for teaching. *New Directions For Evaluation, 125,* 91–100.

Stevahn, L., King, J. A., Ghere, G., & Minnema, J. (2005) Establishing essential competencies for program evaluators. *American Journal of Evaluation, 26,* 43–59.

Sudzina, M. R. (1997). Case study as a constructivist pedagogy for teaching educational psychology. *Educational Psychology Review, 9,* 199–218.

Sudzina, M. R. (1999). Guidelines for teaching with cases. In M. Sudzina (Ed.), *Case study applications for teacher education: Cases of teaching and learning in content areas.* Boston, MA: Allyn & Bacon.

CPSIA information can be obtained
at www.ICGtesting.com
Printed in the USA
FFOW01n1536190616
25145FF

9 781681 233963